Exploring Point Reyes National Seashore
and
Golden Gate National Recreation Area

Tracy Salcedo-Chourré

FALCON®

GUILFORD, CONNECTICUT
HELENA, MONTANA
AN IMPRINT OF THE GLOBE PEQUOT PRESS

A FALCONGUIDE®

Text design by Nancy Freeborn
Maps created by Blue Gecko Graphics © The Globe Pequot Press
All photographs by Tracy Salcedo-Chourré
Photo of the author by Martin Chourré

Library of Congress Cataloging-in-Publication Data

Salcedo-Chourré, Tracy.
  Exploring Point Reyes National Seashore and the Golden Gate National Recreation area / Tracy Salcedo-Chourré.— 1st ed.
      p. cm. — (A Falcon guide)
  Includes bibliographical references (p.).
  ISBN 0-7627-2213-4
    1. Point Reyes National Seashore (Calif.)—Guidebooks. 2. Golden Gate National Recreation Area (Calif.)—Guidebooks. 3. Natural history—California—Point Reyes National Seashore. 4. Natural history—California—Golden Gate National Recreation Area. 5. Point Reyes National Seashore (Calif.)—History. 6. Golden Gate National Recreation Area (Calif.)—History. I. Title. II. Series.

  F868.P9 S35 2002
  917.94'62—dc21

                                                                                2002029729

Manufactured in the United States of America
First Edition/First Printing

Contents

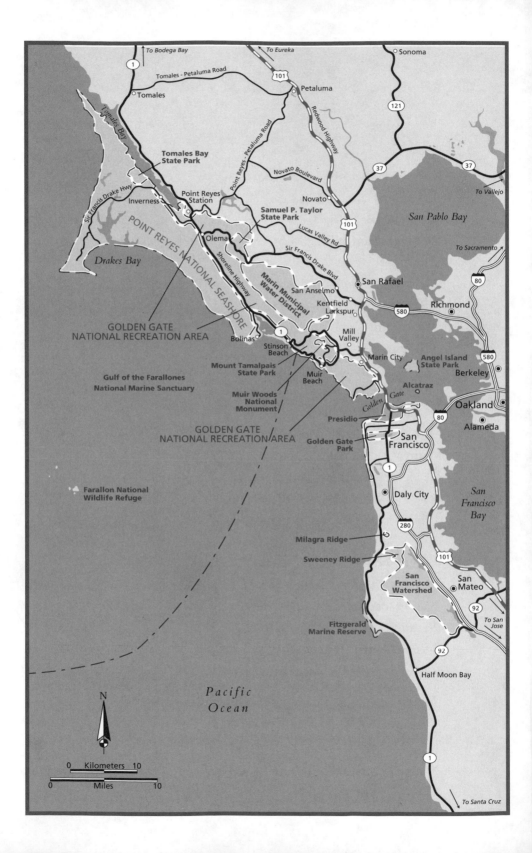

For my father and Walter.
I can only hope that one day
I will know the wilderness around my home
as well as they do.

Acknowledgments

I've called on the resources of a number of knowledgeable people in compiling this guidebook. Some, like folks I've met along the trail over the years or at various functions at Point Reyes or in the Golden Gate National Recreation Area, I cannot name, but I thank them nonetheless for their comments, insights, and recommendations. Others I can name specifically: I'd like to thank John Dell'Osso, chief of interpretation at the Point Reyes National Seashore; Will Elder, park ranger and media specialist at the Presidio National Park; Park Ranger Marcus Combs of the Presidio and Muir Woods National Monument; Mia Monroe, also at Muir Woods National Monument; Naomi Torres at the Crissy Field Center; and Rich Weideman, chief of the Office of Public Affairs and Special Events at the Golden Gate National Recreation Area, all of whom either discussed my work with me or reviewed portions of the manuscript. I'd also like to thank Joanne McGarry for expressing her concerns about dog etiquette in the Golden Gate National Recreation Area; Site Steward John Porter for his informative tour of the Nike Missile Site; and Wolfgang Schubert, a National Park Service docent at the Crissy Field Center, for sharing his knowledge of the Presidio and Lands End with me. Thanks to Jeff Serena at The Globe Pequot Press for his patience and confidence in my abilities as a writer. I'd also like to thank my father, Jesse Salcedo, and our family friend Walter Hoffman, for reminding me of places I'd visited in my youth, and for turning me on to places I haven't visited before; as well as my brothers, Nick and Chris, for sharing their knowledge and experience with me. My gratitude is also due my mother, Judy Salcedo, and my mother-in-law, Sally Chourré, for affording me the time to explore by watching my children or taking care of other business. Finally, I'd like to thank my husband, Martin Chourré, and my sons, Jesse, Cruz, and Penn, for accompanying me on many of my park explorations, and for tolerating my absence while I ventured off into the wild.

Legend

Interstate		Interstate
U.S. Highways		U.S. Highways
Miscellaneous Roads (Paved)		State Roads
Gravel Road		Forest Roads
Unimproved Roads		Cities
Selected Route		Trailhead
Optional Route		Parking
Pipelines		Picnic
Powerlines		Ranger Station
Fence		Rest room
Park Boundary		Overlook
River/Creek		Mountain / Peak
Lakes/Large Rivers		Structures / Point of Interest
Cliffs		Campground
Tunnel		Gate
Boardwalk		Horse Trail
Spring		Bridge
Directional Scale		

Interstate: 5 55 555

U.S. Highways: 5 55 555

State Roads: 55 555

Forest Roads: 41 416 4165

Cities   Capitol   Large   Small

START

N

0   Miles   1

Introduction

I have a powerful bond with both the Point Reyes National Seashore and the Golden Gate National Recreation Area. I've always loved the parks—after all, they were my playgrounds when I was growing up in Marin County. But I didn't realize how fundamental those bonds were until I began researching this guidebook.

It's really an old story, one that's been told many times, of how a person is shaped by the landscape she is raised in. My explorations took me back to places, both real and emotional, that are associated with the milestones of my life. I could hear the laughter of my friends as we enjoyed an illicit afternoon of teenage fun on the beach at Kirby Cove. I could smell the smoky interior of the sweat lodge at Kule Loklo, where, as an undergraduate anthropology student, I helped docents from the Miwok Archaeological Preserve of Marin skin a roadkilled fox with an obsidian knife. I could hear my toddler son squealing at the feel of the sand at Stinson Beach under his toes—the first beach sand this Colorado-born boy had ever experienced. The parks are a part of me. And I'm very, very lucky.

These landscapes—my landscapes—are world renowned for their beauty. They include San Francisco Bay and the Golden Gate Bridge, the convoluted topography of the Marin Headlands, Tomales Point and the Olema Valley, Ocean Beach and the Great Beach. These seascapes—my seascapes—open over the vastness of the Pacific Ocean, washed with sunshine and energized by storms, endlessly engaging, always dynamic. I hope your explorations in these parks leave as deep a mark on your soul as they have on mine.

How to Use This Guide

I have broken this guide into two major sections: The first covers Point Reyes National Seashore, and the second, Golden Gate National Recreation Area. Within each section I've provided brief overviews of the parks, including cultural history, natural history (including geology and weather), amenities, and how to get to and around the park. I've included chapters describing points of interest within the parks—lighthouses, museums, cultural and historical sites, and wildlife-viewing areas. I've also included, where appropriate, brief descriptions of water sport opportunities within the parks, primarily sea kayaking and surfing.

White surf and chocolate sand compliment each other at Tennessee Beach in the Golden Gate National Recreation Area.

But the guide's main focus is trails within the parks, which are described in detail. Not every trail in each park, however, is included—that's where the exploring part comes in. The trails I've selected lead into different corners of the parks, and offer access to other routes that, hopefully, will entice you to venture off the paths I've beaten. Within these trail descriptions I've stated whether they are appropriate for hikers, horseback riders, and/or mountain bikers, so that you can select your favorite mode of travel and go for it.

Mileages

For trails at the Point Reyes National Seashore, I relied on maps, distances listed on trail signs, and the odometers on my mountain bike and car to determine distances from one point to the next. The same is true for the Marin Headlands area of the Golden Gate National Recreation Area (GGNRA). Where the three sources haven't jibed, I've listed the mileages from the park's trail signs. Trails in the Presidio and the southern portions of the Golden Gate National Recreation Area generally don't have mileages listed on trail signs—in some cases, there are no signs at all. In these instances I've relied on maps and my common sense and experience to determine mileages. I believe deviations from actual mileages are minimal, and shouldn't affect your ability to gauge the difficulty or duration of a given hike or ride.

Difficulty Ratings

The trails are rated *very easy*, *easy*, *moderate*, or *hard*. In assigning a label, I took into account elevation gains and losses, trail surfaces, and distances. Generally speaking, very easy trails are flat and less than a mile long. Easy trails are generally a bit longer and mostly flat. Moderate trails involve greater distances and (perhaps) greater elevation changes. Hard trails generally have sustained steep pitches, and cover distances greater than 5 miles.

Keep in mind that every trail is only as difficult as you make it. If you keep a pace within your level of fitness, drink plenty of water, and stoke up on good, high-energy foods, you can make any trail easy.

Route Finding

Trails within the Point Reyes National Seashore and the Golden Gate National Recreation Area are generally very well marked and nicely maintained. The only park in which trails are not clearly signed is the Presidio, and that will probably change as the park matures.

Most of these trails lead to other trails, or can be linked with other trails in routes different from those I've described herein. This guide is about exploring: Use these trails to get out there, and a good map, a compass, and curiosity to break away, if you choose.

Maps

A wealth of maps cover these parks. The USGS topographic maps that pertain to each route are listed in hike descriptions. In some instances, though the map covers the area, the trail may not appear on the map. Still, USGS topos are useful for orienteering and identifying landmarks.

Both the seashore and the GGNRA offer general overview maps, which are good tools for locating trailheads, and serve adequately as trail maps. Tom Harrison has produced an excellent trail map for the Point Reyes National Seashore, and the Golden Gate National Parks Association for the Marin Headlands. You can also pick up a good map of the Presidio, showing roadways, hiking trails, and suggesting bicycling routes, at any of that park's visitor centers.

Share the Trail

Marin County has seen a long-running battle among different trail user groups. Some horseback riders, hikers, and mountain bikers, like preschoolers, have a hard time sharing. My experience has been that conflicts, while not common, do crop up, and when they do they can be very unpleasant. It's a shame, but that's the way it is.

Of course, if all users realized that everyone is on the trail for the same reason—to have fun—and if every trail user treated every other trail user with common courtesy, there would be no conflicts, no trail closures, no nasty words or letters to the editor. But until kindness and respect are as spontaneous as wildflowers blooming in spring, we must abide by some basic rules of trail etiquette.

- Horses have the right-of-way. Hikers should yield by stepping off the trail on the downhill side and allowing horses to pass. Mountain bikers should warn horseback riders of their approach, particularly when coming from behind, in a clear voice, and dismount if the equestrian requests it.
- Mountain bikers must also yield to hikers.

Zero Impact

Point Reyes National Seashore and the GGNRA are among the most visited national parks in the United States. With millions of people walking these trails and beaches each year, the potential for negative impacts is enormous. An urban wilderness can accommodate human use only as long as everybody who visits leaves no trace of his or her passage. It takes only a few thoughtless or uninformed visitors to ruin it for everyone who follows.

A waterfall of fern spills down a cliff alongside the Stewart Trail in the Point Reyes National Seashore.

Nowadays most wilderness users want to walk softly, but some aren't aware that they have poor manners. They litter, they stray from the established path, creating unsightly social trails, they pick up artifacts and pick flowers without thought as to how those items fit into the overall ecology of the place in which they were found. Consequently, a new code of ethics has been developed to cope with unending waves of people who want a perfect park experience, but may not know how to leave no trace of their visit.

Three Falcon Principles of Zero Impact

Leave with everything you brought in.

Leave no sign of your visit.

Leave the landscape as you found it.

- Most of us know better than to litter—in or out of the backcountry. Be sure you leave nothing, regardless of how small it is, along the trail, on the beach, or at your campsite. Pack out everything—orange peels, flip tops, cigarette butts—or deposit it in trash receptacles at trailheads. Also, pick up any trash that others leave behind.
- Follow the main trail. Avoid cutting switchbacks and walking on vegetation beside the trail.
- Don't pick up "souvenirs," such as rocks, antlers, or wildflowers. The next person wants to see them too.
- Avoid making loud noises on the trail or in camps. Be courteous—remember, sound travels easily in the backcountry, especially across water.
- Use rest rooms at trailheads. None of these trails takes you so far from civilization or toilet facilities that you can't easily reach them. If you absolutely must go, use a lightweight trowel to bury your waste 6 to 8 inches deep, at least 300 feet from any water source. Pack out used toilet paper. Keep all waste products (including dishwater, soaps, and toothpaste) at least 300 feet from any water source.
- Camping in these parks is by permit only, and only allowed in designated camp sites.
- Finally, and perhaps most importantly, strictly follow the pack-in/pack-out rule. If you carry something into the backcountry, consume it or carry it out.

Leave no trace—then put your ear to the ground and listen carefully. Thousands of people coming behind you are thanking you for your courtesy and good sense.

Make It a Safe Trip

Both Point Reyes and the GGNRA are located close to towns and cities, and are generally very safe. That doesn't mean, however, that travelers in these parks should venture off on trails or beaches without being prepared.

Being prepared for a hike, mountain bike ride, or horseback ride in these parks means so much more than just throwing a water bottle in a fanny pack and setting off. It means taking the time to learn about the conditions on the trail, carrying gear to protect you from changes in the weather, and making sure, especially if you choose to travel solo, that someone knows where you are going and when you plan to return.

One of the most important facets of preparedness is knowing your limitations. Choose adventures that are well suited to your physical and mental condition. Don't overexert yourself, give yourself plenty of time to reach your destination, and turn around if you have any doubts on either score.

Here are some basic tips to help guarantee that your journey in the parks is a safe and comfortable one:

- Check the weather forecast. It's a good idea to avoid beaches and cliffs during periods of high wind, or during especially violent storms. Avoid traveling during prolonged periods of cold weather.

- Avoid traveling alone.

- Keep your party together.

- Study basic survival and first aid before leaving home.

- Don't eat wild plants unless you have positively identified them.

- Before you leave the trailhead, find out as much as you can about the route, especially the potential hazards.

- Don't exhaust yourself or other members of your party by traveling too far or too fast. Let the slowest person set the pace.

- Don't wait until you're confused to look at your maps. Follow them as you go along, from the moment you start moving up the trail, so you have a continual fix on your location.

- If you get lost, don't panic. Sit down and relax for a few minutes while you carefully check your map and take a reading with your compass. Confidently plan your next move. It's often smart to retrace your steps until you find familiar ground, even if you think it might lengthen your trip. Lots of people get temporarily lost on the trail and then find their way again—usually by calmly and rationally dealing with the situation.

- Stay clear of all wild animals.

- Take along a first-aid kit that includes, at a minimum, the following: a sewing needle, a snakebite kit, aspirin, antibacterial ointment, two antiseptic swabs, two butterfly bandages, adhesive tape, four adhesive strips, four gauze pads, two triangular bandages, codeine tablets, two inflatable splints, moleskin or Second Skin for blisters, one roll of 3-inch gauze, a CPR shield, rubber gloves, and lightweight first-aid instructions.

• Take a survival kit that includes, at minimum, the following: a compass, a whistle, matches in a waterproof container, a cigarette lighter, a candle, a signal mirror, a flashlight, fire starter, aluminum foil, water purification tablets, a space blanket, and flares.

Traveling in these parks, while generally safe, does have its hazards. Specific dangers are addressed below.

Cliffs

Some of the trails and sites described in this guide are on or in the vicinity of seaside cliffs. Subjected to the constant erosive forces of wind and water, and in some cases composed of inherently crumbly rock, the edges of these cliffs can be unstable. The parks have posted warning signs in areas where the cliff hazards are known; save yourself a potentially long fall by taking those warnings seriously. To be on the safe side, avoid cliff edges throughout the parks, whether signed or not.

Surf and Tides

Most people who have lived near the coastline of northern California for any length of time are very aware of the dangers posed by surf and currents, especially along those beaches that open onto the Pacific Ocean. Rip currents and sneaker waves render most beaches in the Point Reyes National Seashore and the GGNRA unsafe for swimmers, and only experienced surfers, sailboarders, and other water recreationalists should venture into the water. The safest beaches for playing on or near the surf are those that open onto bays, like East Beach at Crissy Field, Stinson Beach, and Limantour Beach.

• **Sneaker waves:** Beaches on the Pacific Ocean are occasionally swept by sneaker waves. These unpredictable, extra-large single waves, created by conditions at sea that are unknowable to people on land, pose a considerable danger to the unwary, unwise, or uninformed. There is no way to predict when a sneaker wave will hit, and those unlucky enough to be caught by such a wave will find themselves soaked at best, and washed out to sea at worst.

Park officials in Point Reyes have posted warning signs at trailheads to beaches known for sneaker waves, including both the north and south portions of the Great Beach, McClures Beach, and Kehoe Beach. Beachcombers should stay a safe distance from the breaking surf on these beaches. Within the GGNRA, sneaker waves are known to sweep Ocean Beach, Rodeo Beach, Tennessee Beach, and Muir Beach.

- **Riptides or currents:** The waters off every beach in these parks are subject to riptides. These potentially dangerous currents sweep backward from the beach out to sea, and have been known to drag unwary swimmers or surfers out with them. Again, the beaches where riptides are least likely to pose a great threat are those lie within the confines of a bay, like Stinson Beach, Limantour Beach, and East Beach at Crissy Field.

Poison Oak and Stinging Nettle

Though generally not deadly, poison oak and stinging nettle can cause explorers a great deal of discomfort and annoyance.

- **Poison oak,** identifiable by lobed leaves that grow in sets of three, shiny and green in spring and bright red during late summer and fall, causes an itchy skin rash. The plant grows as a bush, vine, or ground cover, and is most easily avoided by remaining on the trail. If you suspect you have come in contact with the plant, be sure to wash your skin and clothing as soon as possible to remove the plant oils.

- **Stinging nettle** also causes skin irritation, in the form of a stinging or burning sensation that can persist for a day. It's a tall, weed-like plant that blends perfectly into tall grasses in meadows, and the best way to avoid it is to stay on the trail. No way to wash this off—you'll just have to grin and bear it. Stinging nettle poses a more dangerous threat to horses; again, it's best to keep your steed on trails.

Ticks, Mountain Lions, Rattlesnakes, and Deer

Ticks thrive in the grass and brush of Point Reyes National Seashore and the GGNRA. Some are merely creepy; others carry Lyme disease, an infection that, if left untreated, can cause arthritis and tissue damage. Wear light-colored clothing so that you can see the little critters, and tuck your pant legs into your socks so that they cannot sneak up your legs. Inspect your body after hikes to make sure no ticks have snuck on board. If one has attached, remove it carefully, making sure you get the entire parasite, including its head. If a rash appears around the bite site, or if you develop flu-like symptoms, contact your doctor for treatment.

Mountain lions are seen infrequently, but do live in the rangelands of Point Reyes and portions of the GGNRA. Attacks on humans are very rare, but have been documented. Some tips for traveling in mountain lion country include:

- Do not approach a mountain lion. Give the animal the opportunity to move on. Slowly back away, but maintain eye contact. It's best to choose another route or time to hike through the area.

Fog filters through the firs along the Sky Trail in the Point Reyes National Seashore.

- Do not run from a mountain lion. Running may stimulate the animal's predatory response.
- If you encounter a mountain lion, make noise; talk or yell loudly and regularly. Shout to make others in the area aware of the situation.
- Appear larger than you really are. Raise your arms above your head and make waving motions. Raise your jacket or another object above your head. Do not bend over, since this will make you appear smaller and more "preylike."
- If you are with small children, pick them up. Bring the child close to you, maintain eye contact with the mountain lion, and pull the child up without bending over. If you are with other children or adults, band together.
- Defend yourself and others. If attacked, fight back. Try to remain standing. Do not feign death. Pick up a branch or rock; pull out a knife, pepper spray, or other deterrent. Keep in mind that this is a last effort. Defending pets is not recommended.
- Respect any warning signs posted by agencies.
- Teach others in your group how to behave in a mountain lion encounter.
- Report encounters. Record your location and the details of any encounter and notify the nearest landowner or land management agency. The land management agency (federal, state, or county) may want to visit the site and,

if appropriate, post education or warning signs. Fish and wildlife agencies should also be notified because they record and track such encounters.

Rattlesnakes are rare along the coastline, where fog and winds keep temperatures below the levels that venomous snakes prefer. But they may be encountered along trails in inland valleys. These snakes generally do not bite unless provoked: They are probably as afraid of you as you are of them. Bites are usually not fatal, but may result in tissue damage if not treated immediately. When traveling in rocky terrain or cross-country, watch where you step.

Amazingly enough, more people are injured in national parks in encounters with deer than with bears, mountain lions, and other more traditional threatening animals. Everyone seems to think it's okay to approach Bambi, but deer are wild animals, and must be treated as such. Do not approach or try to feed deer in either Point Reyes or the GGNRA, for your own health and safety and the safety of the deer. The animal risks malnutrition and disease if it becomes accustomed to eating "human food."

Giardia

Giardiasis (also known as giardia) is caused by an intestinal parasite, *Giardia lamblia*, which can be found in lakes and streams throughout Point Reyes and the GGNRA. The symptoms of giardiasis include nausea, abdominal cramps, flatulence, lethargy, diarrhea, and weight loss, and usually manifest themselves six to fifteen days after consuming impure water. To prevent giardiasis, boil water before drinking or use a water filter, which can also remove additional bacteria and protozoans. Should you contract giardiasis, see your doctor; symptoms can last for months if untreated.

Weather

Generally the weather along the coastline around the Golden Gate and Point Reyes is not extreme. The maritime influence keeps temperatures relatively moderate, with few days of freezing temperatures in the winter, and few days of extreme heat in summer, relative to the interior valleys and mountains of California. This does not mean, however, that the weather is always comfortable in these national parks. Fog is a possibility regardless of the time of year, and brings with it chilly temperatures and moisture. If you are unprepared, this may be, at best, an inconvenience, and, at worst, a threat. When it's very cold and wet, or when it's very hot, the risks of developing hypothermia or heat stroke increase.

To avoid the potential discomforts—and dangers—of weather extremes, dress in layers. Always pack a warm jacket, hat, and gloves, just in case. Drink plenty of water while hiking, mountain biking, or horseback riding, and pack high-energy snacks to bolster your reserves.

A triumvirate of pelicans flees the incoming fog at the Point Reyes National Seashore.

Adjacent Parks and Open Space

The Point Reyes National Seashore and the Golden Gate National Recreation Area are part of an extensive system of open spaces along the coastline north and south of San Francisco Bay. Mount Tamalpais and Angel Island State Parks both protect major landmarks within the Bay Area; the others may not encompass such conspicuous treasures, but are more than worthy of exploration.

Neighboring parks and open spaces are described here in brief. Please use the contact information provided below to learn more about them. If you wish to stay overnight at any of the parks where camping is permitted, be sure to make reservations. The parks are presented from north to south.

- **Tomales Bay State Park:** Located adjacent to Point Reyes National Seashore, about 40 miles north of San Francisco, the 2,000 acres of Tomales Bay State Park contain lovely beaches and forests fronting on its namesake, Tomales Bay. Open daily from 8:00 A.M. to sunset, the park offers swimming, hiking, picnicking facilities, but no camping. You can contact the park by writing Tomales Bay State Park, Star Route, Inverness, CA 94937, calling (415) 669–1140, or visiting the Web site at cal-parks.ca.gov.

- **Samuel P. Taylor State Park:** Nestled along the banks of Lagunitas Creek and home to thick groves of redwoods, Samuel P. Taylor State Park is a favorite camp spot for Marinites. The park covers more than 2,700 acres and contains swimming holes, hiking and bicycling trails, and camping and picnicking facilities. Like Tomales Bay, this park is located about 40 miles north of San Francisco, and about 5 miles east of the Point Reyes National Seashore. Contact the park by writing to Samuel P. Taylor State Park, P.O. Box 251, Lagunitas, CA 94938, by calling (415) 488–9897, or by visiting the Web site at cal-parks.ca.gov.

- **Mount Tamalpais State Park:** Rising to more than 2,500 feet, Mount Tamalpais is the matriarch of the North Bay. Its slopes are covered in a mixed forest of oak, madrone, and manzanita, with pockets of redwoods in moist canyons. An extensive network of trails winds along the slopes, with fire roads open to mountain bikes. It also has picnicking facilities, several campsites, and an open-air theater that dates back to the early 1900s. For more information, write to Mount Tamalpais State Park, 801 Panoramic Highway, Mill Valley, CA 94941, call (415) 388–2070, or visit the Web site at cal-parks.ca.gov.

- **Marin Municipal Water District:** The Marin Municipal Water District (MMWD) manages extensive open spaces surrounding Mount Tamalpais. The lands encompass five small, pretty reservoirs, where no swimming is permitted, but catch-and-release fishing is allowed. About 130 miles of hiking trails are available; horseback riders are allowed on all fire protection roads and certain trails, and mountain bikers are restricted to fire protection roads. Picnic facilities are available at Lagunitas Lake. Contact the MMWD by writing the Marin Municipal Water District, 220 Nellen Avenue, Corte Madera, CA 94925, calling (415) 945–1455, or visiting the Web site at www.marinwater.org. The telephone number for the Sky Oaks Ranger Station is (415) 945-1181.

- **Angel Island State Park:** The only way to reach this spectacular state park, which sits in the middle of San Francisco Bay, is by ferry or private boat. The island has a rich and diverse history: The Coast Miwok used it as a hunting and fishing base, it harbored Spanish explorer Juan de Ayala, and it was an integral part of the coastal defense system that has left its mark on so many open spaces around the bay. Recreational opportunities on the island include hiking, bicycling, and picnicking. Guided tours of the island are available seasonally. No overnight camping is permitted. For more on the park, including ferry information, call (415) 435–1915 or visit the Web site at cal-parks.ca.gov.

- **San Francisco Watershed:** The Peninsula Watershed extends south from the GGNRA's Sweeney Ridge, protecting more than 23,000 acres of coastal hills and encompassing four large reservoirs. Limited hiking is available within the watershed, but a number of trails border the boundary, including the Sweeney Ridge Trail. For more information on the watershed, visit the Web site at www.ci.sf.ca.us/puc/lrms/pages/penws.htm.

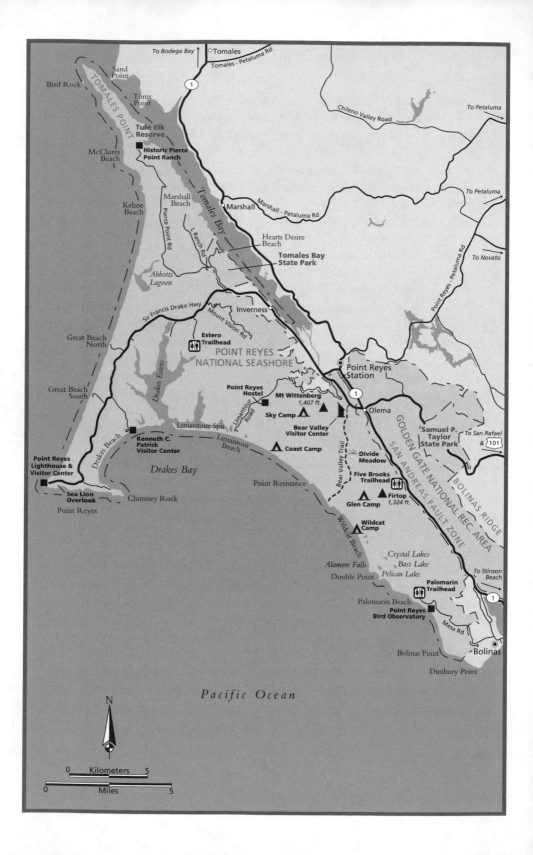

Point Reyes National Seashore

This may sound strange, but in my opinion, February is the best time to play at Point Reyes. Winter is gradually losing its annual battle with spring, the cracks in its armament of cold and bluster allowing days of sunshine and blue skies, and spring has yet to remember that it's a season of enervating winds. In these quiet, brilliant, lengthening days, the grassy hills and pastures are kelly green and velvety, and the bravest wildflowers—Douglas iris, footsteps of spring, California poppies—open tentative petals to the suddenly strong sun.

But sunshine—or February—is not a prerequisite to enjoying the seashore. Both seascape and landscape are spectacularly dramatic when the weather is fitful with winter's squalls, when rainbows are washed in and out of the sky by sun and rain and vigorous winds punish the wave-tops, treetops, and ridgetops. When the fog rolls in—a common occurrence in summer—the seashore softens, fading into a quiet and contemplative place, veiled in a temperate mist that muffles even the thunder of the surf. With views blocked by the dreamy grayness, the park seems small, isolated, and very wild. By autumn, the omnipresent summertime fogs are in retreat, revealing the land and sea in sharp relief. Both air and water heat up, making the beaches and the forest-shrouded trails the most attractive destinations.

In this section of the guide, I've spotlighted the enormous trail system within the Point Reyes National Seashore, which accommodates hikers, equestrians, and, on some routes, mountain bikers. I've also included information on cultural attractions, natural attractions, and other recreational opportunities within the park. I've been as thorough as the parameters of this guide permit; needless to say, there's more to the park than what's included here. To get more information on park amenities, you can write to the Superintendent, Point Reyes National Seashore, Point Reyes Station, CA 94956. The telephone number is (415) 464–5100. The National Park Service maintains a Web site for the park at www.nps.gov/pore.

The Point Reyes National Seashore Association, a nonprofit organization that supports and promotes the park, organizes extensive offerings of ongoing educational and environmental programs within the park, including field seminars and summer camps. To contact the association, write to the PRNSA, Point Reyes Station, CA 94956, or call (415) 663–1155. The Web site is www.ptreyes.org.

The History of Point Reyes

First came the Coast Miwok and their ancestors, an aboriginal people that flourished on the foggy peninsula that would one day be known as Point Reyes. Then came the Spaniards, whose colonial aspirations dealt the Native peoples cultural and physical blows that forever altered their lives and lands. Then came the Mexicans, who divvied up the area into ranchos, thus initiating a ranching tradition that would enable the Americans, who succeeded them, to transform Point Reyes into an empire of dairies. In its latest incarnation, Point Reyes is a national park, encompassing about 70,000 acres of wildlands and pasturelands, edged with spectacular beaches, and dotted with reminders of what has came before.

The Coast Miwok People

In the wilderness that once was Point Reyes, the Coast Miwok Indians developed a complex and successful society long before the arrival of "civilized" Europeans, a way of life hinted at by archaeological evidence and celebrated by its descendants in a re-creation of one of their ancestors' villages.

Indigenous habitation of the California coast in Marin and southern Sonoma Counties by the Coast Miwok Indians and their ancestors dates back thousands of years. Within the boundaries of the national park, the archaeological remains of more than 100 villages have been found; evidence that the land supported a healthy population. The Coast Miwok were hunters and gatherers, harvesting clams, oysters, halibut, and other foodstuffs from the sea using tule canoes, and hunting deer and smaller game on land. They gathered seasonal greens, nuts, and berries, relying heavily on the acorn as a staple food, and wove elaborate, beautiful, and practical baskets for cooking and storage. They built permanent villages, with houses (*kotcas*) of tule and redwood bark, granaries in which to store acorns, sweat lodges and roundhouses for social and spiritual activities. Such structures stand today at Kule Loklo, a re-creation of a Coast Miwok village in the national seashore.

These were the practical aspects of the Coast Miwok lifestyle. But there was so much more. The people made "coins" of shell that were traded throughout California—traded for the obsidian from which to make arrowheads and knives, for example. They gambled for fun and profit. They practiced a vigorous spiritual tradition, which involved ceremonial dances, elaborate costumes, and a rich oral history.

Sir Francis Drake was most likely the first European to encounter the Coast Miwok people. Drake's California landing, along with later explorations of the California coast by other explorers from Spain and Russia, marked the beginning of the tragic decimation of all California's native peoples, including the Coast Miwok. By the eighteenth century, the Spanish had driven the people into missions, subjecting them to disease and virtual slavery. By the time the Mexicans won independence from Spain in 1821, the Coast Miwok way of life was essentially extinct.

But some Coast Miwok survived, as did members of the neighboring Pomo tribe, who lived north of the Coast Miwok homelands in Sonoma County. Their descendants, after years of battling prejudice and bureaucracy, formed the Federated Indians of Graton Rancheria, which was granted full tribal status in 2000 and currently lists more than 500 members. At Kule Loklo, interpretation of Coast Miwok culture is ongoing, under the auspices of the tribe, the park service, and the Miwok Archeological Preserve of Marin (MAPOM).

The Explorers

The arrival of Europeans on the Point Reyes peninsula is much better documented than that of the aboriginal people. Spanish explorer Juan Rodriguez Cabrillo first surveyed the California coast in 1542 but made no note of the existence of Point Reyes, according to park literature. It wasn't until Sir Francis Drake of England, then merely Captain Drake, brought his ship, the *Golden Hind*, into Drakes Bay for repairs that Point Reyes finally made the maps.

That Drake landed in Drakes Bay is the subject of some controversy. I'll admit my prejudices up front: I was raised just off Sir Francis Drake Boulevard, I am a graduate of Sir Francis Drake High School, and, by gum, Sir Francis Drake landed in Drakes Bay. So when I read the convincing arguments set forth in *Discovering Francis Drake's California Harbor* (among other sources), I was happily vindicated in my beliefs. But until the doubters fall lockstep behind me, I must mention that other possible harbors have been proposed as Drake's landing, among them Bodega Bay, Bolinas Lagoon, and (truly), Goleta.

For the purposes of this guide, however, we'll assume that Drake landed at Drakes Bay. That he met and associated with the Coast Miwok. That he spent more than a month here in 1579, repairing his leaking vessel in the calm waters of Drakes Estero.

Drake's "discovery" of Nova Albion, as he called the country around his landing site, was made during his famed circumnavigation of the globe between 1577 and 1580. He'd just raided his way up the Pacific coasts of South America and Mexico, and with millions of dollars in loot on board, he continued north, searching for the fabled Northwest Passage, thought to be the quickest route back to England. It was during his fruitless search for the passage that he sought shelter, lending his name and fame to the bay at Point Reyes.

After Drake came more Europeans. Those who left a lasting impression on the point include Sebastian Rodriguez Cermeño, a Portuguese ship captain and trader charged by Spanish authorities with the task of exploring and claiming lands for the Spanish empire. Cermeño's ship, the *San Augustin*, foundered in

Drakes Bay in 1595, and its cargo, including Chinese pottery, has been washing onto nearby beaches ever since.

Later came Spanish explorer Don Sebastian Vizcaino. He visited Drakes Bay during his explorations of the coast in 1603. Sailing past the rocky headlands on a Catholic holiday known as the Feast of the Three Kings, he dubbed the landform La Punta de los Tres Reyes, the Point of the Three Kings, a name that has been abbreviated to Point Reyes. The king of points. It fits.

The Ranchers

By the early 1800s Spanish rule was well established in California. Though its mission system, which included Mission San Rafael Arcangel, little more than 20 miles from Point Reyes, the Spanish had subdued—or perhaps more correctly, decimated—the Coast Miwok population, and taken over the lands they'd once called home. And they had put their cattle out to graze on pastures at Point Reyes—thus becoming the first in a chain of ranchers on the point that remains intact today.

When the Mexicans took over from the Spanish in 1821, land grants were given to petitioners throughout California. The first grants on Point Reyes were made in 1836; James Berry acquired Rancho Punta de los Reyes in the upper Olema Valley, and Rafael Garcia was granted Rancho Tomales y Baulinas in the lower Olema Valley. A few years later, Antonio Osio acquired Rancho Punta de los Reyes Sobrante, which covered much of today's parkland.

Over the years the boundaries of these land grants shifted among the three owners, and new owners as well. But it wasn't until after the Americans took control of California in 1848, and the land grant system came to an end, that ownership issues on Point Reyes got complicated. Even messy. Park historian Dewey Livingston, in his expansive history *Ranching on the Point Reyes Peninsula*, recounts the story of a doctor named Andrew Randall, who purchased the Osio ranch in 1852, fell into foreclosure, and was eventually shot by one of his creditors.

It took a couple of lawyers named Shafter—and members of their families—to bring order to the land ownership chaos on Point Reyes in the mid- to late 1800s. Oscar Shafter, his brother James, and Oscar's son-in-law Charles Howard eventually came to own most of Point Reyes, and devised a system whereby they leased ranches, numbered from A to Z, to dairymen, many of whom were immigrants from Switzerland and the Azores. Driving through the park today, you pass through these ranches, some still operating, some now simply expanses of pasture, identified with signs that denote their historic status. By the late 1800s Point Reyes dairies were renowned for their butter—indeed, the product was so good that it was counterfeited, according to Livingston. Both butter and cheese were sent by schooner to markets in San Francisco. And the ranches on Point Reyes thrived.

The "Bat House," so called because of the colony of winged mammals that roosts here, was built in the 1880s on the Randall family's Olema Valley dairy ranch.

With the deaths of the family patriarchs around the turn of the twentieth century, the Shafter dairy empire on Point Reyes slowly disintegrated. Ranches were sold to the leaseholders, who held the land until the National Park Service began purchasing properties for the seashore in the 1960s and 1970s. The tables turned again at that point, with the park leasing the ranches it had acquired back to the families who had run cattle on them, in some cases for generations.

Drive through the seashore today—through most of West Marin, for that matter—and you drive through ranchland. It looks so bucolic, so established and secure. But the survival of these ranches has been hard fought, and efforts to preserve them from subdivision and aggressive development are ongoing. The national seashore's willingness to let ranching continue on parkland has been pivotal to the successful preservation of both open spaces and agriculture in West Marin. Equally significant have been the efforts of a grassroots organization called the Marin Agricultural Land Trust (MALT). Established in 1980, MALT has both preserved the pastoral landscapes that buffer the seashore, and enabled small family dairies to stay viable, by purchasing the development rights to ranches throughout West Marin.

Ranching in the park—and outside the park, for that matter—is not exempt from criticism. Concerns about overgrazing, habitat degradation, and the pollution of streams and estuaries are raised on an ongoing basis, with justification. Good stewardship of the park's pastoral zone is vital to the health of all the ecosystems that surround it. Ranches within the park and under MALT's umbrella are monitored to ensure that natural resources are protected. But the vigilance of these two entities will only be enhanced if they must answer hard questions about the environmental impacts of ranches.

The survival of ranching on Point Reyes depends on the survival of ranches throughout west Marin and west Sonoma County, to the north. It's a matter of scale. Without volume, small family dairies can't compete with larger dairies operating in the California's Central Valley. By purchasing food produced locally, consumers help support agriculture throughout the area. Personally, I like knowing that the butter I'm spreading on my toast came from the milk of a cow that grazed on Point Reyes. The alternative just isn't appealing anymore.

The Park

The National Park Service first suggested that the Point Reyes peninsula be preserved as a national park in 1935. At that time park officials estimated that the land could be purchased for $2.4 million, an astonishing figure given land prices in Marin County these days. But the park wouldn't come into being for another thirty years, postponed by the Great Depression, World War II, and rising land prices.

Still, in the interim, small chunks of land within the future park were socked away. Championed by local ranchers, a couple of small parks were created at Drakes Beach and McClures Beach. Between 1945 and 1951, land was acquired for Tomales Bay State Park, now wedged between Tomales Bay and the national seashore.

By the 1950s and early 1960s, real estate developers were eyeing the rolling hills of West Marin with the same desire that a famished teenage boy feels for pizza. A freeway was planned for the top of the Bolinas Ridge, foundations and infrastructure was being built for homes at Limantour Beach, the hills on the east side of Tomales Bay were targeted for residential and commercial development. It was a potential bonanza for the land barons, and a potential disaster for conservationists.

The park service proposed development of a different kind in 1958, when it asked the federal government to buy 35,000 acres on Point Reyes for a national seashore. Congressman Clem Miller of Inverness and California Senator Clair Engle upped the ante to 53,000 acres. The proposed park faced opposition from ranchers, land developers, and local politicians, but the congressman and the senator, along with an army of supporters, persevered. President John F. Kennedy signed a bill creating Point Reyes National Seashore in 1962.

Formal status for the park was a major victory, but the funds initially designated to acquire parkland weren't nearly adequate. More money—lots of it—would be needed to purchase the 64,000 acres authorized by the law. Fearing that a loss of momentum might result in development of lands slated for inclusion in the park, a powerful grassroots advocacy group was formed. Save Our Seashore, with Marin County Supervisor Peter Behr at the helm, gathered a small fortune in signatures supporting the appropriation of more money for parkland acquisition, and parlayed those signatures into cash.

By the time I was old enough to hike its trails and play on its beaches, in the late 1970s, Point Reyes National Seashore was a fixture of West Marin's landscape and a prized part of the remarkable wealth of parklands in the San Francisco Bay Area. Today the park covers more than 70,000 acres. More than 32,000 of those are designated wilderness, and more than 140 miles of trails wind through the park's open spaces. And the legacy of the Coast Miwok, the explorers, and the ranchers remains on the landscape, preserved in perpetuity.

Natural History

Point Reyes encompasses a number of different ecosystems, layered like a cake from the intertidal zones at land's end to the ridgetops more than 1,000 feet above.

At sea level the interface of two habitats creates a third. The first is the Pacific Ocean, an ecosystem far too big and complex to be detailed in this guidebook. Still, Point Reyes draws much of its natural wealth from offshore: sea creatures that make sought-after appearances near or on the point include the Pacific gray whale, northern elephant seals, harbor seals, California sea lions, and Steller sea lions. Seabirds, most conspicuously brown pelicans (from May to December) and gulls, along with various species of grebes, loons, and scoters, skim the waters looking for food.

The second is the coastal strand, characterized by long beaches and steep cliffs dropping into the sea. The coastal strand looks comparatively sterile—in many cases comprised of naked, shifting dunes—but supports a variety of plants, including beach grasses, the non-native ice plant, sand verbena, and beach strawberry, and shrubs like bush lupine, dune lupine, and mock heather. Shorebirds hunt and peck in the sands along the tide line; the species vary by season but may include migratory birds like the dunlin, sanderling, and sandpiper, and nesting birds like the killdeer and the endangered snowy plover. Other creatures living on the beaches include sand crabs, sand dollars, and various clams, mussels, and snails.

Wedged between these two habitats is the intertidal zone, sometimes submerged, sometimes exposed, home to such exotic creatures as the sea star, the giant green anemone, various barnacles, limpets, and crabs, and both red and purple sea urchins. Plants in the tidal zone are primarily algaes, like sea lettuce, and, farther offshore, different species of kelp, including bull kelp, noteworthy for its large bulbous "head."

Moving upland and inland, coastal strand gives way to coastal scrub and rangelands interspersed with pockets of coastal prairie. The coastal scrub is easy to identify, a thick tangle of coyote brush, bush lupine, and fragrant California sage on dry, south- and west-facing slopes, and coyote brush mingled with blackberry brambles, poison oak, and sword fern on wetter, north-facing slopes. A variety of wildflowers bloom amid the shrubs, including yellow monkey flower, California poppies, and the distinctive red cobweb thistle. Many varieties of songbirds call the scrub home, including wrentits, warblers, thrushes, sparrows, towhees, wrens, and quail; their birdsong chorus is omnipresent and cheering.

The rangelands stretch for many acres across the rolling middle of the headlands, a close-cropped grassland that is vividly green when watered by winter rains, and fades from gold to brittle brown as the dry months progress. This once was primarily coastal prairie, a mix of perennial grasses that was overrun by non-native annual grasses brought in on the hooves (literally) of cattle when they were introduced to the point. Several species of blackbirds, along with starlings and sparrows, flock to the rangelands and prairie remnants to feed and breed.

The scrublands and grasslands are flush with fauna. In addition to cattle, the range is also home to the three species of deer that roam the park: the native black-tailed deer, the non-native fallow deer, with a coat so pale in color that it sometimes appears white, and the non-native axis deer, a large animal with a reddish brown coat speckled with white dots. Tule elk, which have their own reserve on Tomales Point, also inhabit the range. Rabbits, raccoons, opossums, rodents, mice, moles and voles—the list is endless. The presence of so much prey, of course, means that these lands are also home to predators, including mountain lions, bobcats, foxes, and coyotes.

Finally, in the highlands on the Inverness Ridge, lush evergreen forests thrive. In the north part of the park, the forest is dominated by the Bishop pine, with an undergrowth of huckleberry, coffeeberry, ceanothus, and the occasional manzanita. The shrubbery provides food and shelter for songbirds, squirrels, raccoons, deer, and other critters.

The south part of the ridge is also covered by an evergreen forest, this one dominated by the Douglas fir and its diverse understory of huckleberry, poison oak, and, in moister areas, sword ferns that grow to primeval sizes. Some of the trees themselves have grown very large, their bases measuring 6 feet in diameter.

These habitats overlay most of the peninsula, but the park boasts habitats within habitats. Streams that course from the ridgelines to the sea support vibrant riparian habitats that harbor alders, cottonwoods, willows, bay laurels and oaks, and support frogs, newts, and other amphibians. Marshes, both fresh-water and saltwater, clogged with a variety of rushes, sedges, cattails, and willows, edge ponds, lakes, and lagoons throughout the park. Oak woodlands reach into Bear Valley and down the Olema Valley, the stately trees throwing great circles of shade over the grasses beneath their canopies.

Gnarly oaks, like this one on the Bear Valley Trail, mingle with many other trees in the dense and complex woodlands of Point Reyes.

This great diversity, a grand museum of wildlife and plant life, contains more than twenty-four threatened and endangered species, including the California red-legged frog and the northern spotted owl. More than 470 different species of birds have been sighted within the park. That such abundance thrives at the back door of one of the greatest metropolitan areas in the United States is a tribute to the dedication of the park service and the loving care of the park's visitors.

The Vision Fire

In October 1995 a black cloud hovered over West Marin. The Inverness Ridge was on fire. The Point Reyes National Seashore was on fire.

The black cloud appeared evil at first, a great tragedy, a senseless conflagration that destroyed a familiar forest and forever changed a landscape that was dearly loved. But the cloud had a silver lining. In the wake of the Vision Fire has come rebirth—a rebirth that, in places, seems almost too exuberant, as fledgling trees and rioting wildflowers and a variety of grasses battle for space on ground enriched by the ashes of their predecessors.

The Vision Fire, so named because it started on the slopes of Mount Vision, was started by human carelessness—an illegal campfire improperly extinguished and run amok. It was fanned by winds that gusted up to 50 miles per hour, extremely low humidity, and abundant fuel. By the time it was extinguished, thirteen days after it ignited, the fire had torched approximately 13,000 acres in the park and destroyed forty-five homes in neighboring Inverness Park.

The landscape looked ruined in the winter that followed—charred, gray, riddled not only with the scars left by the fire but also those left by firefighting efforts. But by April, as before-and-after pictures taken by the park service attest, the rebound had begun, with grasses and wildflowers erupting from soils refreshed with nutrients, under a sun no longer blocked by a canopy of trees. Park officials also employed the talents of specialists in a variety of fields to help both the park and neighboring residents with rehabilitation of the burned areas.

Today, while it's still quite evident fire rampaged through the area—on some trails north of Limantour Road, the smell of ash and charred wood still wafts from the dirt—it's also clear that nature has a plan. The new growth is lush and vibrant beneath what remains of the old. The original landscape can't be replaced, but it is surely being restored.

In its aftermath, the Vision Fire also created a unique environment for learning. Experts delved into a variety of research studies, from the historic role of fire on the point to the fire's effects on butterflies and moths, songbirds, the Bishop pine forest, the Muddy Hollow watershed, and the rare Point Reyes mountain beaver.

Should another wildfire rip through Point Reyes, there is no doubt that lovers of the park would mourn. But for those who have witnessed the aftermath of the Vision Fire, that grief will be tempered by the knowledge that the wildlands are resilient—they will come back.

Geography and Geology

The dominant feature of both the geography and geology of Point Reyes is the San Andreas Fault. It runs down the Olema Valley on the east side of the national seashore, a great rift that ruptured with disastrous effects in 1906, and is sure to rupture again.

The fault marks the line along which two great slabs of the earth's crust meet. The forces of plate tectonics are moving the point, which rides on the Pacific Plate, northward toward Alaska. The neighboring North American Plate is not moving in the same direction, and the friction that builds up between these enormous opposing forces occasionally must be released. In the earthquakes caused by these releases, Point Reyes inches closer to its final destination in the Aleutian Trench. That's what happened in 1906, and that's what will happen again someday. The future temblor already has a name: "The Big One."

Meanwhile, the Olema Valley section of the fault looks bucolic. The fault enters the valley at the Bolinas Lagoon then stretches northward through the ranchlands, between the rippled ridges, before diving beneath finger-shaped Tomales Bay. On the fault's east side rises the Bolinas Ridge, which tops out at more than 1,400 feet; on its west side the Inverness Ridge reaches equal heights. Mount Wittenberg, at 1,407 feet, is the highest point in the park.

The rift valley is geographic evidence of the fault. The geologic evidence is also clear-cut. On the east side of the fault, the rocks are classified by geologists as Franciscan, consisting of graywacke, chert, shale, and other sedimentary deposits. On Point Reyes the bedrock is granite, which originated in an entirely different area—and environment—than the Franciscan rocks just across the valley. According to one park official, Point Reyes is essentially the southern tip of the Sierra Nevada, which has moved northward from near Los Angeles over time.

The Pacific Ocean is the other great sculptor of landforms on Point Reyes, carving out cliffs and depositing beaches along its southern, western, and northern boundaries. In the southern reaches of the park, south of Drakes Bay, the land falls steeply and directly from the top of Inverness Ridge into the sea. North of Drakes Bay the drop pauses on the rangelands, an undulating mesa filled with sediments, the creamy color of which is on display in the cliffs at Drakes Beach. North of the point the mesa slips easily into beach, then into the ocean. But the headlands, made of a harder conglomerate rock formation, form a steep bank of cliffs that plunge precipitously into the sea.

Getting to the Park

Point Reyes National Seashore is the westernmost appendage of Marin County. The park is located about 30 miles north of San Francisco as the crow flies; on the ground, depending where you start and what route you take, the distances vary.

The most direct way to reach the park from points north and south is via U.S. Highway 101 and Sir Francis Drake Boulevard. I call Sir Francis Drake a boulevard here because that's what the freeway sign says, but this road appears on area maps as both the Sir Francis Drake Highway and Sir Francis Drake Boulevard. In my opinion, it's both. On the east side of Marin County, from the point it leaves US 101 in Corte Madera until it reaches the summit of Whites Hill in Fairfax, it's most definitely a boulevard, with all the development and congestion suggested by that name. Once in West Marin, traveling through the open spaces of the San Geronimo Valley, past Samuel P. Taylor State Park, and out through Inverness onto the pasturelands of the Point Reyes peninsula, it's most definitely a highway. Given the geographic focus of this guide, I refer to it most often as the Sir Francis Drake Highway.

Approaching from the north or south on US 101, take the Sir Francis Drake Boulevard/San Anselmo exit in Corte Madera and head west. The boulevard travels through a series of little suburban towns: Kentfield, Ross, San Anselmo, and finally Fairfax. At about 10 miles, the road climbs over Whites Hill and enters the broad San Geronimo Valley. Pass a series of small towns; beyond Lagunitas the valley narrows and enters the Lagunitas Creek drainage. Redwoods crowd the road through Samuel P. Taylor State Park, which is at about the 15-mile mark. A portion of the Golden Gate National Recreation Area abuts the state park on its western border, as the redwoods thin and rolling pasturelands open.

Sir Francis Drake crosses Lagunitas Creek at Tocaloma at about 20 miles, then climbs up and over the Bolinas Ridge, arriving at its junction with California Highway 1 in Olema at about 22 miles. Turn right (north) onto CA 1 (also the Sir Francis Drake Highway), and go about 0.1 mile to Bear Valley Road. Turn left (west) onto Bear Valley Road, and follow it for about 0.5 mile to the national seashore's signed entrance road. The park's administrative offices are in the northwest corner of the intersection; the Bear Valley Visitor Center is about 0.2 mile west on the access road.

You can also reach the park from both north and south via CA 1. Approaching from San Francisco, CA 1 and US 101 are one and the same. Cross the Golden Gate Bridge, and drive north to the CA 1/Stinson Beach exit in Marin City. Go west, under the freeway, on CA 1 (also called the Shoreline Highway), passing through the western reaches of Mill Valley before climbing over a shoulder of Mount Tamalpais and descending to Muir Beach, which is about 8

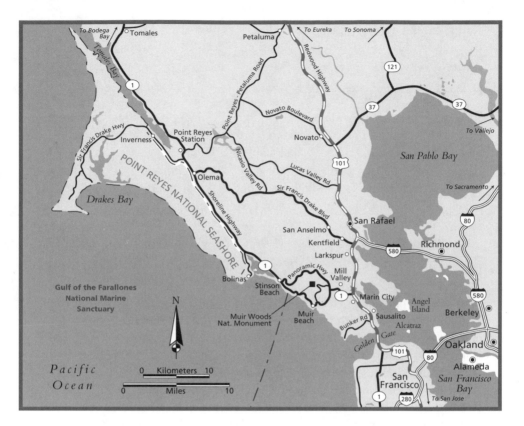

miles from the freeway interchange. CA 1 winds along the scenic coastline to Stinson Beach, then continues up the Olema Valley from Stinson to the stop sign at the intersection with the Sir Francis Drake Highway in Olema. Continue straight on CA 1 to Bear Valley Road, make a left (west) turn, and follow Bear Valley Road for 0.5 mile to the park access road.

From the north, follow CA 1 south to Point Reyes Station, a charming little town that borders both the national seashore and the southern end of Tomales Bay. The CA 1/Bear Valley Road intersection in Olema is about 2 miles south of downtown Point Reyes; make a right (west) turn onto Bear Valley Road, and continue west to the park access road. Alternatively, you can turn right (west) just south of town on the Sir Francis Drake Highway (signs point toward Inverness and the Point Reyes Lighthouse), and follow Sir Francis Drake for 0.7 mile to its intersection with Bear Valley Road. Turn left (south) onto Bear Valley Road, and go 1.7 miles to the access road, which is on the right (west).

You can also reach the park via a web of scenic back roads that break west out of San Rafael and Novato in Marin County, and Petaluma and Santa Rosa in Sonoma County. Arguably the most popular back road to the park is the

Point Reyes–Petaluma Road, which leaves Petaluma via D Street and winds through ranchlands to Point Reyes Station. A detailed California map will help you find your way.

Getting around the Park

Two main arteries provide access to every destination in the Point Reyes National Seashore. The Sir Francis Drake Highway leads into the northern and western reaches of the park, and California Highway 1 is the main route to the south. Secondary roads branching off the Sir Francis Drake Highway include Pierce Point Road, which leads out to the northern tip of the park at Tomales Point, and the Mount Vision Road, a scenic drive to the top of the Inverness Ridge. CA 1 offers access to the Five Brooks and Palomarin areas. The Limantour Road, which breaks west off the Bear Valley Road north of the park's headquarters in Bear Valley, leads to several important trailheads and destinations as well.

California Highway 1: This two-lane highway slices through the bottomlands of the Olema Valley, with the pasturelands of Bolinas Ridge rising on the east and the forested slopes of Inverness Ridge on the west. Approximately 11 miles of the highway front the Point Reyes National Seashore, stretching from Point Reyes Station south to the head of the Bolinas Lagoon.

Major sites and junctions along the highway, as you head south from the stop sign at the intersection with the Sir Francis Drake Highway in Olema, include the Stewart Ranch, on the right (west) at 2.5 miles, the Five Brooks Trailhead access road, on the right (west) at 3.5 miles, and the Randall Trailhead on the left (east) at 5.6 miles. The Thirteen Corners, a stretch that descends through a dense stand of eucalyptus (start counting at the large yellow speed sign) begins at about 6.6 miles. Dogtown and the Olema Valley and McCurdy Trailheads are at 8.2 miles, and the junction with the Olema-Bolinas Road, which offers access to the Palomarin Trailhead, is at 9.1 miles.

Beyond the Olema-Bolinas Road, CA 1 skirts the eastern shoreline of the Bolinas Lagoon, reaching Stinson Beach (part of the Golden Gate National Recreation Area) at about 13 miles. From there it continues down the coastline into San Francisco and beyond.

Sir Francis Drake Highway: The portion of the Sir Francis Drake Highway that runs through the national seashore leads through and to some of the best-known sites in the park, including Drakes Estero and Drakes Beach, the Great Beach, and the Point Reyes Lighthouse.

The road starts in eastern Marin County and ends on its westernmost point. Nearly 20 miles of its length lies within the boundaries of the park. From the stop sign in Olema, the highway is one with CA 1, running north for about 2 miles to the border of Point Reyes Station. It diverges from CA 1 at that point, breaking west and cutting through the Olema Marsh to the Bear Valley Road junction at 2.7 miles.

The highway veers north from that junction, tracing the western shore of Tomales Bay and passing through Inverness Park at 3.4 miles, and Inverness at 5.9 miles. Both of these hamlets, along with the bigger town of Point Reyes Station, offer grocery stores, restaurants, and other shops and conveniences.

At about 7.3 miles, the highway swings west again, passing the junction with Camino Del Mar, which leads to Shell Beach in Tomales Bay State Park. Stay left (west), climbing up and over the Inverness Ridge. Pierce Point Road departs to the right (north) at 8.8 miles, and the first of the historic ranches, M Ranch, is on the right as well, at 9 miles. At 9.4 miles, Mount Vision Road departs to the left (south); the next left, on a ranch road at 10.3 miles, leads to the Estero Trail.

Johnson's Oyster Farm, on the shores of Drakes Estero, is on the left (south) side of the highway at 11.2 miles. The AT&T/MCI radio and telephone station, studded with antennas used for ship-to-shore communications throughout the Pacific, is on the right (west) as the highway swings southward through the rangelands of the park's pastoral zone.

Trailheads and access roads are now interspersed with historic ranches identified by letters of the alphabet. The Bull Point Trailhead, on the left at 13 miles, is on the site of the former F Ranch. At about 14 miles, the access road to North Beach (a portion of the Great Beach) departs to the right (west); pass through the Historic E Ranch to the next intersection, with the road to Drakes Beach and the Ken Patrick Visitor Center at 16.3 miles. Wind down through the pastures to the South Beach access road (again, part of the Great Beach) at 16.8 miles. Proceed through the Historic B and A Ranches; the road to Chimney Rock is at 20.6 miles.

The highway now heads west again, climbing onto its final stretch along the headlands. At 21.4 miles, a small pullout and interpretive sign mark the site of the Sea Lion Overlook. The road ends at 21.7 miles, in the parking lot that serves the Point Reyes Lighthouse and its visitor center.

Pierce Point Road: The Pierce Point Road leads north from the Sir Francis Drake Highway onto Tomales Point. It begins by climbing onto the forested Inverness Ridge, passing the Jepson Trailhead, which drops down into adjacent Tomales Bay State Park, about 1.1 miles from Sir Francis Drake. The entrance to the state park is at 1.3 miles; a right (east) turn leads down to Hearts Desire Beach. Dropping down into pasturelands, the road passes the Historic H Ranch before reaching the Abbotts Lagoon Trailhead on the left (west) at 3.5 miles. Next comes the Historic I Ranch, then the Kehoe Beach Trailhead on the left (west) at 5.6 miles.

The road climbs steeply from the Kehoe Trailhead, passing the Historic J Ranch, then dipping down and leaving the pastoral zone for designated wilderness. This is the range of the tule elk, which enjoy some of the most spectacular views in the park, with Tomales Bay on the east and the Pacific Ocean on the west. The Pierce Point Ranch is at 9.2 miles; the road continues for another 0.2 mile to the west, dead-ending in the parking lot for McClures Beach.

Mount Vision Road: The Mount Vision Road intersects the Sir Francis Drake Highway at 7.6 miles. This narrow strip of asphalt climbs south up the steep slopes of Mount Vision, which stands 1,282 feet above sea level. It climbs steep switchbacks for the first 2 miles or so, first through healthy forest that was relatively untouched by the Vision Fire of 1995, then into open areas where the woodland was incinerated. Once the canopy disappears the views westward become stunning, dropping down across softly undulating pasturelands to Drakes Estero and Bay, and the headlands. A picnic bench on the west side of the roadway at about 2.5 miles is a wonderful vista point; other pullouts alongside the road work nicely for viewing the panorama as well.

The road climbs through the rolling chaparral on the ridgetop, passing small ponds that glitter darkly beneath an unfettered sun. Views open east as well as west, past Bolinas Ridge to Sonoma Mountain and Mount St. Helena, landmarks of the interior valleys of the Coast Range.

The road ends amid the scrub in a large parking lot at about 4 miles. Though blocked by a gate at this point, the Mount Vision Road continues for another 0.5 mile, offering access to the radio installations atop Point Reyes Hill, and to the Bucklin Trail and Inverness Ridge Trail.

Limantour Road: The Limantour Road is nearly 8 miles long, reaching from the Bear Valley Road to the parking area for Limantour Beach. It begins by heading south through a broad meadow that backs up to the Olema Marsh. At 0.9 mile, the road switchbacks north and begins a long, traversing climb up the east face of the Inverness Ridge, the dense trees blocking all but the most fleeting views.

The Sky Trailhead is on the left (south) at 3.5 miles, on the ridgetop; the road curves north, climbing into the burn area, where the views open west of Drakes Bay, Limantour, and the Point Reyes headlands.

The Bayview Trailhead is on the right (north) at 4.5 miles. The road begins a long, westward, downhill run at this point, through a rolling landscape of coastal scrub. A steep, 17 percent pitch drops you at the intersection of the road leading left (south) to the Point Reyes Hostel, Clem Miller Environmental Education Center, and the Laguna and Coast Trailheads, and the road leading right (north) to the Muddy Hollow Trailhead. Climb just as steeply out of the ravine, and continue through the scrublands to the Limantour parking area at 7.7 miles.

There is limited public transportation to the park, provided by Golden Gate Transit. Call (415) 923–2000 for information and schedules.

Finding the Trailheads

All directions to trailheads begin at the Bear Valley Visitor Center. Located on Bear Valley Road about 0.5 mile northwest of Olema and 2 miles southwest of Point Reyes Station, the visitor center is the newest structure on the former W Ranch, also known as the Bear Valley Ranch. In addition to the visitor center, former ranching structures now house the park's administrative offices. The big red barn—a former hay barn built in the late 1800s—is as effective a marker for the access road to the visitor center as the large park signs. You can't miss it.

Bear in mind that, on weekends during whale-watching season, the park operates shuttle buses to the whale-watching sites near the Point Reyes Lighthouse, at the end of the Sir Francis Drake Highway. The shuttles depart from the parking lot at the Ken Patrick Visitor Center, at Drakes Beach. Tickets are available at the Ken Patrick center.

Visitor Centers and Amenities

Bear Valley Visitor Center

The Bear Valley Visitor Center is the nerve center of the Point Reyes National Seashore. An airy, barn-like structure, the center houses a well-stocked book and gift store, a theater, and an exhibit area. The central desk is staffed by knowledgeable rangers who dispense their expertise along with park maps, brochures, and other printed materials. You can also ask about the ranger-led hikes and tours, special activities at the Point Reyes Lighthouse, Kule Loklo, or other sites around the park, and learn about trail, weather, and tidal conditions. In addition, you can make reservations for overnight stays in the park's backcountry camps, and must pick up your backcountry camping permits there.

The visitor center is open Monday through Friday, from 9:00 A.M. to 5:00 P.M., and on weekends and all holidays (except Christmas) from 8:00 A.M. to 5:00 P.M. It's closed on Christmas. The telephone number is (415) 464–5100.

The visitor center is located on the Bear Valley Road, about 0.5 mile northwest of the stop sign in Olema, and 2 miles southwest of Point Reyes Station. From the intersection of California Highway 1 and the Sir Francis Drake Highway in Olema, go north on CA 1 for 0.1 mile, and turn left (west) onto Bear Valley Road. Follow Bear Valley Road west, then north, to the signed access road for the visitor center and park administration buildings. Follow the paved access road west for 0.2 mile to the ample parking area.

From Point Reyes Station, head south on CA 1 to its intersection with the Sir Francis Drake Highway. Turn right (west) onto Sir Francis Drake, and go for 0.7 mile to its intersection with Bear Valley Road. Turn left (south) onto Bear Valley Road, and go 1.7 miles to the visitor center's access road.

For more camping information, call (415) 663–8054.

Ken Patrick Visitor Center

The Ken Patrick Visitor Center has the weather-beaten look of a modern beach house. Its wood exterior has been bleached various shades of gray, blending harmoniously with the grays and greens of the coastal chaparral that surrounds it. Large windows open onto the panorama of Drakes Bay, Drakes Beach, and the distinctive pale cliffs that reportedly made Francis Drake and his English crew feel at home when they landed here in 1579.

The complex houses rest rooms and the Drake's Beach Café, serving oyster stew, oyster burgers, fries, and other staples of cafe fare. Visitor center, rest rooms, and café all open onto an interior courtyard that is protected from wind and weather and decorated with interpretive displays.

The entrance to the visitor center is flanked by a billboard where the park posts information and important notices. Inside you will find interpretive displays about the exploration of the area—some about Drake, others about the ill-fated voyage of Sebastian Cermeño, whose ship, the *San Augustin*, rests beneath the waves of Drakes Bay—as well as natural history displays that include the suspended skeleton of a minke whale. The visitor center also offers books and gifts for sale, and is staffed by a ranger when open.

The Ken Patrick Visitor Center is open from 10 A.M. to 5 P.M. on weekends and holidays year-round, and is closed on Christmas. During summer months (from Memorial Day to Labor Day) the visitor center is open from Friday through Tuesday, and is closed on Wednesday and Thursday (it also closes between noon and 1:00 P.M. for lunch). For more information, call (415) 669–1250.

Lighthouse Visitor Center

Though tiny by comparison to the other visitor centers in the national seashore, the Lighthouse Visitor Center is far from spare. The interior of the tiny white building, which sits in the lee of a rock outcrop above the Point Reyes Lighthouse, isn't much larger than a modest bedroom, but each wall is packed with information. Interpretive displays cover whales, birds, seals, the lighthouse, the lifeboat station, and more, with just enough space left over for a gift shop and a desk for the ranger who staffs the center. Outside, whiteboards hold information on whale sightings, sea lion and elephant seal sightings, and interpretive programs.

The Lighthouse Visitor Center is open from 10:00 A.M. to 4:30 P.M. Thursday through Monday, and is closed on Tuesday and Wednesday and on Christmas Day. To reach the center from the Bear Valley Visitor Center, take the access road east 0.2 mile to its intersection with Bear Valley Road. Turn left (north) onto Bear Valley Road, and drive 1.7 miles to its intersection with the Sir Francis Drake Highway. Turn left (north) onto the highway, and follow it for 19 miles to the lighthouse parking lot at the end of the road. A paved 0.4-mile trail/road continues west, past interpretive signs and park housing, to the visitor center, which is above the steep stairs that lead down to the lighthouse.

The lighthouse area is extremely popular. The parking lot is full on most weekend days and during the week when the whale migration is in full swing. If you can't find a spot in the lot, park alongside the Sir Francis Drake Highway, taking care to leave your vehicle well off the roadway.

On weekends during the whale-watching season, the park service closes the Sir Francis Drake Highway at Drakes Beach and provides a shuttle service from the Ken Patrick Visitor Center at Drakes Beach to the lighthouse parking lot. Tickets for the shuttle, which cost $4.00 in the 2001–2002 season, are available at the Ken Patrick Visitor Center.

For more information on the Lighthouse Visitor Center, call (415) 669–1534.

Clem Miller Environmental Education Center

Named for Congressman Clem Miller, a Marin Country resident who championed the creation of the Point Reyes National Seashore in the early 1960s, this center is a residential facility where students and teachers gather to study the seashore's ecology. It's operated by the Point Reyes National Seashore Association, a nonprofit group dedicated to supporting the park through both preservation projects and educational efforts. The center is located off Limantour Road near the Point Reyes Hostel. For more information, contact the association's field seminars program office at (415) 663–1224, or visit the Web site at www.ptreyes.org. You can pick up one of the association's field seminar brochures at the Bear Valley Visitor Center, or write to the Point Reyes National Seashore Association, Point Reyes Station, CA 94956.

Point Reyes Hostel

Run by Hostelling International, the Point Reyes Hostel offers low-cost overnight accommodations for travelers to the seashore. It sleeps forty-four people, and offers them use of a common room, kitchen, and showers. Reservations are recommended, especially during the summer months and on weekends, and can be made by calling the hostel directly at (415) 663–8811, or by using the telephone tree reservation system at (800) 909–4776.

The hostel is located off of Limantour Road near the Clem Miller Environment Education Center. Follow Limantour Road for about 6 miles from its intersection with the Bear Valley Road, then turn left (south) onto the signed access road. The hostel is about 0.3 mile down the access road.

To get more information, you can write to P.O. Box 247, Point Reyes Station, CA 94956; call the office; or visit the Web site at www.norcalhostels.org/pointreyes.

Mountain bikers, hikers, and equestrians will find a trail to suit their tastes and talents in the Point Reyes National Seashore. This cyclist enjoys the Estero Trail, which leads to Sunset Beach and Drakes Head, among other destinations.

Point Reyes National Seashore maintains an extensive trail system, with routes leading through all its varied ecosystems and to its most spectacular locales and vistas. From the wind-scoured coastal bluffs to the blooming meadows of the pastoral zone, from dense evergreen forests to the gnarly-limbed trees of the oak woodland, from Bass Lake to Alamere Falls to Arch Rock to Tomales Bluff—paths lead to and through each and more.

More than 146 miles of trails wind through the seashore. Most are meticulously maintained, well signed, and well used. The routes described in this chapter do not represent an inclusive list—after all, this is an "exploring" guide. I selected these trails as a sampling of what is available in Point Reyes, and encourage you to venture off the described track.

The trails are presented generally from north to south, beginning with routes off Pierce Point Road and ending with trails beginning from Palomarin.

Off Pierce Point Road

Tomales Point Trail

HIGHLIGHTS: Extending out to windswept bluffs at the northern tip of the seashore, the Tomales Point Trail affords great views of Tomales Bay and the rugged coastline to the north, and the opportunity to see the beautiful and rare tule elk.

TYPE OF JOURNEY: Out-and-back.

TOTAL DISTANCE: 9.4 miles.

DIFFICULTY: Hard.

PERMITTED USES: Hiking, horseback riding.

MAPS: USGS Tomales; Point Reyes National Seashore Map; Tom Harrison Point Reyes National Seashore Map; TOPO! San Francisco Bay Area, Wine Country, and Big Sur.

SPECIAL CONSIDERATIONS: No dogs are allowed. Mountain lions can be found in the area; you are advised not to hike alone, and to verse yourself in the proper response if you encounter a cat.

Tomales Point Trail

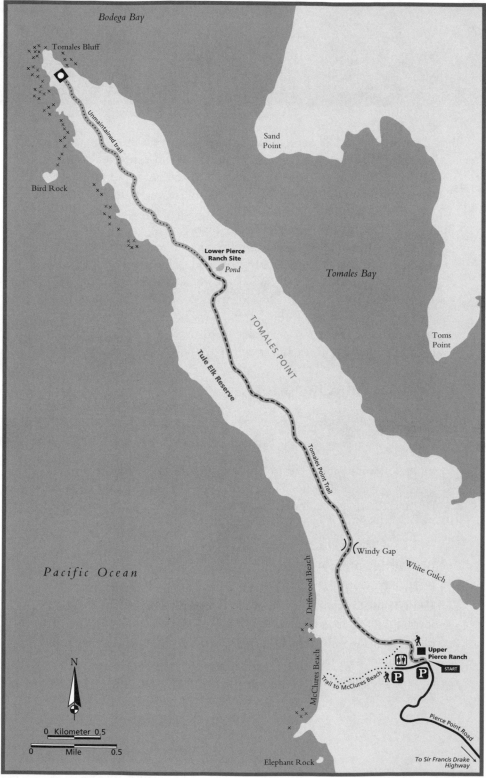

Bodega Bay

Tomales Bluff

Unmaintained trail

Bird Rock

Sand Point

Lower Pierce Ranch Site
Pond

Tomales Bay

Toms Point

TOMALES POINT

Tule Elk Reserve

Tomales Point Trail

Pacific Ocean

Windy Gap

White Gulch

Driftwood Beach

Upper Pierce Ranch

N

McClures Beach

Trail to McClures Beach

START

Pierce Point Road

0 Kilometer 0.5

0 Mile 0.5

Elephant Rock

To Sir Francis Drake Highway

PARKING AND FACILITIES: Parking at the trailhead is ample, but the only amenities are garbage and recycling receptacles and a pay phone. Picnic tables can be found inside the ranch enclosure. Rest rooms are located about 0.1 mile farther down (west) on Pierce Point Road at the McClures Beach Trailhead.

FINDING THE TRAILHEAD: From the Bear Valley Visitor Center, drive east down the access road for 0.2 mile to Bear Valley Road. Turn left (north) onto Bear Valley Road, and follow it for 1.7 miles to its intersection with the Sir Francis Drake Highway. Turn left (north) onto Sir Francis Drake, and follow the highway for 5.5 miles to its intersection with Pierce Point Road. Turn right (north) onto Pierce Point Road, and go about 8.8 miles to the parking area for the Upper Pierce Ranch.

KEY POINTS:

0.0 Trailhead.

0.8 Pass Windy Gap and begin to climb.

3.2 Reach the pond and the site of the Lower Pierce Ranch.

4.0 Begin the cross-country portion of the route.

4.7 Arrive on the bluffs near the tip of Tomales Point.

Amid the bush lupine and cobweb thistle that flourishes at the end of Tomales Point, the Tomales Point Trail scatters into myriad thin sand tracks. Wandering through the thickets on a clear day, the trick of finding the best route only adds to the wildness and beauty of this hike. Your destination is obvious—the end of the narrowing point of land that juts into the ocean, forming the western flank of Tomales Bay—and that makes the maze feel safe, the flowers more colorful and fragrant, the seabirds more entertaining, and the surf benign.

This hike takes you into the seashore's tule elk reserve, home of one of the largest herds of this rare native species in California. The trail also offers you the opportunity to glimpse calving seals in early summer, and in spring boasts a wonderful wildflower display. Sun or fog, it's a journey well worth taking.

Begin by skirting the Upper Pierce Ranch on its west side, passing informational signs that describe the ranch and warn that you'll be traveling in mountain lion territory. A trail sign states that Tomales Point is 4.7 miles ahead.

Beyond the ranch and its sheltering wall of cypress, the broad, sandy track (a former ranch road) traverses a grassy hillside. As you circle above a hollow, you are treated to views of the surf and rocks at McClures Beach to the southwest. Round a bend, and views of the beach give way to the surf-bashed rocks at the base of the west-facing cliffs.

Pass a sign warning of hazardous footing along the cliffs at about the 0.5-mile mark. The trail curls inland, offering glimpses of tempting but inaccessible beaches to the west. Windy Gap is at about 0.8 mile; from the gap White Gulch spills left (east) into Tomales Bay. Tule elk sometimes congregate here. A sculptured ravine careens right (west) into the Pacific, its walls etched with castlelike spires.

The trail begins to climb beyond the gap. The incline is fairly steep at first, then mellows as you pass a game fence, which is on the right (east) on a knoll overlooking the trail. Rock outcrops jut from the scrub as you climb; at about 1.5 miles a side trail veers off to the right (east) to an overlook of Dillon Beach, at the mouth of Tomales Bay. Other outcrops offer views west to the ocean.

At about 2.5 miles the trail crests, and you begin to descend. As the road swings to the east, you can see the pond near the site of the Lower Pierce Ranch below, as well as Dillon Beach and Sand Point, with Bolinas Ridge behind. You pass the pond on its west side at about 3.2 miles. Tule elk, coated in three-toned brown with dark heads and fluffy white butts, congregate here as well. At 3.5 miles the trail descends through a row of cypress and shoulder-high bush lupine. Pass another trail sign, and drop through a gully offering a picture-frame view of the mouth of the bay.

The trail climbs out of the gully, passing through dense poppies and lupine, which by midsummer boasts both yellow blooms and drying seedpods that rattle when brushed—a tambourine to the ocean's percussion. Cross a flat area to another trail sign. The maintained trail ends here, at about the 4-mile mark, but a well-defined route has been pounded into the sand leading up into the scrub. Climb up this sandy path, then pick your way through the bushes. The rounded shrubs of the maze are enlivened with colorful poppies, lupine, thistle (including the stunning red cobweb thistle), insects, birds, and butterflies.

As you approach the tip of the point, Bird Rock, whitewashed with droppings, comes into view. Pelicans and other shorebirds fly overhead. Another well-defined track leads west from the braided trails to an overlook on the left (west), with views down to a lonely crescent beach and Bird Rock.

Continue north to the point; the trails taper out here. Pick a clear sandy spot and watch the surf spill over the dark rocks and pools that bleed from the land into the sea, the pelicans wheel overhead, and the silvery boats skim in the narrow waters of Tomales Bay.

When you can tear yourself away, return to the trailhead via the same route.

Abbotts Lagoon

HIGHLIGHTS: The birdwatching along twin arms of Abbotts Lagoon is among the best in the national seashore. Relaxing on the remote stretch of the Great Beach at trail's end ain't bad either.

TYPE OF JOURNEY: Out-and-back.

TOTAL DISTANCE: 3 miles.

DIFFICULTY: Easy.

PERMITTED USES: Hiking, horseback riding.

MAPS: USGS Drakes Bay and Tomales; Point Reyes National Seashore Map; Tom Harrison Point Reyes National Seashore Map; TOPO! San Francisco Bay Area, Wine Country, and Big Sur.

SPECIAL CONSIDERATIONS: No dogs are allowed.

PARKING AND FACILITIES: The lot on the west side of Pierce Point Road offers plenty of parking. A rest room is available.

FINDING THE TRAILHEAD: From the Bear Valley Visitor Center, drive east down the access road for 0.2 mile to Bear Valley Road. Turn left (north) onto Bear Valley Road, and follow it for 1.7 miles to its intersection with the Sir Francis Drake Highway. Turn left (north) onto Sir Francis Drake, and follow the highway for 5.5 miles to its intersection with Pierce Point Road. Turn right (north) onto Pierce Point Road, and follow it for 3.4 miles to the Abbotts Lagoon parking area.

KEY POINTS:

0.0 Trailhead.

0.2 Cross a footbridge.

1.0 Reach the footbridge at the west end of the first lagoon.

1.5 Arrive on the beach at the mouth of the lagoon.

Abbotts Lagoon is a haven for birds. They sing in the scrub, waddle on the sand, race and peck along the tide line, and skydive into the surf. For any number of coots, grebes, terns, gulls, pelicans, and songbirds, Abbotts Lagoon is either home or the perfect stopover on a long and exhausting migration route.

The lagoon has two arms. The trail first skirts the south side of the upper arm, then crosses a footbridge over the slender waterway that connects to the lower lagoon. The trail essentially disappears at the lower lagoon, but traveling cross-country on the north side of the brackish water leads easily to the beach.

Begin by heading west from the parking area on the broad path, passing an informational sign at the trailhead. Cross a footbridge spanning a seasonal

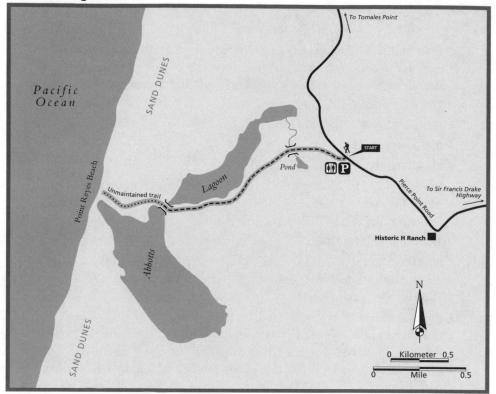

creeklet at about 0.2 mile; a tiny pond is on the left (southeast). The broad sandy path leads gradually downhill, passing a bench and an interpretive sign about the endangered snowy plover. Cows graze in the fenced pasture to the left (south).

As you near the west end of the upper lagoon, the trail leaves the fence line and drops closer to the water. Traverse the base of a steep, scrubby hillside, then drop to the second footbridge at 1 mile; this bridge spans the water-hyacinth-clogged link between the two arms of the lagoon. A narrow side trail breaks off to the left (south) and climbs onto the scrubby hillside; ignore this, and cross the bridge.

On the other side of the bridge, the scrub gives way to the relatively barren sands of the dunes that surround the lower lagoon and form the western boundary of the upper lagoon. The trail disappears, but the route to the beach is clear. Skimming the northern rim of the lower lagoon, you have views west toward the Pacific Ocean, and of the antenna farm that sprouts from the grassy bluff to the south.

A roll of dune separates the lagoon from the ocean; climb over this onto the arcing beach. If the day is clear, you can see south to the Point Reyes headlands, and north toward Elephant Rock and Tomales Point. You can wander up and down the beach as far as you'd like (and the surf safely permits). Brown pelicans sometimes congregate here, clustering on the sands or skimming the water for a meal.

After your stay on the beach, return as you came.

The bird-watching at Abbotts Lagoon is awesome, but some are more interested in what lies beneath than what flies above.

Inverness Ridge Trail

HIGHLIGHTS: The legacy of the 1995 Vision Fire is illustrated in the fledgling forest that has sprung up along the Inverness Ridge Trail.

TYPE OF JOURNEY: Out-and-back.

TOTAL DISTANCE: 6.2 miles.

DIFFICULTY: Moderate.

PERMITTED USES: Hiking, horseback riding, mountain biking.

MAPS: USGS Inverness; Point Reyes National Seashore Map; Tom Harrison Point Reyes National Seashore Map; TOPO! San Francisco Bay Area, Wine Country, and Big Sur.

SPECIAL CONSIDERATIONS: No pets are permitted.

PARKING AND FACILITIES: There is a large parking lot at the Mount Vision trailhead, but no other amenities.

FINDING THE TRAILHEAD: From the Bear Valley Visitor Center, follow the access road east for 0.2 mile to the Bear Valley Road. Turn left (north) onto the Bear Valley Road and go 1.7 miles to its intersection with the Sir Francis Drake Highway near Inverness Park. Turn left (north) onto the Sir Francis Drake Highway, and follow the highway for 7.6 miles, through the town of Inverness, to the Mount Vision Road. Turn left (south) onto the Mount Vision Road, which climbs for 4 miles to the trailhead parking area.

KEY POINTS:

0.0 Trailhead.

0.5 Reach the top of Point Reyes Hill.

1.1 Drop into a saddle.

1.8 Reach the junction with the Drakes View Trail.

2.4 Meet the paved drive.

The Inverness Ridge Trail traces a strip of the urban/wilderness interface on the east side of Point Reyes National Seashore. Lest the reference to development scare you off, fear not: The trail passes only a handful of homes as it follows the ridgeline between the top of Point Reyes Hill and Limantour Road. The vistas that unfold as you follow the route are spectacular, as is the landscape you travel through, a landscape once blackened by the Vision Fire and now undergoing a vigorous regeneration.

Inverness Ridge Trail

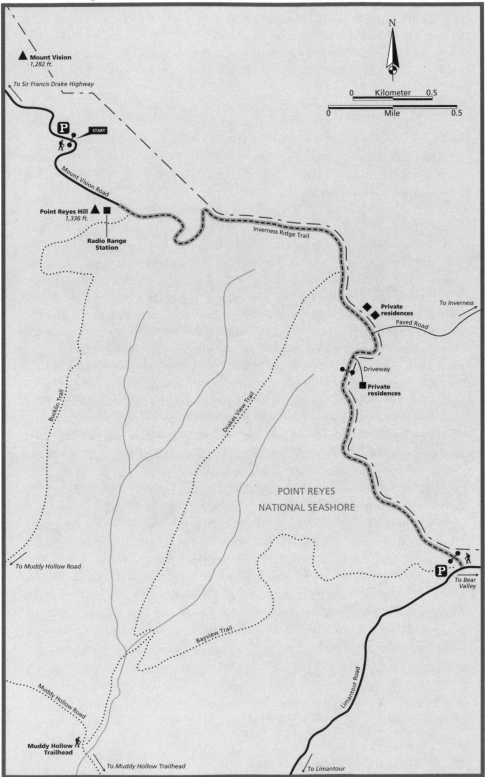

Mount Vision
1,282 ft.

To Sir Francis Drake Highway

P

START

Mount Vision Road

Point Reyes Hill
1,336 ft.

Radio Range Station

Inverness Ridge Trail

N

0   Kilometer   0.5

0   Mile   0.5

Bucklin Trail

Drakes View Trail

To Inverness

Private residences

Paved Road

Driveway

Private residences

POINT REYES

NATIONAL SEASHORE

To Muddy Hollow Road

P

To Bear Valley

Bayview Trail

Limantour Road

Muddy Hollow Road

Muddy Hollow Trailhead

To Muddy Hollow Trailhead

To Limantour

The trail begins behind the gate, following the pavement up through the chaparral toward the crest of Point Reyes Hill, which rises 1,336 feet above sea level. Views on the climb spread down and west to the sea, over rolling pastoral lands and the shimmering limbs of Drakes Estero to the Point Reyes headlands, all painted in pale shades of green, blue, and brown.

The Bucklin Trail departs to the right (west) as you near the crest of the hill, which is at 0.5 mile. The vistas now spread east across Tomales Bay and south to Mount Tamalpais, as well as over the point. Pass the radio installations, enclosed in a chain-link fence on the right (west) side of the trail, as the path dives down the south face of the hill as a narrow singletrack. There is no sign here, but the trail is obvious.

After a brief steep stretch, the pitch of the descent mellows as the trail rounds a switchback on the south side of the knob. More switchbacks drop you to a saddle, where views open north and east across the narrow blue finger of Tomales Bay, and southwest to Drakes Bay. Above and to the southeast, the aftermath of the Vision Fire, both fecund and spare, is graphically illustrated.

The trail plunges into the two-tiered forest—burned snags over thick new growth—at first climbing, then carving a roller-coaster traverse across the upper west-facing slopes of the ridge. Sometimes the path is wide enough to be recognized as the fire road that it is; at other times, a dense understory of manzanita, sage, and coyote brush crowds the path, so thick in places that it forms a tunnel.

At 1.8 miles the trail climbs to its intersection with the Drakes View Trail. Stay straight (south) on the Inverness Ridge Trail; the Drakes View Trail goes right (west), and leads down, eventually, to the Muddy Hollow Road. The first home appears to the left (east) of the trail. Pass a paved parking area below the house, staying right (southwest) on the unmarked trail.

The trail dives steeply downhill, dishing up fabulous views southwest to Limantour Beach and Drakes Bay, to a paved, private drive at 2.4 miles. Turn right (southwest) onto the asphalt, which acts as the trail for about 200 yards, all downhill. The trail reverts to dirt as it climbs to a gate; the paved drive swings left (southeast) to a private residence. Signs point the way.

Now plainly a fire road, the Inverness Ridge Trail rolls south along the west face of the ridge, still open to great views as it loops in and out of gullies cleared by the fire. The trail/road ends at Limantour Road, where a large dirt parking area serves both as a trailhead for the Inverness Ridge Trail and the Bayview Trail. Return as you came.

HIGHLIGHTS: Vast congregations of shorebirds gather on the mudflats off Sunset Beach to rest, feed, and socialize. A perch on the sand or rocks that rim the beach is perfect for human rest, feeding, and socializing.

TYPE OF JOURNEY: Out-and-back.

TOTAL DISTANCE: 7.8 miles.

DIFFICULTY: Moderate to hard.

PERMITTED USES: Hiking, horseback riding, mountain biking.

MAPS: USGS Drakes Bay; Point Reyes National Seashore Map; Tom Harrison Point Reyes National Seashore Map; TOPO! San Francisco Bay Area, Wine Country, and Big Sur.

SPECIAL CONSIDERATIONS: No dogs are allowed. This is a multiuse trail; please be considerate of other trail users.

PARKING AND FACILITIES: There is a large parking area serving the Estero Trailhead. Rest rooms arc available.

FINDING THE TRAILHEAD: From the Bear Valley Visitor Center, take the access road 0.2 mile east to Bear Valley Road. Turn left (north) onto Bear Valley Road and drive 1.7 miles to its intersection with the Sir Francis Drake Highway at Inverness Park. Turn left (north) onto Sir Francis Drake, and travel for 8.5 miles, beyond the town of Inverness, to the signed turnoff for the Estero Trail. Follow the narrow, paved ranch access road for 0.9 mile to the Estero Trailhead parking area, which is on the right (west) side of the road. The ranch road beyond the trailhead parking area is private.

KEY POINTS:

0.0 Trailhead.

0.6 Pass the bench in the trees.

1.1 Cross the footbridge.

2.4 Reach the trail junction.

3.5 Pass the lagoon.

3.9 Arrive on Sunset Beach.

Drakes Estero harbors a staggering abundance of bird life—thick clusters of sanderlings and sandpipers hunting and pecking in the mudflats, brown pelicans and gulls gliding low over the water searching for food, lone herons and egrets hungrily stalking the rushes. The Estero Trail, which begins behind the

Estero Trail to Sunset Beach, Estero Trail to Drakes Head

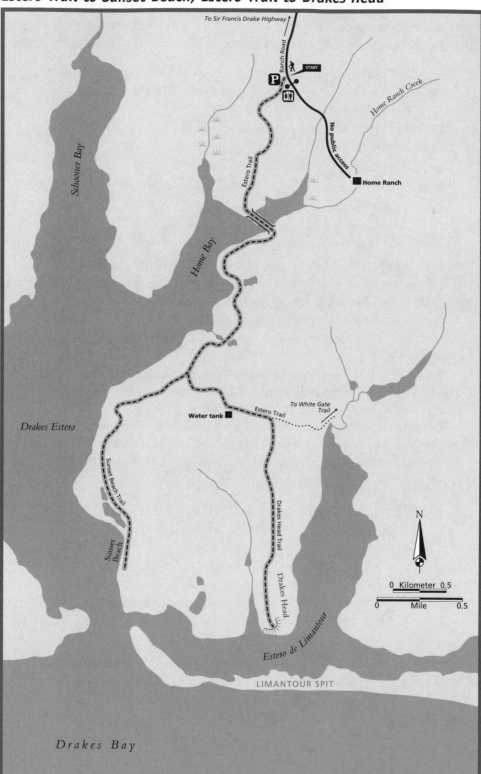

To Sir Francis Drake Highway

Ranch Road

START

P

Home Ranch Creek

No public access

Home Ranch

Estero Trail

Schooner Bay

Home Bay

To White Gate Trail

Water tank

Estero Trail

Drakes Estero

Sunset Beach Trail

Drakes Head Trail

Drakes Head

Sunset Beach

N

0 Kilometer 0.5

0 Mile 0.5

Estero de Limantour

LIMANTOUR SPIT

Drakes Bay

information board in the southwest corner of its gravel parking lot, offers ample opportunity to enjoy the avian spectacle.

The trail climbs gently away from the lot, leveling after about 0.3 mile and traversing a grassy knoll knotted with grasses, wildflowers, and bracken fern that overlooks the pastures of Home Ranch. The doubletrack then circles west into a thick stand of evergreens at about 0.6 mile; a bench is stationed in the dense shade. The path is softened with duff, threading through alternating open areas and glades. The waters of Home Bay sparkle through the trees.

Drop to a scenic wooden footbridge that spans the neck of Home Bay at 1.1 mile. From benches built into the bridge, you can watch flocks of birds frolicking and feeding in the tidelands. Ranch buildings are visible to the east, and the widening bay shimmers to the west. The first of a triumvirate of short hill climbs follows—a steep 0.5-mile climb broken by a couple of brief flats and one short drop before a last pitch passes you through a notch. When the trail flattens you have wonderful views of the estero.

Drop quickly to a dike over a finger of the bay at 1.8 miles, and turn sharply right (south) across a little timber bridge. Beyond the bridge lies the second climb, and beyond that, another swift drop to another dike. Ascend to more estero views at a gate and a stile that serves as passage for trekkers—and an interesting obstacle for cyclists—at 2.3 miles.

The junction of the Sunset Beach Trail and the Estero Trail is at 2.4 miles. The Estero Trail to Drakes Head breaks off to the left (east); continue straight (southwest) on the Sunset Beach Trail.

Descend through a lovely bloom of coastal scrub and grassland to a gate and stile at 3.3 miles. Beyond the gate, the trail curves down to overlook a glittering lagoon, then drops lagoonside at 3.5 miles. Views of Drakes Estero through the break in the bluffs at the mouth of the lagoon are gorgeous.

Beyond the lagoon, the trail curves south and becomes entrenched in tall, thick brambles before emerging on the narrow, pickleweed-laced shore of Sunset Beach at 3.9 miles. The shallow beach is sheltered by bluffs on the southeast, opening northwest onto the forever-moving waters of the estero and to Drakes Bay, with the Point Reyes headlands in the distance. The views are grand, but it's the birds that will capture your attention—at times they are as thick as ants on a peach at a picnic, moving in waves like the surf.

Return to the trailhead via the same route.

OPTION: If you have the time, which is more than possible if you are traveling by mountain bike, tie this trail in with the trail to Drakes Head (the trail description follows) for a journey of 11.8 miles.

See map on page 46

HIGHLIGHTS: Towering almost 150 feet above the narrow strip of water separating the Limantour Spit from the mainland, Drakes Head offers absolutely awesome views of the sweeping arc of Drakes Bay.

TYPE OF JOURNEY: Out-and-back.

TOTAL DISTANCE: 8.8 miles.

DIFFICULTY: Moderate to hard.

PERMITTED USES: Hiking, horseback riding, mountain biking.

MAPS: USGS Drakes Bay; Point Reyes National Seashore Map; Tom Harrison Point Reyes National Seashore Map; TOPO! San Francisco Bay Area, Wine Country, and Big Sur.

SPECIAL CONSIDERATIONS: No dogs are allowed. This is a multiuse trail; please be considerate of other trail users.

PARKING AND FACILITIES: A large parking area serves the Estero Trailhead. Rest rooms are available.

FINDING THE TRAILHEAD: From the Bear Valley Visitor Center, take the access road east for 0.2 mile to Bear Valley Road. Turn left (north) onto Bear Valley Road and drive 1.7 miles to its intersection with the Sir Francis Drake Highway at Inverness Park. Turn left (north) onto Sir Francis Drake, and travel for 8.5 miles, though the town of Inverness, to the turnoff for the Estero Trail. Follow the narrow, paved ranch access road south for 0.9 mile to the signed Estero Trailhead parking area, which is on the right (west) side of the road. The ranch road beyond the trailhead parking area is private.

KEY POINTS:

0.0 Trailhead.

0.6 Pass the bench in the trees.

1.1 Cross the footbridge.

2.4 Reach the Sunset Beach Trail junction.

3.0 Reach the Drakes Head Trail intersection.

4.4 Arrive at the Drakes Head overlook.

From the crest of Drakes Head on a clear day, the panoramic splendor of Point Reyes and the Gulf of the Farallones is displayed with cartographic clarity. Southernmost in your sights is Lands End; moving northward, the sea sweeps into the great indent of the Golden Gate and expands westward to the saw-

A hiker enjoys well-earned views of the Limantour Spit, Estero de Limantour, and Drakes Bay from the crest of Drakes Head.

toothed rocks of the elusive Farallon Islands. The rugged Marin County coastline stretches into the national seashore, mellowing into the golden arc of Limantour Beach and the green expanse of Drakes Bay. The creamy Limantour Spit, directly below the head, is framed on the inside by the turquoise shallows of the Estero de Limantour; looking west, Drakes Bay is edged by milky cliffs that swing southward to the hazy headlands of the point.

Begin by following the Estero Trail as described in the hike to Sunset Beach. Briefly, the doubletrack starts behind the information board in the southwest corner of the gravel parking lot, climbing up and around a grassy knoll overlooking Home Ranch. Head west into a thick stand of evergreens, passing a bench at about 0.6 mile. At 1.1 mile, drop to a wooden footbridge that spans the neck of Home Bay. The trail is a roller coaster beyond the bridge, with sharp ups and downs and wonderful views of the estero and its bird life.

The trail splits at 2.4 miles. The Estero Trail to Drakes Head goes left (southeast); the trail to Sunset Beach heads straight (southwest) and is described in greater detail in the Sunset Beach Trail description.

To reach Drakes Head, stay left on the narrow Estero Trail and head southeast. The path climbs for a 0.25 mile to a fence, trail sign, and cattle watering basin—passage through the fence is via a stile—then continues through a broken fence (a stile is available here too). The path veers to the east and follows the fence line across the top of the bluff, with wooded Inverness Ridge in the distance. Cross a ranch road, staying alongside the fence on the overgrown road that serves as the trail. Blue signs with white arrows keep you on track.

At 3 miles you reach another stile and a trail intersection. The Estero Trail continues straight (east) to the Glenbrook Trail and Muddy Hollow. Turn right (south) onto the Drakes Head Trail.

Head south through the thick grasses, shoulder high and speckled with wildflowers in spring, bleached blond by midsummer, gray and crackling dry in autumn. Lands End reclines dark on the southeastern horizon. Cattle tracks diverge from the main route at various points along the trek to the overlook: At the first, you'll want to stay on the high road; at the second, veer to the right, climbing onto the rolling grassy hump of the head. Estero de Limantour hems the land in on the right, blue and turquoise with blooms of kelp staining it with swathes of brown.

The tip of Drakes Head is at 4.4 miles—a sun-splashed knob of grass overlooking the blue shallows of the Limantour estero, the end of Limantour Spit, Drakes Bay, and points south. It's the perfect place to spread a lunchtime picnic or simply sit for a spell. When you can peel yourself away, return as you came.

OPTIONS: Add a trip out to Sunset Beach for a daylong trek of 11.8 miles (see the preceding hike description). Or, if you want to venture into even more remote parts of the seashore, explore the remainder of the Estero Trail, which continues to the Muddy Hollow Trail near Limantour Beach.

Bull Point

HIGHLIGHTS: Tracing the eastern bluffs of Creamery Bay, the Bull Point Trail wanders through pasturelands—and the cows that graze them— to expansive views of Drakes Estero and Drakes Bay.

TYPE OF JOURNEY: Out-and-back.

TOTAL DISTANCE: 3.6 miles.

DIFFICULTY: Moderate.

PERMITTED USES: Hiking, horseback riding, mountain biking.

MAPS: USGS Drakes Bay; Point Reyes National Seashore Map; Tom Harrison Point Reyes National Seashore Map; TOPO! San Francisco Bay Area, Wine Country, and Big Sur.

SPECIAL CONSIDERATIONS: No dogs are allowed. The trail is open to mountain bikes, which must yield to hikers and horseback riders, but is more than wide enough to be shared amicably by all user groups. The route passes through pasturelands; cows use and surround the trail. If you are uncomfortable with large bovines, you might want to choose another route.

PARKING AND FACILITIES: The parking area is on the left (southeast) side of the Sir Francis Drake Highway. There are no facilities.

FINDING THE TRAILHEAD: From the Bear Valley Visitor Center, drive east 0.2 mile to Bear Valley Road, and turn left (north). Follow Bear Valley Road for 1.7 miles to its intersection with the Sir Francis Drake Highway near Inverness Park. Turn left (north) onto Sir Francis Drake. The highway winds along the west shore of Tomales Bay, through the towns of Inverness Park and Inverness, then veers west into the park. The Bull Point Trailhead is 10.4 miles from the Bear Valley Road/Sir Francis Drake Highway intersection, on the left (southeast) side of the road.

KEY POINTS:

0.0 Trailhead.

0.2 Pass the gate.

1.0 The trail levels on the bluff.

1.8 Reach Bull Point.

The complex dynamic that has allowed Point Reyes and the surrounding landscapes of West Marin to remain relatively untouched by development comes into sharp focus along the Bull Point Trail. It's a bovine nature walk, combining what makes Point Reyes desirable as open space (vistas, wildlife) with what has preserved those open spaces (agriculture). The meadowlands that surround the path are cropped not by tule elk or deer, as you might expect in a national park, but by roaming cattle that mark both pasture and trail with fragrant patties and study hikers with implacable patience. The scene is bucolic but provocative, affording the perfect opportunity to contemplate the benefits and pitfalls of ranching in the park.

The trail begins in the northeast corner of the parking area, adjacent to an informational sign. Follow the path north to the break in the fence, then veer southeast and down into the pastures on the old ranch road.

At about 0.1 mile the trail drops onto a circle of pounded earth surrounding a water basin; the cows congregate here. The main trail continues to the left (east); a less defined road/trail heads right (southwest), soon narrows to singletrack within the scrub, then peters out after about 0.5 mile at a soggy ditch that feeds Creamery Bay.

Bull Point Trail

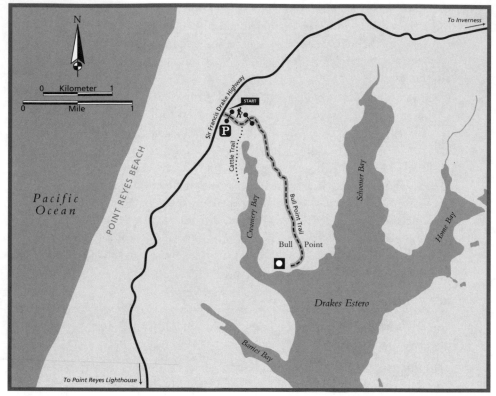

The main road drops over a culvert and climbs to a gate at about 0.2 mile. Pass through the gate and follow the grassy ranch road as it curves south above the east shore of Creamery Bay.

The trail climbs gently along the scrubby bluffs, with views south and west across the bay. By 1 mile you have topped the bluff and earned views into the broader waters of Drakes Estero, flanked by the bright cliffs of the headlands.

As you near trail's end, the track slopes gently downhill toward the water. If the tide is low, the surf breaks in white streaks at the mouth of the bay, and mud-flats open along the shores. Cows wander the pasture here too, breaking new trails through the brambles, but the main track, dropping south, is obvious.

The trail arcs west at its tip and drops to the cliffs at the water's edge. It dead-ends in a gully choked with coyote brush, fern, willow, blackberry brambles, and poison oak at 1.8 miles.

Enjoy the views from the blunt end of the point, then return as you came.

Chimney Rock

HIGHLIGHTS: Famed for its springtime wildflower blooms, the trail to Chimney Rock also features fabulous views of Drakes Bay and the Pacific Ocean.

TYPE OF JOURNEY: Out-and-back.

TOTAL DISTANCE: 2 miles.

DIFFICULTY: Easy.

PERMITTED USES: Hiking.

MAPS: USGS Drakes Bay; Point Reyes National Seashore Map; Tom Harrison Point Reyes National Seashore Map; TOPO! San Francisco Bay Area, Wine Country, and Big Sur.

SPECIAL CONSIDERATIONS: No dogs are allowed. The trail is exposed in brief sections and passes near unstable cliffs; remain on the designated route. When the Pacific gray whales are migrating, from January to April, the overlook is a popular whale-watching spot.

PARKING AND FACILITIES: A large parking lot serves as trailhead for this hike and for the Elephant Seal Overlook and the Historic Lifeboat Station. Rest rooms are available.

FINDING THE TRAILHEAD: From the Bear Valley Visitor Center, drive east on the access road for 0.2 mile to Bear Valley Road. Turn left (north), and follow Bear Valley Road for 1.7 miles to its intersection with the Sir Francis Drake Highway. Turn left (north) onto the highway, and follow it for a total of 17.7 miles to the Chimney Road turnoff, passing along the west shore of Tomales Bay before heading west onto the rolling pasturelands of the point. Turn left (east) onto the Chimney Rock access road, and go 0.9 mile to the trailhead and parking area.

KEY POINTS:

0.0 Trailhead.

0.5 Reach the top of the bluff and the trail intersection.

1.0 Arrive at the bench overlooking Chimney Rock.

In spring the trail to Chimney Rock passes through the premier wildflower display on the Point Reyes peninsula. The palette is dazzling, featuring a rainbow bloom set against verdant grasses and the bright blues of sea and sky. But the hike is delightful at any time, winding through coastal scrub to an overlook with views of the white cliffs and dazzling waters of Drakes Bay, the sweep of the coast south past the Golden Gate to Lands End, and the shimmering Pacific.

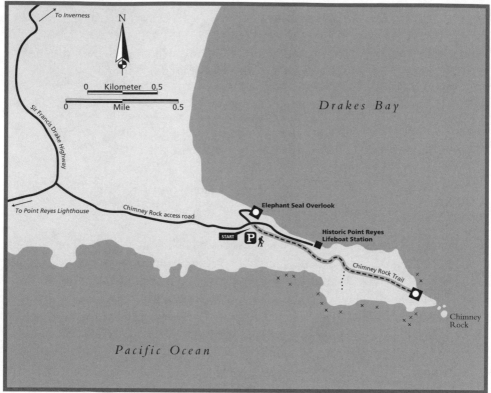

The hike begins in the southwest corner of the parking lot; the routes to Elephant Seal Overlook and the Historic Lifeboat Station begin to the northeast, down the paved road. Climb up onto the hillside, then begin a mostly flat traverse, enjoying views of Drakes Bay, dotted with fishing and pleasure boats, and the whitewashed buildings of the lifeboat station. These views are briefly blocked by a brace of gnarly old cypress trees, but open again once the trees are passed. The trail is buffered on the south by a grassy bluff.

Round a bend into a saddle at about the 0.25-mile mark; a break in the bluff allows the brightness of the ocean to flood the trail. Cliffs rise on both flanks of the oceanside opening, and signs caution you away from the precipice. The main trail stays below the edge, well within the safety zone, but offers ample views out to the Pacific. Avoid the side trails that lead to the cliff's edge, for safety's sake and to reduce erosion.

A short, steep pitch climbs steeply away from the ocean and toward the bay side of the point, passing a large bush lupine. The trail tops out on the bluff at about 0.5 mile. At the trail intersection, stay left (east), following the arrow that points to the Chimney Rock overview. The two side trails that break off to the right (south) lead to ocean overlooks worthy of a visit either now or on the return hike, if you have the time and inclination.

The trail flattens as it heads toward the end of the point, with the broad bay on the left (northeast) meeting the ocean that spreads endlessly on the right (south). The sounds of surf and wind are punctuated by the low, lonely throb of a buoy.

At about 0.8 mile, the trail descends gently to a shallow saddle. Social paths lead right and left to cliffside overlooks. The main path climbs up and over the last hillock to the fence at the brink of the headlands at 1 mile.

A sun-bleached bench rests on the reddish earth of the point just inside the fence, a respite for weary or contemplative hikers. The vistas, of course, are wonderful. Chimney Rock, the largest of a small cluster of sea stacks just off the tip of the point, is battered by the surf, but that doesn't seem to bother the clusters of seabirds that gather on its craggy top. The rugged coastline, green and brown, stretches southward toward the Golden Gate, and, looking west, curves in the sun-splashed or fog-shrouded walls of Point Reyes. Once you've taken it all in, return as you came.

OPTION: As mentioned above, you can break off the main route to visit the headlands overlook; this trail heads south at about the midpoint of the Chimney Rock Trail. This jaunt will add about 0.4 mile to your hike.

White water spills through an arch in a small sea stack on the ocean side of the Chimney Rock promontory.

Sky Trail to Sky Camp and Mount Wittenberg

HIGHLIGHTS: Arguably the easiest climb to a backcountry camp in Point Reyes National Seashore, this section of the Sky Trail wanders through a portion of the forest destroyed by, and now recovering from, the 1995 Vision Fire.

TYPE OF JOURNEY: Out-and-back.

TOTAL DISTANCE: 3.6 miles to Sky Camp and back; 6 miles to Mount Wittenberg summit and back.

DIFFICULTY: Moderate to hard.

PERMITTED USES: Hiking, horseback riding, mountain biking to Sky Camp. Horseback riders have access to the trails surrounding Mount Wittenberg, but are not permitted on the summit trail.

MAPS: USGS Inverness; Point Reyes National Seashore Map; Tom Harrison Point Reyes National Seashore Map; TOPO! San Francisco Bay Area, Wine Country, and Big Sur.

SPECIAL CONSIDERATIONS: No dogs are allowed. Horses are not permitted on the Mount Wittenberg summit trail. Overnight camping at Sky Camp is restricted to hikers and mountain bikers.

PARKING AND FACILITIES: The parking area is located on the southwest side of Limantour Road, and holds ten to twelve vehicles. Additional parking is available along the road. No rest rooms are available.

FINDING THE TRAILHEAD: From the Bear Valley Visitor Center, drive east on the visitor center road for 0.2 mile to Bear Valley Road. Turn left (north), and follow Bear Valley Road for 1.3 miles to its intersection with Limantour Road. Turn left (south) onto Limantour Road, and follow it for 1.3 miles to the trailhead.

KEY POINTS:

0.0 Trailhead.

1.2 Reach the intersection with the Fire Lane Trail.

1.3 Pass the Horse Trail intersection.

1.8 Arrive at Sky Camp.

2.4 Reach the Mount Wittenberg Trail junction.

2.8 Arrive at the Z Ranch and summit trail junction.

3.0 Arrive on the Mount Wittenberg summit.

Sky Trail to Sky Camp and Mount Wittenberg

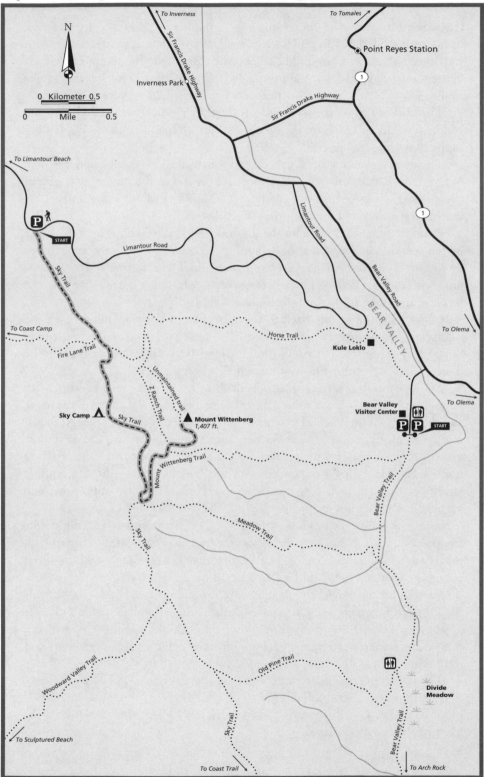

If you want to keep your options open as to the length and difficulty of a hike or ride at Point Reyes, this trail is the perfect choice. Make it short and easy with a gentle climb to Sky Camp; add challenge by climbing to the summit of Mount Wittenberg; complete a lollipop loop by following the Z Ranch and Horse Trails back to Sky Trail and the trailhead. Each possibility is sure to delight.

The trail begins on the south side of the parking lot. Pass through the gate and begin a gentle climb on the broad dirt service road that does double duty as the Sky Trail.

The open evergreen forest that shrouds the trail allows a thick undergrowth of fern, poison oak, and blackberry to thrive. Breaks in the canopy to the right (west) reveal views of hills scoured by the Vision Fire of 1995 and, in the distance, Drakes Bay and the Point Reyes headlands.

Round a switchback at about the 0.5-mile mark; the climb is broken briefly by flat sections, and is never too strenuous. At about 0.7 mile the trail curves up eastward and traverses above a steep ravine thick with foliage and trees dripping with the lace lichen known colloquially as old-man's beard. Views on the traverse are of the rolling hills of Bolinas Ridge.

Cross a shallow saddle back to the west side of the ridge, and reach the intersection with the Fire Lane Trail at 1.2 miles. Stay left (south) on the broad Sky Trail, reaching the junction with the Horse Trail, which branches off to the left (south) at 1.3 miles. Stay right (southwest) on the Sky Trail.

Another forested ravine—this one shallower than the previous—opens to your right (west) as you continue on the now flat trail. Pass a small meadow, and the legacy of the Vision Fire comes into sharp focus. The blackened standing snags left by the fire rise on either side of the road, with a dense undergrowth thriving beneath their naked branches. Views west of Drakes Bay are unimpeded, unless fog has tangled with the boughs. When the fog is in, it envelopes the damaged forest in a Sleepy Hollow beauty, mysterious and vaguely unsettling, but lovely nonetheless.

The trail climbs again briefly, then drops to Sky Camp at 1.8 miles. The camp is equipped with toilets and a water spigot, and campsites outfitted with picnic tables, grills, and critterproof food storage boxes. Detailed information about Sky Camp is found in the Point Reyes backpacking chapter.

You can turn around here, or head onward and upward to Mount Wittenberg. From the camp, the trail etches a traversing, view-laden climb along a meadowy hillside. Pass briefly through a cool glade thick with western sword fern, then reenter meadow again, climbing steadily but easily toward the crest of the ridge.

The next trail crossing, on the ridgeline, is at 2.4 miles. The Sky Trail continues to the right (south), linking up with the Meadow Trail, Woodward Valley Trail, and eventually the Coast Trail. Turn left, switching back north on the Mount Wittenberg Trail.

Young hikers check out a giant fir tree on the north side of Mount Wittenberg.

The Mount Wittenberg Trail climbs across the upper reaches of the same hillside that hosts the Sky Trail, which runs parallel below and to the left (west). Round a bend, then climb to a saddle and another trail intersection at 2.8 miles. Here the Mount Wittenberg Trail drops right (east), descending steeply to Bear Valley; the Z Ranch Trail, a broad service road/trail, veers left (northwest). The signed Mount Wittenberg summit trail breaks to the right (north) from the Z Ranch Trail.

The narrow singletrack summit trail climbs briefly through fledgling fir trees to the rounded summit of Mount Wittenberg, where views west of Drakes Bay are limited, but you can look over the tops of the young trees to the sprawling Bolinas Ridge. Enjoy the summit before returning as you came.

OPTION: If you'd like to add variety to your return trip, you can descend to the Sky Trail via the Z Ranch Trail and Horse Trail. Drop back to the Z Ranch Trail intersection at the base of the summit trail, and turn right (north) onto Z Ranch. The trail drops for 0.7 mile to the Horse Trail. Go left (northwest) on the Horse Trail, which traverses a sharp ravine, passing an old broken fir tree and offering scattered views of Tomales Bay. Reach the Sky Trail at 0.4 mile and turn right (north), following the Sky Trail back to the parking area. The complete lollipop loop is about 5.4 miles in length.

HIGHLIGHTS: The airy heights of the Douglas fir forest on the west-facing slopes of Mount Wittenberg and the open expanses of Limantour Beach are linked by this rugged route.

TYPE OF JOURNEY: Shuttle or out-and-back.

TOTAL DISTANCE: 6.8 miles (shuttle); 13.6 miles (out-and-back).

DIFFICULTY: Hard.

PERMITTED USES: Hiking, horseback riding.

MAPS: USGS Inverness and Drakes Bay; Point Reyes National Seashore Map; Tom Harrison Point Reyes National Seashore Map; TOPO! San Francisco Bay Area, Wine Country, and Big Sur.

SPECIAL CONSIDERATIONS: No dogs are allowed on the Sky Trail or the Fire Lane Trail. Dogs are permitted, however, on the southern stretches of Limantour Beach.

PARKING AND FACILITIES: The parking area is located on the southwest side of Limantour Road and holds ten to twelve vehicles. Additional parking is available along the road. No rest rooms are available.

FINDING THE TRAILHEAD: From the Bear Valley Visitor Center, drive east on the access road for 0.2 mile to Bear Valley Road. Turn left (north), and follow Bear Valley Road for 1.3 miles to its intersection with Limantour Road. Turn left (south) onto Limantour Road, and follow it for 1.3 miles to the trailhead.

KEY POINTS:

0.0 Trailhead.

1.2 Reach the intersection with the Fire Lane Trail.

3.4 Reach the junction with the Laguna Trail.

4.5 Arrive at the Coast Trail near Coast Camp.

6.8 Reach the parking area at Limantour Beach.

Pass down the lovely and lonely Fire Lane Trail and you'll journey through nearly every ecosystem that the Point Reyes National Seashore encompasses: a moist, vivid fir forest; the skeletal landscape left by the Vision Fire; the impenetrable coyote brush and stunted oak carpeting the coastal bluffs; and the naked sands bordering Drakes Bay.

I recommend this trail as a shuttle hike, starting at the Sky Trailhead on Limantour Road and ending 6.8 miles later and about 1,000 feet lower at the parking lot at Limantour Beach. If you opt to make this a round-trip journey, I

Fire Lane Trail to Limantour Beach

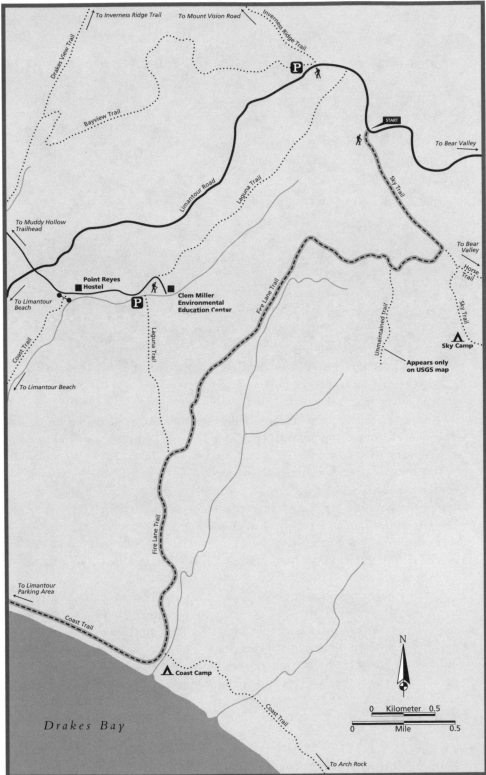

To Inverness Ridge Trail

To Mount Vision Road

Inverness Ridge Trail

Drakes View Trail

Bayview Trail

P

START

To Bear Valley

Limantour Road

Laguna Trail

Sky Trail

To Muddy Hollow Trailhead

To Bear Valley

Horse Trail

Point Reyes Hostel

P

Clem Miller Environmental Education Center

Fire Lane Trail

Unmaintained trail

Sky Trail

Sky Camp

To Limantour Beach

Coast Trail

Laguna Trail

To Limantour Beach

Appears only on USGS map

To Limantour Parking Area

Fire Lane Trail

Coast Trail

Coast Camp

N

Coast Trail

0   Kilometer   0.5

0   Mile   0.5

Drakes Bay

To Arch Rock

Hikers drop down along the Fire Lane Trail to its junction with the Laguna Trail.

suggest you begin at Limantour Beach, climb up to the Sky Trail, then return as you came. The round trip is brutal both in length and elevation gain and loss, but well worth the effort if you're in shape and up for a long day's challenge.

The route is described here one way from the Sky Trail to Limantour. Begin at the Sky Trailhead parking area. Pass through the gate and climb the broad dirt service road that doubles as the Sky Trail. A thick undergrowth of fern, poison oak, and blackberry thrives beneath an open evergreen forest. Breaks in the canopy to the right (west) reveal views of hills scoured by the Vision Fire of 1995, and, in the distance, Drakes Bay and the headlands of Point Reyes.

Round a switchback at about the 0.5-mile mark; at about 0.7 mile, the trail curves eastward and skirts a ravine overgrown with verdant foliage and trees draped in old-man's beard. Cross a shallow saddle back to the west side of the ridge, and reach the junction with the Fire Lane Trail at 1.2 miles. The Sky Trail continues left (south) to Sky Camp; turn right (west) onto the Fire Lane Trail, a narrow singletrack that plunges into the thick green of the Douglas fir forest.

The trail begins to drop almost immediately, though gently at first. Wild-flowers battle with the ferns and brambles, their colorful heads tangled and reaching, and lacy lichens add a pale gray hue to a palette of kelly, moss, lollipop, and golf course greens. The vigor of the forest is betrayed by fire scars as the path drops into a burned area. Hike through a gully with views west toward Limantour Beach, then the trail skims the top of a ridge where burned-out branches frame views that probably didn't exist before the 1995 blaze.

Drop steeply down a section of trail bordered by young firs; the trail flattens at a large fire-blackened snag, then veers north into coastal scrub. At about the 2-mile mark, the trail dips into another gully thick with coyote brush and monkey flower, climbs past more charred snags, and, crowded by young trees, descends again. As you climb out of this gully, you get a firsthand lesson in how wildfire affects the landscape: A verdant undergrowth thrives beneath the snags, new trees, and older trees that survived the conflagration.

The trail continues to roller coaster westward through the scrublands, tracing a steep ravine that drops away to the left (southeast). At about 2.5 miles, pass through a saddle that offers views north and down into the former Laguna Ranch, now site of the Point Reyes Hostel and the Clem Miller Environmental Education Center, with the Limantour Road snaking along the hillside above.

Up and down and around the trail goes, ever closer to the edge of the continent. If the day is clear, you can see the Farallon Islands from high points along the route. The roller coaster ends with a plunge into a broad grassy swale. The trail curves west toward a lonely copse of charred trees, intersecting the Laguna Trail at 3.4 miles.

The Laguna Trail branches right (north) toward the hostel and the education center. Stay left (southwest) on the Fire Lane Trail, which passes the dark stand of trees and crosses a flat expanse that, though the grass is sparse, could pass as a meadow. Now a doubletrack, the path circles a bluff to the southwest and begins a gentle decline; a brief glimpse of Point Lobos and the Golden Gate is permitted before the hills and shrubs hide them.

The trail traces a ravine as it continues westward to its junction with the Coast Trail near Coast Camp at 4.5 miles. Rest rooms are available at Coast Camp, which lies 0.1 mile to the left (south), in the lee of a bluff. Turn right (northwest) onto the Coast Trail to reach Limantour Beach.

The wide dirt road that serves at the Coast Trail arcs west to the oceanfront, then heads north along the blufftop, parallel to the beach, with the pale cliffs of Drakes Bay and the dark knob of Chimney Rock visible in the distance. Though you can hear the surf pounding the shoreline, the strand is below and out of sight. About a mile up the Coast Trail, you'll reach a point where you must drop left (west) onto the beach to reach the Limantour parking lot. If you continue on the Coast Trail, you'll end up at the youth hostel.

Follow the beach for another 1.2 miles to the Limantour parking area, which is at 6.8 miles.

HIGHLIGHTS: These relatively little-used trails feature views that extend out over Drakes Bay and the Point Reyes headlands, and an explorer-esque wilderness feel.

TYPE OF JOURNEY: Loop.

TOTAL DISTANCE: 4.9 miles.

DIFFICULTY: Hard.

PERMITTED USES: Hiking, horseback riding.

MAPS: USGS Inverness and Drakes Bay; Point Reyes National Seashore Map; Tom Harrison Point Reyes National Seashore Map; TOPO! San Francisco Bay Area, Wine Country, and Big Sur.

SPECIAL CONSIDERATIONS: No pets are permitted on the trail. The Inverness Ridge Trail portion of the loop is multiuse; please be courteous to fellow trail users.

PARKING AND FACILITIES: A large unpaved parking area serves both the Bayview Trailhead and the Inverness Ridge Trailhead. No other facilities are available.

FINDING THE TRAILHEAD: From the Bear Valley Visitor Center, take the access road east for 0.2 mile to Bear Valley Road. Turn left (north) onto Bear Valley Road, and go 1.3 miles to the Limantour Road. Turn left (south) onto the Limantour Road, and climb to the Bayview/Inverness Ridge Trailhead parking area, which is on the right (north) side of the road at 4.5 miles.

KEY POINTS:

0.0 Trailhead.

0.7 Reach the paved drive; climb 200 feet to the trail's continuation.

1.3 Arrive at the junction with the Drakes View Trail.

3.1 Reach the Bayview Trail and begin the long ascent.

4.9 Finish the loop at the parking area.

This loop distinguishes itself in two ways. It feels remarkably remote, with few tracks left by fellow hikers but plenty by deer and other wild critters. But perhaps more significantly, the sweet, smoky scent left by the Vision Fire infuses the soil at trail's end. The wildlands may be recovering—as evidenced by the young trees that sometimes grow so closely packed that nothing larger than a jackrabbit can squeeze between the narrow trunks—but the essence of the fire, like garlic in a savory sauce, is well incorporated in the landscape.

Drakes View–Bayview Loop

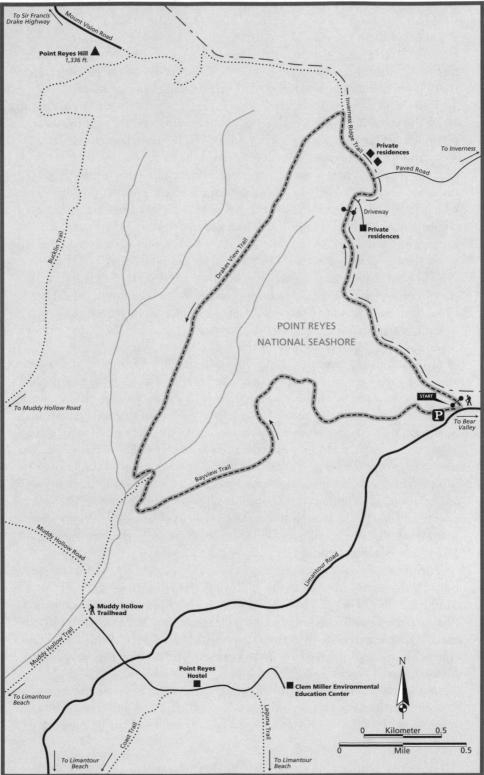

The route begins on the Inverness Ridge Trail, the broad fire lane behind the gate on the north side of the parking lot. The Bayview Trail, the return portion of this loop (which is described here traveling counterclockwise, though it's equally fun the other way) is on the west side of the parking area; a trail sign here indicates the distances to various points farther afield.

Pass the gate on the Inverness Ridge Trail and begin a very, very easy climb along the broad dirt road, which curves in and out of ravines near the crest of the ridge. With the passage of the Vision Fire, views have been revealed spreading westward down the rolling coastal hills to the sea.

The fire road dips to a paved drive at 0.7 mile; climb straight (north) up the drive for about 200 yards to the continuation of the Inverness Ridge Trail, which heads left (northwest) off the pavement. Now a singletrack, the trail climbs steeply through dense brush and the sparse shade of trees spared the ravages of the wildfire. A few of the private homes that have been sprinkled along the top of the ridge sit above the trail on the right (east).

The trail flattens as it approaches the Drakes View Trail crossing, with a paved road on the right (east) offering access to another home. The Drakes View Trail intersection is set amid a dense cluster of fledgling pines at 1.3 miles; the trail sign indicates that the Bayview Trail is 1.8 miles distant. The Inverness Ridge Trail continues northward to Mount Vision.

Turn left (west) onto the Drakes View Trail. The route is flat for a brief stretch, arcing westward, then begins an unbroken descent of various degrees of steepness. The seemingly impenetrable wall of young evergreens is enlivened periodically by the red bark and shiny leaves of the manzanita, which puts forth tiny bell-like white and pink blooms in late winter and early spring.

As you descend, stands of new trees alternate with patches of chaparral. The trail is alternatively steep and not so steep, the shallower sections offering blessed relief to knees and hips. The final portion of the descent is through coastal scrub, highlighted with wildflowers in spring and summer. The scat of coyote and other wild animals litters the track—watch your step. Views stretch west along the silvery ribbon of Muddy Hollow as it reaches out toward Limantour Beach and the sea.

Riparian species—bunchgrasses, bays, oaks, blackberry brambles—edge into the chaparral as you near the end of the descent in the upper portion of Muddy Hollow. The trail switchbacks down alongside a no-name creek surrounded by willow. Cross a little arcing bridge in a stand of tall cottonwoods; the Drakes View Trail ends at its junction with the Bayview Trail at 3.1 miles. A bench at the trail intersection is the perfect place to enjoy the seclusion and bolster yourself for the upcoming climb.

At the trail intersection, turn left (east) on the Bayview Trail; the westward leading stretch of trail leads to the Muddy Hollow Road and Trail. The trail sign states that both the Limantour Road and the trailhead are 1.8 miles above.

Yes, it's a long way up from the bottomlands, but the ascent is briefly delayed as the trail traces the south side of the willow-shrouded creek. The climb begins with a switchback, ascends through a bower of brambles to another switchback, then curves back eastward on a scrubby ridgetop.

Once on the open slopes, the Bayview Trail climbs like the Drake's View Trail descended, in fits and starts. It runs atop the ridge directly north of the one that holds the Limantour Road, and road noise detracts from the wilderness feel captured on the descent—a slow reintroduction to civilization. You will climb for more than a mile; the trail then curves into the lee of the ridge it's ridden atop since the last switchback. The hillside buffers the trail from the Limantour Road and focuses the eye on the steep ravine to the north, with the ridge ridden by the Drakes View Trail in the foreground, and Point Reyes Hill blocking the northern horizon. Signs and smells of the Vision Fire become evident here, with charcoaled stumps barely visible in the undergrowth, the bare branches of torched trees overhead, and the faint scent of ash kicked up with the dust underfoot.

The trail flattens as it traverses south, then east, back to the trailhead, which is at 4.9 miles.

Laguna–Coast Trail Loop

HIGHLIGHTS: This exploration of the coastal habitats near Limantour Beach includes passage through a dense stand of alders.

TYPE OF JOURNEY: Loop.

TOTAL DISTANCE: 4.9 miles

DIFFICULTY: Moderate.

PERMITTED USES: Hiking, horseback riding, mountain bikes on the Coast Trail portion of the route.

MAPS: USGS Inverness; Point Reyes National Seashore Map; Tom Harrison Point Reyes National Seashore Map; TOPO! San Francisco Bay Area, Wine Country, and Big Sur.

SPECIAL CONSIDERATIONS: Pets are permitted on Limantour Beach but not on any of the trails. The Coast Trail is used by hikers, mountain bikers, and equestrians; be courteous to your fellow trail users by yielding the trail when necessary.

PARKING AND FACILITIES: The parking lot at the Laguna Trailhead holds about thirty cars. If the lot is full, park alongside the access road. There is no lot at the Coast Trailhead, but you can park alongside the road here too. There are no other facilities at either trailhead.

Laguna–Coast Trail Loop

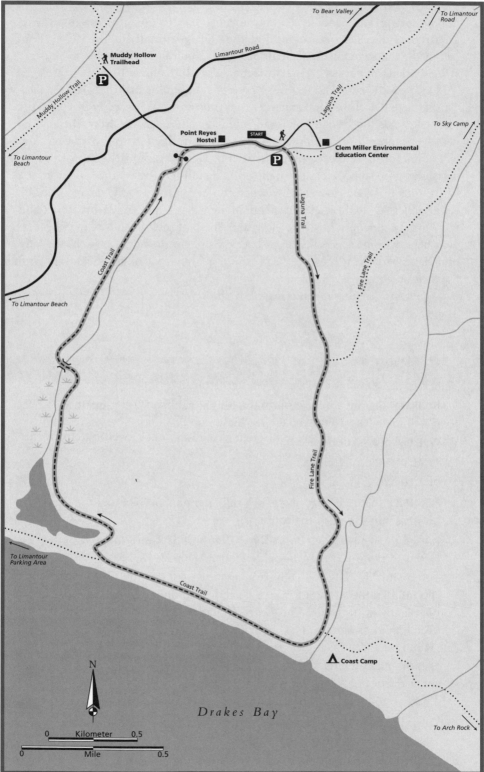

FINDING THE TRAILHEAD: From the Bear Valley Visitor Center, drive east on the visitor center road for 0.2 mile to Bear Valley Road. Turn left (north), and follow Bear Valley Road for 1.3 miles to its intersection with Limantour Road. Turn left (south) onto Limantour Road, and follow it for 6 miles to a signed four-way intersection at the base of a very steep hill. Turn left (south) onto the road to the Point Reyes Hostel and the Clem Miller Environmental Education Center; the road to the right (north) leads to the Muddy Hollow Trailhead. Follow the access road for 0.5 mile to the parking area at the Laguna Trailhead, which is on the right (south) and across the little bridge.

KEY POINTS:

0.0 Trailhead.

0.8 Reach the intersection with the Fire Lane Trail.

1.8 Descend to the intersection with the Coast Trail.

2.8 Pass the spur trail onto Limantour Beach.

3.1 Turn east, away from the beach, at the pond.

4.6 Arrive at the Coast Trailhead near the Point Reyes Hostel.

4.9 Return to the Laguna Trailhead.

Shade is a sparse commodity in the coastal scrublands of Limantour. But at the beach end of the nameless creek that gathers high on Inverness Ridge, runs down through Laguna Ranch, and traces the Coast Trail to the ridge of dunes at the beach front, alders grow in great profusion. They swell out from the banks of the creek, crowding against the sides of the valley. When leafed out, the trees throw dense shade over the trail; when naked, the boughs filter the sun in a intricate latticework.

The loop is described here in a clockwise direction, but can be traveled just as easily either way. Begin at the Laguna Trailhead, passing park residences, and veering right at the trail signs. The short side track that leads to the Clem Miller Environmental Education Center also begins here, breaking off to the left (east), while the Laguna Trail climbs to the right (south).

The trail, an old two-track ranch road, leads into a narrow valley drained by a seasonal stream that gurgles gently in winter and early spring, but disappears by summer, with only a few bunchgrasses and willows attesting to its passage. The trail climbs along the lower west-facing slopes of the drainage, with the riparian plants giving way to scrub as you gain altitude.

The pitch of the path steepens in the narrowing upper reaches of the valley, and the trail's surface is rutted by runoff and erosion. Crest the saddle, with an impressive rock outcropping on the west side of the route. A cluster of fire-scarred trees spills down a slope up and ahead; this marks the intersection with the Fire Lane Trail at 0.8 mile.

Go right (southwest) onto the Fire Lane Trail and a dry, meadowy plateau. The trail surface is alternatively solid and sandy. Skirt a bluff to the southwest and begin to descend, enjoying a view of Lands End and the Golden Gate at a fleeting break in the hills and shrubs.

The trail traces a ravine to its junction with the Coast Trail at 1.8 miles. Coast Camp is 0.1 mile to the left (south), in the lee of a bluff; you will find picnic facilities, rest rooms, and water at the camp, if you need them.

To continue the loop, go right (west) on the Coast Trail, which quickly reaches the bluffs above Limantour Beach, then turns northwest to parallel the beach. From the broad roadway, views open onto the deep blue waters and pale cliffs of Drakes Bay and the abrupt drop of the Point Reyes headlands into the sea at Chimney Rock. If the air is clear, you can make out the black, jagged forms of the Farallon Islands on the horizon.

Spur roads take off right (west) from the main track, traveling 50 or 100 yards into the scrub before ending—remnants of the infrastructure that was to support an extensive subdivision once planned for the Limantour area—a development thankfully aborted.

At 2.8 miles, a sandy, signed spur trail breaks off the Coast Trail to the west, offering access to the beach. This is your last chance to sink your toes into the sands, for the Coast Trail is separated from the beach by a bluff beyond this point. The road sweeps down long, lazy S-curves to the marshy border of a large, reed-rimmed pond that is separated from the beach by a short bank of dunes at 3.1 miles.

Beyond the broad marshes that hem in the eastern reaches of the pond, the trail drops to run alongside its inlet stream—a relatively energetic watercourse that supports a thick stand of alders along its braided bed. The trees, which are on the left (north) side of the trail, cast welcome shade on hot hikers when the sun is out, in addition to presenting an interesting juxtaposition to the otherwise treeless landscape. On the south side of the trail, coastal scrub prevails, accented by thickets of blackberry.

At 3.5 miles the trail veers sharply north across both the riparian band and the creek, which runs under the roadway through a culvert. The trail then turns back to the northeast, with the stream on its right (south) side, now screened from sight by a wall of willow and an occasional stand of cattails.

Wedged between the northern slope of the valley and the riparian zone of the creek, the trail makes a straight shot to the Coast Trailhead near the Point Reyes Hostel at 4.6 miles. Pass the gate onto the paved access road and turn right (east), following the road toward the Laguna Trailhead, which is at 4.9 miles.

From Bear Valley Trailhead

Earthquake Trail

HIGHLIGHTS: The volatile geology of the Point Reyes peninsula is illustrated along this short, paved interpretive trail.

TYPE OF JOURNEY: Loop.

TOTAL DISTANCE: 0.6 mile.

DIFFICULTY: Very easy.

PERMITTED USES: Hiking.

MAPS: USGS Inverness; Point Reyes National Seashore Map; Tom Harrison Point Reyes National Seashore Map; TOPO! San Francisco Bay Area, Wine Country, and Big Sur.

SPECIAL CONSIDERATIONS: No dogs are allowed. The trail is wheelchair accessible.

PARKING AND FACILITIES: The Bear Valley Trailhead has huge parking areas, picnic facilities, rest rooms, water, and a visitor center.

FINDING THE TRAILHEAD: The trailhead is wedged between the rest rooms and the picnic area at the southeast end of the dirt parking lot at the Bear Valley Visitor Center. The lot is on the south side of the paved access road. An informational sign also marks the trailhead.

KEY POINTS:

0.0 Trailhead.

0.1 Cross the bridge over the little creek.

0.3 Take the spur trail up to the dislocated fence line.

0.5 Return to the intersection near the trailhead.

In 1906 the San Andreas Fault snapped, unleashing an earthquake of legendary power. The infamous San Francisco temblor, and the fire that followed, destroyed much of the city by the bay. But the damage wasn't limited to San Francisco; communities throughout northern California were affected by the quake. And graphic evidence of the violent rupture can be found in the Point Reyes National Seashore.

The Earthquake Trail documents the legacy of the 1906 quake. Interpretive signs along the easy, paved path illustrate the quake's effects on San Francisco and the Olema Valley, bed of the culprit fault, as well as on the geology that will one day transport the Point Reyes peninsula into Alaska's Aleutian Trench. Fascinating on a variety of levels, the trail showcases graphic physical evidence

Earthquake Trail

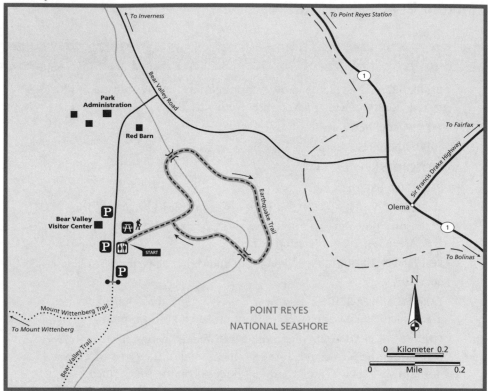

of the power of the fault line. Perfect for families, the hike is a provocative experience no matter your age.

The hike begins by passing an interpretive sign showing the San Andreas Fault in relief. Pass through an arm of the meadow that surrounds the visitor center; after about 50 yards the trail forks. Stay left (east), following the arrows on the pavement. The grasses of the meadow harbor the vivid California poppy, among other wildflowers, in spring and summer.

The next interpretive sign contains pictures of the devastation caused by the quake. Beyond, the trail dips into a forest of bay and oak, with blackberry brambles edging the pavement. Drop to the bridge that spans a nameless tributary of Olema Creek at about 0.1 mile. Pass another interpretive sign on the east side of the bridge, then the trail swings south, wedged between a wall of willows and a rustic fence line. Pass several more interpretive signs—one describing a local legend of bovine distress that is a treat to read—before reaching a short dirt footpath at about 0.3 mile. Take the spur to check out the 16-foot break in the fence line—a graphic illustration of the earthquake's power.

More interpretive signs describe quake dynamics before the trail crosses another bridge and reenters the meadow. The broad, multilimbed base of a great bay laurel is a great place for the kids to play before you arc back north toward the trail intersection near the trailhead, passing the two last interpretive signs. Turn left (northwest) at the intersection at 0.5 mile, and climb gently back to the trailhead.

The Earthquake Trail, one of the most popular in the Point Reyes National Seashore, charms and educates visitors of all ages.

Mount Wittenberg and Meadow Trail Loop

HIGHLIGHTS: Leading to the highest point in the park, the summit trail on Mount Wittenberg serves up tree-framed views of the Olema Valley, Drakes Bay, and the Point Reyes headlands.

TYPE OF JOURNEY: Loop.

TOTAL DISTANCE: 5.1 miles.

DIFFICULTY: Hard.

PERMITTED USES: Hiking, horseback riding.

MAPS: USGS Inverness; Point Reyes National Seashore Map; Tom Harrison Point Reyes National Seashore Map; TOPO! San Francisco Bay Area, Wine Country, and Big Sur.

SPECIAL CONSIDERATIONS: No dogs are allowed. Horses are not permitted on the summit trail or on the Meadow Trail on Saturday, Sunday, or holidays.

PARKING AND FACILITIES: The Bear Valley Trailhead has huge parking areas, picnic facilities, rest rooms, water, and a visitor center.

FINDING THE TRAILHEAD: The Bear Valley Trailhead is at the west end of the two big parking lots that serve the Bear Valley Visitor Center. A gate and an informational billboard are stationed at the beginning of the wide dirt track.

KEY POINTS:

0.0 Trailhead.

0.2 Reach the Mount Wittenberg Trail.

1.8 Arrive at the saddle.

2.2 Reach the summit of Mount Wittenberg.

2.8 Head down on the Meadow Trail.

4.3 Meet the Bear Valley Trail.

5.1 Return to the Bear Valley Trailhead.

Standing on the summit of Mount Wittenberg is a bit like standing on a monk's head. A fringe of young evergreens sprouts in a ring around the rocky clearing on the mountaintop, like hair around a bald man's pate. If you peek through the treetops to the east, you can see the rolling hills and pastures of West Marin. Looking southeast, you gaze down the Olema Valley. Views west to Drakes Bay and the ocean, and views to the north foretell the summit's future, which flies in the face of the fate of your typical balding man: The firs grow ever taller and thicker, blocking all vistas and offering shelter from the wind and sun.

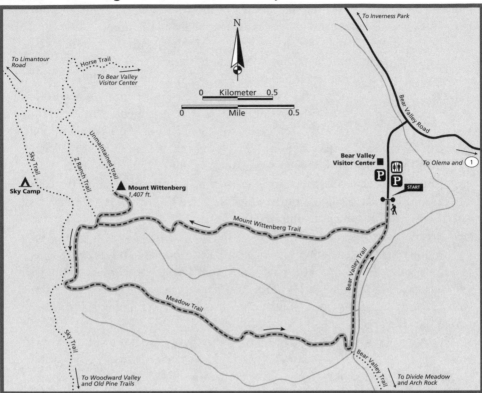

This loop begins on the wide, flat Bear Valley Trail, which heads into the meadow southwest of the Bear Valley Visitor Center. At 0.2 mile the Mount Wittenberg Trail breaks off to the right (northwest); the Bear Valley Trail goes straight (southwest), leaving the meadow for the trees.

Turn right (northwest) on the Mount Wittenberg Trail, and begin to climb, first through meadow, then through the blessed shade of a mixed evergreen forest. The trail flattens briefly beneath the thickening canopy, then climbs steeply again, swooping up alongside a ravine that drops off to the right (east). Climb around a broad switchback; then snaking curves lead to a bench chainsawed from a section of fallen log.

At about the 1-mile mark, you round a switchback shored up by a retaining wall, then another. Winds blown off the ocean stir the tops of the trees in melodic waves. When the trail switchbacks to the east, you can see the smooth hills on the east side of the Olema Valley; when it switchbacks west, there are no views—just trees that grow less dense and an understory that grows thinner the higher you climb.

A last steep section brings you to a traverse through arcing laurels; in late spring and early summer, the tall stalks of foxglove enliven the understory in the gulch that yawns to the left (south) of the trail. The trail widens to two tracks as it enters grassland and ascends to a saddle at 1.8 miles.

At the three-way intersection, go right (northwest) onto the Z Ranch Trail, then quickly right onto the Mount Wittenberg summit trail. The Z Ranch for which the trail is named was once owned by the Wittenberg family, for whom the mountain is named. The Mount Wittenberg Trail continues to the left (south), leading to the Meadow Trail and Sky Trail. Again you climb, this time across grassy hillsides with views west to Point Reyes, the Limantour Spit, Drakes Estero, and Drakes Bay. You can also check out the scars of the Vision Fire, still very obvious on the landscape leading out toward Limantour.

Round a switchback; the trail is crowded by rattlesnake grass (so called because the dried seedpods rattle when they are disturbed). Pass some trail restoration signs, and circle onto the summit at 2.2 miles.

After checking out the views through the mountain's halo of new firs—on a clear day you can see south and east past Black Mountain and the folds of the Bolinas Ridge to Mount Tamalpais and Mount Diablo—backtrack to the trail intersection in the saddle at 2.4 miles. You can return as you came, or continue on the loop by going right (south) onto the Mount Wittenberg Trail to the Meadow Trail.

Heading south on the broad Mount Wittenberg Trail, you will enjoy great views of the beaches, estero, and point to the west; below, the Sky Trail switch-backs down toward Sky Camp. Traverse gently downhill to a four-way trail intersection at 2.8 miles. The Sky Trail leads right (northwest) to Sky Camp and the Limantour Road, and continues straight (southwest) toward the Baldy Trail. Turn left (southeast) onto the signed Meadow Trail.

A couple of informational trail signs mark the beginning of the Meadow Trail and the descent. The path drops into a thick forest of lichen-hairy firs and bent laurels, with the same fragrant understory that graces the Mount Witten-berg Trail. About 0.5 mile down the trail, you will break out into the broad meadow for which the route is named, laden with wildflowers in spring and scorched gold in summer and fall.

Leaving the meadow for the woods again, the trail continues its relentless descent, passing gnarly old bay trees as it drops. As you near the trail's end, the path loops southward into the canyon that cradles the Bear Valley Trail, and traverses down the canyon's left (northwest) face. Cross several small creeklets before you reach the bridge spanning the creek alongside the Bear Valley Trail at 4.3 miles.

Turn left (northeast) onto the Bear Valley Trail and follow the flat path alongside the creek back to the trailhead at 5.1 miles.

Bear Valley Trail to Divide Meadow

HIGHLIGHTS: One of the most popular and accessible routes in the park, the Bear Valley Trail leads through a dense riparian woodland to picturesque Divide Meadow.

TYPE OF JOURNEY: Out-and-back.

TOTAL DISTANCE: 3.2 miles.

DIFFICULTY: Easy.

PERMITTED USES: Hiking, horseback riding, mountain biking.

MAPS: USGS Inverness; Point Reyes National Seashore Map; Tom Harrison Point Reyes National Seashore Map; TOPO! San Francisco Bay Area, Wine Country, and Big Sur.

SPECIAL CONSIDERATIONS: No dogs are allowed. This route is popular and often crowded. Be considerate of all other users, including mountain bikers and equestrians. The trail is closed to horses between the Mount Wittenberg and Glen Trail junctions on weekends and holidays.

PARKING AND FACILITIES: Parking is plentiful in the large lot at the Bear Valley Visitor Center. You will find rest rooms, picnic facilities, water, and more in and around the visitor center.

FINDING THE TRAILHEAD: The trailhead is located at the west end of the parking area for the Bear Valley Visitor Center. Cars are barred from the wide dirt track by a gate.

KEY POINTS:

0.0 Trailhead.

0.2 Pass the Mount Wittenberg Trail.

0.8 Pass the Meadow Trail.

1.6 Reach Divide Meadow.

The journey from the Bear Valley Visitor Center to Divide Meadow is a quintessential Point Reyes experience. If you live near the park, you've done it a thousand times. You've walked it in the rain, through the fog, and under a blazing Indian summer sun. If you've never hiked at the national seashore, this is the perfect introduction. The broad and relatively flat trail, perfect for sharing a conversation with a hiking companion, leads through shady forest to a broad sloping meadow flush with wildflowers in the spring.

The Bear Valley Trail begins by heading southwest through the meadow that surrounds the Bear Valley Visitor Center. At 0.2 mile the Mount Wittenberg Trail breaks off to the right (northwest); continue southwest on the broad

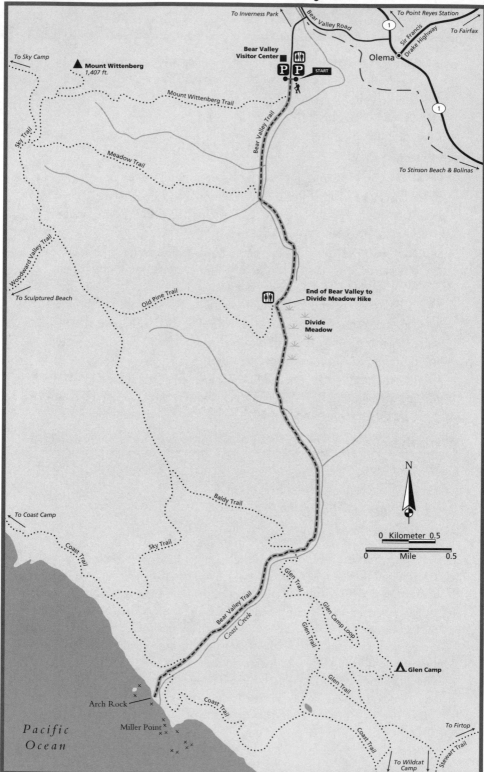

To Inverness Park
Bear Valley Road
To Point Reyes Station
Sir Francis Drake Highway
To Fairfax
Olema
To Sky Camp
▲ Mount Wittenberg
1,407 ft.
Bear Valley Visitor Center
START
To Stinson Beach & Bolinas
Mount Wittenberg Trail
Bear Valley Trail
Sky Trail
Meadow Trail
Woodward Valley Trail
To Sculptured Beach
Old Pine Trail
End of Bear Valley to Divide Meadow Hike
Divide Meadow
N
To Coast Camp
Baldy Trail
Coast Trail
Sky Trail
0 Kilometer 0.5
0   Mile   0.5
Bear Valley Trail
Glen Trail
Glen Camp Loop
Coast Creek
Glen Trail
Glen Trail
▲ Glen Camp
Arch Rock
Coast Trail
Miller Point
To Firtop
Pacific Ocean
Coast Trail
Glen Trail
Coast Trail
To Wildcat Camp
Stewart Trail

track, which leaves the meadow and is enveloped in the shade of the riparian plants and trees that grow along a trickling unnamed tributary feeding Olema Creek to the east.

At 0.8 mile the Meadow Trail departs to the right (northwest), crossing a bridge and beginning a steep climb to the Sky Trail. Stay straight (southwest) on the Bear Valley Trail, which continues a very gentle ascent through the woods. Moss-covered logs occasionally span the creek, which burbles along the right (west) side of the path before crossing to the left and petering out. The only steep part of the climb comes in the form of a few broad curves before you reach Divide Meadow at 1.6 miles.

Divide Meadow, rimmed in tall firs, once was the site of the Bear Valley Country Club. No obvious sign of the camp, which operated from the late 1800s to 1940, remains on the site, though park historian Dewey Livingston makes note of a pair of fruit trees and "a deteriorating two-room outhouse." Instead, you'll find more modern rest rooms tucked into the woods on the northwest side of the meadow, and rustic log benches scattered in shade at the head of the meadow. The perfect destination for short day hike, the meadow is also a trail intersection, with the Old Pine Trail, a former ranch road, heading right (northwest) from the top of the divide. Arch Rock lies 2.5 miles ahead on the Bear Valley Trail.

If you chose to, hike on. Otherwise, return as you came.

Divide Meadow is one of the most popular destinations in the Point Reyes National Seashore.

Bear Valley Trail to Arch Rock

See map on page 78

HIGHLIGHTS: The well-loved Bear Valley Trail continues beyond Divide Meadow to Arch Rock, where a clifftop perch affords expansive views of the coast and ocean.

TYPE OF JOURNEY: Out-and-back.

TOTAL DISTANCE: 8.2 miles.

DIFFICULTY: Moderate.

PERMITTED USES: Hiking, horseback riding, limited mountain biking.

MAPS: USGS Inverness; Point Reyes National Seashore Map; Tom Harrison Point Reyes National Seashore Map; TOPO! San Francisco Bay Area, Wine Country, and Big Sur.

SPECIAL CONSIDERATIONS: No dogs are allowed. This route is popular and often crowded. Be considerate of all other users, including mountain bikers and equestrians. The trail is closed to horses between the Mount Wittenberg and Glen Trail junctions on weekends and holidays. Mountain bikes are not permitted beyond the Glen Trail intersection.

PARKING AND FACILITIES: Parking is plentiful in the large lots at the Bear Valley Visitor Center. You will find rest rooms, picnic facilities, water, and more in and around the visitor center.

FINDING THE TRAILHEAD: The trailhead is located at the west end of the parking area for the Bear Valley Visitor Center. Cars are barred from the wide dirt track by a gate.

KEY POINTS:

0.0 Trailhead.

0.2 Pass the Mount Wittenberg Trail.

0.8 Pass the Meadow Trail.

1.6 Reach Divide Meadow.

3.2 Reach the intersection with the Glen and Baldy Trails.

4.1 Arrive at Arch Rock.

On Arch Rock, an open overlook of the Pacific, seagulls wait with ground squirrels for castaways from picnics. And picnickers, so entranced by the wonderful views, are likely not to care. On a clear day, vistas open across shimmering Drakes Bay to the headlands and Limantour. In the fog, with the surf crashing on narrow strips of chocolate sand beneath hollowed cliffs and beat-

Even on a foggy day, Arch Rock is a wonderful place for a picnic.

ing against the sea stacks off Miller Point, the rock's allure is more subtle and a bit mystical, but just as engaging.

To reach Arch Rock, follow the Bear Valley Trail from the Bear Valley Visitor Center to its end. The first part of the trail is detailed in the Divide Meadow trail description. In short, the trail heads southwest from the visitor center, passing the Mount Wittenberg Trail at 0.2 mile, and the Meadow Trail at 0.8 mile, both of which depart to the right (northwest). Stay straight (southwest) on the Bear Valley Trail, which climbs easily to Divide Meadow at 1.6 miles.

The Old Pine Trail heads right (northwest) from the top of the Divide Meadow; stay straight (southwest) on the Bear Valley Trail. The former ranch road skirts the marsh at the base of the meadow before reentering the shady riparian zone along Coast Creek and flowing with the creek downhill to the sea.

At 3.2 miles, reach the intersection with the Glen and Baldy Trails. This is the end of the line for mountain bikers, who must lock their trusty machines to the bike rack and hoof it to whatever destination they have in mind. The Glen Trail heads left (south) to Glen Camp, Wildcat Camp, and eventually Palomarin; the Bear Valley Trail continues straight (southwest); and the Baldy Trail parts ways to the far right (north), leading up to the Sky Trail.

Stay on the Bear Valley Trail as it follows the creek, which cascades through a green veil of willow and cottonwood on the left (south). The trail then leaves the stream, climbing into a small, brush-filled meadow. Ascend through a gap into rolling hills covered with coastal scrub brightened with yellow monkey flower into late summer.

The trail begins a gentle descent, reaching an intersection with the Coast Trail at 3.9 miles. The Coast Trail heads right (northwest) toward Sky Trail and Coast Camp, and left (southwest) to Arch Rock and Wildcat Camp. Stay left, still descending. The creek drops out of sight to the left (south), under thick cover of willow.

The trail forks again, with the Coast Trail continuing left (southwest) and the spur trail to Arch Rock leading straight (west). Climb up and around the last bluff; views open of the broad top of the rock, with the ocean spread beyond. Climb onto the top of the rock at 4.1 miles, settle into a rocky seat, and enjoy.

Unless you plan to explore other routes near Arch Rock, return as you came.

Woodward Valley Loop

HIGHLIGHTS: Ridgetop and valley bottom, healthy forest and forest devastated by fire, coastal bluffs with views that stretch forever—this long trek passes through all this and more.

TYPE OF JOURNEY: Loop.

TOTAL DISTANCE: 12 miles.

DIFFICULTY: Hard.

PERMITTED USES: Hiking; horseback riding on weekdays.

MAPS: USGS Inverness and Double Point; Point Reyes National Seashore Map; Tom Harrison Point Reyes National Seashore Map; TOPO! San Francisco Bay Area, Wine Country, and Big Sur.

SPECIAL CONSIDERATIONS: Horses are not permitted on several of these trails on weekends; equestrians should plan to do this route during the week. No pets are permitted. The Bear Valley Trail portion of this route is very popular; please be courteous to fellow trail users, regardless of their mode of travel.

PARKING AND FACILITIES: Parking is plentiful in the two large lots at the Bear Valley Visitor Center. You will find rest rooms, picnic facilities, water and more in and around the visitor center.

FINDING THE TRAILHEAD: The trailhead is located at the west end of the two large parking areas that serve the Bear Valley Visitor Center. Cars are barred from the wide dirt track by a gate.

KEY POINTS:

0.0 Trailhead.

0.2 Pass the Mount Wittenberg Trail.

0.8 Arrive at the Meadow Trail junction.

2.3 Reach Sky Trail.

3.0 Meet the Woodward Valley Trail.

4.8 Finish the descent at the Coast Trail.

5.3 Pass the trail that leads down to Sculptured Beach.

7.8 Reach the junction with the westernmost end of the Sky Trail.

8.3 Arrive at the junction with the Bear Valley Trail.

9.1 Pass the Baldy and Glen Trail intersections.

10.7 Arrive at the top of Divide Meadow and the Old Pine Trail junction.

11.5 Return to the Meadow Trail junction.

12.3 Reach Bear Valley and trail's end.

This route will enchant anyone who agrees that wandering in the wilderness, like eating chocolate mousse and falling in love, is one of the most pleasurable experiences on the planet.

And for those who think I tend toward hyperbole . . . well, I do. But I challenge you: If you're in shape and you've got the time, try it before you knock it.

The route begins on the Bear Valley Trail, heading southwest along the wide former ranch road. Pass the Mount Wittenberg Trail at 0.2 mile, then plunge into the woodlands that shade most of the Bear Valley route, hitting the Meadow Trail at 0.8 mile.

Turn right (northwest) onto the Meadow Trail, crossing the little footbridge and climbing, almost immediately, up a heavily forested slope. The trail ascends steeply at times, crossing a couple of creeklets then weaving beneath an intricate canopy of bay laurel and other evergreens. Set a comfortable pace and enjoy the workout.

Woodward Valley Loop

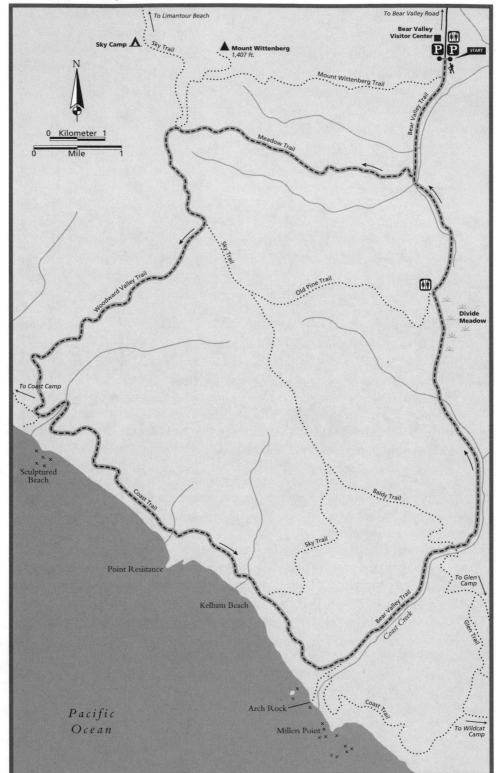

To Limantour Beach

Sky Camp

Sky Trail

Mount Wittenberg
1,407 ft.

To Bear Valley Road

**Bear Valley
Visitor Center**

P P

START

N

Mount Wittenberg Trail

Bear Valley Trail

Meadow Trail

0   Kilometer   1

0   Mile   1

Woodward Valley Trail

Sky Trail

Old Pine Trail

**Divide
Meadow**

To Coast Camp

Sculptured
Beach

Coast Trail

Baldy Trail

Sky Trail

To Glen
Camp

Point Resistance

Glen Trail

Kelham Beach

Bear Valley Trail

Coast Creek

*Pacific
Ocean*

Arch Rock

Coast Trail

Millers Point

To Wildcat
Camp

About a mile up the trail, the forest backs away from the path, opening into the broad meadow that lends the route its name. Thick with wildflowers in spring, brittle blond in summer and fall, here the sunlight that falls unimpeded is welcome and welcoming. Above the meadow, the trail reenters the woodland and remains amid the thick shade and aromatic undergrowth until it meets the Sky Trail and the Mount Wittenberg Trail atop the ridge at 2.3 miles.

Turn left (south) onto the Sky Trail; the Mount Wittenberg Trail and the other branch of the Sky Trail head right (north) to the summit of Mount Wittenberg and Sky Camp, respectively. The south portion of the Sky Trail rolls along the ridgetop, through impressive stands of ramrod-straight Douglas fir, to the junction with the Woodward Valley Trail at 3 miles.

The Woodward Valley Trail breaks west through a small herb-scented meadow flanked by columns of fir; a huge bay laurel provides nice shade in which to rest or snack near the trail intersection. The meadow is squeezed to a grassy border along the track before the trail plunges down into the woods again, woods at first healthy and vital, then stripped of greenery by the Vision Fire. On a clear day hikers are treated to glimpses of the Farallon Islands, which appear big and close through the boughs, set on the edge of a deep blue sea corrugated by wind.

The trail begins to drop in earnest as it leaves the forest. Turn a corner to the north, and staggering vistas open of Limantour and Drakes Bay. Round a switchback down a steep north-facing slope, cross a saddle, then hike briefly southward beneath burned trees. Switchback north and south again, descending into and around hunkering pillows of coastal scrub. You are still hundreds of feet above the surf, but its influence is now wonderfully obvious, blowing wind, sound, and mist up onto the hillsides.

As the trail traverses west along a scrub slope—a rolling heath of fragrant herbs and fragile wildflowers—you can look down on the arc of Drakes Bay and the snaking Coast Trail. Switchbacks drop you down to the Coast Trail intersection at 4.8 miles.

Turn left (south) onto the Coast Trail, a broad, flat, and easy road/trail set atop the coastal bluffs. The path skims a washed-out ravine, where water has carved the sandy rock into a Gothic ramparts, then narrows to singletrack before reaching the intersection with the trail to Sculptured Beach at 5.3 miles.

Sculptured Beach is a great place to break for lunch, with its wonderfully eroded cliffs and life-filled tide pools adding to any culinary experience—even one that consists only of gorp and water. The trail leading down to the beach is about 0.5 mile, direct and easy to follow.

Whether you visit the beach or not, the loop continues to the south. Circle through a ravine, where a bridge crosses a seasonal stream, then climb back out onto the bluffs. The next gully has been touched by the long reach of the

Views of Drakes Bay through the burned snags left by the Vision Fire enrich a hike on the Woodward Valley Trail.

Vision Fire, which left in its wake torched trees and vibrant scrub. Then it's back out to the bluffs, then inland through another ravine, this one the site of another bridge spanning a stream that has cut a narrow path through the scrub and trees shading the north-facing slope.

The Coast Trail heads back to the coast, where views stretch south along the cliffs and over clusters of sea stacks hammered by a relentless sea. The trail sticks close to the coastline for a good stretch before dipping in and out of a couple more gullies, the last shaded by a great old eucalyptus with massive, twisted branches and a base at least 6 feet in diameter. This tree, planted circa 1890, according to park documents, marks the site of the former Y Ranch. The ravine also sports a steep rock outcropping, a creek, and a bridge.

Back on the blufftops, the Coast Trail intersects the western end of the Sky Trail, which breaks off to the left (east) at 7.8 miles. Stay straight (south) on the Coast Trail, which continues for another 0.5 mile to its intersection with the Bear Valley Trail at 8.3 miles.

To return to the trailhead, stay straight (east) on the Bear Valley Trail; the Coast Trail continues south to Arch Rock, Wildcat Camp, and Palomarin.

The Bear Valley Trail, detailed in earlier trail descriptions for Divide Meadow and Arch Rock, traces Coast Creek east, reaching the intersection with the Baldy and Glen Trails at 9.1 miles, and climbing to the top of Divide Meadow and the Old Pine Trail junction at 10.7 miles. At 11.5 miles, on the downhill run, the trail passes the base of the Meadow Trail. And at 12.3 miles you will have reached Bear Valley and the trail's end.

OPTIONS: You can also reach the Sky Trail atop Inverness Ridge by following the Mount Wittenberg Trail up from Bear Valley, or the Old Pine Trail, which departs from Divide Meadow.

The portion of the Coast Trail that stretches from the end of the Woodward Valley Trail near Sculptured Beach to the Bear Valley Trail near Arch Rock is both remote and lovely.

Glen Camp Loop

HIGHLIGHTS: Become intimately acquainted with the mixed evergreen forest that thrives on Inverness Ridge as you climb up and around Glen Camp.

TYPE OF JOURNEY: Lollipop loop.

TOTAL DISTANCE: 10 miles.

DIFFICULTY: Hard.

PERMITTED USES: Hiking, horseback riding, mountain biking on the Bear Valley Trail.

MAPS: USGS Inverness and Double Point; Point Reyes National Seashore Map; Tom Harrison Point Reyes National Seashore Map; TOPO! San Francisco Bay Area, Wine Country, and Big Sur.

SPECIAL CONSIDERATIONS: The Glen Camp Loop is an excellent bike-and-hike route. Mountain bikers can leave their bikes at the intersection of the Bear Valley and Glen Trails, where a rack is provided. Mountain bikers on the Bear Valley Trail, which is extremely popular and sometimes crowded, should alert other users of their presence by speaking loudly and clearly. No pets are permitted on any of these trails.

PARKING AND FACILITIES: Parking is plentiful in the two large lots at the Bear Valley Visitor Center. Rest rooms, picnic facilities, and water are available at the visitor center.

FINDING THE TRAILHEAD: The Bear Valley Trail begins at the west end of the twin parking areas at the Bear Valley Visitor Center. A gate and informational billboards mark the beginning of the trail.

KEY POINTS:

0.0 Trailhead.

0.2 Pass the Mount Wittenberg Trail.

0.8 Pass the Meadow Trail.

1.6 Reach Divide Meadow.

3.2 Reach the intersection with the Glen and Baldy Trails.

3.7 Arrive at the Glen Camp Loop trail.

4.6 Take a break at Glen Camp.

5.4 Reach the Glen Trail intersection.

6.3 Return to the Glen Camp Loop trail intersection.

Glen Camp Loop

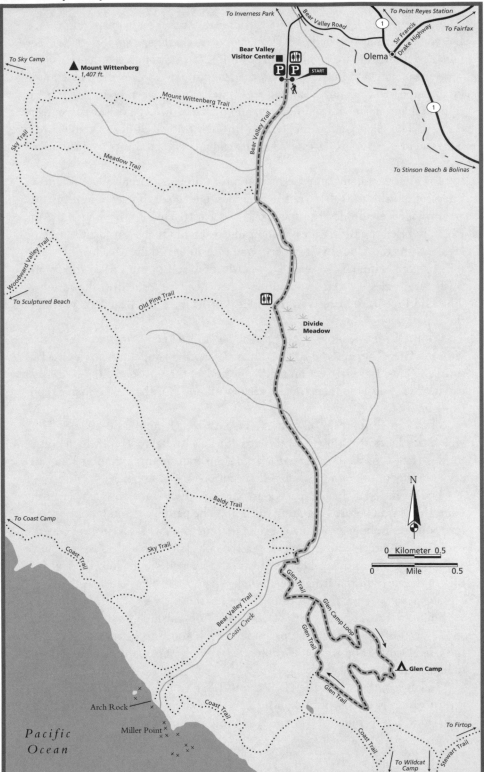

To Inverness Park
To Point Reyes Station
To Fairfax
Bear Valley Road
Sir Francis Drake Highway
Olema
To Sky Camp
Bear Valley Visitor Center
START
To Stinson Beach & Bolinas
Mount Wittenberg
1,407 ft.
Mount Wittenberg Trail
Bear Valley Trail
Sky Trail
Meadow Trail
Woodward Valley Trail
Old Pine Trail
To Sculptured Beach
Divide Meadow
N
Baldy Trail
To Coast Camp
Coast Trail
Sky Trail
0 Kilometer 0.5
0 Mile 0.5
Bear Valley Trail
Coast Creek
Glen Trail
Glen Camp Loop
Glen Trail
Glen Trail
Glen Trail
Glen Camp
To Firtop
Arch Rock
Coast Trail
Miller Point
Coast Trail
Stewart Trail
Pacific Ocean
To Wildcat Camp

The Inverness Ridge, when viewed from a distance, presents a straight face. Draped in dense woodlands, its facade appears seamless, a smooth dark green barrier defining the western boundary of Tomales Bay and the Olema Valley.

But up close and on the ground, the ridge smiles and yawns. The straight line it appeared to define becomes convoluted, lost in steep ravines that break right and left, north and south, down and up and down again as it descends to the sea. The Glen Camp Loop winds through this maze of draw and forest, with the briefest of breaks offered at the camp itself, a dollop of sunshine in a sea of green.

To reach the Glen Camp Loop, you must follow the Bear Valley Trail to its intersection with the Glen Trail at 3.2 miles. Details of this section of the trail are provided in the descriptions of the routes to Divide Meadow and Arch Rock. In brief, the Bear Valley Trail heads west from the visitor center parking area, passing the Mount Wittenberg Trail (0.2 mile) and the Meadow Trail (0.8 mile) before climbing to scenic Divide Meadow at 1.6 miles. Rest rooms and trash receptacles, as well as a couple of benches, are located in the meadow. The Old Pine Trail departs to the right (north) from the Bear Valley Trail at the top of the meadow.

From Divide Meadow, the Bear Valley Trail descends to the intersection with the Glen Trail and the Baldy Trail at 3.2 miles, paralleling Coast Creek as it drops. This trail intersection marks the end of the portion of the route that can be ridden on a mountain bike; a rack is provided for those who wish to continue on foot.

The Glen Trail breaks off to the left (southwest) from the Bear Valley Trail, which continues straight (west) to Arch Rock. The Baldy Trail, which climbs to Sky Trail, is to the right (north). Trail signs indicate the distances to a variety of destinations from this hub; Glen Camp is 1.4 miles ahead.

The Glen Trail dips across Coast Creek, which runs through a culvert beneath the trail before beginning to climb. The path leads southwest through fern and overarching aromatic bay, then flattens as it crosses a clearing covered with coyote brush and meadow grasses—the first shadeless spot you've encountered since leaving Divide Meadow. The trail climbs into the trees on the south side of the clearing, then switches back on itself to crest a ridge overlooking a steep ravine that drops to the right (south).

Follow the trail east along the rolling ridgetop, through fir and oak and bay, to the head of the ravine. The path then bends south to its intersection with the Glen Camp Loop trail at 3.7 miles. A sign indicates that Glen Camp is 0.9 mile distant.

Go left (southeast) on the Glen Camp Loop; the Glen Trail, which is the return route, is to the right (southwest). Of course, you can travel the loop either way, but it is described here in a clockwise direction.

Dense forest surrounds the grassy clearing at Glen Camp, which makes the perfect destination for both a day hike and an overnight trip.

The Glen Camp Loop trail begins as a flat, narrow singletrack that parallels a small meadow sloping upward to the north. The meadow quickly narrows into an evergreen-shrouded draw, and the path is enclosed once again in woodland.

A gentle decline becomes more abrupt as the trail approaches a seasonal stream that traces the bottom of the draw. Switchback across the stream, which, when fed by winter rains, gurgles merrily through a culvert beneath the path. Climb out of the draw to the east, trace another ravine, then cross another creek choked with oak and willow. The trail zigs and zags through a convoluted but universally verdant world, sometimes descending but mostly climbing as it wanders toward Glen Camp.

Skirt a clearing, crowded with brush but free of the shady canopy that overhangs the trail, then parallel another draw. A quick descent drops you through a fragrant glade of eucalyptus, and another clearing—a vernal pool in winter—opens to the right (west) of the track. Hitch up the other side of the basin that cradles the pool/meadow to Glen Camp, which is at 4.6 miles.

A seat at one of the picnic tables scattered around the meadowy expanse of Glen Camp makes a perfect spot for a snack—provided that camp isn't crowded with backpackers. When you are rested, make your way back to the trail, which skims the north border of the camp. A sign here indicates that the Bear Valley Trail lies 1.4 miles distant if you return as you came (to the right/northeast), and that if you head out left (north) on the Glen Camp Loop trail, you will reach the

Greenpicker Trail in 0.7 mile and the Glen Trail 0.1 mile beyond that. To continue the loop go left, following the broad road that climbs up and southwest, then north, toward the Greenpicker and Glen Trails.

Views open of the wooded valleys of Inverness Ridge to the north as you climb away from Glen Camp—the first expansive views you enjoy on the loop. The trail continues generally up and north to yet another switchback; now headed south, the trail continues its gentle ascent, flattening only when it reaches the Greenpicker Trail intersection at 5.3 miles. The Greenpicker Trail breaks off the loop to the left (east), and climbs 1 mile to Firtop; stay straight (south) on the broad Glen Camp Loop trail.

The trail drops alongside a brush-filled seasonal stream for 0.1 mile and ends at its intersection with the Glen Trail in a small clearing. The Glen Trail appears to be an extension of the service road that has served as the Glen Camp Loop; it continues for 0.5 mile south to the Stewart Trail. You will return on the north-heading branch of the Glen Trail, which switches back to parallel the Glen Camp Loop on the other side of the stream. Another trail, the Coast/Glen Spur South, leads right (west) off the Glen Trail at this intersection as well; it travels 0.3 mile to the Coast Trail.

Turn sharply right (north) onto the Glen Trail, passing a short section of split-rail fence and crossing the seasonal stream. A narrow singletrack, the path traverses the wooded hillside above the little stream. The forest parts briefly in a clearing—if you can call it that—stuffed with coyote brush that grows 7 feet high on either side of the trail. The Coast/Glen Spur North departs to the left (west) off the Glen Trail in the midst of the shrubbery at about 5.8 miles; stay right (north and downhill) on the Glen Trail. A sign indicates that the Bear Valley Trail is 1 mile ahead.

The descent becomes sharper, tracing the east-facing wall of a steep wooded valley, with great views across the deep draw to Inverness Ridge— views you should stop to enjoy, because the steep path requires your focus. It's pretty much a straight shot down to the intersection with the northern terminus of the Glen Camp Loop at 6.3 miles.

From this intersection, you will retrace your steps to the Bear Valley Trailhead. You'll catch your only brief glimpse of the ocean from this last section of the Glen Trail, which drops to the Bear Valley Trail at 6.8 miles. Turn right (east) onto the Bear Valley Trail to return to the Bear Valley Visitor Center and the parking area at 10 miles.

From Five Brooks Trailhead

Olema Valley Trail

HIGHLIGHTS: This roller-coaster ride takes you down the rift zone of the San Andreas Fault.

TYPE OF JOURNEY: Out-and-back.

TOTAL DISTANCE: 10.4 miles.

DIFFICULTY: Hard.

PERMITTED USES: Hiking, horseback riding, mountain biking.

MAPS: USGS Inverness, Double Point, and Bolinas; Point Reyes National Seashore Map; Tom Harrison Point Reyes National Seashore Map; TOPO! San Francisco Bay Area, Wine Country, and Big Sur.

SPECIAL CONSIDERATIONS: This singletrack trail is shared by all users, and though not common, there is the potential for conflicts. Please be courteous to all travelers.

PARKING AND FACILITIES: The parking lot at Five Brooks is huge, but fills up on weekends. Rest rooms and trash and recycling receptacles are available in the parking area.

FINDING THE TRAILHEAD: From the Bear Valley Visitor Center, return to Bear Valley Road via the access road (0.2 mile), and turn right (east) onto Bear Valley Road. Follow the Bear Valley Road for 0.5 mile to its intersection with California Highway 1. Turn right (south) onto CA 1 for 0.1 mile to the stop sign at its intersection with the Sir Francis Drake Highway in Olema. Continue straight on CA 1 for 3.5 miles to the signed turnoff for the Five Brooks trailhead and stables. Turn right (west) onto the dirt Five Brooks access road, and follow it for 0.1 mile to the parking lot.

KEY POINTS:

0.0 Trailhead.

0.4 Leave the Stewart Trail for the Olema Valley Trail.

0.5 Reach the three-way junction near the stables.

1.7 Climb to the Bolema Trail intersection.

2.9 Pass the Randall Trail spur.

4.3 Cross Pine Gulch Creek.

4.4 Pass Teixeira Ranch.

Olema Valley Trail

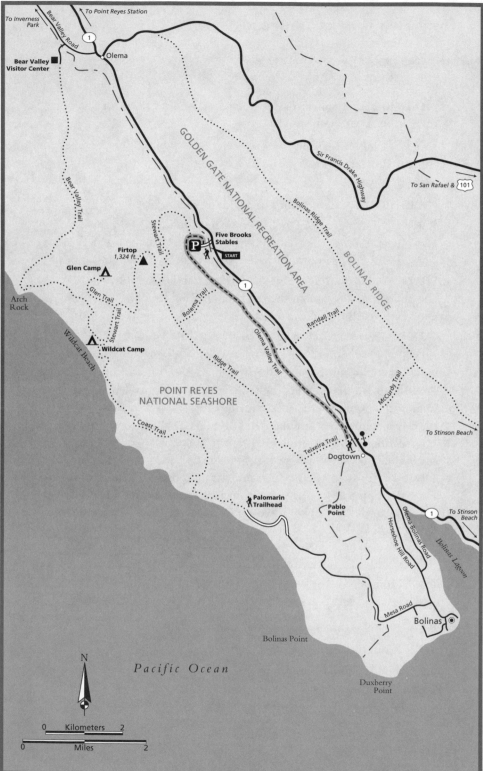

Though there isn't a huge amount of elevation gain or loss on this route, the Olema Valley Trail boasts its share of ups and downs. Popular with horseback riders and cyclists, the twisting singletrack combines short, steep pitches with sweeping descents, and encroaching underbrush with broad views. Toss in a couple of creek crossings near trail's end and you've got a route that will charm and challenge hikers of all abilities, and both intermediate and advanced equestrians and mountain bikers.

To reach the Olema Valley Trail, begin on the Stewart Trail, a dirt road/trail that begins at the north end of the Five Brooks parking area. Pass the gate and head north on the road, passing its intersection with the Rift Zone Trail on the right (east) at 0.1 mile. The Stewart Trail meets the Olema Valley Trail at 0.4 mile at a three-way intersection. Go left (southwest) on the Olema Valley Trail.

At the next three-way trail intersection, at about 0.5 mile, a trail sign overgrown with cow parsnip and blackberry brambles points toward the Five Brooks Ranch, which is down the road to the left (southeast); the manure on the trail will clue you in soon enough if you miss the sign. Take the singletrack trail to the right; the Bolema Trail intersection is 1.2 miles ahead, Teixeira Trail is at 4.8 miles, and Dogtown is 5.2 miles distant.

The first mile undulates through the broad, shady, and verdant bottomland that cradles Olema Creek. Just beyond the 1-mile mark, cross a bridge over a creek tributary; a rather significant climb begins on the other side of the bridge. Note to cyclists: If you don't shift down, or if you lose it midway up, the hill morphs into a hike-a-bike.

After 0.3 mile the pitch lessens and the trail traverses the hillside above the creek to the intersection with the Bolema Trail at 1.7 miles. The Bolema Trail breaks off to the right (northwest) and is off limits to bicyclists; stay left (south) on the Olema Valley Trail.

Lose the elevation you just gained swiftly, dropping into a sunny meadow. The trail is sandy in spots here—a reminder that, though all you see around you is meadow and forest, you are recreating in a national *seashore*. The route roller coasters through alternating meadows and clusters of oak, madrone, and manzanita, with a devilish undergrowth of stinging nettle and poison oak dotting the seemingly innocuous grasses. Don't stray from the path!

At 2.9 miles, after a winding downhill that weaves through the meadowlands, you reach the intersection with the Randall Spur Trail. The spur trail leads left (southeast) to the Randall Trail in a little less than a 0.5 mile; the Randall Trail then climbs to the Bolinas Ridge Trail. Continue right (south) on the Olema Valley Trail; the sign says Dogtown is 2.7 miles ahead, but it's actually about 2.3 miles distant.

Climb briefly from the Randall Trail spur, then begin a mostly downhill run through the Pine Creek Gulch drainage. The surrounding foliage is densely

The Olema Valley Trail stretches between Five Brooks and Dogtown.

riparian, oaks and bay laurels and blackberry brambles and poison oak; this portion of the route, which is basically a singletrack etched into an overgrown ranch road, may be muddy during and after the rainy season.

At about 3.5 miles the trail traverses a moist gully and drops through a stand of mossy-trunked bay laurels. A second gully follows at about 3.7 miles, then the trail flattens amid thickets of willow. Descend through another pocket of bay and fern; a tiny footbridge spans a seasonal stream in the gully at the 4-mile mark.

At 4.3 miles the trail passes a private property boundary sign, then dips through the bed of alder-lined Pine Gulch Creek. Fording the creek is very straightforward in summer months, when the flows are low or nonexistent, but you may find yourself wading through ankle-deep riffles in the rainy season. If the water is too high to cross safely, then this, obviously, is trail's end.

A short 0.1 mile beyond the creek crossing, the path leaves the riparian zone for the meadowlands of the Teixeira Ranch. The rusty-roofed barns are on the left (east) side of the trail, with the ranch house on the hill above.

Reach the Teixeira Trail intersection at 4.8 miles, in the midst of the moist meadow. The Teixeira Trail climbs right (west) onto Inverness Ridge; stay straight (south) on the Olema Valley Trail. The second creek crossing, if the water is high, can be a bit deeper and more challenging than the first, but again, by summertime the streambed may be dry. Climb up through another patch of meadow to the trail's end at 5.2 miles, at a gate on the west side of California Highway 1. The tiny cluster of buildings that makes up Dogtown lies directly south of the trailhead, and you can cross the road to the McCurdy Trail, which climbs east onto the Bolinas Ridge. Unless you plan to link this trail into a more ambitious loop (see the option below), return as you came.

OPTION: You can add altitude, distance, and views to a long day hike by linking this trail with the Bolinas Ridge Trail in a lollipop loop. From the southern end of the Olema Valley Trail, climb up the McCurdy Trail to the Bolinas Ridge Trail, head north along the Bolinas Ridge Trail to the Randall Trail, and descend the Randall Trail back to CA 1. The Randall Spur Trail hitches you back up with the Olema Valley Trail, which you follow north back to the Five Brooks Trailhead. This lollipop loop is about 13 miles long and involves an elevation gain (and loss) of more than 1,200 feet.

Stewart and Greenpicker Trails Loop

HIGHLIGHTS: Fern, fir, and huckleberry knit these trails together, weaving a shady route perfect for a hot Indian summer's day.

TYPE OF JOURNEY: Loop.

TOTAL DISTANCE: 7.4 miles.

DIFFICULTY: Hard.

PERMITTED USES: Hiking and horseback riding on the entire loop; mountain biking on the Stewart Trail only.

MAPS: USGS Inverness and Double Point; Point Reyes National Seashore Map; Tom Harrison Point Reyes National Seashore Map; TOPO! San Francisco Bay Area, Wine Country, and Big Sur.

SPECIAL CONSIDERATIONS: No pets are permitted on this trail. The Stewart Trail is a multiuse trail that is extremely popular with equestrians. Please be courteous to your fellow trail users; mountain bikers should yield to all other travelers, and hikers should yield to horseback riders.

PARKING AND FACILITIES: There is a huge parking area at the Five Brooks Trailhead, but it can fill quickly on weekends. Rest rooms and trash and recycling facilities are provided.

FINDING THE TRAILHEAD: From the Bear Valley Visitor Center, return to Bear Valley Road via the access road (0.2 mile), and turn right (east) onto Bear Valley Road. Follow the Bear Valley Road for 0.5 mile to its intersection with California Highway 1. Turn right (south) onto CA 1, and drive 0.1 mile to the stop sign in the heart of Olema. The signed turnoff for the Five Brooks trailhead and stables is 3.5 miles south of the intersection in Olema on CA 1. Turn right (west) onto the dirt Five Brooks access road, and follow it for 0.1 mile to the parking lot.

Stewart and Greenpicker Trails Loop

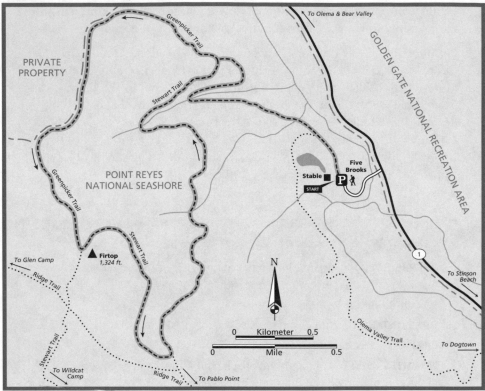

KEY POINTS:

0.0 Trailhead.

0.4 Reach the intersection with the Olema Valley Trail.

1.6 The Stewart Trail meets the base of the Greenpicker Trail.

3.4 Climb to the junction with the Stewart Trail on Firtop.

4.2 Descend to the intersection with the Ridge Trail.

6.1 Return to the intersection with the Greenpicker Trail.

Whether bathed in bright sunlight or wreathed in fog, the Douglas firs that envelop the slopes of Firtop have a mystic quality. The venerable trees filter sunlight, sharp or diffuse, through a prism of green, dappling the forest floor and nourishing a thick undergrowth of berry brambles and fern.

The Stewart and Greenpicker Trails ramble through this ethereal woodland, breaking free of the forest only in a clearing at the summit of Firtop. On this high point along Inverness Ridge, the trees frame a tiny meadow perfect for picnicking and resting, especially if the sun is out and warming the grasses.

Begin on the Stewart Trail, the broad dirt road that leaves the Five Brooks parking area and heads north. Pass the gate and the intersection with the Rift Zone Trail (hiking only) on the right (east) at 0.1 mile. Pass the Five Brooks Pond, screened by thick rushes on the left (south) side of the trail, and continue to the intersection with the Olema Valley Trail at 0.4 mile. Stay right (north) on the Stewart Trail; a sign here indicates that the Greenpicker Trail begins 0.8 mile ahead.

The wide path/road crosses a creeklet, then passes a gated trail on the right (east) that leads to the Stewart Horse Camp and the Rift Zone Trail. The Stewart Trail begins to climb—an ascent that, while never too strenuous, doesn't let up until you reach the summit of Firtop. The trail traces the path of a nameless creek to the west, then curves through a switchback and passes a cliff hung with a thick curtain of fern, so vibrantly green in winter and early spring that it almost hurts to look at.

Bend back around to head west again, meeting the intersection with the Greenpicker Trail at 1.6 miles. Both the Stewart Trail and the Greenpicker Trail head up to the summit of Firtop; the loop is described here counterclockwise, beginning on the Greenpicker Trail and ending with a descent on the Stewart Trail. Go right (north) on the Greenpicker Trail to begin the loop.

The pitch of the Greenpicker Trail, a narrow singletrack that winds into the trees, immediately increases. Huge, lichen-dressed firs border the path—the base of the trunk of one is at least 6 feet in diameter. The limbs of the firs, as well as the bay laurels, arc over the trail as it ascends.

Yes, you made it: A hiker checks out the marker on the summit of Firtop.

A couple of switchbacks take you up to a section of trail covered with sword fern so thick and tall it lends the forest floor a prehistoric atmosphere. The trail keeps rising in a northwesterly direction, traversing a hillside where breaks in the trees offer glimpses eastward of the Olema Valley and Bolinas Ridge to the east.

The path switches back and heads west, entering a bower of huckleberry brambles and fern. The undergrowth forms thick hedgerows that crowd the steep, narrow track on both sides. Social paths and drainage ditches break off right and left from the main route; stay west on the obvious, ever-ascending, and rustic Greenpicker Trail.

As you crest the top of the ridge, the steep incline gives way to a heavily wooded roller coaster. A trail breaks off to the right (north); a gate indicates that the path leads into a restricted area, and a sign warns that you risk getting lost if you venture past the gate.

Stay left on the Greenpicker Trail, which rolls south for another 0.2 mile to its intersection with a spur trail to Glen Camp (this trail was closed due to hazardous conditions in late 2001; check with at the visitor center about its status). Stay left (straight and south) on the Greenpicker Trail, which continues for about 0.1 mile to its junction with the Stewart Trail in the meadow on the summit of Firtop at 3.4 miles.

The small meadow holds a sign, in the shade of a fir tree, giving the summit elevation of 1,324 feet. The Stewart Trail is the broad track that runs along the south border of the meadow, heading left (east) back to Five Brooks and right (west) down to Wildcat Camp. Take the time you need to explore, rest, and rejuvenate before beginning the long downhill run on the Stewart Trail.

The second part of the loop begins with a short climb to the left (eastward) on the Stewart Trail, which then circles down through the trees to the east face of Inverness Ridge. Heading south on a steady, easy decline, patches of asphalt emerge from the dirt, harking back to when this was a paved road leading to Glen Camp. The Ridge Trail intersection is at 4.2 miles. Stay left on the Stewart Trail, which curves northward; the Ridge Trail bears right (south), continuing down the crest of Inverness Ridge toward Pablo Point and the Palomarin Trailhead.

The descent continues through a wildly fruitful forest, the firs towering over a tangle of berry bushes—elderberry, huckleberry, thimbleberry—entwined with bay laurel and wildflowers that vary with the season. Openings in the forest reveal views of the Bolinas Ridge and Black Mountain.

The Stewart Trail veers west into a draw crowded with sword fern as it nears the bottom of the east-facing slope of Inverness Ridge, then curves back east, then briefly north, to meet the bottom of the Greenpicker Trail at 6.1 miles. The loop is complete.

To return to the trailhead, retrace your steps down and southeast on the Stewart Trail, reaching the Five Brooks Trailhead and parking area at 7.4 miles.

HIGHLIGHTS: Forested mountaintop and crashing surf are linked together by the steep up and down of the Stewart Trail.

TYPE OF JOURNEY: Out-and-back.

TOTAL DISTANCE: 13.4 miles.

DIFFICULTY: Hard.

PERMITTED USES: Hiking, horseback riding, mountain biking.

MAPS: USGS Inverness and Double Point; Point Reyes National Seashore Map; Tom Harrison Point Reyes National Seashore Map; TOPO! San Francisco Bay Area, Wine Country, and Big Sur.

SPECIAL CONSIDERATIONS: This is a popular multiuse trail—especially with horseback riders. Treat your fellow trekkers with courtesy, regardless of their mode of travel.

PARKING AND FACILITIES: There is a huge parking area at the Five Brooks Trailhead, but it can fill quickly on weekends. Rest rooms and trash and recycling facilities are provided.

FINDING THE TRAILHEAD: From the Bear Valley Visitor Center, return to Bear Valley Road via the access road (0.2 mile), and turn right (east) onto Bear Valley Road. Follow Bear Valley Road for 0.5 mile to its intersection with California Highway 1. Turn right (south) onto CA 1, and drive 0.1 mile to the stop sign in Olema. The signed turnoff for the Five Brooks Trailhead and Stables is 3.5 miles south of the inter-section in Olema on CA 1. Turn right (west) onto the dirt Five Brooks access road, and follow it for 0.1 mile to the parking lot.

KEY POINTS:

0.0 Trailhead.

0.4 Reach the intersection with the Olema Valley Trail.

1.6 Arrive at the junction of the Stewart Trail and the Greenpicker Trail.

4.1 Reach the summit of Firtop.

5.0 Pass the Old Out Road.

5.5 Reach the junction with the Glen Trail.

6.0 The Stewart Trail ends at the Coast Trail.

6.7 Arrive at Wildcat Camp.

Stewart Trail to Wildcat Camp

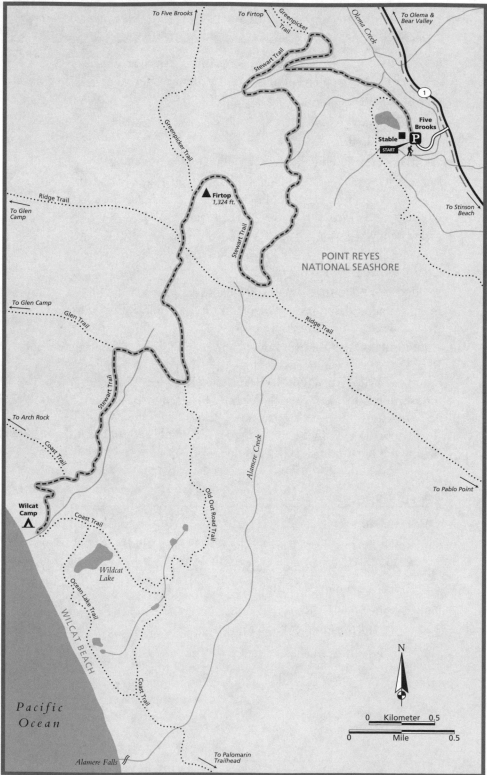

To Five Brooks

To Firtop

Greenpicker Trail

Stewart Trail

Olema Creek

To Olema & Bear Valley

1

Five Brooks

Stable

START

P

Greenpicker Trail

To Stinson Beach

Ridge Trail

To Glen Camp

▲ Firtop
1,324 ft.

Stewart Trail

POINT REYES
NATIONAL SEASHORE

To Glen Camp

Glen Trail

Ridge Trail

Stewart Trail

To Arch Rock

Coast Trail

Alamere Creek

Old Out Road Trail

To Pablo Point

Wilcat
Camp

Coast Trail

Wildcat
Lake

Ocean Lake Trail

WILCAT BEACH

Coast Trail

Pacific
Ocean

N

Kilometer
0   0.5

Mile
0   0.5

Alamere Falls

To Palomarin
Trailhead

It's a very, very long haul, but with its challenging terrain, spectacular views, and superlative landmarks—the shady summit of Firtop, the raucous surf at Wildcat Beach—the Stewart Trail from Five Brooks to Wildcat Camp is a seashore favorite.

Begin on the wide, dirt Stewart Trail, which heads north out of the Five Brooks parking area. Pass the intersection with the Rift Zone Trail on the right (east) at 0.1 mile. Five Brooks Pond is set behind a screen of willow and reed on the left (south) side of the trail.

The intersection with the Olema Valley Trail is at 0.4 mile. Stay right (north) on the Stewart Trail, which crosses a small creek, then passes a gated trail on the right (east) that leads to the Stewart Horse Camp and the Rift Zone Trail. The Stewart Trail begins to climb—a relentless but relatively moderate ascent that leads to the summit of Firtop. The road parallels a no-name creek, then curves through a switchback and passes a cliff down which spills a fall of vivid green fern.

The intersection with the Greenpicker Trail is at 1.6 miles. The Green-picker Trail heads right (northwest) from the intersection, also climbing to the summit of Firtop (this route is described earlier in this chapter). Stay left (southwest) on the Stewart Trail, which climbs back through the fern-thick gully, crossing the nameless stream about 200 feet higher in its draw.

The Stewart Trail then makes a long, south-trending, traversing ascent up the east face of Inverness Ridge, where occasional breaks in the forest and undergrowth allow views east across the Olema Valley to Bolinas Ridge and beyond. At 3.5 miles the trail curves west to meet the Ridge Trail; stay right (north) on the Stewart Trail.

The evergreens mingle with dense thickets of huckleberry as the ascent continues. Patches of asphalt—harking back to a time when this was a paved roadway—emerge from the dirt. The trail slowly curves westward, circling onto the 1,324-foot summit of Firtop at 4.1 miles.

Catch your breath (or allow your trusty steed to do so) in the small meadow atop Firtop. The Greenpicker Trail heads north out of the meadow, leading 3.4 miles back down to Five Brooks. Stay straight (west) on the Stewart Trail; the sign says Wildcat Camp is 2.8 miles ahead.

A steep, straight 0.2-mile downhill run through the firs drops you to a set of intersections with the spurs to the Greenpicker Trail, which breaks off to the right (north), and the Ridge Trail, which takes off to the left (south). Stay straight (west) on the Stewart Trail.

The pitch of the descent mellows beyond the trail junction, with pavement again peeking through the dirt. A brief climb leads to a more earnest downhill traverse southward across the face of the ridge, with the expanse of the ocean visible through the trees to the west. Round a broad switchback, and continue

Thick trees and sea mist shroud the Stewart Trail on the descent to Wildcat Camp.

the descending traverse to the north. The intersection with the Old Out Road is at about 5 miles; this popular horse route departs to the left (southwest), leading down to the Coast Trail. Stay right (northwest) on the Stewart Trail.

Drop through and around a couple of forested ravines before meeting the Glen Trail at 5.5 miles. The Glen Trail breaks off to the right, switchbacking to the northeast from the Stewart Trail and leading to Glen Camp and Bear Valley. The Stewart Trail continues left (west) and downhill; the sign says Wildcat is 1.2 miles ahead, but it's obviously still a long way to sea level.

The next section of the descent offers views of green hills dropping into the shimmering blue Pacific. The Stewart Trail ends at its intersection with the Coast Trail at the 6-mile mark, with the right (north) fork of the Coast Trail leading to Arch Rock and Bear Valley, and the left (west) fork continuing down to Wildcat Camp.

The final 0.7-mile approach to Wildcat Camp involves dropping down a scrub-covered slope via three steep switchbacks. The last switchback deposits you on the little plateau, open to the wind and just a bit above Wildcat Beach, upon which the picnic benches and barbecue braziers of the camp are scattered. Inverness Ridge abuts the back of the camp—a daunting wall of scrub and forest that you must climb to return to Five Brooks. But before you tackle that obstacle, rest on the beach, bolster yourself with food and water—heck, take a nap, if you want to. The ascent isn't as formidable as it appears.

From Palomarin Trailhead

Coast Trail to Bass Lake

HIGHLIGHTS: This pleasant ramble along the seaside bluffs ends in a small meadow on the north shore of pretty Bass Lake.

TYPE OF JOURNEY: Out-and-back.

TOTAL DISTANCE: 5.8 miles.

DIFFICULTY: Moderate.

PERMITTED USES: Hiking, horseback riding.

MAPS: USGS Bolinas and Double Point; Point Reyes National Seashore Map; Tom Harrison Point Reyes National Seashore Map; TOPO! San Francisco Bay Area, Wine Country, and Big Sur.

SPECIAL CONSIDERATIONS: No pets are permitted.

PARKING AND FACILITIES: The large parking area at the Palomarin Trailhead, like many parking lots at the seashore, fills quickly on weekends. If no parking is available, you can park alongside the road, or in the small parking area for the Point Reyes Bird Observatory (if there's room), located 0.6 mile back (south) on Mesa Road. Rest rooms and trash and recycling receptacles are provided.

FINDING THE TRAILHEAD: From the Bear Valley Visitor Center, head east on the access road for 0.2 mile to Bear Valley Road. Turn right (southeast) onto Bear Valley Road and go 0.5 mile to California Highway 1. Turn right (south) onto CA 1 for 0.1 mile to the stop sign at the intersection with Sir Francis Drake Highway in Olema. Continue straight (south) from Olema on CA 1 to its intersection with the Olema-Bolinas Road at about 9 miles. This Y-intersection is unmarked. Go right (southwest) on the Olema-Bolinas Road for 1.3 miles to the stop sign at Horseshoe Hill Road. Turn left (south) and continue on the Olema-Bolinas Road to the stop sign at its intersection with Mesa Road. Turn right (west) onto Mesa Road, and follow it for 4.5 rolling miles to its end at the Palomarin Trailhead. The pavement ends at about 3.5 miles, and the parking area for the Point Reyes Bird Observatory is at 3.9 miles.

Coast Trail to Bass Lake

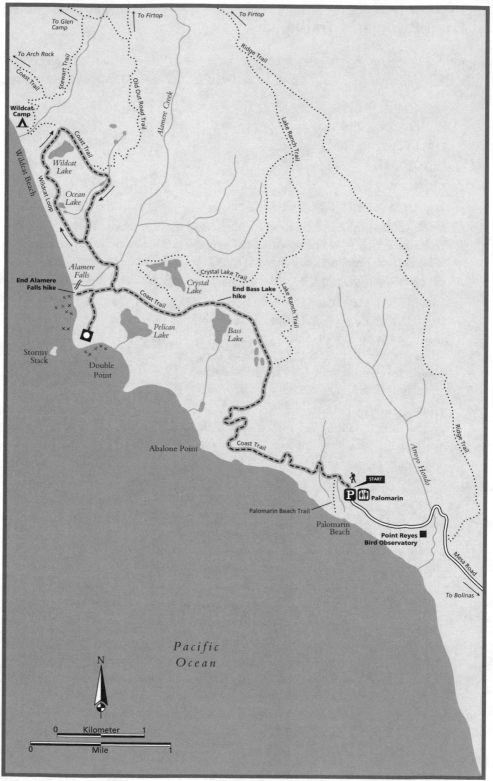

KEY POINTS:

0.0 Trailhead.

0.1 Pass the trail that leads down to Palomarin Beach.

2.2 Meet the Lake Ranch Trail.

2.9 Reach the meadow on the north shore of Bass Lake.

When considering a body of water as a destination at the Point Reyes National Seashore, a lake generally doesn't come to mind. But the southern portion of the park is dotted with lovely lakes, Bass Lake being one of the prettiest and certainly the easiest to reach. Insulated by thick riparian plants and dense fir forest, the waters of the lake are opaque, antique bottle green under the sun and almost black in the fog, nearly always still and reflective. Access to the shoreline is difficult—there is no beach—but trekkers can reach the waterside from a small meadow on the north side of the lake. It's perfect place to enjoy a picnic or to rest before the trek back to Palomarin.

The quickest route to Bass Lake follows the Coast Trail from Palomarin. The trail begins by climbing a short staircase adjacent to the rest rooms on the east side of the parking lot; the broad road/trail immediately turns north and enters a thick stand of eucalyptus. Signs inform trail users that no pets or bikes are allowed on this stretch of the Coast Trail, which runs through designated wilderness. Another couple of informational and interpretive signs are found at the intersection with the trail that leads left (west) down to Palomarin Beach at 0.1 mile. Stay straight (north) on the Coast Trail.

The trail briefly follows the contours of the brushy, wooded hillside, curving in and out of gullies that are dry in summer and boast small streams in winter, before breaking out onto bluffs cloaked only in low-growing coastal scrub. Views of the Pacific stretch north, south, and west, with gray-green hillsides rising to the east.

As it continues north, the path skims the cliff's edge, with views dropping more than 200 feet to the beach. It then cuts inland into a gully, where a footbridge spans a small creek. The trail forks as you head out toward the seashore again; stay on the high road, as the fence and arrow dictate. The next gully, also featuring a small footbridge, is at about the 1-mile mark. As it curves back toward the ocean, the path passes through lush riparian growth.

Pacific views are left behind as the Coast Trail climbs steeply up and east, rounding a couple of sweeping curves as it ascends inland. Small stands of Monterey pine shade the steady, fairly rigorous climb, which curves around to the back side of a substantial hill. A steep, rocky ravine opens to the right (south); then steep slopes hem the path in on both flanks. Climb through a narrow cleft between the two hillsides to a saddle; trees on the west side appear young and short, while those growing above and to the east are taller and more mature.

Fog shrouds the still waters of Bass Lake, its fringe of evergreens reflected with perfect clarity on the inky surface.

The Coast Trail descends from the saddle, passing a vernal pool tucked into tall grasses on the left (west) before it meets the Lake Ranch Trail at 2.2 miles. The Lake Ranch Trail heads right (northeast) to the Ridge Trail, and eventually to Five Brooks. Stay left (northwest) on the Coast Trail.

Several more ponds, their waters a thick, fertile green, appears on the left (west) as you continue on the flat track. The ponds are separate in the dry season—indeed, some of the more ephemeral dry out completely—but in the rainy season, the waters spill from one basin to the next. The shores are clogged with brush, but social trails lead to informal picnic areas shaded by evergreens above the shorelines, and to relatively clear places that pass for beaches.

Remain on the Coast Trail; patches of old asphalt erupt from the gravel surface as the trail threads between marshes (vernal pools in the rainy season) and small ponds. Frogs populate the wet areas, filling the air with their croaks when the water (and their passion) is high. Cross a narrow stream straddled by cottonwoods; the trail descends alongside the stream, the watercourse hidden in a tangle of brush.

Both stream and trail flatten as they approach Bass Lake, which opens to the west. A thicket of willow separates the dark waters of the lake from the trail, which traverses above the east side of the lakeshore, crossing buried culverts that channel water draining into the lake from the eastern hills.

At the north shore of the lake, a signed footpath breaks off to the left (west) at 2.9 miles. The path punches through a stand of Douglas fir before emptying into a small, tree-rimmed meadow. A steep, eroded trail—once a staircase—leads down from the west side of the clearing to a narrow landing at the lakeshore, where calla lilies bloom in winter. Enjoy the lake and its environs, then return as you come.

OPTION: Bass Lake is one of many destinations along the 16-mile length of the Coast Trail, which stretches north to Limantour. The trail to Alamere Falls and Wildcat Camp is described next, but you can go as long and far as you desire on this scenic route.

Alamere Falls and Double Point Overlook

See map on page 106

HIGHLIGHTS: The Coast Trail offers access to a dynamic duo: Alamere Falls, the most spectacular waterfall on the Point Reyes peninsula, and the lofty Double Point Overlook, offering bird's-eye views of Double Point Cove, Pelican Lake, and the landscapes of the southern seashore.

TYPE OF JOURNEY: Out-and-back.

TOTAL DISTANCE: 8.5 miles.

DIFFICULTY: Hard.

PERMITTED USES: Hiking, horseback riding along the Coast Trail.

MAPS: USGS Bolinas and Double Point; Point Reyes National Seashore Map; Tom Harrison Point Reyes National Seashore Map; TOPO! San Francisco Bay Area, Wine Country, and Big Sur.

SPECIAL CONSIDERATIONS: No pets are allowed on this route. The Alamere Falls Trail and the unsigned trail to the Double Point Overlook are rugged and unmaintained, and should be attempted only by experienced hikers.

PARKING AND FACILITIES: The large parking area at the Palomarin Trailhead fills quickly on weekends. If no parking is available, park alongside Mesa Road, or in the small parking area for the Point Reyes Bird Observatory, located 0.6 mile back (south) on Mesa Road. Rest rooms and trash and recycling receptacles are provided.

FINDING THE TRAILHEAD: From the Bear Valley Visitor Center, go east on the access road for 0.2 mile to Bear Valley Road. Turn right (southeast) onto Bear Valley Road and travel 0.5 mile to California Highway 1. Turn right (south) onto CA 1, and go 0.1 mile to the stop sign at the intersection with Sir Francis Drake Highway in Olema. Continue straight (south) on CA 1 from Olema to an unmarked intersection with the Olema-Bolinas Road at about 9 miles. Go right (southwest) on the Olema-Bolinas Road for 1.3 miles to the stop sign at Horseshoe Hill Road. Turn left (south) and continue on the Olema-Bolinas Road to the stop sign at its intersection with Mesa Road. Turn right (west) onto Mesa Road, and follow it for 4.5 miles to its end at the Palomarin Trailhead, passing the Point Reyes Bird Observatory at 3.9 miles.

KEY POINTS:

0.0 Trailhead.

0.1 Pass the trail to Palomarin Beach.

2.2 Reach the Lake Ranch Trail intersection.

2.9 Pass the north shores of Bass Lake.

3.1 Pass the Crystal Lake Trail.

3.6 Reach the Alamere Falls Trail.

4.1 Arrive at the falls.

4.6 Return to the Double Point Overlook Trail.

5.0 Reach the overlook.

5.4 Return to the Coast Trail.

Alluring and challenging. Alamere Falls, like a wild rose, displays its beauty without reservation, but is prickly and must be approached with caution. Its waters tumble over a series of terraces before taking a final plunge onto Wildcat Beach, where the surf vigorously pounds the strand. The harmonizing thunder of both ocean and fall is distant on the exposed summit overlooking Double Point Cove, the second destination on this route, from which you look down nearly 500 feet to the sea.

Both Alamere Falls and the Double Point Overlook are reached via the Coast Trail. The route begins by climbing a short staircase adjacent to the rest rooms on the east side of the Palomarin Trailhead parking lot. The broad road/trail immediately turns north and enters a glade of eucalyptus, passing several information signs before meeting the trail that leads left (west) to Palomarin Beach at 0.1 mile.

Stay straight (north) on the Coast Trail, which follows the contours of the coastline, weaving inland through gullies and out onto the bluffs overlooking the ocean for more than a mile before climbing steeply up and east, rounding a couple of sweeping curves as it heads inland. Ascend past a steep, rocky ravine on the right (south), then through a narrow cleft between the two hillsides to a saddle.

The Coast Trail descends from the saddle where the Lake Ranch Trail breaks off to the right (northeast) at 2.2 miles. Stay left (northwest) on the Coast Trail, passing a series of ponds and vernal pools as the trail descends to Bass Lake at 2.9 miles. A signed footpath breaks off to the left (west) before the Coast Trail begins to climb away from the lake through a thick mixed evergreen forest. This section of the route is detailed in the Bass Lake trail description.

The Coast Trail flattens above the Bass Lake basin, and arcs westward. The Crystal Lake Trail intersection is at 3.1 miles; this trail, which heads right (north and east) toward the Ridge Trail, was closed as of late 2001 due to dangerous conditions. Continue straight (northwest) on the Coast Trail, which drops out of the dense woodlands back into the coastal scrub. Pelican Lake lies cupped in a bowl below and to the left (west); you can see a snapshot of the ocean through a V-shaped break in the bluffs.

The easy descent continues, shaded in spots by thickets of broom and scrub, and the sounds of the nearby surf are carried into the bluffs by the wind. Pass an unmarked social trail that breaks off to the left (southwest)—this path leads to the Double Point Overlook, where you'll venture on the return trip. The signed but unmaintained trail to Alamere Falls branches off to the left (west) about 100 feet below the Double Point trail, at about 3.6 miles. Watch carefully for the trail and trail sign because they blend into the landscape and are easy to miss.

Thick brambles of coyote brush encroach on the eroded singletrack trail, but it's clear and easy to follow. Alamere Creek runs through the willow-choked basin to the right (north). The track heads steeply downhill and, given both the ruts and pitch, is more difficult than it looks. Pass through head-high bowers of thick brush to the brink of the falls, where the path becomes a real challenge, skittering down an eroded cliff adjacent to the upper reaches of the falls. It's a hands-on affair that's not for the neophyte.

Pick your way down twisting clefts in the cliff onto terraces misted by the adjacent falls; these rocky platforms overlook both the ocean and the cascades. To reach the beach, you must pick your way across the creek as it flows over the terraces, then drop the final hundred feet to Wildcat Beach. When the water is high, this crossing is a significant obstacle for all but the most confident and adventurous hikers; many are content to rest on the terraces above the beach, savoring the views west of the Pacific and back east at the tumbling cascades. Whether you settle on the rocks along the upper cascades or rest on the beach at its base, Alamere Falls, at 4.1 miles, is an invigorating destination. Water is everywhere—washing the sand, tumbling from the cliffs, cascading through channels.

When you can tear yourself away, return to the Coast Trail as you came. Turn right (south) and climb back to the unsigned Double Point Overlook trail at 4.6 miles. An arrow on a short section of split-rail fence indicates where the Coast Trail bends north, toward the Alamere Falls Trail and Wildcat Camp; the footpath to the overlook skirts the fence and plunges into waist-high coyote brush and bush lupine. Push through the scrub to a clear stretch of trail, which passes above the north shore of Pelican Lake. Wade through several more thick stands of scrub as you head toward a steep hillside—the trail looks like it might get swallowed in the greenery, but it never does.

The trail is clear of crowding brush as you climb westward, with the ocean spread to the west and the Alamere Creek canyon dropping away to the right (north). The path curves southward and again weaves through rounded bushes before emptying into a clearing where the trail appears to split. Stay up and right (west); the left fork disappears into the brush overlooking Pelican Lake.

The path climbs and bends back to the west, opening to stunning views west and north. The sounds of the surf pummeling Wildcat Beach and the strip of sand cradled in Double Point Cove are carried up to you by the wind. Atop

Muddy with runoff, Alamere Falls begins its tumble to Wildcat Beach and the sea.

the summit, at 5 miles, the views open in every direction, up and down the rocky, craggy coastline, down the steep strawberry-blond cliffs into inaccessible Double Point Cove, and east onto the serene waters of Pelican Lake. It's a lonely, exposed spot, not for those afraid of heights. And of course, if you happen to climb to the overlook in the fog (as I once did), you won't see a thing. Such is life at the seashore.

To return to the trailhead, retrace your steps to the Coast Trail, then follow the trail back south to the Palomarin parking area.

Wildcat Loop

See map on page 106

HIGHLIGHTS: Call this a lakes tour: the trail skirts Bass Lake, Pelican Lake, Wildcat Lake, and Ocean Lake, and features great coastal vistas as well.

TYPE OF JOURNEY: Lollipop loop.

TOTAL DISTANCE: 11 miles.

DIFFICULTY: Hard.

PERMITTED USES: Hiking, horseback riding.

MAPS: USGS Bolinas and Double Point; Point Reyes National Seashore Map; Tom Harrison Point Reyes National Seashore Map; TOPO! San Francisco Bay Area, Wine Country, and Big Sur.

SPECIAL CONSIDERATIONS: No pets are allowed on this route.

PARKING AND FACILITIES: The large parking area at the Palomarin Trailhead fills quickly on weekends. If no parking is available, park alongside Mesa Road, or in the small parking area for the Point Reyes Bird Observatory, located 0.6 mile back (south) on Mesa Road. Rest rooms and trash and recycling receptacles are provided.

FINDING THE TRAILHEAD: From the Bear Valley Visitor Center, go east on the access road for 0.2 mile to Bear Valley Road. Turn right (southeast) onto Bear Valley Road and travel 0.5 mile to California Highway 1. Turn right (south) onto CA 1, and go 0.1 mile to the stop sign at the intersection with Sir Francis Drake Highway in Olema. Continue straight (south) on CA 1 from Olema to an unmarked intersection with the Olema-Bolinas Road, which is about 9 miles from Olema. Go right (southwest) on the Olema-Bolinas Road for 1.3 miles to the stop sign at Horseshoe Hill Road. Turn left (south) and continue on the Olema-Bolinas Road to the stop sign at its intersection with Mesa Road. Turn right (west) onto Mesa Road, and follow it for 4.5 miles to its end at the Palomarin Trailhead, passing the Point Reyes Bird Observatory at 3.9 miles.

KEY POINTS:

0.0 Trailhead.

0.1 Pass the trail to Palomarin Beach.

2.2 Reach the Lake Ranch Trail intersection.

2.9 Pass the north shore of Bass Lake.

3.1 Pass the Crystal Lake Trail.

3.6 Arrive the Alamere Falls Trail junction.

4.2 Reach the Ocean Lake Loop Trail.

5.3 Return to the Coast Trail.

5.5 Drop to Wildcat Camp.

5.7 Climb back to the Coast/Ocean Lake Loop Trail junction.

6.8 Reach the southern Coast/Ocean Lake Loop intersection.

11.0 Return to the trailhead.

Each of the lakes you'll pass on this long, scenic trek has a different character. Bass Lake has a mountain tarn feel, completely enclosed in trees. Pelican Lake, sunken in a bowl of coastal scrub below the steep flanks of Double Point, rings with the sound of an ocean that is yet out of sight. Little Ocean Lake, insulated by a thick border of reeds, is exposed to wind, sky, fog, and, when the air is clear, lengthy coastal views. And Wildcat Lake, hugged by bluffs on the west and Inverness Ridge on the east, is a sheltering haven for birds and trekkers alike.

Save a relatively short stretch on the Ocean Lake Loop trail, most of this route follows the Coast Trail. The first section of the route has been detailed in the Bass Lake and Alamere Falls hike descriptions, so I'll set forth only a summary here.

The Coast Trail leaves the parking lot via a short staircase adjacent to the rest rooms. Turn left (north) onto the broad trail/road, which passes through a glade of eucalyptus to the intersection with the Palomarin Beach Trail at 0.1 mile. Continue north on the Coast Trail, which follows the contours of the coastline for more than a mile before climbing steeply up and inland. Pass through a saddle, then drop to the Lake Ranch Trail junction at 2.2 miles.

Hikers enjoy the views from the high point on the Ocean Lake Loop trail.

Stay left (northwest) on the Coast Trail, which passes a series of ponds before reaching Bass Lake at 2.9 miles. Continuing north, the Coast Trail climbs out of the lake basin and arrives at the Crystal Lake Trail intersection at 3.1 miles. Stay left (northwest) on the Coast Trail, dropping out of the woods into the coastal scrub above Pelican Lake. An unmarked social trail to the Double Point Overlook breaks off to the left (west) about 100 feet above the intersection with the signed trail to Alamere Falls at about 3.6 miles. The Alamere Falls Trail also departs to the left (west).

Again, stay right (north) on the Coast Trail, which drops through the willowy bottomlands to cross Alamere Creek, then climbs through the scrub to the intersection with the Ocean Lake Loop trail at 4.2 miles. Turn left (northwest) onto the Ocean Lake Loop trail, a narrow footpath that boasts unobstructed views across the waters to the pale cliffs bordering Drakes Bay. When the surf is up on Wildcat Beach, which stretches below the bluff upon which the trail rides, the waves roar like jet engines.

The trail flattens in a marshy basin, with a steep cliff on the east side. Reeds choke the southern portion of the hollow, with tiny, glassy Ocean Lake barely visible through the foliage. A berm runs parallel to the trail on the ocean side.

The trail curls inland, then employs a steep, north-trending traverse to mount the cliff wall on the east. There's a bit of exposure here, but it's short, and the trail is plenty wide. Atop the bluff, the park service has thoughtfully erected a bench for the visitors' viewing pleasure. The vistas stretch south to Double Point, with the frothy spill of Alamere Falls in the foreground, north past the dark strand of Wildcat Beach to Limantour Beach, and west to the cliffs of the Point Reyes headlands.

The trail turns eastward, heading toward the forested slopes of Inverness Ridge, then descends along the western shores of Wildcat Lake. You have only a quick view of the lake before the trail winds down the north side of the basin through tall grasses and shrubs. Cross the lake's outlet stream, then meet the Coast Trail at 5.3 miles. Turn left (north) onto the Coast Trail; it's a quick but steep 0.2-mile drop along the outlet stream from here to Wildcat Camp. A short trail offers easy access to Wildcat Beach for a little R&R before beginning the journey back to the trailhead.

To complete the loop, climb south out of Wildcat Camp on the Coast Trail, returning to the Coast/Ocean Lake Loop intersection at 5.7 miles. Stay left (south) on the Coast Trail, climbing a bit more to views of Wildcat Lake from its east shore. From the lakeside trail you can watch ducks ply the waters, their wakes slashing white V's on the opaque surface.

Thick brush borders the two-track trail as it continues to climb southward, with patches of asphalt visible through the dirt. The intersection with the Old Out Road is at about 6.2 miles; this trail leads left (east) and up onto Inverness

Ridge. Stay straight (south) on the Coast Trail, which leaves the scrubland for the shade of the mixed evergreen forest as it loops through a steep-sided gully. Pass a pond on the right (west) side of the trail that appears to be in the process of giving way to marsh and meadow, its surface vividly green with algae and water plants.

Out of the ravine, the trail curves south again, crossing the sun-drenched (or fog-shrouded) blufftops. The steep cone of Double Point rises on the horizon, with the willows of Alamere Creek strung along its base. The southern intersection with the Ocean Lake Loop is at 6.8 miles. Unless you want to do laps, continue straight (south) on the Coast Trail, retracing your steps to the Palomarin Trailhead at 11 miles.

On Adjacent Golden Gate Lands

Bolinas Ridge Trail to the Randall Trail

HIGHLIGHTS: The top of Bolinas Ridge offers bird's-eye views up and down the San Andreas Rift Zone.

TYPE OF JOURNEY: Out-and-back or shuttle.

TOTAL DISTANCE: 12.5 miles to the Randall Trail and back; 22.2 miles to the Bolinas-Fairfax Road and back.

DIFFICULTY: Moderate to hard.

PERMITTED USES: Hiking, horseback riding, mountain biking.

MAPS: USGS Inverness, San Geronimo, and Bolinas; Point Reyes National Seashore Map; Tom Harrison Point Reyes National Seashore Map; TOPO! San Francisco Bay Area, Wine Country, and Big Sur.

SPECIAL CONSIDERATIONS: Dogs are permitted on this trail; please keep them on a leash. The trail passes through pastureland; you may encounter cows on or near the trail. Please close all gates behind you.

PARKING AND FACILITIES: Parking for about ten cars is available in a pullout at the trailhead. Other pullouts alongside the Sir Francis Drake Highway provide additional parking a bit farther afield. No other facilities are available.

FINDING THE TRAILHEAD: To reach the trailhead from the Bear Valley Visitor Center, take the access road east to Bear Valley Road and turn right (southeast). Follow the Bear Valley Road for 0.5 mile to its end at California Highway 1. Turn right (south) onto CA 1 and go 0.1 mile to the stop sign at its junction with the Sir Francis Drake Highway in the heart of Olema. Turn left (east) onto Sir Francis Drake, and climb

Bolinas Ridge Trail to the Randall Trail

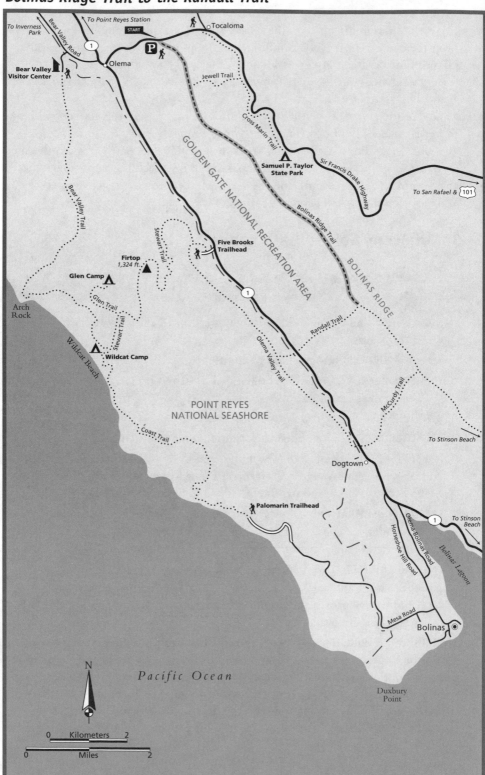

To Inverness Park

Bear Valley Road

To Point Reyes Station

Tocaloma

START

1

P

Olema

Bear Valley Visitor Center

Jewell Trail

Cross Marin Trail

GOLDEN GATE NATIONAL RECREATION AREA

Samuel P. Taylor State Park

Sir Francis Drake Highway

To San Rafael & 101

Bear Valley Trail

Stewart Trail

Bolinas Ridge Trail

Five Brooks Trailhead

Firtop 1,324 ft.

Glen Camp

Glen Trail

BOLINAS RIDGE

Arch Rock

Stewart Trail

1

Wildcat Beach

Wildcat Camp

Olema Valley Trail

Randall Trail

McCurdy Trail

To Stinson Beach

POINT REYES NATIONAL SEASHORE

Coast Trail

Dogtown

Palomarin Trailhead

Horseshoe Hill Road

Olema-Bolinas Road

1

To Stinson Beach

Bolinas Lagoon

Mesa Road

Bolinas

N

Pacific Ocean

Duxbury Point

0   Kilometers   2

0   Miles   2

for 1 mile to the top of the hill. The trailhead and parking pullout are on the right (south) just beyond the crest of the ridge, about 1.1 miles from Olema.

KEY POINTS:

0.0 Trailhead.

1.3 Reach the junction with the Jewell Trail.

2.2 Pass through one of many gates.

4.2 Pass through a stand of eucalyptus.

5.0 Reach the junction with the trail down to Shafter Bridge.

6.2 Arrive at the Randall Trail and turnaround point.

The San Andreas Fault displays geometric perfection as it divides the Olema Valley. The bottomlands, angled southeast to northwest, delineate a straight-edged separation between twin ridges, the wooded Inverness Ridge on the west side, and the grassy Bolinas Ridge on the east. Looking down from the Bolinas Ridge Trail, the notorious fault hardly appears dangerous; rather, it has sculpted a lovely, undulating terrain cloaked in forest and meadow, a landscape than sinks slowly beneath the waters of Tomales Bay in the north, and Bolinas Lagoon in the south.

The trail, which is also part of the Bay Area Ridge Trail, begins by passing a trail sign listing mileages to various trail intersections (the Randall Trail is 6.2 miles ahead), then follows a narrow track through the pasture to the fire road that serves as the trail, upon which you head left (southeast). Climb up and around a small corral before veering to the south. Pass through an open gate—the first of many, some that you'll have to open and close, others circumvented via stiles—and a soft, rolling ascent along the ridgeline commences. The grass-lands on either side of the broad fire road have been cropped close by soft-eyed, fearless cows; the landscape is heath-like, with outcrops of gray-green rock scattered like random mystical statues among the grasses.

At 1 mile the trail forks at a gate and another Bay Area Ridge Trail sign. Go right (southeast) through the gate, being careful to close it behind you. The signed Jewell Trail breaks off to the left (east) at 1.3 miles, dropping 0.9 mile to meet the Cross Marin Trail at Lagunitas Creek. Stay right, climbing steeply southwest on a gravelly patch of roadway; the Randall Trail is 4.9 miles distant.

The views change with the orientation of the trail, which weaves through the contours of the ridgeline—now of the Lagunitas Creek canyon, now of Inverness Ridge, now of Tomales Bay to the north. Pass an open gate at 1.5 miles, then follow a fence line to the next gate at 1.8 miles (making sure to close it once you've passed).

The roller coaster trail ascends to the next gate at 2.2 miles. The fence line that has paralleled the trail now demarcates an abrupt change in ecosystem, a pastoral/wilderness interface that graphically illustrates how grazing transforms the land. Evergeen woodlands and coyote brush creep up the ridge toward the trail on the left (east) side, while the close-cropped pastures drop off the ridge to the right (west).

The mixed evergreen forest and coyote brush envelop the trail as you continue, providing welcome shade if the day is hot and clear. Beyond the next fence, at 3.3 miles, the trail reenters pastureland. This crossing offers the option of using a stile if you don't want to open and close the gate. A little pond with a clump of reeds growing from its center fills a little hollow on the right (west) side of the trail.

Climb past a second pond, then up onto a hump in the ridgeline where the pasture broadens and flattens. To get good views down into the Olema Valley, break off the trail to the right (west) to an informal overlook.

Roll onward and upward, passing a couple of old eucalyptus at 4.3 miles, and reaching a rock outcropping with an oak growing from a cleft at 4.5 miles— another wonderful place to stop and take in the views. Pass through another gate (with a stile) and proceed through another section of unpasture-ized land to the intersection with the Bolinas Ridge Trail and the Shafter Bridge Trail at 5 miles. The Shafter Bridge Trail, which departs to the left (east), travels through Mount Tamalpais watershed lands that abut the Golden Gate National Recreation Area. Stay straight (south) on the Bolinas Ridge Trail.

Redwood trees mingle with the other evergreens as the trail rolls on toward the Randall Trail, which is on the right (west) at 6.2 miles. The Randall Trail leads 1.5 miles downhill and west to CA 1.

Unless you plan to explore that route, or continue along the Bolinas Ridge Trail to its end at the Bolinas-Fairfax Road, this is the turnaround point. On the return trek, you'll be treated to wonderful, unobstructed views of Tomales Bay, with Inverness and Bolinas Ridges stretching north on either side, and the grassy slopes of Black Mountain to the northeast.

OPTIONS: Unless you are an aerobic animal or plan to hike or ride for most of a long summer's day, shuttle hikes or rides are in order if you continue past the Randall Trail intersection. The Bolinas Ridge Trail continues for another 5.9 miles along the ridgeline before ending on the winding Bolinas-Fairfax Road. You can also use the Randall Trail to link to the Olema Valley Trail, which ends at Five Brooks, and the Rift Zone Trail, which will take you back to Bear Valley.

Cross Marin Trail (Sir Francis Drake Bikeway)

HIGHLIGHTS: Paved, flat, and shaded by redwoods, the Cross Marin Trail is perfect for a family outing.

TYPE OF JOURNEY: Out-and-back.

TOTAL DISTANCE: 4 miles to the state park boundary and back; 9 miles to Shafter's Bridge and back.

DIFFICULTY: Very easy to park boundary; moderate to Shafter's Bridge.

PERMITTED USES: Hiking, mountain biking, horseback riding.

MAPS: USGS Inverness and San Geronimo; Point Reyes National Seashore Map; Tom Harrison Point Reyes National Seashore Map; TOPO! San Francisco Bay Area, Wine Country, and Big Sur.

SPECIAL CONSIDERATIONS: Pets must be on leashes.

PARKING AND FACILITIES: Parking at Tocaloma is in a pullout alongside Platform Bridge Road. You also can access the trail from Samuel P. Taylor State Park, but will have to pay a fee. The park has picnic facilities, campsites, and rest rooms.

FINDING THE TRAILHEAD: To reach the Tocaloma trailhead from the Bear Valley Visitor Center, head east for 0.2 mile down the access road to Bear Valley Road. Turn right (east) onto Bear Valley Road and drive for 0.5 mile to its intersection with California Highway 1. Turn right (south) onto CA 1 for 0.1 mile to the junction with the Sir Francis Drake Highway in Olema. Turn left (east) onto Sir Francis Drake, and go about 2 miles to its intersection with Platform Bridge Road. Turn left (north) onto Platform Bridge Road; the parking pullout is less than 0.1 mile down Platform Bridge Road, on the left (west).

KEY POINTS:

0.0 Trailhead.

1.4 Pass the Jewell Trail intersection.

2.0 Reach the boundary of the state park.

3.0 Pass through the campground.

3.5 Cross the overpass.

4.0 Pass the Ridge Trail to Mount Barnabe.

4.5 Arrive at Shafter's Bridge.

The riparian habitat that flourishes along Lagunitas Creek envelopes the northern reaches of the Cross Marin Trail so completely that travelers seldom glimpse any of the surrounding terrain—the rolling pasturelands roamed by

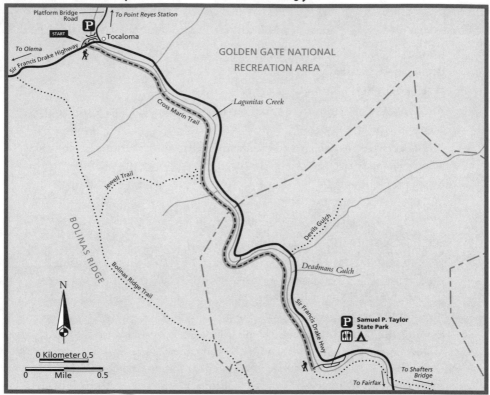

dairy cows, the nearby highway, sometimes the creek itself. The route is flat, paved, and easy, set upon the former bed of the Northern Pacific Railroad, which boosted the paper milling enterprise of Samuel Penfield Taylor, for whom the nearby state park is named.

The route begins by crossing a wonderful old bridge that spans Lagunitas Creek from Platform Bridge Road to the trailhead proper. On the east side of the bridge, turn left (southeast) onto the signed Cross Marin Trail.

The paved path, split down the middle by a single yellow line, dives under a modern bridge supporting the Sir Francis Drake Highway, then climbs onto the railroad grade that traces the banks of Lagunitas Creek. The first part of the path passes through a thick riparian forest crowded with bay trees and dotted with small redwood groves, then courses through a narrow meadow. On the far side of a stand of eucalyptus, at 1.4 miles, you will reach the Jewell Trail intersection, with the dirt Jewell Trail breaking away to the right (west) on a steep climb to the Bolinas Ridge Trail. Continue straight (southeast) on the Cross Marin Trail.

The boundary with Samuel P. Taylor State Park (and the end of the portion of the trail contained within the GGNRA) is at 2 miles, but chances are you won't want to stop there. Stay on the main park road, ignoring other paved roads that lead to park housing and facilities, and passing the marker at the site of the Pioneer Paper Mill on the left (northeast). The Ox Trail departs to the right (southwest) opposite the marker.

The trail/road leads into the campground proper, shaded by impressive stands of redwoods, at about the 3-mile mark at a gate; this is where you will find campsites, picnic facilities, and rest rooms. Stay on the right (south) side of the creek, passing the Redwood Grove Picnic Area and through another gate. The Pioneer Tree Trail departs to the right (south) on the far side of the gate.

The pavement ends, and the trail rises to cross an overpass spanning the Sir Francis Drake Highway at 3.5 miles. Pass the Irving Group Picnic Area, continuing on what is now a rather rough dirt road that parallels the creek on its north bank. Pass the junction with the Ridge Trail, which climbs onto Mount Barnabe, at about the 4-mile mark.

The broad track ends 0.5 mile beyond the Ridge Trail, at a gate and a Kent Lake trail sign. Take the narrow footpath down to the creek, where you can cool your heels in the swimming holes below Shafter's Bridge. During the rainy season, a lively cascade spills from pool to pool, and you may be lucky enough to see salmon and steelhead spawning in the clear waters of the stream.

Return as you came.

Cyclists look down on Lagunitas Creek from the old bridge in Tocaloma.

Camping in the Point Reyes National Seashore allows you more time to enjoy its treasures, like the tide pools at Sculptured Beach south of Coast Camp.

Point Reyes Recreation

While the trails that weave through Point Reyes are the focus of much recreational activity within the park, there are other ways to enjoy the national seashore. This chapter summarizes some of those other opportunities for fun. For a couple of the activities—backpacking and horseback riding—trails are integral; what's included here is information specific to these pastimes (such as camps and stables). The park is also a destination for sea kayakers and road bikers; popular routes for these recreationalists are also discussed in this chapter.

Backcountry Camps

Most national parks have at least one well-outfitted car-friendly campground, crowded with vehicles shaped like silver torpedoes and shoe boxes, clusters of colorful camp chairs and coolers, picnic tables outfitted with such luxuries as high-wattage lanterns and mosquito screens.

You won't see this in Point Reyes. Its four backcountry camps can only be reached via trails, and you (or your horse) must carry in all gear. That you gain far more than you lose in this exchange of wheels for feet is evidenced by the intense popularity of these camps: On weekends, year-round, they are often booked up, and in summertime you must make your reservations far in advance.

Reservations: Given that the park is heavily used by the hefty population of the greater Bay Area, sites in the camps are frequently booked, particularly in summer months. Reservations are highly recommended, and can be made up to three months in advance. You can make reservations by visiting the Bear Valley Visitor Center, which is open from 9:00 A.M. to 5:00 P.M. seven days a week, or by calling (415) 663–8054 between 9:00 A.M. and 2:00 P.M. on weekdays.

You also can visit the Point Reyes National Seashore Web site at www.nps.gov/pore/recreation/camp2/ and follow the links to the fax form, which you can fill out, print, and fax to the park at (415) 464–5149. The camping section of the Web site also includes detailed information on each camp, including aerial photos of the sites and all camping rules and regulations.

Payment for a site is due when you make your reservation. The fee for one night at a single site (for up to six people), is $10. Group camps serving seven to fourteen people run $20 per night, and group camps serving fifteen to twenty-five people cost $30 per night. You must have a valid permit to camp.

Point Reyes and Backcountry Camps

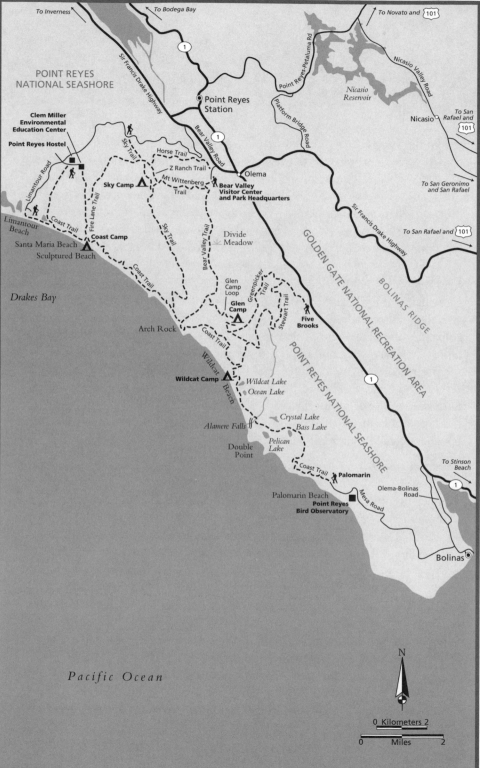

Amenities: All camps have picnic tables, food storage lockers, and grills for barbecues, as well as pit toilets and water spigots. The water at the camps is usually potable, but you should check with the park rangers before drinking it. Otherwise, park officials recommend that you boil water before drinking. As always, don't drink untreated water from streams or lakes—it is likely contaminated with giardia.

Sky Camp

Situated on a brushy slope below the summit of Mount Wittenberg, views from Sky Camp spread west past Limantour Beach and across Drakes Bay to the distant headlands and the Pacific beyond. A bunch of trails converge near the camp, with the summit of Mount Wittenberg, the crest of Inverness Ridge, and Limantour Beach—all comfortable and enticing day-hike options.

The camp is on the site of the former Z Ranch (a trail bearing this name traverses higher slopes on Mount Wittenberg). Campers will find twelve sites here, including one group site. All the sites look down on hills and draws scorched by the Vision Fire of 1995. The camps are well spaced, with a couple perched in open meadow, and the rest tucked into clearings surrounded by thick coyote brush and berry brambles. The camp has toilets, a water spigot, and a hitching post. Campsites are equipped with picnic tables, grills, and critterproof food storage boxes.

The quickest and easiest route to Sky Camp is via the Sky Trail from the Sky Trailhead on Limantour Road. To reach this trailhead from the Bear Valley Visitor Center, follow Bear Valley Road north for 1.3 miles to Limantour Road, then take Limantour Road west for 1.3 miles to the trailhead. The 1.8-mile route is described in detail in the Point Reyes Trails chapter. If you want a workout, load your pack and head to Sky Camp from Bear Valley. Variations on this route, too, are detailed in the Point Reyes Trails chapter; regardless of the trail you climb, Sky Camp is about 2.8 miles from Bear Valley.

Coast Camp

The heart of Coast Camp is cuddled against a protective bluff. A broad strip of cropped grass grows between the bluff on the west, and the steep hills on the east, cradling a smattering of the fourteen sites in the camp. It's here that campers come to use the bathrooms and get water, walking in from other sites tucked amid the scrub above and east of the small meadow. It's a wilderness version of the village green.

Its spectacular coastside setting is foremost in its appeal—Coast Camp is five minutes' hike from Limantour Beach—but the relatively easy hikes that lead to it also factor into its popularity. A lone, majestic eucalyptus, the only vestige of the U Ranch, which operated here until the 1930s, marks the foot-

The Coast Trail traces the eastern edge of Coast Camp.

path that leads down to the strand, site of a daily exodus by those who've spent the night in camp. The awesome cliffs and tide pools of Sculptured Beach lie about a mile south of the camp—an easy day hike along the beach (at low tide) or along the Coast Trail.

In addition to those in the green, Coast Camp boasts sites along the Coast Trail as it continues southeast, and more sites set amid the scrub on the eastern hillside. The sites are well spaced, and all are outfitted with food storage lockers, braziers, and picnic tables. There is no shade here; all camps are open to sun, fog, and the stars at night. The hitching posts are at the northern edge of the camp, near the trail to the beach.

The most direct way to reach Coast Camp is to follow Limantour Beach south from the Limantour Road for 2.3 miles to the small trail that climbs east from the beach to the camp. The multiuse Coast Trail also leads to the camp: This route begins at the Coast Trailhead in Laguna Ranch, near the Point Reyes Hostel. The broad service road/trail follows a stream westward for 1.5 miles to the seaside, then bends south, paralleling Limantour Beach. The Coast Trail rides atop scrubby bluffs for about mile before curving inland to meet the Fire Lane Trail. Plunge through a little gully that cradles another creek, and at 2.9 miles you stand amid the sites of Coast Camp.

Yet another option takes the inland route to Coast Camp, following the Laguna and Fire Lane Trails. This route begins at the Laguna Trailhead, which is located in Laguna Ranch about 0.2 mile east of the Point Reyes Hostel, and 0.5 mile from the intersection of the hostel access road and Limantour Road. This short trek is detailed in the Point Reyes Trails chapter.

Glen Camp

Glen Camp, unlike the other backcountry camps in the Point Reyes National Seashore, is all about trees. The camp, on the former site of the Glen Ranch, is embedded in the heavy forest that covers Inverness Ridge, completely view-free. What it lacks in vistas, it more than makes up for in seclusion: It's a quiet, private place, off the most well-beaten paths in the park and far from any crowd.

The twelve sites that make up Glen Camp ring a meadowy clearing, with a stately oak shading the southernmost sites and a single site plopped in the middle of the clearing. The sites are relatively close together, and close to the rest room and water facilities. As with the other camps, each site has a picnic table, food storage cabinet, and barbecue grill. No group sites are available here, and no horses are permitted.

The most direct route to Glen Camp begins at the Bear Valley Trailhead, and is detailed in the Glen Camp Loop trail description in the Point Reyes Trails chapter. The camp is a 4.6-mile trek from the Bear Valley Trailhead.

You also can reach Glen Camp from the Five Brooks Trailhead. From Five Brooks, climb the Stewart Trail up and west over Firtop to its junction with the Glen Trail at 5.5 miles. Go north on the Glen Trail to its intersection with the Glen Camp Loop trail, and continue on the loop trail to the camp at 6.2 miles.

Wildcat Camp

By happy coincidence, given its name, Wildcat Camp is the wildest in the seashore. It's a long way from any trailhead, separated from civilization by ridges and ravines and miles and miles. It's hard to believe that a small ranch once operated on the remote site, but the Wildcat Ranch did, for nearly a century.

Perched on a small, treeless plateau overlooking Wildcat Beach, the camp is open to extremes of sun, wind, cold, and fog. The thunder of the waves pounding the beach, varying in intensity as the sets roll in, can be deafening at times. A fine sea mist issues from the surf and hangs in the air, softening the edges of the steep, harsh landscape.

Wildcat is small, with a scant seven sites (three of them group sites). Despite the rigors of the trails leading to the camp, it's a popular destination, and the sites fill quickly. Each site holds a picnic table (or two), a barbecue brazier, and a food storage cabinet. Rest rooms, water, and trash receptacles are provided. A couple of hitch rails line the west side of the camp, and water for horses is available in a cistern just across the creek on the south side of the camp.

Wildcat Camp, set on a bluff above Wildcat Beach, is open and exposed to sun and surf.

A short, rutted footpath leads down along the no-name creek to noisy Wildcat Beach. Seldom crowded, the beach stretches a mile or more in either direction, depending on the tides. Alamere Falls, the most impressive waterfall in the park, spills onto the beach to the south and is a good destination for a day hike. The Wildcat Loop, which passes both Wildcat Lake and Ocean Lake and features fabulous views up and down the coastline, is another great day-hike option; this loop is detailed in the Point Reyes Trails chapter.

Arguably, the most scenic route to Wildcat Camp is from the Palomarin Trailhead via the Coast Trail. The trail skirts the coastline before turning inland to pass the Lake Ranch Trail junction at 2.2 miles, Bass Lake at 2.9 miles, the intersection with the Crystal Lake Trail at 3.1 miles, and the trail to Alamere Falls at 3.6 miles. Beyond Alamere Falls, the trail splits, with the Coast Trail taking the inside track and the Ocean Lake Loop trail hugging the coast-line before hooking back up with the Coast Trail above Wildcat Camp at about the 5-mile mark. The camp is 5.5 miles from Palomarin.

You can also reach Wildcat Camp from the Five Brooks Trailhead, without a doubt the most strenuous route. Climb the broad fire road that serves as the Stewart Trail for about 4 miles to the top of Firtop on the crest of Inverness Ridge, then plunge steeply down the other side, losing more than 1,300 feet on the 2.7-mile descent to sea level. The Stewart Trail ends at the Coast Trail at the 6-mile mark; follow the Coast Trail the final 0.7 mile southwest to the camp.

The Coast Trail to Alamere Falls, the Stewart Trail to Wildcat Beach, and the Ocean Lake Loop trail are all described in more detail in the Point Reyes Trails chapter.

Horse Ranches and Rides

The trail system in the Point Reyes National Seashore is vast and diverse, sometimes strenuous, and sometimes lonely. But distance, difficulty, and loneliness all fall by the wayside when you travel the trails on horseback.

Horseback riding in the national seashore has two hubs: in Bear Valley, where the Morgan Horse Ranch is located, and at the Five Brooks Ranch in the Olema Valley. Both have parking lots that can easily accommodate horse trailers, and offer easy access to popular routes that begin at the Bear Valley Trailhead and the Five Brooks Trailhead. Some of these trails are described in the Point Reyes Trails chapter; others link several trails together for longer equestrian routes.

Traveling by horse along the park's trails is generally safe and easy, but equestrians, like all trail users, need to be attentive to trail conditions, the condition of their horse, and the presence of other trail users. The park has set forth some safety and etiquette tips for riders:

- Avoid contact with stinging nettle. Touching the plant is bothersome for humans, but dangerous—and potentially fatal—for horses. Riders can avoid the plant by staying on trails, and should familiarize themselves with trails upon which the nettle encroaches.

- Though confrontations with other trail users haven't been a big problem in the park, horseback riders should be aware of proper trail etiquette. Both hikers and mountain bikers must yield to equestrians. Mountain bikers should announce their presence, especially when approaching from behind, in a clear voice, and dismount if horseback riders ask them to. Hikers should step onto the downhill side of the trail and wait for the horses to pass.

- Shortcutting causes erosion. Stay on designated trails.

- For the safety and comfort of both yourself and your horse, ride with a friend, and make sure you have plenty of time to complete your ride. Plan for rest stops for your horse, especially if you are riding over the Inverness Ridge.

Certain trail restrictions apply to horses and pack animals within the park. Several trails are closed to horses on weekends and holidays, including the Bear Valley Trail between the Mount Wittenberg Trail and the Glen Trail, the Meadow Trail, and the Old Pine Trail. Interpretive trails, including the Earthquake Trail and the Woodpecker Trail, are always off limits to horses.

Drakes Beach is the only beach closed to horses, though seasonal closures of other beaches for wildlife protection are enforced. Horses can't be ridden in the dunes or on vegetated areas of any beach within the park. Horses are not allowed above the tide line on the Great Beach between June 15 and September 15, when the endangered snowy plover nests. And South Beach is closed to

Point Reyes Horse Ranches and Rides

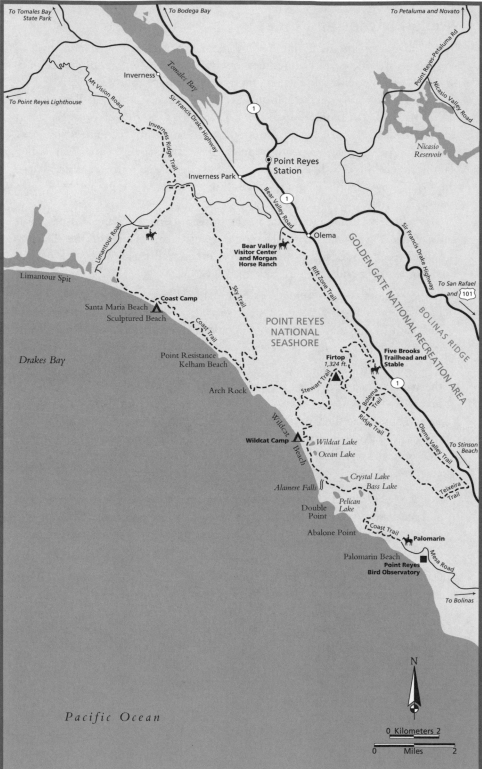

horses when occupied by elephant seals, generally in winter and spring. Check with a ranger for details.

Horses are allowed in Coast Camp, Sky Camp, and Wildcat Camp, but not at Glen Camp. Like humans, horses must have a permit to spend the night in these camps. Horses are not permitted off trail in campgrounds, nor can they be left unattended for long periods of time in camps without a permit. A maximum of six horses is allowed at each camp. Water and hitching posts are provided. Grazing is not permitted in the wilderness areas of the park, so you must pack in your animal's feed. That feed should be weed-free, so that non-native plants are not propagated within the park.

You and your steed can also camp overnight at the Stewart Horse Camp in the Olema Valley, located just north of the Five Brooks Ranch. You can reach this privately owned facility by calling (415) 663–1362.

Morgan Horse Ranch

The Morgan Horse Ranch, set atop a knoll overlooking the meadow at Bear Valley, now houses only a handful of the nut-brown Morgan horses used by the rangers to patrol the trails at Point Reyes. But in its heyday the ranch was a breeding facility for Morgans that were sent out to other parks in the national park system, as well as a training ground for the rangers who would ride them.

The Morgan horse, a 200-year-old American breed that dates back to a single sire, has a "calm temperament" that makes it perfect for patrolling park trails and for trail maintenance work, according to the park service. The Morgans in Point Reyes are used in the wilderness areas for these two purposes.

The Morgan Horse Ranch is open from 9:00 A.M. to 4:30 P.M., and offers interpretive displays and demonstrations. For more information about the ranch, contact the Bear Valley Visitor Center at (415) 464–5100.

Though you can't rent the Morgans for trail rides, the ranch is adjacent to the Bear Valley Trailhead, which offers access to popular riding trails in the north part of the park. These trails include:

- **The Bear Valley Trail to Arch Rock,** an extremely popular 8.2-mile round trip to an overlook at the coastline.

- **The Mount Wittenberg Trail Loop,** which climbs to the shoulder of the mountain via the Horse Trail and Z Ranch Trail, then descends to Bear Valley on the Mount Wittenberg Trail (or the other way around). The summit trail is off limits to horses. This route is about 4.5 miles in length.

- **The Sky Trail,** which can be reached via several trails that climb out of Bear Valley to the crest of Inverness Ridge. The Sky Trail drops along the wooded ridgelines to the Coast Trail just north of Arch Rock; the loop returns to Bear Valley on the Bear Valley Trail. Exact mileages vary depending on whether you ride the Mount Wittenberg Trail, Meadow Trail, or Old Pine Trail onto the ridge, but you can bank on covering at least 10 miles.

- **The Rift Zone Trail,** which heads south through the bottomlands of the Olema Valley to Five Brooks and back, is an 8.6-mile round-trip journey.

Five Brooks Ranch

You can tell by the size of the stables and arena. You can tell by the trailers packing the parking lot at the trailhead. You can tell by the number of horses on the surrounding trails. Five Brooks is where the equestrians come to ride in Point Reyes.

The stables, with outdoor paddocks and a huge barn just south of the Five Brooks Pond, offer a variety of trail riding options, hayrides, boarding services, and sponsorship opportunities. Guided rides take you along the Stewart Trail, to Firtop, along the Glen Trail, and down to Wildcat Beach. Rates range from $30 for the shortest ride to $150 for an all-day ride (slightly more for private guided rides). Reservations for guided rides are recommended.

The stables, a park service concession, are open from 9:00 A.M. to 5:00 P.M. daily. The mailing address for the Five Brooks Ranch is P.O. Box 99, Olema, CA 94950; the telephone number is (415) 663–1570. For more information, you also can visit the Web site at www.fivebrooks.com.

Popular horse routes from Five Brooks include:

- **The Stewart Trail to Wildcat Camp,** a 13.4-mile ride that takes you over Firtop to the beachside campground.

- **The Greenpicker Trail,** a narrow path that climbs more than 3 miles to the summit of Firtop, a favorite of those working at the ranch.

- **The Olema Valley/Bolema Trail loop,** a 6.3-mile loop heads south out of Five Brooks along Olema Creek on the Olema Valley Trail, climbs up to Inverness Ridge on the Bolema Trail, then returns to Five Brooks via the Ridge and Stewart Trails.

- **The Teixeira Loop,** a 13.5-mile loop that takes the Olema Valley Trail south to the Teixeira Trail, climbs onto Inverness Ridge, and returns to Five Brooks via the Ridge and Stewart Trails.

- Riders also use the **Olema Valley Trail** to reach the **Randall Trail,** which climbs onto Bolinas Ridge. The **Bolinas Ridge Trail,** a fire road that runs atop the ridgeline, offers great long-distance trail riding opportunities.

- **Palomarin** also offers great trail riding opportunities. The **Coast Trail**, a 16-mile-long route that traces the western edge of the park from Palomarin to Limantour, offers access to Bass Lake and the Lake Ranch Trails, both popular destinations.

Road Biking

On cool sunny mornings, the roads leading into and out of the Point Reyes National Seashore host nearly as many cyclists as they do motorists. They travel, sometimes singly, sometimes in packs, on the Petaluma–Point Reyes Road between Nicasio Reservoir and Point Reyes Station, on the Sir Francis Drake Highway between Fairfax and Olema, on California Highway 1 between Olema on Stinson Beach. They come seeking open highways and spectacular views, the chance to exercise their bodies and free their minds. And they couldn't pick a better place to do it.

Roadways in and around the Point Reyes National Seashore are narrow, two-laned affairs. But what they lack by way of shoulder they more than make up for in scenery, challenging climbs, and fast descents. Only two roads within or immediately adjacent to the park see a lot of bike traffic, however, with most cyclists enjoying the pastoral highways that weave through nearby areas of West Marin.

The roads that do attract cyclists—the Limantour Road and the stretch of CA 1 between Point Reyes Station and Stinson Beach—travel through rather different country. The **Limantour Road (Route 1),** an 18-mile round trip that takes you up and over Inverness Ridge, then down through the coastal scrub to Limantour Beach, offers a long climb up to the ridgetop, at nearly 800 feet, and a long winding descent down to the beach.

CA 1 between Point Reyes Station and Stinson Beach (Route 4), in contrast, is a longer ride at about 26 miles round trip, and might be described as a roller coaster on a bell curve. The road undulates upward from Point Reyes, gaining nearly 400 feet in elevation as it winds through open pasture-lands and intermittent stands of oak and bay laurel in the northern part of the Olema Valley. It descends to Stinson Beach in a more straightforward manner, passing several historic ranches and plunging down through the eucalyptus at Thirteen Corners before reaching the north shore of the Bolinas Lagoon. Cool down on the flat stretch along the western shores of the lagoon, rest on Stinson Beach, then use that flat lagoonside meander to warm up for the climb back toward Point Reyes Station.

While **Pierce Point Road (Route 2)** and the **Sir Francis Drake Highway (Route 5)** certainly offer the ups, downs, and scenery that cyclists crave, their rough surfacing and complete lack of shoulder make them less desirable than other routes in and around the park. A fat-tire bike might be a better choice for the Pierce Point Road, in particular, but then that defeats the purpose, for both on- and off-road cyclists. All four of the main roads through the park are described, with waypoints and mileages, in the introduction to the Point Reyes section of this guide.

The **Cross Marin Trail (Route 3),** part of the Golden Gate National Recreation Area, is a nice option for the cyclist who is limited on time or

Point Reyes Road Biking

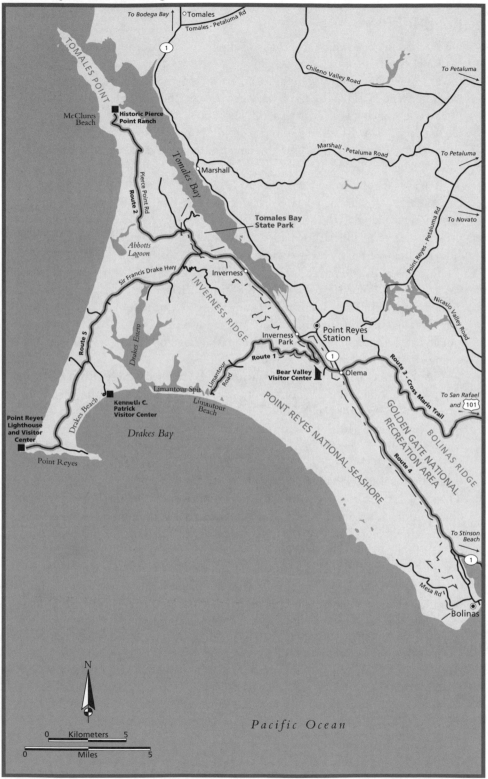

doesn't wish to share the roadway with automobiles. This route, the paved section of which runs from Tocaloma to Samuel P. Taylor State Park, follows an old railroad grade through the Lagunitas Creek canyon. At only about 7 miles round trip, it hardly presents a challenge to a cyclist seeking a workout, but for a leisurely family ride, or a quick stretch for the limbs and mind, it fits the bill perfectly. This route is detailed in the Point Reyes Trails chapter.

Sea Kayaking

Maybe, as the nose of your kayak edges into the water, you will find Tomales Bay glassy green and shrouded in calming fog. Maybe you will find it lit by a brilliant sun and whipped by brisk winds. And maybe, in the course of the time you spend paddling, the bay's foggy cloak will burn away to hours of sunglass weather before the ubiquitous wind whips the fog back over the water and you find yourself swathed in grayness again. You might catch sight of bat rays and sharks cruising in shadowy blue-green waters, or swarms of colorful jellyfish, their white umbrellas open to reveal lacy pink and purple frills. Seals dive and forage for meals, revealing themselves only when they break the surface of the bay to look back at you. And above it all, pelicans and gulls hover watchfully, diving pell-mell into the waves when dinner reveals itself.

Sea kayaking, especially on Tomales Bay, has become very popular—so popular, in fact, that the bay waters are almost crowded on summer days. Such heavy use has had an impact on the both water quality and the quality of the habitat for the creatures that call the 15-mile long bay home. Staving off adverse effects from this increase in use means that paddlers are subject to restrictions. These include:

- Put boats in the water at one of the designated launch areas on the bay. On the east side, paddlers can launch from Millerton Point in Tomales Bay State Park, Miller County Park (also known as Nicks Cove), and Lawson's Landing, near Dillon Beach. On the west side, launch points are at Hearts Desire Beach in Tomales Bay State Park, the Golden Hinde Inn and Marina in Inverness, and White House Pool near Inverness Park. Some of these launch points are within parks that charge day-use fees, or at private marinas that may charge a launch fee.
- Hog Island is "critical wildlife habitat." The west side of the island is open for day use only.
- Both Hearts Desire Beach and Indian Beach are open for day use only.
- Overnight camping is allowed on some beaches within the seashore with a permit. Beaches where overnight camping is allowed are Kilkenny Beach, Marshall Beach, Tomales Beach, Fruit Tree Beach, Blue Gum Beach, and Avalis Beach, which is near the mouth of Tomales Bay. Overnight camping is not permitted elsewhere along Tomales Bay.

- No parking is available within the Point Reyes National Seashore or Tomales Bay State Park for overnight boat campers.
- Be sure to use rest room facilities on shore. Most launch sites have toilet facilities, as do some of the destination beaches, including Marshall Beach and Tomales Beach. Otherwise, human waste and toilet paper must be packed out.
- Pack out all trash, including leftover food.

Finally, the Marine Mammal Protection Act requires that you stay at least 300 feet from any marine mammal. During the harbor seal pupping season, which runs from mid-March to June, you may see a pup alone on a beach. Do not disturb it; its mother is probably just out feeding. If you are concerned that a pup has been abandoned, or that a seal is injured, contact a park ranger.

One of the most popular paddles on Tomales Bay is on the west side, stretching between Hearts Desire Beach and Marshall Beach. Another popular Tomales Bay paddle begins on the eastern shore at Nicks Cove and spans the breadth of the narrow waterway, ending on park lands in the Tule Elk Reserve on Tomales Point.

Paddling Drakes Estero is generally more challenging than Tomales Bay, the territory of more experienced kayakers. Local guides advise that kayakers "do their homework" before venturing onto these waters, given the complexities of the tides and winds. But the rewards are remarkable. All three of the estero's fingers—Home Bay, Schooner Bay, and Creamery Bay—are surrounded by the scenic rangelands of the park's pastoral zone and flush with wildlife to be observed and appreciated. The estero is closed each year from March to June when the harbor seals pup. The put-in spot is at Johnson's Oyster Farm, located off the Sir Francis Drake Highway about 11 miles west of the Bear Valley Visitor Center.

To make boat camping reservations, visit the Bear Valley Visitor Center, which is open daily from 9:00 A.M. to 5:00 P.M. You can also make reservations by calling (415) 663–8054 between 9 A.M. and 2 P.M. Reservations may be made up to three months in advance. Fees range from $10 per night (for one to six people) to $30 per night (for groups of fifteen to twenty-five people).

Two sea kayaking purveyors, offering tours, classes, and kayak rentals, operate on Tomales Bay. Tamal-Saka is located in Marshall on the east shore of the bay, and can be reached by calling (415) 663–1743. The company's Web site is www.tamalsaka.com. Blue Water Kayaking is located on the west shore of Tomales Bay near Inverness, and can be contacted by calling (415) 669–2600; the Web site is www.bwkayak.com. Both outfitters offer tours of Tomales Bay and Drakes Estero, and range farther afield as well.

There are lots of reasons to visit the Point Reyes National Seashore. There are wonderful trails, abundant wildlife, fabulous historic sites and cultural exhibits.

And then there are the beaches. The amazing, tumultuous, mesmerizing beaches.

The beaches of Point Reyes, despite the fact that they aren't so distant from each other in mileage, vary wildly in size, orientation, and attitude. Those fronting directly on the Pacific, like the Great Beach, possess an edginess that isn't present on bayfront beaches like Limantour and Stinson. Some require that beachgoers hike in a short distance, which generally means they are free of the clutter of people and things found on beaches within a few hundred feet of a parking lot. Not to deride those beaches, because there ain't nothing wrong with spreading a beach towel next to the cooler and watching humanity frolic in the sand.

Beaches hemmed in by cliffs, beaches that stretch for miles, beaches with tide pools, beaches energized by dangerous surf, beaches with views of the Farallon Islands and the Point Reyes headlands, beaches that quiet the soul . . . they are all here. And in this guide they are introduced from north to south along the peninsula.

McClures Beach

With its abrupt boundaries and narrow confines, McClures Beach more resembles the rugged coves of the Marin Headlands than the expansive beaches found elsewhere in the Point Reyes National Seashore. Steep cliffs of dark red rock barricade it on three sides, brooding over moist sand and a churning surf that pummels the 0.5-mile long strand , as if trying to carve out more room for the sea behind it. The incessant waves captivate, crashing into sea stacks just offshore and into sentinel rocks that guard the northern and southern boundaries of the beach, shooting up in fountains as great gray waves disintegrate into thick white foam. The setting is both beautiful and vaguely enervating.

The 0.6-mile trail that leads down to McClures Beach is challenging, much like the beach itself. The sandy path begins at the western border of the parking lot, descending steeply alongside a steep, scrub-choked gully side-cut by other steep, scrub-choked gullies. The scrub is varied and colorful depending on the time of year, composed of bush lupine, coyote brush, blackberry brambles, and wildflowers.

The path levels briefly as you veer westward toward a gap in the steep bluffs, and the sounds of the surf careen up the canyon. The stream that has carved the gully comes into view as you round another bend, as does the ocean and an interpretive sign describing the dangers of the surf and the great white sharks that patrol the Gulf of the Farallones just offshore. Heed the warnings about sneaker waves on this stretch of beach.

The creek that traces the path to McClures gets more rambunctious as it nears its terminus, spilling onto the sand with the trail at 0.6 mile. From trail's end, you can walk a short distance north or south on the narrow strip of sand, resting on driftwood logs if they are dry, patches of sand, or rough seats of exposed rock. Low tide exposes tide pools here and in neighboring coves, but extensive exploring is discouraged by park officials, who rescue people stranded by incoming tides each year. Remain on the beach to stay safe.

To reach McClures Beach from the Bear Valley Visitor Center, follow the visitor center access road for 0.2 mile east to Bear Valley Road. Turn left (north) onto Bear Valley Road, and go 1.7 miles to its intersection with the Sir Francis Drake Highway. Turn left (north) onto Sir Francis Drake, and follow the highway for 5.5 miles to Pierce Point Road. Turn right (north) onto Pierce Point Road, and drive for 8.8 miles to the parking area for the Upper Pierce Ranch. The road veers sharply left (west), and drops for about 0.1 mile to the McClures Beach parking lot. There is ample parking, along with rest rooms and trash and recycling bins, at the trailhead.

Kehoe Beach

Washed by an endless stream of disorganized waves, the sands of Kehoe Beach serve as playground and feeding ground for teams of pelicans and gulls and other shorebirds. People visiting the open, wind-whipped, expansive southern reaches of the beach often pause to watch the birds coast on the sea breezes and dive into the waves, then walk on, and on, and on.

Those walking north will soon encounter a different aspect of the beach. Rounded bluff and soft dune quickly give way to eroded rock walls, then to steep cliffs of an unyielding gray granite, shot with dikes of luminous white quartz. These cliffs enclose a cove at the northern edge of the beach, then plunge jaggedly into the surf and bar further passage north on any but the lowest tides. The expansiveness of the Great Beach meets the abrupt edges of McClures Beach; the union is at Kehoe.

The trail to Kehoe Beach is 0.6 mile in length, and traces the border of a lush, overgrown marsh that is a basketweaver's bonanza; on the right (north) side of the path, hills covered in scrub stretch slowly up and away. Flocks of blackbirds or starlings feed in and above the marsh, flying with the synchronicity of a school of fish, silvery when moving in one direction, black when

Point Reyes Beaches

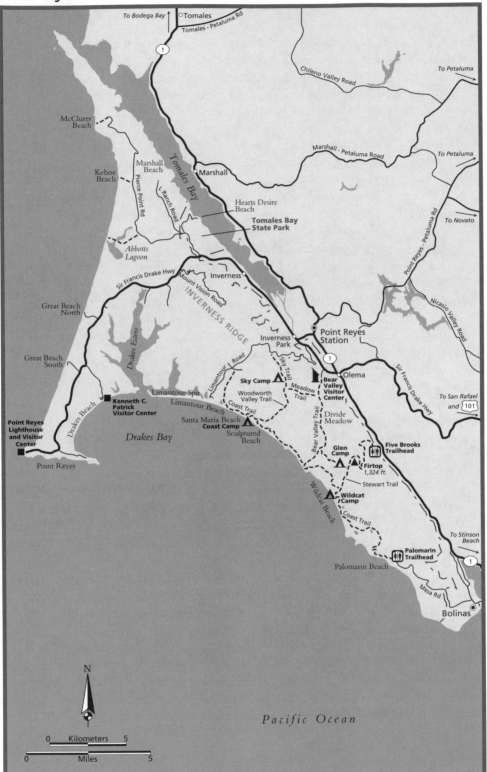

swooping in another, momentarily disappearing against the dark hills as they turn. The singletrack gradually climbs above the marsh; you can see the tidal lagoon and the beach through a break in the bluffs to the west.

The trail widens to a two-track, then broadens into a sand-surfaced road. Pass a bench at about 0.5 mile, crest the barrier dune, and drop down a wide sandy ramp onto the beach at 0.6 mile. A narrow estuary fed by the waters of the marsh drains to the north, emptying into a surly Pacific breaking in unstructured waves on the beach. The larger breakers form and crash farther out. Again, as elsewhere along the Pacific front of the seashore, don't swim, and beware of sneaker waves.

The broad open strand reaches south toward Point Reyes, and north toward the imposing cliffs of Tomales Point. The cliffs just north of the trail, composed of pale sandstone, are undercut with shallow caves, and grow taller and more craggy as you head north. A trio of deep grottoes pocks the cliff face about a 0.5 mile from the trail and marsh; the northernmost two look out at the ocean with the gaze of a great stony owl.

The cliffs change character north of the owl eyes, melting from a crumbling orange to a deep gray granite spiked with white dikes, alpine in character, steep and relatively sheer. They arc into a shallow cove, then drop into the surf, where they mingle with short sea stacks battered by whitewater.

To reach Kehoe Beach from the Bear Valley Visitor Center, follow the visitor center access road for 0.2 mile east to Bear Valley Road. Turn left (north) onto Bear Valley Road, and go 1.7 miles to its intersection with the Sir Francis Drake Highway. Turn left (north) onto Sir Francis Drake, and follow the highway for 5.5 miles to Pierce Point Road. Turn right (north) onto Pierce Point Road, and drive for 5.4 miles to the Kehoe Beach trailhead. Parking is available in pullouts on either side of the road; the trailhead is on the left (west). Rest rooms are tucked in a copse of evergreens at the trailhead, along with trash and recycling receptacles. Bikes are permitted on the trail. Dogs are allowed on the trail and on the beach north of the trail.

The Great Beach

Fully exposed to the incessant pounding of the Pacific, a broad strand stretches for more than ten miles along the western edge of Point Reyes. Known as the Great Beach, this strip of sand at the interface of land and sea is renowned for its endless views and ferocious, thunderous, mesmerizing surf.

The ocean is as capricious here as a temperamental god, sometimes in the mood for order, more often seeking chaos, demanding constant attention: The dangerous surf doesn't permit playful jumping in the waves, building sand castles near the surf, or spreading blankets for sunbathing close to the tide line. It's a beach that demands, and deserves, caution and respect.

The Great Beach offers misty views of the Point Reyes headlands.

The Great Beach was the site of the original lifeboat station on Point Reyes. The brave men who staffed the station used hand-pulled surfboats, along with other types of lifesaving equipment, to rescue shipwreck survivors between 1890 and 1894; operations were moved to Drakes Bay in 1894 (see the Point Reyes Points of Interest chapter for more information).

Also known as Point Reyes Beach and Ten Mile Beach, the Great Beach is served by two parking areas. Approaching from the north on the Sir Francis Drake Highway, the first access is at North Beach, 11 miles west of the intersection of Sir Francis Drake and the Bear Valley Road. The huge parking lot is 0.6 mile down the access road; you'll find rest rooms and trash receptacles here. The cliffs of Tomales Point dominate the vista as you walk north on the beach, first following a line of shallow embankments—maybe 10 feet high—buttressed by sand. The clifflets give way to dunes anchored by waving beach grasses and non-native ice plant. Walking south, the views are of the Point Reyes headlands, and of waves that fold haphazardly onto the beach. There is no break, no gentle swoosh and silence of a calmer sea.

The second access point is at South Beach, where, again, a large parking area, outfitted with rest rooms and trash receptacles, allows visitors to spread out along the expansive sands. The South Beach access road is about 13.6 miles west of the intersection of the Sir Francis Drake Highway and Bear Valley Road; the parking area is 0.7 mile from the highway via the access road. Here again, you can walk for miles in either direction, staying, of course, well away from the unpredictable surf.

Pets are allowed at both beaches, subject to seasonal restrictions to permit the unmolested nesting of the endangered snowy plover. No dogs are allowed north of the parking lot at North Beach.

Drakes Beach

The dramatic cliffs that, legend has it, reminded explorer Francis Drake of the White Cliffs of Dover are the signature of Drakes Beach. The crumbling walls tower over the narrow arc of sand, presenting a kaleidoscope of pale colors that vary depending on the aspect and intensity of the sunlight. In bright sun, orange and golden hues become more vivid; in flat light the cliffs are a chalky white, the scrub that caps them and tumbles into their clefts contrasting black against their creaminess.

The beach, like most on the seashore, can be crowded on sunny summer weekends. Most visitors cluster in the shadows of the cliffs closest to the parking area, sunning, picnicking and beachcombing. You can find solitude, however, by traveling left (east) or right (southwest) along the sands. The shallow waters of Drakes Estero, about 1 mile distant, form the easternmost border of the beach, and the rugged topography of the headlands overshadow the stretch of beach to the west. It's a walking person's beach; swimming is not advisable.

The Ken Patrick Visitor Center sits on the eastern side of the beach's large parking lot. The visitor center, open from 10:00 A.M. to 5:00 P.M. on weekends and holidays, offers interpretive displays and information. The weather-bleached complex also houses rest rooms, and the Drake's Beach Café, serving oyster stew, oyster burgers, fries, and other staples of cafe fare.

To reach Drakes Beach from the Bear Valley Visitor Center, drive east 0.2 mile to Bear Valley Road, and turn left (north). Follow Bear Valley Road for 1.7 miles to its intersection with the Sir Francis Drake Highway near Inverness Park. Turn left (north) onto Sir Francis Drake. Travel for 13.7 miles along the highway, which winds through the towns of Inverness Park and Inverness, then continues out into the rolling pastureland on the Point Reyes peninsula. At the signed intersection with the Drakes Beach access road, turn left (southeast), and drive 1.5 miles down to the beach parking area.

Limantour Beach

The sweeping arc of Limantour Beach is the front porch of Point Reyes. From a seat on its welcoming dunes, you look out across Drakes Bay to the Pacific much as you might look across your front lawn to the street beyond. Some days, the gentle surf rolls in low from a glassy sea, like the waves of neighbors on a quiet cul-de-sac; other days the bay and beach are assaulted by oceanborn turbulence, noisy and energetic as a busy boulevard.

On sunny summer days, the section of the beach around the short access trail is crowded with visitors. The surf is generally safe here, so kids of all ages head for the water, jumping small waves, riding boogie boards or body surfing on the larger waves, and even swimming if their skin is thick enough to withstand the cold. Shade umbrellas and beach blankets spread on the sand in a colorful mosaic. The air is busy with Frisbees, volleyballs, footballs, foraging gulls, and, if there is a breeze, fluttering kites. Walk a 0.5 mile north or south on the beach, however, and the crowds thin and become more contemplative. Those walking south most likely have a dog or two in tow; this is one of the few places in Point Reyes where dogs on leashes are welcome.

Visit the beach on a stormy day, and you'll likely find but a sprinkling of people on its 5-mile length, where storm-fed surf thumps the shore, warning you to keep your distance. The beach stretches south for more than 2 miles before it melds into Santa Maria Beach at the mouth of Santa Maria Creek near Coast Camp. If the tide is out, you can cross the rocky tide pool area onto Sculptured Beach, which is described below. The landscape to your left (northeast) changes from open coastal plain to rolling coastal bluffs, then to exposed, eroded cliffs that grow ever taller as you head south. About 1.2 miles down the beach, just as the rolling bluffs give way to cliffs, you can turn left (northeast) and pick up the Coast Trail, a broad track that parallels the beach and leads south to Coast Camp.

Heading northwest from the parking area, you enter the dunes on the Limantour Spit. Part of the Philip Burton Wilderness Area and Research Natural Area, this part of the beach is off limits to dogs. The spit forms a shallow barrier between the waters of Drakes Bay and the Estero de Limantour. You'll have the

Tide pools mark the end of Limantour Beach and the beginning of its neighbor, the spectacular Sculptured Beach.

opportunity to enjoy an abundance of bird life, as well as unsurpassed views west of the pale cliffs that surround Drake's Beach, the headlands, and Chimney Rock. Near the tip of the spit, about two miles west of the parking area, the rocky face of Drakes Head hovers above.

To reach Limantour from the Bear Valley Visitor Center, drive east from the center for 0.2 mile to Bear Valley Road and turn left (north). Follow Bear Valley Road for 1.3 miles to Limantour Road, and turn left. The road winds up and over Inverness Ridge, and down past the road to the Point Reyes Hostel, to end at the Limantour parking area at 7.7 miles. From the parking area, a 0.25-mile path, partly paved, leads west past the rest rooms to the beach.

Sculptured Beach

Sculptured Beach, a distant outpost south of Limantour Beach, is one of the best—and safest—tide pooling areas within the national seashore. Low tides expose rocky outcroppings that jut out into Drakes Bay, and reveal a wealth of tidal creatures—sea stars, anemones, urchins, barnacles, kelp, and a variety of less familiar creatures and plants.

But the tide pools are only one facet of this beach's unique architecture. The steep cliffs that rise from pebble-strewn sands have been sculpted by wind and water into cathedral-like formations, glowing deeply orange in the sunshine, and a paler tan when the fog is in. Curtains of greenery cling to the cliffs where moisture—and the hardiness of the plants—allows.

The two shortest routes to Sculptured Beach begin off the Limantour Road. If the tide is low enough, you can walk all the way south from the Limantour parking area along Limantour Beach—a good 6-mile round-trip hike on an absolutely beautiful strand. The cliffs grow higher and more eroded as you proceed southward, until the intricately convoluted rock faces and dark, knobby clumps of tide pool rocks signal your arrival at Sculptured Beach.

Or you can reach Sculptured Beach via the Coast Trail, which parallels Limantour Beach but rides the bluffs above and to the east. The spur trail to Sculptured Beach begins 3.9 miles west and south of the Coast Trailhead at Laguna Ranch (or about 3 miles from the Limantour parking lot); there is a trail sign and a hitching post at the trail junction. From the Coast Trail, the Sculptured Beach Trail descends through shrubbery that grows into a bower overhead before giving way to wind-clipped grasses. Descend a steep pitch (wet in winter), and a short flight of stairs to reach the heart of Sculptured Beach.

You can also approach from the south, via the Bear Valley Trail and Coast Trails, but this is a long trek of approximately 7 miles from the Bear Valley Trailhead. Likewise, hiking up and over Inverness Ridge via the Woodward Valley Trail—an absolutely wonderful hike described in the chapter on Point Reyes Trails—is a strenuous 5.3-mile one-way journey.

Sea mist softens the edges of the cliffs that drop onto Wildcat Beach, one of the most remote strands in the Point Reyes National Seashore.

Wildcat Beach

The surf is big at Wildcat Beach—big thumping sets of waves that, in their crashing, create a perpetual mist that shrouds and softens the light that falls on the beach, the cliffs that rise above it, and nearby Wildcat Camp. It litters the sand with smooth pebbles; rocks and stacks of driftwood are piled against the base of the orange-Creamsicle cliffs. To the west, across the tireless, thunderous surf, rise the white cliffs surrounding Drakes Bay, from here as pristine and striking as they doubtless were to the famed explorer who sought refuge in the bay in the sixteenth century.

From the access trail at Wildcat Camp, depending on the tides and the weather, you can walk for a mile or more in either direction. Heading northward, the strand hugs the cliffs that stretch toward Miller Point and Arch Rock. Southward spills Alamere Falls, tumbling down terraces before making its final plunge to the beach. Beyond Alamere Falls, the beach is blocked by the 500-foot-high cliffs of Double Point. Off the point, Stormy Stack is buffeted by white plumes of seawater, as are the smaller stacks to the north.

The best access to Wildcat Beach is via Wildcat Camp, which is a long walk from any trailhead. The tiny outlet stream from Wildcat Lake, which rests in a shallow, brushy bowl above and to the southeast of Wildcat Camp, drains through a little ravine that borders the south side of the camp. The trail is a scant 200 yards long, rutted but easily negotiated.

To reach Wildcat Beach from Palomarin, follow the Coast Trail north, passing Bass Lake at 2.6 miles and the trails to Alamere Falls and Double Point at 4.1 miles, finally reaching Wildcat Camp and the access trail at 5.5 miles. If you are an experienced hiker, you can use the unmaintained Alamere Falls Trail to reach the beach.

You can also reach Wildcat Beach from Five Brooks—a 6.7-mile one-way journey that leads up and over Firtop, one of the highest points on Inverness Ridge. The Firtop summit is 4 miles from Five Brooks; Wildcat Camp is a 2.7-mile descent beyond.

Palomarin Beach

Nature layers itself on Palomarin Beach. The steep cliffs that line the eastern boundary of the beach are the first layer, warning beachgoers not to sit at their base by occasionally spilling thin streams of broken rock down their faces. The next layer is heaped at the base of the cliffs: a jumble of driftwood, gray pebbles tumbled smooth in the surf, and the bleached carcasses of bull kelp. The dark

A green anemone studded with bits of shell waits amid the rocks of the tide pools at Palomarin Beach for the tide to come in.

sand that forms the third layer is flecked with white specks of pulverized seashells. Tide pools, dark, rough, and slippery with sea grass, form the fourth layer, stretching from the sand to the last layer, that of the surf and sea, which sweeps onto shore in booming pulses of whitewater.

To reach Palomarin Beach, follow the Coast Trail north out of the Palomarin Trailhead parking lot for a scant 0.1 mile, passing through a non-native woodland of eucalyptus and broom. The 0.6-mile-long trail to Palomarin Beach breaks off to the left (west), plunging down two switchbacks into a hollow lush with willow and oak; then following a little stream southward to the sea.

To reach the Palomarin Trailhead from the Bear Valley Visitor Center, go east on the access road for 0.2 mile to Bear Valley Road. Turn right (southeast) onto Bear Valley Road and travel 0.5 mile to California Highway 1. Turn right (south) onto CA 1, and go 0.1 mile to the stop sign at the intersection at with Sir Francis Drake Highway in Olema. Continue straight (south) on CA 1 from Olema to an unmarked intersection with the Olema-Bolinas Road at about 9 miles. Go right (southwest) on the Olema-Bolinas Road for 1.3 miles to the stop sign at Horseshoe Hill Road. Turn left (south) and continue on the Olema-Bolinas Road for 0.5 mile to the stop sign at its intersection with Mesa Road. Turn right (west) onto Mesa Road, and follow it for 4.5 miles to its end at the Palomarin Trailhead. Dogs are permitted if they are on a leash.

Stinson Beach (Golden Gate NRA)

Stinson Beach is where Marin comes to play. On a sunny summer's day, you'll find the beach packed with people—people tossing footballs and Frisbees, walking their dogs, building sand castles as close to the surf as they dare, lying back on colorful beach blankets getting tans that will set their dermatologists' teeth on edge, dozing in low-slung chairs with books balanced on bellies. The usually friendly waves invite the exploits and expertise of surfers, boogie boarders, body surfers, and wave jumpers, some still in diapers. Stinson, more than any other beach described in this book, has that southern California groove.

Though only about a mile of the beach lies within the Golden Gate National Recreation Area, it stretches for more than 3 miles, from rock outcrops and cliffs on its southern boundary to a spit as it nears its western terminus, with Bolinas Lagoon on one side, and Bolinas Bay and the Pacific on the other.

A large parking lot separates the beach from California Highway 1 in the tiny town of Stinson Beach, where public access is easiest. In addition to copious parking (though the string of lots do fill up on sunny weekends), this section of the beach has picnic and barbecue facilities, rest rooms, water, and access to shopping and restaurants in town. The gate opens at 9:00 A.M., but closing time varies depending on the season. Fires are not allowed on the beach, and dogs must be kept on leashes.

To reach Stinson from the Bear Valley Visitor Center, follow the Bear Valley Road east to CA 1 in Olema. Stinson Beach is 13.5 miles south of the intersection of CA 1 and the Sir Francis Drake Highway at the stop sign in downtown Olema. The drive is spectacular, running down the pastoral Olema Valley to the Bolinas Lagoon, then tracing the eastern shore of the lagoon into town and the beach parking lot.

Young folk, under the watchful eye of a local mom, check out a crab on Stinson Beach.

Point Reyes Points of Interest

The beaches and trails of Point Reyes garner huge amounts of praise and attention, but the park has much more to offer. The wildlife-viewing opportunities, whether you are looking for whales, sea lions, or birds, are superb. The park has several historic sites, including the Point Reyes Lighthouse and a re-creation of a Coast Miwok Indian village, that both fascinate and educate.

Historic and Cultural Sites

Kule Loklo

In the heat of summer, Native peoples gather beneath the spreading shade of twisted oaks in the village of Kule Loklo. They chant and stomp the ground in ritual dances; feathered skirts fly and beaded headdresses crackle as they circle and twirl. The smoke from the pit in which a deer slowly roasts wafts over the clearing they've pounded smooth with their bare feet. They dance for hours, even as the attention of their non-Native audience wavers. It's the Big Time, and the Coast Miwok and their neighbors have gathered to celebrate their heritage.

These modern Indians have helped re-create a village typical of those occupied by their ancestors, the Native peoples who once flourished north of San Francisco Bay, at Kule Loklo. Coast Miwok and Pomo Indians have served as cultural interpreters at the village, and participate in the annual events held there, including the Big Time and the Strawberry Festival, a continuation of gatherings that brought tribes together to renew cultural and social links before the arrival of Europeans.

When Kule Loklo doesn't ring with the chants of celebrants, it can be a lonely place, evocative of the tragedy that overtook those who once lived in villages like it. Visitors may find themselves alone among the unfamiliar structures that were central to village life for the Coast Miwok: *kotcas* (huts made of tule or redwood bark), granaries where acorns were stored, a sweat lodge, and a roundhouse. It's a living village, not a museum, so all but the roundhouse are open for exploration, described by interpretive signs. The village is authentic and genuine, but when empty, it becomes the poignant shell of a culture that no longer exists.

The trail to Kule Loklo, which means "Bear Valley" in Coast Miwok, begins at the east end of the easternmost Bear Valley Visitor Center parking lot. The

Point Reyes Points of Interest

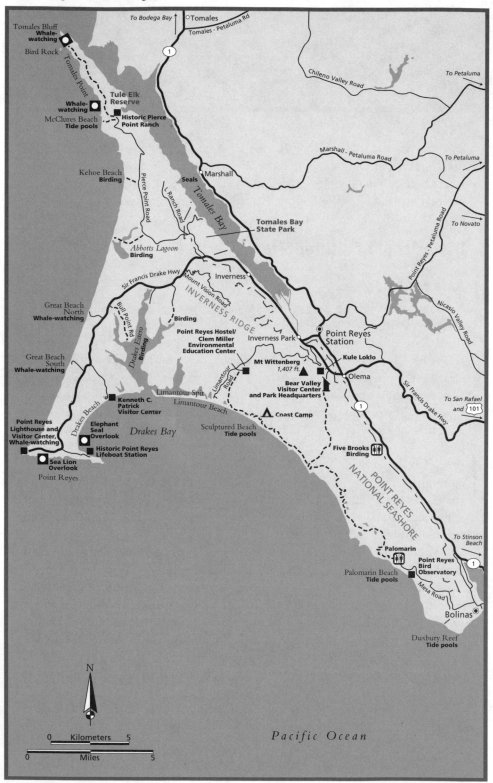

trailhead is marked with an interpretive sign, as well as a trail sign indicating that the village lies 0.3 mile ahead (0.4 mile if you take the Horse Trail).

Climb the broad track northward into the shade of oaks and bay laurels, with a fenced pasture to your left (west). A great moss-covered tree limb arcs over the path; all but children will have to duck to pass.

At about 0.2 mile, the trail curves west and parallels a bank of eucalyptus. At the next interpretive sign, head right (north), through the peeling trunks. The trail arcs back to the west, and the clearing that holds the village comes into view.

When you've explored the *kotcas*, granaries, sweat lodge, and other structures, or enjoyed a picnic beneath the bough-draped shelters or oaks dripping with old-man's beard, head back as you came.

For more information about the Big Time celebration, the Strawberry Festival, which is held at Kule Loklo in spring, or other interpretive programs, contact the Bear Valley Visitor Center or visit the park's Web site.

Pierce Point Ranch

Once the only ranch on the Point Reyes peninsula that was not owned by the Shafter family, the Pierce Ranch was established in 1858 by Solomon Pierce and later operated by his son, A. J. Like most Marin dairies in the nineteenth century, the Pierce ranch produced a "gourmet" butter, which was transported by schooner to San Francisco for sale (the skim milk that remained, now favored by breakfast cereal lovers everywhere, was fed to the hogs). The McClure family, for whom the spectacular beach located 0.6 mile to the west is named, owned the ranch from 1929 to 1966, when it was turned over to the fledgling Point Reyes National Seashore. It is on the National Register of Historic Places, and is in the process of being restored.

A short interpretive trail—maybe a 0.25 mile in length, if you visit every building—loops through the ranch. An interpretive sign welcomes you just inside the lichen-encrusted gate, with the huge hay barn looming on your left (west). The path is a loop, which can be traveled in either direction, and is described here walking counterclockwise.

Begin by passing the old dairy and creamery. Behind that, to the east, is the ranch house; a survivor of the 1906 earthquake, it's now a private residence and off limits to visitors. The washhouse and north bunkhouse are also behind the fence that delineates the public/private boundary.

The one-room schoolhouse, where children from surrounding ranches as well as the Pierce children were educated, is at the west end of the ranch compound. Curving southward, you will pass the wagon shed, which still houses ranch wagons that probably got little use. Ranch residents and visitors, like the butter, got around via the water, boarding boats and ships at a wharf in nearby White Gulch. Beyond the wagon shed is another bunkhouse, the blacksmith's shop and store, and the calf shed, which was used to nurse sick calves.

The dominant feature of the ranch—the massive white barn—is at the southern boundary of the compound. Supported on a rough foundation of rock, its timbers secured with wooden pegs, the barn dates back to the 1870s. Built as a milking barn—the interpretive sign notes that one man could milk twenty to thirty cows in an hour— the building was converted to a hay barn in 1945, when the ranch forsook dairy cows for beef cattle. The tour ends at the neighboring new creamery building.

To reach the Upper Pierce Ranch from the Bear Valley Visitor Center, follow the visitor center access road east for 0.2 mile to Bear Valley Road. Turn left (north) onto Bear Valley Road, and go 1.7 miles to its intersection with the Sir Francis Drake Highway. Turn left (north) onto Sir Francis Drake, and follow the highway for 5.5 miles to its intersection with Pierce Point Road. Turn right (north) onto Pierce Point Road, and go about 8.8 miles to the parking area for the Upper Pierce Ranch.

Amenities at the ranch include ample parking, a pay phone, and trash and recycling receptacles. Picnic tables are located inside the ranch enclosure. Rest rooms are located 0.1 mile farther down Pierce Point Road, in the McClures Beach parking area. The Tomales Point Trail begins at the Upper Pierce Ranch parking lot, circling the ranch on its west side before launching out through the Tule Elk Reserve toward Tomales Point.

Point Reyes Lighthouse

Shipwrecks were an appallingly frequent occurrence in the early days of navigation along the rugged coast of northern California. The maritime carnage around Point Reyes began in 1595, with the wreck of the *San Augustin* in Drakes Bay, and continued up until, and even after, the lighthouse was built in the late nineteenth century. The hidden rocks, turbulent currents, and infamously thick fogs, not to mention the fact that the point juts more than 10 miles west from the neighboring coastline, all contributed to a plethora of wrecks—fifty-six between 1841 and 1934 alone, according to park service documents.

Congress, prodded by commercial ship owners struggling to preserve precious cargo during the glory days of the California gold rush, approved funds for construction of the lighthouse in the 1850s. But various delays—problems acquiring the property, difficulties in building on the site—meant the lighthouse didn't begin operation until 1870. Its distinctive signal, flashed out to sea by a beautifully faceted Fresnel lens, enabled seafarers to identify their position, and steer clear of the dangerous waters off the point. A foghorn augmented the warning capabilities of the lighthouse.

The lighthouse operated for more than a century before it was shut down in 1975. These days, an automated light and foghorn, located in a building below the lighthouse, warn vessels away from the jagged coast. But the old Fresnel light still works, the "last functioning intact light of its kind on the West Coast."

A seemingly endless staircase leads down to—and up from—the Point Reyes Lighthouse.

The lighthouse is reached via a 0.4-mile long trail/access road that begins west of the main parking area at the end of the Sir Francis Drake Highway. Walk around a gate and follow the road west, passing several interpretive signs, through an open landscape of coastal scrub that allows great views west and north when the fog is out.

At about the halfway point, you'll pass through a tunnel of cypress that has been sculpted by incessant winds into an arch over the roadway. Beyond lies park housing: A two-story apartment building with spectacular views is on the right (northwest), and garages are on the left (southeast), the driveway sporting a painting of a whale.

The tiny Point Reyes Lighthouse Visitor Center is stationed in the lee of a large rock outcrop about 100 yards west of the park housing complex. It marks the beginning of a flight of 308 narrow stairs that leads down to the lighthouse itself, anchored onto a pillar of rock at very tip of the peninsula.

The lighthouse stairs and exhibits are open from 10:00 A.M. to 4:30 P.M. Thursday through Monday, weather and staffing permitting, and closed on Tuesday and Wednesday. For information about weather conditions, which may affect whether the facilities are open, call (415) 669–1534.

The lighthouse and all of its associated amenities—overlooks, parking lots, visitor center, even rest rooms—are extremely popular. Though the main parking lot is ample, it is packed on most weekend days. If you can't find a spot in the lot, park alongside Sir Francis Drake Highway, taking care to make sure your vehicle is safely off the roadway.

On weekends in whale-watching season, the park service closes the end of the Sir Francis Drake Highway and provides a shuttle service from the Ken Patrick Visitor Center at Drakes Beach to the lighthouse parking lot. Tickets for the shuttle are available at the Ken Patrick Visitor Center.

To reach the lighthouse parking lot from the Bear Valley Visitor Center, take the access road east 0.2 mile to its intersection with Bear Valley Road. Turn left (north) onto Bear Valley Road, and drive 1.7 miles to its intersection with the Sir Francis Drake Highway. Turn left (north) onto the highway, and pass through Inverness as you trace the western shore of Tomales Bay. Climb up and over Inverness Ridge, then through the rolling pasturelands, traveling a total of 19 miles to the lighthouse parking lot.

Historic Lifeboat Station

Historic records of efforts to rescue mariners whose ships ran afoul of the rocks, beaches, and turbulent water off Point Reyes date back to the mid-1800s, long before either the Point Reyes Lighthouse or the Historic Lifeboat Station was built. According to a history of the lifeboat station produced by the National Park Service, local ranchers came to the aid of the crew of the *Ayacucho* when the ship foundered at Limantour Beach in 1841 (the beach now bears the name of the *Ayacucho's* captain). For many years the ranchers at Point Reyes were the only hope seamen had of rescue if their vessels ran aground.

It was hoped that construction of the Point Reyes Lighthouse would put an end to the legacy of shipwrecks at the point, but they continued—more than forty in the sixty years after the light was built, according to the park service. So, in 1889, the U.S. Life-Saving Service built a lifeboat station on the Great Beach at Point Reyes, and the tradition of heroic lifesaving efforts at Point Reyes was formalized.

Working as a surfman at the lifeboat station was a dangerous, difficult job. Every rescue demanded strength and bravery, from dragging heavy surfboats into the treacherous surf at the Great Beach to rigging the breeches buoy from shore to troubled ship. Tragically, four men died in the early years of the lifeboat station's operation.

The difficulties of operating a lifeboat station on the Great Beach eventually resulted in the abandonment of that station and the construction of a second, more modern station at Drakes Bay. The new facilities, which overlook the bay today, included a boathouse with a marine railway on its first story, and quarters for the men on its second story. The accommodations and railway enabled men to quickly launch their 36-foot motor lifeboats; they saved crews from more than forty-five ships in the lifeboat station's first ten years, as well as conducting the rescue of the survivors of a plane crash on the point in 1938, according to *The History and Architecture of the Historic Lifeboat Station*, a park service publication by Dewey Livingston and Steven Burke.

Rail lines spill from the Historic Lifeboat Station into Drakes Bay and the fog.

Of course, the job was still a dangerous one. In 1960 two men died when their lifeboat capsized, then righted itself and went on without them. But the successful missions launched from the station far outnumber the tragic ones.

The Point Reyes Lifeboat Station fell into disuse following the construction of the U.S. Coast Guard Station at Bodega Bay in 1963. By 1968 it was closed, and in 1969 it became part of the national seashore. Designated a National Historic Landmark in 1990, the station is now used for special events, environmental education, and field seminars, including those sponsored by the Point Reyes National Seashore Association. Accommodations include a kitchen, small meeting rooms, and sleeping quarters on the second floor.

The lifeboat station is about 0.5 mile east of the Chimney Rock parking lot via the paved access road. Descend from the parking lot for about 50 yards to the T-intersection; the road to the left (northwest) leads to the Elephant Seal Overlook, and the road to the right (east) leads to the Historic Lifeboat Station. Signs here point the way.

The road to the station passes a gate, then runs below the two-story house that once was the residence of the station's officer-in-charge and now is a park residence. Pass another gate below the house, climb a small rise, then drop to the lifeboat station at about the 0.5-mile mark. Though closed to the public, you can peek through the windows of the white-and-green building; a restored 36-foot motor lifeboat is stored inside. You can also walk around the grounds, and check out the railway that leads down into the dark waters of the bay.

To reach the Chimney Rock parking area from the Bear Valley Visitor Center, drive east from the visitor center for 0.2 mile to Bear Valley Road. Turn left (north) onto Bear Valley Road, and go 1.7 miles to the Sir Francis Drake Highway. Turn left (north) onto the Sir Francis Drake Highway, and follow it for 17.7 miles to the Chimney Rock turnoff, which is just south of the Historic A Ranch. Turn left (east) onto the Chimney Rock access road, and drive 0.9 mile to the large parking area, which also serves the Elephant Seal Overlook and the Chimney Rock Trail. Rest rooms are available in the parking lot. For more information, contact the Lighthouse Visitor Center at (415) 669–1534.

Natural History Sites

Whale-watching

Surprisingly, given that most other national parks are swamped in summer months, the number of visitors to Point Reyes National Seashore swells in winter, when the Pacific gray whale makes its annual migration from Alaska to Mexico—the longest of any marine mammal on earth. Stung by frigid winds blowing off a frigid sea, the whale watchers wait, some lucky enough to witness the passing, others disappointed, all invigorated by the experience.

The migration begins in Alaska, northern feeding grounds for these baleen whales, and culminates 5,000 miles to the south, in Mexico, where calves are born. The whales travel along the Pacific coast of North America, sometimes within 200 feet of the coastline, passing Point Reyes between late December and early February on the southbound journey, and on the northward between mid-March and April. Sightings on the southbound journey generally peak in mid-January, and on the northbound journey in mid-March.

The observation deck above the Point Reyes Lighthouse is a popular whale-watching site, but can be bustling during the height of the migration. Several short trails lead from the main lighthouse parking area to other overlooks on the point, where the viewing may be just as good, but the crowds a bit smaller. A 100-yard-long footpath on the south side of the parking lot leads to perch on a south-facing cliff, where, on clear days, views open south to the Marin Headlands, the Golden Gate, and Lands End, and southwest to the Farallon Islands—plenty of sea in which to spot a spyhopping cetacean.

Another whale-watching spot can be reached via a short path—perhaps 200 yards in length—that departs from the north side of the lot at an interpretive sign. It leads down to a promontory guarded by a lichen-encrusted fence, with views west out into the Gulf of the Farallones and north along the baked-brick colored sands of the Great Beach. Whales also can be sighted from the Great Beach itself, which stretches north from the Point Reyes headlands, and from Chimney Rock, on the east side of the headlands.

Bear in mind that, on weekends during whale-watching season, the park operates shuttle buses to the whale-watching sites near the Point Reyes Lighthouse, at the end of the Sir Francis Drake Highway. The shuttles depart from the parking lot at the Ken Patrick Visitor Center at Drakes Beach; tickets are available at the visitor center.

During the week, however, you should be able to find parking in the lot that serves the lighthouse, or alongside the Sir Francis Drake Highway.

Bird-watching

They are everywhere—in the grass, in the bushes, in the trees, on the beach, diving into the surf, soaring over the grasslands, paddling on the lakes. With more than 370 resident and migratory species having been spotted within the national seashore's boundaries, even those who don't know much about birds can't help but be impressed by both the abundance and the variety.

Songbirds, seabirds, shorebirds, birds of prey—they are, simply, everywhere. Which is not to say that some places within the park, like those listed in this section, aren't better for bird-watching than others.

- **Point Reyes Bird Observatory (PRBO):** Before you head off into the wild with binoculars and field guides, you should visit the PRBO, located near the Palomarin Trailhead in the southern portion of the park. Though the observatory, a nonprofit organization dedicated, as the sign says, "to the story and conservation of birds," conducts research internationally, its Point Reyes research station contains a wealth of information about the bird life in its own backyard.

    In addition to descriptions of the long-term studies being conducted on bird ecology, both locally and abroad, exhibits in the observatory include bird nests, bird skulls, study skins (dead stuffed birds), and a collection of garbage that was brought to the Farallon Islands by gulls. A short nature trail, which departs from the observatory parking lot, allows you to both enjoy the shade and beauty of Fern Canyon and look for birds that have been banded for study by observatory staff.

    For more information on the PRBO, or to participate in educational field trips or check out a bird-banding demonstration, call (415) 868–0655. Activities and hours vary seasonally, so call before you head out. You can also visit the observatory's Web site at www.prbo.org.

- **Abbotts Lagoon,** with sheltered waters and proximity to the beach, harbors a wide variety of resident and migratory birds. Songbirds gather in the coastal scrub along the upper lagoon; gulls and pelicans scour the beaches and surf, and hawks can be spotted flying over the bluffs. The lagoon is located in the north part of the park off Pierce Point Road. The 3-mile round-trip trail leading around the lagoon is described in the Point Reyes Trails chapter.

- **Five Brooks Pond** rings with bird call morning and evening. Ducks ply the calm, sheltered water of the pond, which is wreathed in willows and reeds. A picnic table sits about 0.1 mile north of the parking lot that serves the Five Brooks Stables and trailhead, on the southwest side of the Stewart Trail: From the table, you can enjoy lunch while you watch ducks, swallows, thrushes, herons, and other winged visitors. Five Brooks is located in the Olema Valley, about 4 miles south of the Bear Valley Visitor Center via Bear Valley Road and California Highway 1.

- **Olema Marsh:** A quiet little viewing area has been set up at the Olema Marsh, which borders the south end of Tomales Bay about 1.5 miles north of the Bear Valley Visitor Center on the Bear Valley Road. No hiking is permitted here, but from the viewing area you can watch red-winged blackbirds, herons, egrets, and other shorebirds and migratory birds go about their business in the reeds and cattails.

- **Drakes Estero** is another birding hot spot. Several trails lead out across the pasturelands to the various bays of the estero, where shorebirds and seabirds commonly feed and rest. Both the Bull Point Trail and the Estero Trail to Drakes Head and Sunset Beach offer great bird watching opportunities (these are described in the Point Reyes Trails chapter of this guide). The estero is also the site of a large mainland colony of harbor seals. The estero is located off the Sir Francis Drake Highway in the western reaches of the park.

Other good birding sites include Bear Valley, the Limantour Spit (where the endangered snowy plover nests), the Kehoe Marsh, and the Palomarin area. Outside the park, Audubon Canyon Ranch and Bolinas Lagoon are good birding locales.

Sea Lion Overlook

A narrow perch has been carved into the south-facing cliff near the western tip of Point Reyes. From this overlook, you can gaze hundreds of feet down to a rocky cove at the base of the cliff, where California sea lions regularly haul out to sun themselves on the rocks.

California sea lions aren't the only visitors to this rocky patch of land. Steller sea lions, generally larger than their cousins, have also been sighted here, as have a variety of seabirds, and you might also catch a glimpse of a migrating whale if you visit on a clear day between January and April. But the California sea lions are generally here year-round, sunning, feeding, floating, and making lots of noise.

The Sea Lion Overlook is not a place for those afraid of heights. A flight of stairs drops steeply from the Sir Francis Drake Highway to the small fenced overlook area at the edge of the cliff. To get a good bird's-eye view of the action below, you must look down hundreds of feet—a frightening prospect for some. And if the fog is in, forget it. Read the interpretive sign, listen for the barks, then move on to the next attraction.

To reach the Sea Lion Overlook from the Bear Valley Visitor Center, take the access road east 0.2 mile to its intersection with Bear Valley Road. Turn left (north) onto Bear Valley Road, and drive 1.7 miles to its intersection with the Sir Francis Drake Highway. Turn left (north) onto the highway, and follow it for 18.7 miles to the Sea Lion Overlook, a tiny pullout on the south side of the road marked only by an interpretive sign. Additional parking is on the north side of the highway along the roadway.

Elephant Seal Overlook

Elephant seals and whales have quite a bit in common. They are both huge marine mammals that migrate for long distances from feeding grounds to breeding grounds, and are capable of diving thousands of feet below the ocean's surface to hunt. Both species were decimated by humans seeking their valuable oil, but since being granted government protection have rebounded substantially. And both are part of the ecology of the Point Reyes National Seashore.

The park's Elephant Seal Overlook, located on a hillside overlooking a stretch of Drakes Beach, offers great views of a colony of elephant seals that returns each year between December and March to breed and have their pups. Impressive to look at, given their bulk (full-grown males may weigh as much as 5,000 pounds), they are even more curious to hear. Clunking, snorting, bleating, chortling, hiccuping, bellowing—they sound for all the world like plumbing gone horribly wrong.

According to park documents, approximately 1,200 northern elephant seals winter on beaches at the seashore, with as many as 100 animals gathering below the Elephant Seal Overlook. Female elephant seals come ashore during the winter months to give birth, nurse, and wean their pups. They mate again before returning to the open ocean, where they spend the bulk of the year, like the males, feeding and migrating. The pups, left behind by their mothers, must learn to swim and feed on their own.

A short trail leads from the parking lot at the Chimney Rock Trailhead to the overlook. Follow the paved road down about 50 yards from the parking lot to where the road splits and turn left (northwest), following the signs directing you to the viewing area. About 100 yards farther down the pavement, the gravel Elephant Seal Overlook Trail breaks off to the left (northwest). Pass through a stile; the trail traverses the scrubby hillside overlooking Drakes Bay for about 0.3 mile to the fenced viewpoint. The overlook is staffed by docents on weekends and holidays during the pupping season (December to March).

To reach the Elephant Seal Overlook from the Bear Valley Visitor Center, drive east from the center for 0.2 mile to Bear Valley Road. Turn left (north), and follow Bear Valley Road for 1.7 miles to its intersection with the Sir Francis Drake Highway. Turn left (north) onto the Sir Francis Drake Highway, and follow it for 17.7 miles to the Chimney Road turnoff. Turn left (east) onto the Chimney Rock access road, and go 0.9 mile to the large parking area, which also serves the Historic Lifeboat Station and the Chimney Rock Trail. Rest rooms are available in the parking lot.

Harbor Seals

There is no overlook for these shy creatures, but harbor seals also frequent the beaches and waterways of the Point Reyes National Seashore. A large colony has established itself in Drakes Estero, and they can also be seen in Tomales Bay and the Bolinas Lagoon. Most visitors encounter them on beaches in and around the park, where the seals haul out to warm themselves in the sun, and to give birth.

The seals bear their pups between March and June, resulting in the closure of some sensitive areas during that time. Drakes Estero is closed to boating, canoeing, and kayaking from March 15 to June 30, as is the Double Point area. Tomales Point and the Limantour Spit are also pupping sites, but are not closed to park visitors. Park officials ask that anyone venturing into these areas take care not to disturb the seal moms and their babies. As with elephant seals and sea lions, harbor seals fall under the purview of the Marine Mammal Protection Act, and cannot be harassed or killed. Harassment can be defined as simply getting to close to the animals: Stay at least 300 feet from any seal you encounter.

And don't be unduly concerned if you spy a lone pup on the beach during the spring and early summer. Mothers leave their pups behind when they venture into the water to feed. Moving or touching a pup may jeopardize its life, as it is difficult to reunite mother and offspring, and even harder to raise a pup in captivity. If you do suspect that something is amiss with harbor seal or pup, contact a park ranger or the Marine Mammal Center at (415) 289–7325.

Tule Elk Reserve

Yet another animal that was hunted nearly to extinction, the tule elk too has made a remarkable comeback, both throughout California and within the Point Reyes National Seashore. A herd of more than 500 tule elk now ranges across 2,600 acres on Tomales Point, protected within the park's Tule Elk Reserve. Some of the males sport huge racks of antlers, covered in velvet in the spring, hard and imposing for the fall rut, and shed by the winter. The females don't sport racks but are still intriguing, with pale brown coats and distinctive white rump patches, perhaps caring for a fawn in early summer.

Experts estimate that, before the gold rush, 500,000 tule elk roamed the grasslands of California. But hungry forty-niners hunted them mercilessly, and transformed their rangelands into farmland. By 1870 it was thought that no tule elk remained. But a private landowner found a few of the rare creatures on his property, and in, a farsighted act of conservation, protected them. When the fledgling herd became too large for him to manage, he shipped them to other locales, and a statewide population that now numbers more than 3,200 was reestablished.

Tule elk were reintroduced to Point Reyes in the late 1970s. The first years were rough, because the area was hit by drought, but with the rains came better range and a boost in the size of the Tomales herd. It's now one of the largest in the state. A smaller herd has also been established in the Limantour area.

The Tomales Point Trail runs through the Tule Elk Reserve, offering great opportunities to check out these large, graceful animals. Details of the trail route are provided in the Point Reyes Trails chapter. To reach the Tule Elk Reserve from the Bear Valley Visitor Center, drive east down the access road for 0.2 mile to Bear Valley Road. Turn left (north) onto Bear Valley Road, and follow it for 1.7 miles to its intersection with the Sir Francis Drake Highway. Turn left (north) onto Sir Francis Drake, and follow the highway for 5.5 miles to its intersection with Pierce Point Road. Turn right (north) onto Pierce Point Road, and go about 8.8 miles to the parking area for the Pierce Point Ranch. The Tomales Point Trail begins on the southwest side of the big white barn.

Tide Pools

We are familiar with the realms of most of the creatures that live in Point Reyes. We walk the same beaches and trails that they do; we live beneath the clear skies through which they fly.

But the creatures of the tidal zone are different. In some ways they are easier to see—they can't hide in the brush, run off into the woods, or fly over the hill. They are fixed in place, faceless so they show no fear or uncertainty when we approach them or touch them. They are exposed at semiregular intervals, those times noted in tide charts that we can hold in our hands. Yet they seem mysterious and elusive. When we visit a beach with tide pools, we are drawn with the receding waters into their world, where we hunker down, searching the pools for barnacles, anemones, urchins, and sea stars. Perhaps it is their very facelessness and predictability that attracts us to them; they are exotic, yet safe. Or perhaps we are drawn to them because they live in an environment that we can't abide, that we can't even see once the tide rolls in.

Within the park, you'll find good, safe tide pooling at Sculptured Beach, Chimney Rock, and Palomarin Beach. Duxbury Reef, located in Bolinas, has the best tide pooling in the region.

Perhaps the easiest way to reach **Sculptured Beach** is via Limantour Beach. From the Limantour parking lot, you can walk south along the strand for 2.5 miles to the tide pools. To reach the Limantour parking lot from the Bear Valley Visitor Center, drive east from the center for 0.2 mile to Bear Valley Road and turn left (north). Follow Bear Valley Road for 1.3 miles to Limantour Road, and turn left. The road heads south, then west, winding up and over Inverness Ridge to the Limantour parking area at 7.7 miles. Sculptured Beach can also be reached from the Coast Trail, either from Coast Camp or from Bear Valley; check the Point Reyes Trails chapter for trail descriptions.

The tide pools at **Chimney Rock** are located off the beaches near the Historic Lifeboat Station, which is about 0.5 mile east of the Chimney Rock parking area. These tide pools are off limits in the winter months when the elephant seals are pupping. To reach the Chimney Rock parking area from the Bear Valley Visitor Center, drive east from the center on the access road for 0.2 mile to Bear Valley Road. Turn left (north), and follow Bear Valley Road for 1.7 miles to its intersection with the Sir Francis Drake Highway. Turn left (north) onto the highway, and follow it for 17.7 miles to the Chimney Road turnoff. Turn left (east) onto the Chimney Rock access road, and go 0.9 mile to the trailhead and parking area.

The tide pools at **Palomarin Beach** are reached via a 0.6-mile trail that drops off the Coast Trail near the Palomarin Trailhead. These are a bit less exotic than the others, and a bit more remote too. To reach Palomarin from Bear Valley, turn right (southeast) onto Bear Valley Road and go 0.5 mile to California Highway 1. Go right (south) on CA 1 for 0.1 mile to the stop sign at the junction with the Sir Francis Drake Highway in Olema. Continue south on CA 1 to its intersection with the Olema-Bolinas Road at 9 miles. Turn right (southwest) onto the Olema-Bolinas Road, and go 1.3 miles to the stop sign at Horseshoe Hill Road. Turn left (south) and continue on the Olema-Bolinas Road to the stop sign at its intersection with Mesa Road. Turn right (west) onto Mesa Road, and follow it for 4.5 rolling miles to its end at the Palomarin Trailhead.

Duxbury Reef lies off Agate Beach in Bolinas. To reach these extensive tide pools from Bear Valley, follow the directions above to the intersection of the Olema-Bolinas Road and Mesa Road. Turn right (west) onto Mesa Road, and go 0.6 mile to Overlook Drive. Turn left (south) onto Overlook, and go 0.5 mile to Elm Avenue. Turn right (west) onto Elm, and go 0.9 mile down to the Agate Beach parking area.

When tide pooling, wear shoes that grip well when wet. Check tide charts before you venture into intertidal zones, and be sure to return to shore before the tide comes in. Watch for sneaker waves. To protect the animals that live in the tide pools, watch where you step. If you handle one of the creatures, be sure to put it back exactly as you found it.

Golden Gate National Recreation Area

The Golden Gate National Recreation Area (GGNRA) is massive. It stretches from Tomales Bay in the north to Woodside in the south, encompassing more than 75,000 acres of beaches, bluffs, forests, and historic sites in the San Francisco Bay Area, and is touted in park literature as the "largest national park adjacent to an urban area in the world."

Within these many acres you can hike through an ancient redwood forest, tour military installations that date from the Civil War to the Cold War, ride a horse through fragrant coastal scrub, watch the sun set from a broad beach or a tiny cove or a windblown blufftop, step into prison cell, visit a historic lighthouse, surf, ride a mountain bike . . . the GGNRA is a bonanza that would take a lifetime to fully explore (or describe). Some will have that much time, others will have less, but all can appreciate the wealth of recreational and educational opportunities the park has to offer.

The parks and national historic areas that fall under the umbrella of the GGNRA include Muir Woods National Monument, the Presidio of San Francisco, Fort Point National Historic Site, and Alcatraz Island. The recreation area is dotted with forts and batteries, from those overlooking the Marin Headlands to those at Fort Funston. At Rodeo Beach you can watch the surfers; at Ocean Beach you can watch the sun set. Trails for hikers, bicyclists, and equestrians weave though the hills of the Marin Headlands and across Sweeney Ridge and Milagra Ridge, offering incomparable vistas of San Francisco Bay and the Gulf of the Farallones. The bounty is so rich and diverse, the United Nations has recognized the park as the Golden Gate Biosphere Reserve.

Some of the recreational opportunities and points of interest within the park fit nicely into categories—Marin Headlands, Muir Woods National Monument, the Presidio of San Francisco—and are described in sections under those titles. Other attractions—Alcatraz Island, Fort Mason, Lands End, Sweeney Ridge, and Milagra Ridge, among others, are described in the section titled GGNRA San Francisco and Points South. I've left more remote outposts of the park—the hamlet of Hamlet, a historic railroad station on Tomales Bay at the extreme northern boundary, and the Phleger Estate, near Woodside at the park's extreme southern boundary—for you to explore on your own.

The National Park Service maintains an excellent Web site for the GGNRA, which is at www.nps.gov/goga. You can also call the park at (415)

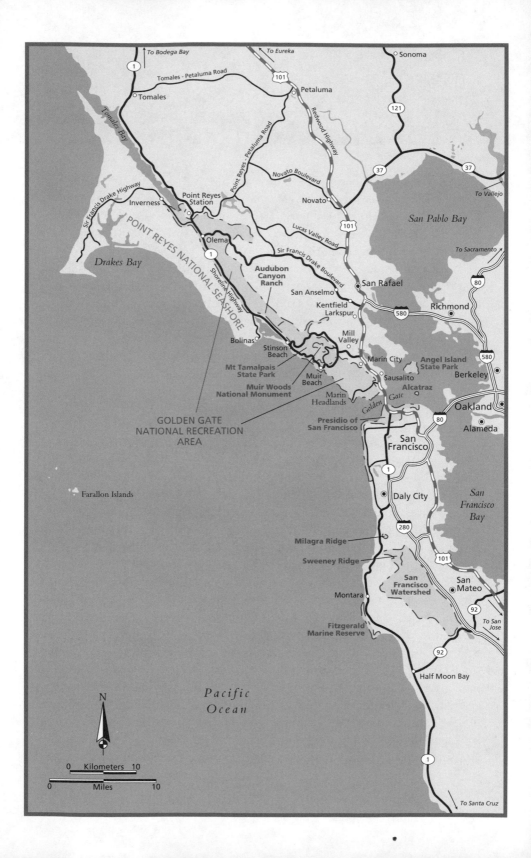

561–4700 for more information. The park is headquartered at Fort Mason, Building 201, San Francisco, CA 94123.

The park is supported by the nonprofit Golden Gate National Parks Association, which conducts educational programs, and works to preserve both habitat and historic sites within the park. The association's mailing address is Golden Gate National Parks Association, Building 201, Fort Mason, San Francisco CA 94123. The telephone number is (415) 561–3000. The association's Web address is www.ggnpa.org.

Details about how to contact specific parks or areas contained within the GGNRA are provided with descriptions of those features. For additional resources, check appendix A.

The History

The history of the Golden Gate National Recreation Area is as sprawling as its boundaries. Two indigenous peoples—the Coast Miwok and Ohlone—thrived on the land for many generations before the arrival of Europeans in the late 1700s. The Spanish established a garrison at what is now the Presidio, built missions, and subdued the Native people before being ousted by the Mexicans, who in turn were booted by the Americans in the mid-1800s. With the gold rush came the rush to protect the precious resources of San Francisco Bay, and the coastline both north and south of the Golden Gate was fortified, then refortified, then fortified again. Finally, in the early 1970s, the Golden Gate National Recreation Area was formed, and the many layers of culture on the land were preserved within the park.

The Ohlone and Coast Miwok Peoples

Both the Ohlone, who lived on the San Francisco peninsula on the south side of the Golden Gate, and the Coast Miwok, who lived north of the Golden Gate in Marin County, were hunting and gathering societies. The tribes enjoyed similar ways of life, dictated by their similar landscapes, but in terms of linguistics, the organization and composition of their societies, and their spiritual beliefs, the tribes were unique.

And their cultures were much more complex than a simple classification like *hunters and gatherers* can express. Yes, they hunted and gathered, but they also enjoyed elaborate spiritual traditions, operated within a complex social structure, created sophisticated weapons and tools, wove baskets so expertly they were considered works of art as well as utilitarian items, and operated within a system of trade that extended far beyond their home turf.

Spanish missionaries descended on the Ohlone and Coast Miwok world in the late eighteenth century, and a way of life hundreds—perhaps thousands—of years old was over. Native people throughout California, including the Ohlone and the Coast Miwok, were gathered to missions, where they were converted to Christianity, forced to work for the friars, and exposed to the diseases that would eventually decimate their populations. Neither the Mexicans nor the Americans who followed treated the Indians any better. Today descendants of these tribes still remain within the region, but little remains of their cultures.

The Explorers

Emissaries from the European empire-building countries—Spain, Great Britain, Russia—conducted exploratory sea voyages along the California coast for many years before anyone discovered the narrow Golden Gate and San Francisco Bay. Indeed, the first European to see the great bay would come over-land, from southern California, where the Spanish had already established missions, presidios, and pueblos. An expedition led by Gaspar de Portola set out from Monterey in late 1769 in search of additional sites for Spanish missions: On November 4, 1769, he and his men crested Sweeney Ridge, later a part of the GGNRA, and gazed down upon the bay. Though Portola didn't establish an outpost at that time, his discovery meant that colonization was imminent. Still, it would be more than five years before Juan Manuel de Ayala would "discover" the Golden Gate, the opening that links the bay to the sea.

In 1774 Juan Bautista de Anza blazed an exploratory overland route to the San Francisco Bay Area from Sonora in Mexico. He followed up with a colonizing expedition in 1775, in which he led 240 settlers north to the missions that had already been established in California. He selected sites for a future presidio and mission on the shores of the bay, sites upon which a presidio and mission still abide.

The Military

It was de Anza's lieutenant, José Joaquin Moraga, who built the first Spanish military outpost in what would later become the GGNRA. His presidio, completed in September 1776, was the northernmost outpost of the Spanish empire in California. The Spanish would also establish forts on the sites of the present-day Fort Point and Fort Mason, and set the stage for more than 200 years of military development at the Golden Gate.

When Mexico won independence from Spain in 1821, it took over the military garrisons established by the Spanish on the bay shore. Though the Presidio was abandoned when General Mariano Vallejo moved military operations north to Sonoma, the adobe structures were still there, waiting to be occupied by the Americans when they took control of California in 1848.

Military development at the Presidio, as well as at other sites around the Golden Gate and on the headlands, took off when gold was discovered in the

Sierra foothills. Three massive brick forts were planned for strategic sites around the bay, but only two were completed, one at Fort Point, on the site of the former Spanish fort El Castillo de San Joaquin, and one on Alcatraz Island.

During and after the Civil War, the idea of strong coastal defensive works on the bluffs overlooking the Pacific Ocean and the Golden Gate gained momentum. Batteries built of brick and earth were constructed both north and south of the mouth of the bay. By the turn of the twentieth century, new weaponry meant that new batteries had to be built. More than thirty-five batteries were erected between 1885 and 1916, a string of concrete fortifications fronting the water both outside and inside the Golden Gate.

The development of aerial warfare in World War I led to another construction frenzy, this time of casemated batteries, where the guns and the soldiers who manned them were protected in caves of concrete and earth that camouflaged them from above.

The final episode in the military history of the Golden Gate National Recreation Area came with the Cold War, when the military bases on the Golden Gate headlands were outfitted with Nike missiles. Some armed with conventional warheads, others with nuclear warheads, the missiles were intended to defend the coast from a Soviet attack that, thankfully, never materialized.

The Park

When the weapons of war took on global proportions, coastal defenses were rendered obsolete. In the late 1960s the military began to explore disposing of its lands at the Golden Gate. It seemed only logical to advocates of open space that these "surplus" lands should be added to a burgeoning coastal greenbelt that included Point Reyes National Seashore, Mount Tamalpais State Park, and Angel Island State Park.

But developers had other ideas. Plans were afoot to build a huge residential and commercial complex in the Marin Headlands; another plan called for construction of a huge archives building at Fort Miley, and grassroots movements grew up to fight these projects. In 1971 the federal government proposed setting aside 4,000 acres for a gateway park at the Golden Gate, but that wasn't nearly adequate as far as open-space advocates were concerned.

In the same year Fort Miley neighbor Amy Meyer, with the support of conservationist Dr. Edgar Wayburn, formed People for a GGNRA and began an ultimately successful campaign for establishment of the park. They found a powerful ally in Congressman Phillip Burton, who proposed that 34,000 acres be set aside for the gateway park, acreage that would link more that 115,000 acres of open space along the coastline from south of the Golden Gate north to Point Reyes. Burton's bill eventually became law, and the Golden Gate National Recreation Area became a reality in 1972.

Natural History

Swept by incessant winds and haunted by cooling fogs, the plants and animals that live in the headlands around the Golden Gate tend to hunker close to the ground. It's a landscape that, with the exception of eucalyptus, pine, cypress, and palm trees that have been planted by humans, is composed of coyote brush, sage, toyon, coffeeberry, bush lupine, poison oak, and mock heather, a gray-green brushland studded with wildflowers in spring and summer.

Coyotes, foxes, and bobcats hunt the rabbits, mice, voles, and other small mammals that range through the shrubbery, while raptors soar above, and seabirds and shorebirds cruise the coastline. Black-tailed deer and their primary predator, the mountain lion, also roam the landscape. The animals are difficult to see, camouflaged perfectly against the mottled grays, browns, and greens of the countryside, but they thrive in pockets of urban wilderness.

Bird life in the Golden Gate National Recreation Area is abundant. Many of the birds you'll see along the coastlines are sea- and shorebirds—gulls, pelicans, cormorants, murres, grebes, and the like. Western gulls nest en masse on the south side of Alcatraz Island; Bird Island, off South Rodeo Beach in the Marin Headlands, is thickly painted with the guano of the thousands of gulls, pelicans, and cormorants that roost there.

The Marin Headlands lie on the Pacific Flyway, a highway for migrating raptors and other birds. Red-tailed hawks, northern harriers, and turkey vultures are relatively common sights year-round, soaring over the valleys on an incessant hunt for prey, but during fall months the skies fill with migrating raptors of all descriptions. Volunteers note their passage for research from the summit of Hawk Hill, while other visitors simply gather on the hilltop to enjoy the spectacle.

In addition to supporting more common fauna, the low-lying, flowering scrub of the headlands is prime habitat for the endangered mission blue butterfly, and signs from the Rodeo Valley south to Milagra Ridge warn visitors to stay on the trail so the fragile habitat won't be destroyed. Other rare creatures found within the GGNRA include the San Francisco garter snake and the California red-legged frog. A number of rare and endangered plant species are also found within the park, including Raven's manzanita, San Francisco spineflower, and Marin dwarf flax. Given the park's proximity to urban landscapes and mobs of people, that these threatened species still exist is a tribute to the efforts of conservationists and park officials.

The park service has been working diligently to preserve and restore native habitats throughout the GGNRA. This ongoing work is on display in the Presidio. Once wide open, similar in appearance to the landscapes that dominate the Marin Headlands and Sweeney Ridge, the Presidio was subject to a beau-

The steep cliffs and jagged rocks of the Marin Headlands belie the rich variety of flora and fauna that flourishes here.

tification project instituted by the U.S. Army that resulted in the planting of more than 100,000 non-native trees, including Monterey cypress, Monterey pine, and eucalyptus. Those trees now cover much of the 800 acres of open space within the Presidio, creating an orderly and parklike forest. About 145 acres of the Presidio are devoted to native plant communities, some of which, like the serpentine grasslands off Inspiration Point and the coastal dune community along Lobos Creek, are undergoing extensive rehabilitation. The Presidio Trust and the National Park Service hope to increase the size of both open-space areas and native habitats by 2010.

Rehabilitation is in its advanced stages at Milagra Ridge, where, in conjunction with a local high school, volunteers with the park's site stewardship program work diligently to re-create the native biota in a nutshell. Surrounded on all sides by development laden with exotic plants and animals, the challenges are great, but not insurmountable.

To support its proactive program to rehabilitate areas like the Presidio and Milagra Ridge with native plants, the GGNRA operates several native plant nurseries in different areas of the park, which specialize in germinating and propagating plants native to that particular ecosystem. Native plant nurseries are located at Fort Funston, the Presidio, Tennessee Valley, Rodeo Valley, and in Muir Woods. For more information or to volunteer at any of these native plant nurseries, write to Native Plant Nurseries, c/o Golden Gate National Recreation Area Volunteer Program, Fort Mason, Building 201, San Francisco, CA 94123.

Geography and Geology

The geography of the Golden Gate National Recreation Area is as much the geography of an urban area as it is of mountain and valley. The cities that surround the park are as much a part of the landscape as the landforms they overlay, yet it is those landforms, shaped by fault lines and erosion, that help define the development that sits atop them.

Like that of neighboring Point Reyes National Seashore, the topography of the GGNRA has been shaped by the movement of big chunks of the earth's crust. According to the theory of plate tectonics, these chunks, or plates, move along fault lines— the primary mover and shaker in the San Francisco region being the San Andreas Fault. As the North American Plate and the Pacific Plate have ground past each other over millennia, they have folded and lifted the landscape, creating the steep headlands and coastal mountains within the park. Erosion has also played a part, etching ravines in the hills and sculpting cliffs that plunge into the sea at the Marin Headlands and Lands End.

The sea has sculpted an arch in a wall of pillow lava off the tip of Point Bonita.

The major geographic feature of the GGNRA, albeit outside the park boundaries, is San Francisco Bay. Until relatively recently, geologically speaking, the bay was a valley, with a great river flowing out through the Golden Gate to a seashore at the Farallon Islands. The valley became a harbor when it flooded with ocean water at the end of the last ice age, about 600,000 years ago, according to park documents. The boundaries of the bay were relatively static until the gold rush, when forty-niners began a systematic alteration of the environment that continues today. The bay has been filled in over the years, with marsh, tidal flat, and even open water giving way to development. Still, the bay retains much of its original beauty, the centerpiece on a table piled high with visual bounty.

The Marin Headlands are dominated by several ridgelines, topping out at more than 1,000 feet, that separate narrow, scrub-covered valleys. The southernmost ridge separates the Rodeo Valley from the Gerbode Valley, Wolf Ridge separates both the Gerbode and Rodeo Valleys from Tennessee Valley, and Tennessee Valley is bounded on the north by Coyote Ridge. The coastline of the headlands, exposed to the corrosive powers of wind and water, is nicked with coves, some of which contain small beaches.

On the south side of the Golden Gate, the parklands hug the coastline, which is characterized by steep cliffs and beaches tucked into little coves on its northern front, facing the Golden Gate. On the Pacific front, Ocean Beach forms a gentler transition, stretching south from Point Lobos to Fort Funston. GGNRA lands at Sweeney Ridge and Milagra Ridge are, as their names indicate, on ridgetops that are part of the Coast Range.

The linchpin of the urban overlay is San Francisco. Its splendid homes and financial and economic hubs are densely packed on the northern tip of the peninsula, with suburban cities and towns, nearly as densely packed, spreading in a great collar of concrete and asphalt around the bay. The city forms the cultural backdrop for the Presidio, Fort Mason, GGNRA sites near Lands End, and Fort Funston. Sweeney Ridge and Milagra Ridge, located on the peninsula south of the city, are surrounded by the tracts of the San Bruno and Pacifica. In the North Bay the trendy, upscale cities of Mill Valley and Sausalito, and the more modest Marin City, abut the Marin Headlands and Tennessee Valley.

Geologically, the GGNRA is built on the Franciscan Complex, which consists of graywacke, chert, shale, and serpentine. These rocks have been molded, and continue to be shaped, by earthquake activity along fault lines and erosion.

In the Marin Headlands pillow basalts, dark and convoluted, are exposed on Point Bonita. A particularly impressive arch of pillow basalt erupts from the sea below the suspension bridge leading to the Point Bonita Lighthouse. Beds of chert, which underlie the scrub along Conzelman Road, have been elaborately folded and contorted, then exposed in roadcuts. These rocks contain fossils that can be seen with a hand lens.

On the south side of the Golden Gate, impressive outcroppings of serpentine, a lovely mottled green rock, jut from the bluffs above Baker Beach. In the Presidio serpentine underlays a rare native grassland. Elsewhere on the headlands, sandstone and chert, like that on the Marin side of the Golden Gate, is exposed to the elements.

The park has produced a fascinating brochure that elaborates on the geology of the headlands via a driving field trip, featuring stops on both the Marin and San Francisco sides of the Golden Gate. The brochure can be downloaded from the park's Web site.

Dogs

Dogs are not permitted on most trails in most national parks, and when they are, they must be kept on leashes. Protection of valuable plant and wildlife resources, and the comfort and safety of park visitors, are the primary—and proven—reasons for these restrictions.

But in the Golden Gate National Recreation Area, this rule hasn't been strictly adhered to. Since 1979 dogs have been allowed to run off their leashes, under "voice control," in certain areas of the GGNRA, including Crissy Field, Fort Funston, Rodeo Beach, and Oakwood Valley. The off-leash policy, recommended by a citizens advisory committee and mistakenly implemented by the park, was declared "null and void" in 2001.

The perceived "change" in the park's leash law policy has resulted in confusion, controversy, and limited compliance with the regulation. Some dog owners insist that their pets should be allowed to continue to run off-leash in areas where it was previously permitted, citing, among other things, the importance of the freedom to run to a dog's health and well-being. Advocates for keeping dogs on their leashes within the park, including conservationists, cite the threats posed by free-ranging canines to fragile habitats and wildlife, as well as the fact that a number of visitors have been bitten, knocked over, and frightened by unrestrained dogs.

The controversy has resulted in a review of pet management options in the GGNRA. Options being explored include keeping the tried-and-true NPS leash law intact, adding new areas where dogs are allowed on leashes, closing additional areas to dogs, and designating some areas as places where dogs can run off-leash. The public comment phase of the process was set to end in April 2002; check with park rangers when you visit for an update on the regulations.

As both a dog lover (and former owner) and a conservationist, I strongly advocate keeping dogs leashed in national parks. Habitat and wildlife conservation is my primary concern; I also support restricting human access to sensitive wildlife and habitat areas. In the case of the more urban GGNRA, I would add that the park is simply too crowded to allow pets to roam unrestrained.

It makes sense, however, to designate an area within the park where dogs could be allowed to run free, under owner supervision and preferably within an enclosure, provided that area doesn't contain sensitive species or ecosystems. If such an area exists within the boundaries of the GGNRA, it should be set aside for that use.

Under the existing leash law, there is an expectation that all dogs in the park will be leashed. Dog owners should respect that. It is simply irresponsible and rude to expose every other park user, particularly those who are afraid of dogs, who have small children, or whose dogs are on a leash, to an unrestrained pet, especially when the sign says that pets should be leashed.

Getting around the Park

You can reach every nook and cranny of the Golden Gate National Recreation Area from U.S. Highway 101 or from California Highway 1. US 101 is *the* major north–south highway through this part of the state, and while it may not be the most direct route to every trailhead and destination within the park, it certainly comes close. Ditto CA 1, though this highway, while scenic, is narrow, winding, and may not be the most expeditious choice. The two highways merge at the Golden Gate Bridge, which is a good place to start as you pick your route.

Because the park is so far reaching and urbanized, however, describing every access road within its bounds in this section would not only be next to impossible, it would make for incredibly boring reading. I have, instead, described routes specific to certain areas, such as Bunker Road in the Marin Headlands, and Lincoln Boulevard in the Presidio, within those sections. In addition, overview maps and written directions to trailheads and destinations are intended to give you a general idea of what access routes you'll need to follow to reach them. If you are concerned about locating a specific site or trailhead, you can call the park for directions or pick up a detailed road map (like a Thomas Bros. Map) at a retail outlet.

Public transit is a good option for getting to the park, particularly in San Francisco, where parking can be nightmarish. Within the city, the San Francisco Municipal Railway (MUNI) offers access to many park sites. Call (415) 673–MUNI, or visit the Web site at www.sfmuni.com. In the North Bay, Golden Gate Transit offers ferry and bus service to San Francisco and MUNI lines, and to areas around the Marin Headlands. Call (415) 455–2000 for more information or visit the Web site at www.goldengate.org. From the East Bay, you can take either the Bay Area Rapid Transit (650–992–2278; www.bart.gov), or A/C Transit buses (510–817–1717; www.actransit.org) into the city, and hook up with MUNI lines to the park. CalTrain and Sam Trans offer access to the city and MUNI from the South Bay; call (800) 660–4287 or visit the Web site at www.caltrain.com.

The Presidio Trust offers a comprehensive shuttle service within the Presidio. PresidiGo shuttles, free of charge and available to both residents and visitors, run weekdays from 6:20 A.M. to 9:00 P.M., and weekends from 9:00 A.M. to 6:00 P.M. The shuttles are equipped with bike racks and wheelchair lifts, and link to MUNI and Golden Gate Transit routes. Route maps and schedules are available on-line at www.presidiotrust.gov/shuttle/, or you can call (415) 561–5300 for more information.

Spectacular vistas, like this across the Marin Headlands from Conzelman Road, await those who explore the Golden Gate National Recreation Area.

The rugged ridges and valleys of the Marin Headlands have, remarkably, retained a wilderness feel despite nearly 200 years of development by the military and development pressures from the private sector.

Military fortifications on the headlands date back to the mid-1800s, when earthworks were erected and mounted with cannon, and a Fort Point-style fortification was planned for Lime Point. Next came massive concrete batteries, which were erected starting in the late 1800s. Following World War I a new battery style was developed, with huge casemates to protect the guns and the artillerymen who manned them. During the Cold War the headlands were outfitted with two Nike missile launch sites.

While the feared enemy attack never materialized, another kind of threat reared its ugly head after the military began to pull out of the headlands. In the 1960s an ambitious developer proposed a massive residential and commercial complex for the hills overlooking the Rodeo and Gerbode Valleys. Dubbed Marincello, this proposed "city" of more than 25,000 people gained the approval of local government, if not of local conservationists, and construction of roadways and utility corridors began. An energetic grassroots effort to preserve the natural aspect of the headlands, coupled with financial hardships and, eventually, the death of the developer, ultimately quashed Marincello. By the mid-1970s both the former development and the former military lands were part of the newly created Golden Gate National Recreation Area.

Lands in the southern and western quarters of the headlands are divided into three separate forts, though no clear lines on the ground separate where one fort ends and the next begins. Fort Baker extends from the bayshore east of the Golden Gate Bridge on San Francisco Bay west to Hawk Hill, and includes the Bay Area Discovery Museum, the Battery Spencer Overlook, and Kirby Cove. Hawk Hill and Battery 129 lie within the boundaries of Fort Barry, which reaches west to the coast, and north to Bunker Road and the Rodeo Lagoon. Fort Barry encompasses Batteries Alexander, Wallace, and Mendell, among others, as well as the Point Bonita Lighthouse, the Nike Missile Site, and the Marin Headlands Visitor Center. Fort Cronkhite reaches north from Rodeo Lagoon to Muir Beach, and east to Hill 88; it includes Battery Townsley and the Marine Mammal Center. Most of Tennessee Valley and Gerbode Valley fall outside the boundaries of the forts.

Marin Headlands Visitor Center

The Marin Headlands Visitor Center, located in the former chapel building in Fort Barry, is the nerve center for information about the headlands portion of the Golden Gate National Recreation Area. Several rangers staff the usually busy information desk at all times; the visitor center also houses a variety of interpretive displays and an extensive bookstore and gift shop. The visitor center is open every day except for Thanksgiving and Christmas. Daily hours are subject to change; call (415) 331–1540 for more information.

Getting around the Headlands

Most of the trails and amenities of the Marin Headlands are located on the west side of U.S. Highway 101 as you exit the Golden Gate Bridge in Marin County. From the northbound lanes of the highway, take the Alexander Avenue exit, and take either the first left (west) turn, onto Conzelman Road, or the second left (west) turn, onto Bunker Road. From the southbound lanes, take the Sausalito/Golden Gate National Recreation Area exit (the last exit before you get on the bridge), which deposits you at the base of Conzelman Road.

Conzelman Road is winding and scenic, traversing the south face of the headlands for a little more than 4 miles before it ends on Field Road near the end of Point Bonita. More than 2 miles of the road are one-way only.

Bunker Road leads both west to the Marin Headlands Visitor Center and Rodeo Beach, and east into East Fort Baker. Heading westbound, it passes through a one-lane tunnel (traffic is subject to five-minute delays), emerging in Rodeo Valley after 0.7 mile. The road traces the valley bottom to its intersection with McCullough Road at 1.3 miles. Continuing west, the road passes the old balloon hangar at the Presidio Riding Club, then reaches a junction with Field Road at 2.4 miles. Stay right (northwest) to reach Rodeo Beach and Fort Cronkhite, which is 0.9 mile ahead, or go left (southeast) on Field Road.

Field Road offers access to the Marin Headlands Visitor Center and other amenities, all of which are accessible from the junction of access roads 0.1 mile from the intersection of Bunker and Field Roads. Continuing southwest on Field, the Nike Missile Site is at 0.4 mile, and the parking area for Battery Alexander is at 1 mile. Field Road intersects Conzelman Road at 1.1 miles, then continues to the Point Bonita Lighthouse Trail at 1.2 miles, Battery Mendell at 1.3 miles, and the Bird Island overlook at 1.4 miles.

Tennessee Valley is located farther north of the Golden Gate, off California Highway 1 in Mill Valley. Take the CA 1/Stinson Beach exit from either the northbound or southbound lanes, and head west from the freeway on CA 1 for about 0.4 mile to the signed *Tennessee Valley Road*. The road heads southwest from the highway, ending after about 1.7 miles at the Tennessee Valley Trailhead.

Marin Headlands Trails

Trails crisscross the Marin Headlands, many of them old ranch roads now pressed into service as fire protection roads and trails. They link the three major valleys of the headlands, Tennessee Valley in the north, Gerbode Valley in the middle, and Rodeo Valley to the south. Some trails are extremely short, leading to different military installations that dot the headlands. Others, of various durations, lead to the three small beaches that have been etched into the otherwise impenetrable coastline. And still others ride the ridges, with vistas of San Francisco Bay, the Golden Gate, and the Pacific Ocean vying for the attention of hikers, mountain bikers, and equestrians.

Tennessee Valley Trailhead

Oakwood Valley Loop

HIGHLIGHTS: Oakwood Valley is host to vigorous cascades in winter and the fragrant shade of eucalyptus and bay laurel in summer.

TYPE OF JOURNEY: Loop.

TOTAL DISTANCE: 3 miles.

DIFFICULTY: Moderate.

PERMITTED USES: Hiking only on the Oakwood Valley Trail; mountain bikes and horseback riders are permitted on the broad Fire Road Trail.

MAPS: USGS Point Bonita; Golden Gate National Recreation Area Map; Marin Headlands Map and Guide to Sites, Trails and Wildlife; TOPO! San Francisco Bay Area, Wine Country, and Big Sur.

SPECIAL CONSIDERATIONS: This is an extremely popular trail among the canine crowd. Pets should be on a leash or respond to voice commands.

PARKING AND FACILITIES: Park on the northwest side of Tennessee Valley Road near Rhubarb Park. There are no rest room facilities for people, but there are "dog stations," equipped with plastic bags and receptacles, at the trailheads. Picnic tables are at the Fire Road Trailhead.

FINDING THE TRAILHEAD: To reach the trailhead from U.S. Highway 101 traveling northbound or southbound, take the California Highway 1/Stinson Beach exit in Marin City, at the border of Sausalito and Mill

Oakwood Valley Loop

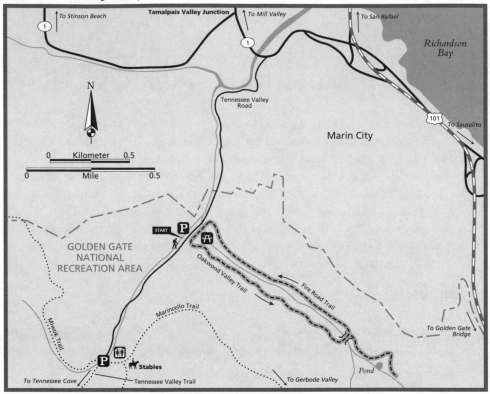

Valley. If approaching from the northbound lanes, follow the frontage road west for 0.7 mile to the arterial on the west side of the freeway; from the southbound exit, stay right, circling north to the intersection in 0.3 mile. Now on CA 1, also known as the Shoreline Highway, continue for 0.3 mile to the Tennessee Valley Road turnoff. Turn left (southwest) onto Tennessee Valley Road, and go 1.3 miles to the Oakwood Valley Trailhead.

KEY POINTS:

0.0 Trailhead.

0.5 Cross the footbridge.

1.0 Reach the junction with the Fire Road Trail.

1.2 Pass the pond.

1.5 Arrive at the staircase and the cascade.

Poor Rover. So many of the trails in Bay Area parks are off limits to dogs that he's likely to find himself left home or confined to the car while the master and mistress check out the wonders of the parks. But not in Oakwood Valley. Here, Sparky finds freedom; here, Fluffy can run off her leash, provided she stays on the trail and responds well to voice commands.

What's good for Spot, of course, is also good for Spot's owner. The trail is interesting and varied, looping up through mixed woodlands to a pond and a cascade that flows vigorously in the rainy season and trickles away to nothing by late summer. It's described here as a loop beginning on the singletrack Oakwood Valley Trail and finishing on the broad Fire Road Trail, but it can be done in the other direction as well.

A large sign marking the Tennessee Valley park boundary also marks the Oakwood Valley Trailhead. Pass the pet litter pickup station as you head through the grasses of a small meadow, then climb stairs into the dense shrubbery of the oak woodland. The trail quickly drops back into the meadow, which can be soggy in winter and spring. The creek that waters the valley is hidden by thickets of willow.

The trail again leaves the meadow after about 0.2 mile, and traverses a wooded hillside as it gently climbs into the valley. Ferns cluster around the path. A use trail branches off to the right (southwest), and other trails branch off left (northeast) to the brush-bordered creek; stay straight (southeast) on the main trail. At about 0.5 mile, drop into a moisture-laden thicket, crossing a footbridge over a seasonal creek, then climb out of the dell on a short log staircase.

Views up and across the valley open and close as thickets crowd in, then draw back from the path. At about 1 mile cross another, bigger bridge spanning the main creek, and reach the intersection with the Fire Road Trail. This makes a nice turnaround spot for a very short hike; you can either return as you came, or turn left (northwest) onto the Fire Road Trail and return to Tennessee Valley Road via that route.

But otherwise, turn right (southeast) onto the Fire Road Trail and continue to climb alongside the creek in the shade of oak and bay laurel. This is a multiuse trail, so be prepared to meet equestrians and mountain bikers on the route.

The Fire Road Trail climbs steadily and steeply, with the creek on the right (southwest). When full, the stream tumbles raucously over the rocks that litter its narrow bed. At 1.2 mile, you can interrupt the climb by taking a seat on a bench overlooking a small pond, which may be no more than a pea-green puddle by late autumn, before the rains hit.

Beyond the pond the trail keeps climbing. Round a switchback, enjoy a brief flat section, then climb to a second switchback, where the trail branches off to the right (south). A steep staircase leads up to a view of the cascade, a gentle fall through the shade of fern and oak. Though the trail forks at this point, this is the end of the line for dogs and bikes, and for a great many hikers as well. See the options below if you wish to hike higher.

Hikers cross the oak-shaded bridge that links the singletrack Oakwood Valley Trail with the broad Fire Road Trail

To complete the Oakwood Valley loop, retrace your steps down to the trail junction at the bridge, enjoying views of Mount Tamalpais as you descend. Stay straight (right) on the broad Fire Road Trail, which descends along the north side of the creek. Stands of eucalyptus—not a native tree, but one that thrives in Marin County's climate—border the road beyond a brief meadow; the trees creak and groan in the gentlest wind. The creek flows through the draw to the left (south), a much more visible part of the landscape on this side of the valley.

The trail ends in a small clearing adjacent to Tennessee Valley Road, where you will find picnic tables, a trail map, and another pet litter station. Go left (south) on Tennessee Valley Road to return to the Oakwood Valley Trailhead and parking area.

OPTIONS: From the trail fork atop the staircase at the cascade, hikers can go right (southeast) and climb to the Alta Avenue Fire Road. This trail offers access to other routes in the Golden Gate National Recreation Area, including the Bobcat Trail, which drops into Gerbode Valley and ends near Rodeo Lagoon. Don't bother going left from the staircase junction, however: What starts out as a promising fire road soon narrows to singletrack, then to little more than a dirt game trail overgrown with bowers of broom.

HIGHLIGHTS: The beach at the end of Tennessee Cove is the perfect destination for a short and easy afternoon hike.

TYPE OF JOURNEY: Out-and-back.

TOTAL DISTANCE: 3.8 miles.

DIFFICULTY: Easy.

PERMITTED USES: Hiking, horseback riding, mountain biking.

MAPS: USGS Point Bonita; Golden Gate National Recreation Area Map; Marin Headlands Map and Guide to Sites, Trails and Wildlife; TOPO! San Francisco Bay Area, Wine Country, and Big Sur.

SPECIAL CONSIDERATIONS: No dogs are allowed on the Tennessee Valley Trail. This is a popular multiuse trail; be considerate of others.

PARKING AND FACILITIES: There is a large parking lot at the Tennessee Valley Trailhead, but it often overflows on weekends, with cars spilling down both sides of Tennessee Valley Road. If you can't find a space in the lot, please park safely along the roadway. Rest rooms are available, along with trash and recycling receptacles.

FINDING THE TRAILHEAD: To reach the trailhead from U.S. Highway 101 traveling northbound or southbound, take the California Highway 1/Stinson Beach exit in Marin City, at the border of Sausalito and Mill Valley. If approaching from the northbound lanes, follow the frontage road west for 0.7 mile to the arterial on the west side of the freeway; from the southbound exit, stay right, circling north to the intersection in 0.3 mile. Now on CA 1, also known as the Shoreline Highway, continue for 0.3 mile to the Tennessee Valley Road turnoff. Go left (southwest) on Tennessee Valley Road for 1.7 miles to its end in the parking area.

KEY POINTS:

0.0 Trailhead.

0.3 Pass the Fox Trail.

0.7 The trail turns west and becomes unpaved.

0.9 Reach the junction with the Tennessee Valley Seasonal Trail.

1.1 Pass the intersection with the Coastal Trail and Coastal Fire Road.

1.5 The seasonal trail and main trail merge.

1.9 Arrive on the beach.

Tennessee Valley Trail

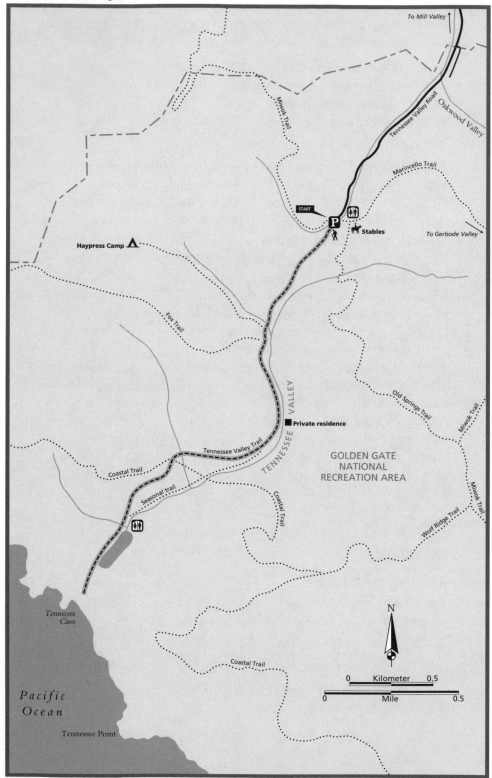

To Mill Valley

Miwok Trail

Tennessee Valley Road

Oakwood Valley

Marincello Trail

To Gerbode Valley

START

P

Stables

Haypress Camp

Fox Trail

Old Springs Trail

Miwok Trail

Private residence

TENNESSEE VALLEY

GOLDEN GATE
NATIONAL
RECREATION AREA

Miwok Trail

Tennessee Valley Trail

Coastal Trail

Seasonal trail

Coastal Trail

Wolf Ridge Trail

N

Tennessee
Cove

Coastal Trail

Pacific
Ocean

Tennessee Point

0   Kilometer   0.5

0   Mile   0.5

The Tennessee Valley rivals the Rodeo Valley for popularity in the Marin Headlands, attracting any number of hikers, mountain bikers, and equestrians to its trails on sunny weekends. The most popular and well-used trail within the valley, by far, is the Tennessee Valley Trail, which winds along the bottomlands from the trailhead to the sea. For most trekkers on the trail, the goal is lovely Tennessee Beach at trail's end.

The Tennessee Valley Trail departs from the southwest corner of the parking lot by the information signs. Pass the gate and head downhill on the paved path, which traces the right (west) side of a eucalyptus-lined creek. Pass the trail to Haypress Camp at 0.25 mile, and the Fox Trail at 0.3 mile, both of which head to the right (northwest). Stay left (southwest) on the Tennessee Valley Trail.

The trail/road continues gently downhill to a private residence—a remnant of a dairy ranch leased back to the owners after the park took over—at 0.7 mile. The signed Tennessee Valley Trail veers right (west), away from the residence on the left (east), and the pavement gives way to dirt. A bench and a trash receptacle sit just off the trail on the right (northwest) at this juncture, allowing hikers the opportunity to rest and enjoy the beauty of the upper valley.

The trail continues alongside the creek, which also bends west seeking the sea. The Tennessee Valley Seasonal Trail breaks off to the left (southwest) at 0.9 mile, sticking close to the waterway and offering hikers, who have sole access to this singletrack, a more intimate interface with the willows, reeds, and other flora of the riparian zone. The price of this intimacy involves large quantities of muck if you venture on the creekside trail in the rainy season; it is best used in summer and autumn. The main Tennessee Valley Trail parallels the seasonal trail, crossing higher, drier ground to the north. Choose the trail that best suits your mood and mode of travel; I describe the main trail here since it's open to all users.

The cove and the little lagoon that rests in its lee become visible ahead as the trail undulates along the lower slopes of the south-facing valley wall. Pass a portable rest room in the shade of a pair of Monterey pines at 1.1 miles, then cross a seasonal stream that runs through a culvert. The Coastal Trail bisects the Tennessee Valley Trail at this point, coming down from the left (south) off Wolf Ridge, crossing the floor of Tennessee Valley, and climbing onto Coyote Ridge to the right (north) as the Coastal Fire Road. Stay straight (west) on the Tennessee Valley Trail.

The trail plunges down to merge with the seasonal trail at 1.5 miles, at the edge of the thick marsh that buffers the eastern end of the boxy little lagoon. A final, relatively flat section of trail, hemmed in by the steep coastal hills, leads to the western end of the marsh as you near the beach. The stream issuing from the pond curves from the south side of the narrow valley floor to the north, cutting a shallow cliff through the thick sand at the back side of the beach before spilling into the Pacific. Pick a path across the stream and mount the embankment—it's only 4 feet tall, for the most part—to reach the small beach at 1.9 miles.

Tennessee Beach, named, like the valley, for the wreck of a nineteenth-century vessel dubbed the *Tennessee*, is perhaps 300 yards long. A keyhole is notched in the upper reaches of the northern cliff; a narrow path leads up stairs and past a bench before climbing steeply up the slope behind the cliff and topping out at a viewpoint near an abandoned bunker. The cliffs to the south are equally impressive, with a couple of sea stacks rising just offshore. Enjoy the beach, then return as you came.

Marincello–Bobcat–Miwok–Old Springs Loop

HIGHLIGHTS: With great views and relatively easy climbing, these trails offer great hiking or horseback riding. But it's for mountain bikers that this loop really shines.

TYPE OF JOURNEY: Loop.

TOTAL DISTANCE: 7.3 miles.

DIFFICULTY: Hard.

PERMITTED USES: Hiking, horseback riding, mountain biking.

MAPS: USGS Point Bonita; Golden Gate National Recreation Area Map; Marin Headlands Map and Guide to Sites, Trails and Wildlife; TOPO! San Francisco Bay Area, Wine Country, and Big Sur.

SPECIAL CONSIDERATIONS: On sunny weekends—even on weekdays— portions of this multiuse trail loop can be very crowded. Please treat your fellow trail users with respect.

PARKING AND FACILITIES: There is a large parking lot at the Tennessee Valley Trailhead, but it often overflows on weekends, with cars spilling down both sides of Tennessee Valley Road. If you can't find a space in the lot, please park safely along the roadway. Rest rooms are available, along with trash and recycling receptacles.

FINDING THE TRAILHEAD: To reach the trailhead from U.S. Highway 101 traveling northbound or southbound, take the California Highway 1/Stinson Beach exit in Marin City, at the border of Sausalito and Mill Valley. If approaching from the northbound lanes, follow the frontage road west for 0.7 mile to the arterial on the west side of the freeway; from the southbound exit, stay right, circling north to the intersection in 0.3 mile. Now on CA 1, also known as the Shoreline Highway, continue west for 0.3 mile to the Tennessee Valley Road turnoff. Go left

Marincello–Bobcat–Miwok–Old Springs Loop

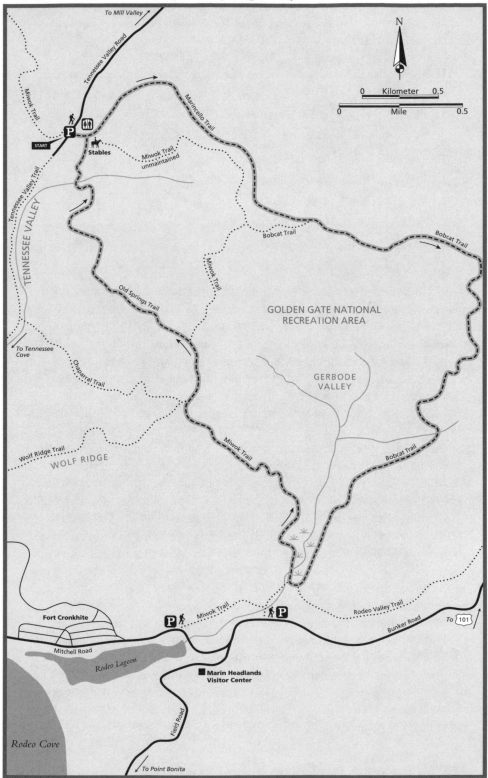

(southwest) on Tennessee Valley Road for 1.7 miles to its end in the trailhead parking area.

KEY POINTS:

0.0 Trailhead.

1.6 Reach the Bobcat Trail intersection.

1.9 Pass the junction with the trail to Hawk Camp.

2.5 Reach the Alta Trail junction.

2.6 Pass the Rodeo Valley Cutoff Trail.

4.7 Arrive at the Miwok Trail.

5.8 Pass the Wolf Ridge Trail intersection.

6.1 Meet the Old Springs Trail.

7.2 Arrive at the Miwok Stables.

This will probably set the teeth of some hikers and equestrians on edge, given that multiuse trails are notoriously contentious in Marin County, but the loop that tours the ridges of Tennessee Valley and the Gerbode Valley is a fabulous mountain bike ride. The trails twice climb—and, more thrillingly, descend— more than 600 feet from valley floor to ridge. Long and moderate, the terrain will engage any hardy fat-tired aficionado. Of course, the trails present the same challenges and rewards to hikers and equestrians, along with fabulous views, the opportunity to watch soaring raptors in autumn, and brilliant wild-flower displays in spring.

The trail begins in the northeast corner of the parking lot behind a white gate. The access road for the Miwok Stables goes to the right (southeast); the Marincello Trail, a signed fire road, heads left (northeast), up through scrub and the sparse shade of evergreens. A second sign identifies the Marincello Trail, along with a portion of the Bobcat Trail, as part of the Bay Area Ridge Trail, a work in progress that, someday, will link ridgetop trails encircling San Francisco Bay. But there is no sign that describes the source of the trail's name: Marincello was the moniker affixed to a massive housing development planned in the 1960s that thankfully fell victim to the preservation efforts of dedicated conservationists and the bad luck of the developer.

Ascend the trail/fire road—a moderate but steady grade shaded on the left (north) by evergreens—to the northeast for about 0.5 mile, where views open of Mill Valley and Mount Tamalpais, with the shallows of Richardson Bay in the foreground. The trail arcs southward, still climbing, now flanked by a line of eucalyptus and pine. The trees grow more intermittent as you climb, and as they fade away views open east and south of the East Bay hills and San Francisco Bay. Climb on steadily, relentlessly, but certainly not painfully.

A cyclist crosses the first of a series of boardwalks at the top of the Old Springs Trail.

At 1.6 miles you crest the ridge at the intersection with the Bobcat Trail; the Marincello Trail ends here. Again, you've got lovely views to the north and east, and to the south, you can see the skyline of San Francisco and the north tower of the Golden Gate Bridge, as well as the spindly upreaching arms of Sutro Tower. The Bobcat Trail is closed to cyclists heading north, but open to all trail users as it begins its descent to the south. Continue straight (south) on the Bobcat Trail.

At 1.9 miles, you arrive at the intersection with the trail to Hawk Camp, which departs to the right (west). The Bobcat Trail continues straight (south), and down, then climbs past a little rock outcrop that offers vistas of the North and East Bays and down the Gerbode Valley to the Pacific Ocean. The junction with the Alta Trail, another link in the Bay Area Ridge Trail, is about 50 yards south of the outcrop, on the left (east) at 2.5 miles.

Again, stay straight (south and down) on the Bobcat Trail. The intersection with the Rodeo Valley Cutoff Trail is at 2.6 miles; stay to the right (down and now west) on the Bobcat Trail.

The long, snaking descent hooks in and out of gullies in the scrub, passing through a lonesome but welcome patch of shade, courtesy of a grove of eucalyptus, at 3.1 miles. A couple of relatively tight S-curves follow at 3.3 miles. The trail flattens out in another eucalyptus grove at 4.3 miles (GGNRA literature indicates this was once part of the Silva dairy ranch), and skirts the riparian zone that thrives along the creek draining the Gerbode Valley.

At 4.6 miles the Rodeo Valley Trail breaks off to the left (south); stay right (west) on the Bobcat Trail, which slices through the tall willow of the riparian zone, crosses the creek, and ends at the Miwok Trail junction at 4.7 miles.

Turn right (north) onto the Miwok Trail, which almost immediately begins a long climb through the folds of the east-facing wall of the Gerbode Valley. The Miwok Trail, like the Marincello Trail, follows a fire road, so the grade, while relentless and sure to bring on a thigh burn, is never terribly steep. The landscape is dominated by low-growing and fragrant scrub; you'll find no shade along this section of the route.

The Wolf Ridge Trail intersection is a scant 100 yards below the end of the climb, at 5.8 miles. Wolf Ridge stretches dark and high to the left (west); its namesake singletrack, for hikers only, traverses below the crest of the ridge, providing access to the radar installations on Hill 88 (detailed in the Coastal/Miwok Loop description). Stay right (northeast) on the Miwok Trail, which mounts a final, washed-out incline. A social trail breaks off to the right (southwest), climbing to the top of a rocky hill with commanding views across the ridges to the Golden Gate and the ocean beyond.

At 6.1 miles you'll arrive at the intersection with the Old Springs Trail. The Miwok Trail continues right (northeast) and up, and is restricted to hikers and equestrians only. Turn left (north) onto the Old Springs Trail, which crosses a series of plank boardwalks that protect small, delicate, spring-fed wetlands from trampling by tires, feet, and hooves. Views to the southwest are of Wolf Ridge and the fortifications atop Hill 88; to the west, through clefts in the hills, you can see out to the Pacific.

The Old Springs Trail is a relatively narrow track—not quite singletrack but also not quite a service road—that winds down through the scrub into Tennessee Valley. More boardwalks protect fragile vegetation at about 6.6 miles, then a relatively steep pitch drops you onto a green hillside that, in the rainy season, evokes the Scottish Highlands: Low, lichen-stained gray rocks erupt from verdant grasses and vibrant wildflowers, stretching below and above the route in a streak of Old Country romance. Down the valley to the west, you can see the small lagoon that borders Tennessee Beach.

At about 6.8 miles the descending path is raised and bordered by logs as it passes through a meadow. A final twisting downhill run drops you to the Miwok Stables at about 7.2 miles.

The four old springs from which the trail gets its name water the stables, and contribute to the muck that sometimes clots the final stretch of the route, especially in winter and spring. Damage control is essential if the trail is muddy: You should walk your bike up and down this 50-yard stretch if it's wet.

One sign on the stable fence asks cyclists to dismount and walk through the stable grounds; a second, indicative of the vitriol that sometimes taints trail use in Marin County, reminds cyclists that this section of the route is not a #&@*& freeway. Stay left on the main road through the stables, dropping a last 0.1 mile to the Tennessee Valley parking lot at 7.3 miles.

Coyote Ridge Loop

HIGHLIGHTS: Valley and ridgetop, ocean and bay—the views along this invigorating trail are expansive and unobstructed.

TYPE OF JOURNEY: Loop.

TOTAL DISTANCE: 5.2 miles.

DIFFICULTY: Hard.

PERMITTED USES: Hiking, horseback riding, mountain biking.

MAPS: USGS Point Bonita; Golden Gate National Recreation Area Map; Marin Headlands Map and Guide to Sites, Trails and Wildlife; TOPO! San Francisco Bay Area, Wine Country, and Big Sur.

SPECIAL CONSIDERATIONS: Pets are allowed only on the Coastal Fire Road and Miwok Trail portions of this route. The trail is multiuse: Please treat your fellow trail user with respect. The lack of trees, and thus shade, renders this an extremely hot trail on sunny summer days. On a crisp winter day, however, it couldn't be more wonderful.

PARKING AND FACILITIES: There is a large parking lot at the Tennessee Valley Trailhead, but it often overflows on weekends, with cars spilling down both sides of Tennessee Valley Road. If you can't find a space in the lot, please park safely along the roadway. Rest rooms are available, along with trash and recycling receptacles.

FINDING THE TRAILHEAD: To reach the trailhead from U.S. Highway 101 traveling northbound or southbound, take the California Highway 1/Stinson Beach exit in Marin City, at the border of Sausalito and Mill Valley. If approaching from the northbound lanes, follow the frontage road west for 0.7 mile to the arterial on the west side of the freeway; from the southbound exit, stay right, circling north to the intersection in 0.3 mile. Now on CA 1, also known as the Shoreline Highway, continue west for 0.3 mile to the Tennessee Valley Road turnoff. Go left (southwest) on Tennessee Valley Road for 1.7 miles to its end in the parking area.

Coyote Ridge Loop

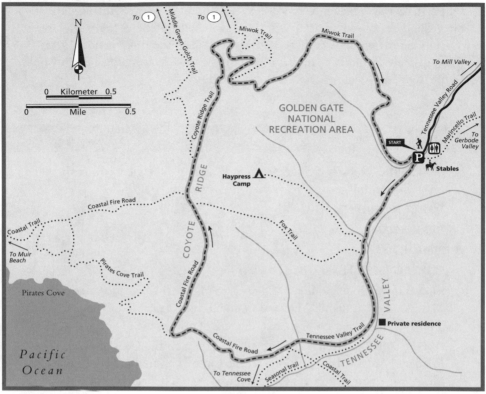

KEY POINTS:

0.0 Trailhead.

0.3 Pass the Fox Trail.

1.1 Arrive at the intersection with the Coastal Fire Road.

1.9 Reach the junction with the Pirates Cove Trail.

2.7 Arrive at the intersection with the Coyote Ridge Trail.

3.6 The Coyote Ridge Trail ends on the Miwok Trail.

4.4 Pass the County View Trail.

5.2 Return to the trailhead.

This route encompasses rigorous and exposed terrain, climbing steeply from the floor of Tennessee Valley to the ridgetop, and descending with equal vigor back to the valley bottom. By exposed I mean it's hot: The only shade is along the first part of the loop in Tennessee Valley, and at the very end, along the Miwok Trail. Regardless of your mode of travel, you'll have to pace yourself— which is not a problem, given that a rest stop enables you to better enjoy lovely views of the glittering Pacific and the Farallon Islands, Pirates Cove and the cove at Muir Beach, and, in the distance, the Point Reyes headlands.

The loop begins by following the Tennessee Valley Trail, which departs from the southwest corner of the parking lot. Pass the gate and head downhill on the paved path. Pass the Haypress Camp turnoff at 0.25 mile, and the Fox Trail turnoff at about 0.3 mile, both of which head off to the right (northwest). Stay left (southwest) on the Tennessee Valley Trail, which continues downhill, passing a private residence on the left (east) at 0.7 mile. The signed trail veers right (west), and the pavement gives way to dirt.

Continue west on the Tennessee Valley Trail, passing the junction with the Tennessee Valley Seasonal Trail at 0.9 mile. The intersection with the Coastal Fire Road is at 1.1 miles. Greater detail on this portion of the trail is provided in the Tennessee Valley Trail description.

Turn right (northwest) onto the Coastal Fire Road. The trail/road starts with a very steep climb, broken by a couple of painfully short breaks in the pitch—but the views are great, dropping down and west to the lagoon and Tennessee Cove. Watch for raptors cruising the hillsides; in my explorations, I've seen a number of northern harriers and red-tailed hawks riding the air currents.

The intense climb—you gain upwards of 600 feet in less than a mile—ends at the intersection of the Coastal Fire Road and the Pirates Cove Trail at 1.9 miles. The views are absolutely beautiful, looking north into the stony arc of Pirates Cove and beyond, and west across the sea; on a clear day, the Farallon Islands etch an inky silhouette on the horizon.

The Coastal Fire Road curves inland, climbing at a more humane pitch along the top of Coyote Ridge. At 2.2 miles views open of San Francisco Bay and the hills of the North Bay, with the Richmond–San Rafael Bridge spanning the mouth of San Pablo Bay.

The intersection of Fox Trail and the Coastal Fire Road is at 2.6 miles. Looking to the south, a portion of the skyline of San Francisco, including the distinctive point of the Transamerica Building, are framed between flat-topped Slacker Hill and the ridge that climbs to Hawk Hill.

Stay left (north) on the Coastal Fire Road, continuing another 0.1 mile to the junction with the Coyote Ridge Trail. Views have opened north to the densely wooded slopes of Mount Tamalpais. Turn right (northeast) onto the broad fire road that serves as the Coyote Ridge Trail, bordered by a rustic fence on the right (south) side. The Coastal Fire Road continues to the left (west), eventually dropping to Muir Beach.

The Middle Green Gulch Trail takes off to the left (northwest) at about 2.9 miles; a no-name trail, signed for no dogs or bikes, departs to the right (south) through a break in the fence line about 25 feet beyond the junction. Remain on broad, obvious Coyote Ridge Trail, which continues straight (northeast).

The Coyote Ridge Trail cuts to the south side of the fence line at about 3.2 miles. A little social path climbs atop a rock-crowned knob here—yet another spot from which to enjoy the views. The trail begins a descending traverse across the south face of Coyote Ridge, passing a few nameless singletrack trails that are off limits to both cyclists and dogs.

The Coyote Ridge Trail ends at its intersection with the Miwok Trail—again, a broad fire road—at about 3.6 miles. The Miwok Trail, part of the Bay Area Ridge Trail, goes left (north and up) toward Mount Tamalpais, and right (southeast and down) toward the Tennessee Valley. Stay right, continuing the descent. At 3.8 miles pass a Bay Area Ridge Trail sign at a singletrack dropping right (south) into the Tennessee Valley. Stay straight (east) on the Miwok Trail, which circles a knob crowned in eucalyptus, then switches back into an extension of the blue gum glade that spills down the east-facing slope of the knob. The trail steepens significantly as it drops through the dense shade and passes a moss-covered water tank.

Another no-name track intersects the Miwok Trail at about 4.2 miles; again, ignore it. The Miwok Trail climbs briefly, clearing the eucalyptus, to a junction with a cluster of unsigned trails. The County View Trail, a wide track that goes straight/left (northeast) to a paved residential street, is at about 4.3 miles. Stay right (southwest) on the Miwok Trail, climbing onto a hilltop overlooking the Tennessee Valley. Little social paths branch off the main route, lacing through the scrub to viewpoints overlooking the valley.

The trail narrows, steepens, and is scarred with ruts and littered with rocks as it drops—mountain bikers will find this section a technical challenge. A couple of steep switchbacks, mitigated by stairs, lead into a grove of eucalyptus at about the 4.8-mile mark. Cross a little footbridge, then leave the trees behind, negotiating the rough trail down to a more substantial footbridge spanning the creek that runs alongside Tennessee Valley Road. Climb briefly and steeply up from the bridge; the trail runs alongside the paved road, reaching the parking area and trailhead at 5.2 miles.

Golden Gate Overlook at Battery Spencer

HIGHLIGHTS: The overlook is about as close as you can get to the north tower of the Golden Gate Bridge without actually being on the bridge.

TYPE OF JOURNEY: Out-and-back.

TOTAL DISTANCE: 0.4 mile.

DIFFICULTY: Very easy.

PERMITTED USES: Hiking.

MAPS: USGS Point Bonita; Golden Gate National Recreation Area Map; Marin Headlands Map and Guide to Sites, Trails and Wildlife; TOPO! San Francisco Bay Area, Wine Country, and Big Sur.

SPECIAL CONSIDERATIONS: No pets are permitted.

PARKING AND FACILITIES: Parking for this extremely popular locale is in a pullout on the south side of Conzelman Road. Because of its popularity—and the popularity of the trail to Kirby Cove, which also begins here—traffic frequently backs up as people pull in and out of parking spaces. Please exercise caution, care, and courtesy while parking or waiting to park. More parking is available farther up (west on) Conzelman Road. Rest rooms and trash and recycling receptacles are available.

FINDING THE TRAILHEAD: From U.S. Highway 101 southbound, take the Sausalito/Golden Gate National Recreation Area exit (the last exit before you drive onto the Golden Gate Bridge). At the stop sign, turn left, then quickly right onto Conzelman Road, which climbs steeply for 0.3 mile to the pullout for parking at Battery Spencer. From US 101 northbound, take the Alexander Avenue exit. Go less than 0.1 mile, and turn left (the first left turn you can make). Go 0.2 mile, passing under the freeway via a tunnel, to Conzelman Road. Turn right onto Conzelman, and go 0.3 mile to the trailhead.

KEY POINTS:

0.0 Trailhead.

0.2 Reach the bridge overlook.

The overlook at Battery Spencer affords the classic view of the Golden Gate Bridge and the San Francisco skyline—the one you see on postcards, on television and in the movies, in all the coffee table picture books. The clatter of

Golden Gate Overlook at Battery Spencer, Kirby Cove

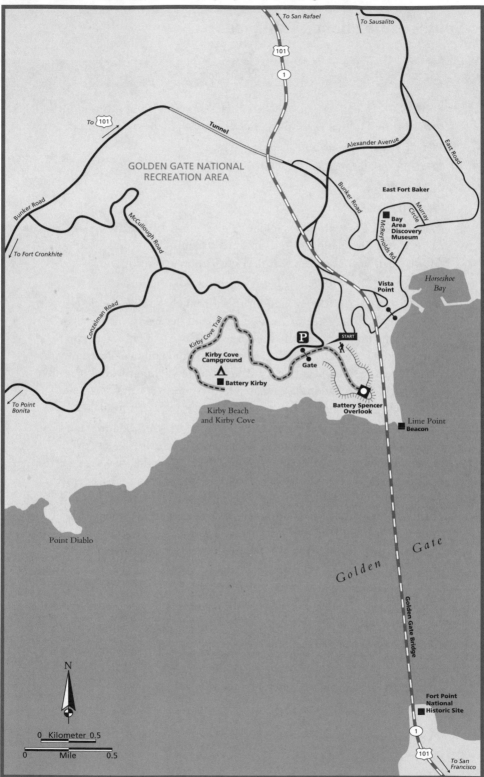

camera shutters capturing honeymooners, visitors, and even guidebook authors with the north tower of the Golden Gate Bridge looming behind is almost as loud as the roar of traffic on the span below.

So easy it barely qualifies as a hike, the short path through the well-groomed fortifications of Battery Spencer is extremely popular. On any sunny weekend afternoon, regardless of the season, you'll be hard pressed to find a parking spot within 0.25 mile of the battery, so be prepared to walk alongside Conzelman Road for a spell.

The trail begins at an information sign; the rest rooms are tucked into a fortified nook on the right (west). Pass through a gate; about 10 yards beyond, you will reach a trail intersection. Choose either the low road or the high road, and circle back on the other. The route is described here starting on the high road to the left (southeast). Head up the stairs to a viewing area; looking down, you'll see cars zipping along on the ramps of the Golden Gate Bridge, with East Fort Baker and its harbor behind. Head south on the broad path, which looks like it leads onto the second tier of the north tower of the bridge. A classic panorama spreads before you: Belvedere Island and the point of Tiburon in the north, Angel Island and Alcatraz Island in the foreground as you scan east, then south to the storied San Francisco skyline, Treasure Island, and the Bay Bridge. The trail starts out flat, then arcs gently upward like the thick cables supporting the bridge to a promontory overlooking the Golden Gate at 0.2 mile.

On the promontory a broad concrete apron stretches to near the cliff's edge, where a cable bars further passage. The views, again, are fabulous: Add to the panorama described above an expansive vista to the west, out past the convoluted topography of the headlands to the sea. Snap your photo; the pictures will stay in your mind for a long time too.

You can return as you came, or use the wooden staircase on the southeast side of the apron to descend onto a gun platform within the enclosure of Battery Spencer. A second staircase, this one concrete, drops you to the ground level of a two-story semicircular enclosure carved into the bluff. The fortifications are painted an olive green, perhaps to match the surrounding coastal scrub but most likely to cover the graffiti that plagues battery walls throughout the headlands. Battery Spencer was part of the Golden Gate's extensive defensive assemblage from 1897 to 1943, and you'll find the concrete of more recent fortifications mixed with the earthworks of earlier battlements.

The broad track leads north through a column of thick-walled structures, with views of the Waldo Grade and the Rainbow Tunnels. The scrub is broken by gun emplacements (interpretive signs show the big, big guns that were installed here), and signs request that you refrain from climbing on the historic earthworks. The path ends at about 0.4 mile at the roadside trailhead.

OPTION: To get a different perspective on the Golden Gate Bridge, as well as more exercise, couple this walk with a hike or mountain bike down into Kirby Cove, which is described below.

Kirby Cove

See map on page 196

HIGHLIGHTS: There's no better beach in the North Bay from which to watch cargo ships and pleasure craft pass under the Golden Gate Bridge.

TYPE OF JOURNEY: Out-and-back.

TOTAL DISTANCE: 1.8 miles.

DIFFICULTY: Moderate.

PERMITTED USES: Hiking, mountain biking, horseback riding.

MAPS: USGS Point Bonita; Golden Gate National Recreation Area Map; Marin Headlands Map and Guide to Sites, Trails and Wildlife; TOPO! San Francisco Bay Area, Wine Country, and Big Sur.

SPECIAL CONSIDERATIONS: Dogs are not permitted on this trail. Kirby Cove hosts a day-use picnic area, as well as a small group campground (see the Marin Headlands Recreation chapter for more information on camping in the headlands).

PARKING AND FACILITIES: The trail to Kirby Cove shares the same roadside parking area as the Battery Spencer overlook— a pullout on the south side of Conzelman Road—and thus also shares its limitations. Because of the popularity of the two attractions, traffic may bottleneck here as people jostle in and out of spaces in the pullout. Please use caution, courtesy, and care while parking and waiting to park. More parking is available farther up (west on) Conzelman Road. Rest rooms and trash and recycling receptacles are available at Battery Spencer and in the camp at Kirby Cove.

FINDING THE TRAILHEAD: From U.S. Highway 101 southbound, take the Sausalito/Golden Gate National Recreation Area exit (the last exit before you drive onto the Golden Gate Bridge). At the stop sign, turn left, then quickly right onto Conzelman Road, which climbs steeply for 0.3 mile to the pullout for parking at Battery Spencer. From US 101 northbound, take the Alexander Avenue exit. Go less than 0.1 mile on the exit ramp, then turn left (the first left turn you can make). Go 0.2 mile, passing under the freeway via a tunnel, to Conzelman Road. Turn right on Conzelman, driving for 0.3 mile to the Battery Spencer/Kirby Cove trailhead.

KEY POINTS:

0.0 Trailhead.

0.8 Reach the campground.

0.9 Arrive on Kirby Beach.

Gazing upward from the beach at Kirby Cove, the span of the Golden Gate Bridge looks impossibly long and fragile. This is especially startling if you've prefaced your hike into Kirby Cove with a visit to the overlook at Battery Spencer (a natural starting point), or with a drive or walk across the bridge itself. Up close the bridge retains its grace, but is substantial and dominant.

Of course, there's more to contemplate on the hike into Kirby Cove than changing perspectives on the bridge—there is the narrow, hospitable beach, there are the abandoned fortifications of Battery Kirby, and there is the endless of parade of cargo vessels, ferries, tugs, sailboats, and yachts passing through the gate between bay and sea.

The trail begins at the west end of the parking area. Pass a closed gate on a broad service road, and descend through coastal scrub. At about 0.2 mile the trail curves north, and the noise of traffic on the bridge gives way to that of the surf pounding the base of the headlands. The smell of pine briefly envelopes the trail as it drops through a brace of evergreens.

Hook through a steep-walled ravine, curving from north to south; tree-framed views of the cove and the mouth of San Francisco Bay lie ahead. Pass through a dense stand of conifers, then enter a eucalyptus grove. When the vegetation is wet and warm, it becomes especially fragrant—aromatherapy, pungent enough to clear the sinuses.

At 0.8 mile the trail forks, with the left (east) fork leading to the small group campground, and the right (south) fork passing around a gate before dropping to Kirby Beach. Stick to the right path; you will catch a glimpse of the gray concrete of Battery Kirby through the scrub before climbing up and over a dune capped with a bike rack. The day-use picnic area is on the right (west), in a grove of Monterey pine. From the top of the dune, two short flights of stairs drop onto the narrow brown arc of the beach.

Take a seat in the sand to watch the boats parade under the Golden Gate, explore the battery, which is hunkered in the dunes, or stroll along the strand. Once you've taken it all in, return as you came. It's all uphill, but if you take your time and enjoy the scenery, it won't be arduous at all.

Slacker Hill

HIGHLIGHTS: Enjoy unparalleled 360-degree views of San Francisco Bay, the Golden Gate, and the Pacific Ocean from the summit of Slacker Hill.

TYPE OF JOURNEY: Out-and-back.

TOTAL DISTANCE: 1 mile.

DIFFICULTY: Hard.

PERMITTED USES: Hiking, horseback riding, mountain biking.

MAPS: USGS Point Bonita; Golden Gate National Recreation Area Map; Marin Headlands Map and Guide to Sites, Trails and Wildlife; TOPO! San Francisco Bay Area, Wine Country, and Big Sur.

SPECIAL CONSIDERATIONS: No dogs are permitted on this trail.

PARKING AND FACILITIES: Park on the west-side shoulder of McCullough Road, taking care to leave the roadway clear. There are no facilities. The trail begins on the east side of the road at the gate.

FINDING THE TRAILHEAD: From U.S. Highway 101 southbound, take the Sausalito/GGNRA exit (the last exit before you drive onto the Golden Gate Bridge). At the stop sign, turn left, then quickly right onto Conzelman Road. Climb 1.2 miles to the intersection of Conzelman and McCullough Roads. Turn right (north) onto McCullough and go about 0.1 mile to the trailhead, which is on the right (east). From US 101 northbound, take the Alexander Avenue exit. Go less than 0.1 mile on the exit ramp, then turn left (the first left turn you can make). Go 0.2 mile, passing under the freeway via a tunnel, to Conzelman Road. Turn right onto Conzelman, and follow the directions above to the trailhead. To reach the trailhead from the Marin Headlands Visitor Center, go east on Bunker Road for about 1.5 miles to the intersection of Bunker Road and McCullough Road. Turn right (southeast) onto McCullough Road, and climb for 0.9 mile to the trailhead and parking area.

KEY POINTS:

0.0 Trailhead.

0.3 Reach the SCA Trail intersection.

0.4 Pass an unsigned dirt road.

0.5 Arrive atop Slacker Hill.

From the spacious summit of Slacker Hill, you look down on the best the Bay Area has to offer in terms of vista: the Golden Gate Bridge, the San Francisco

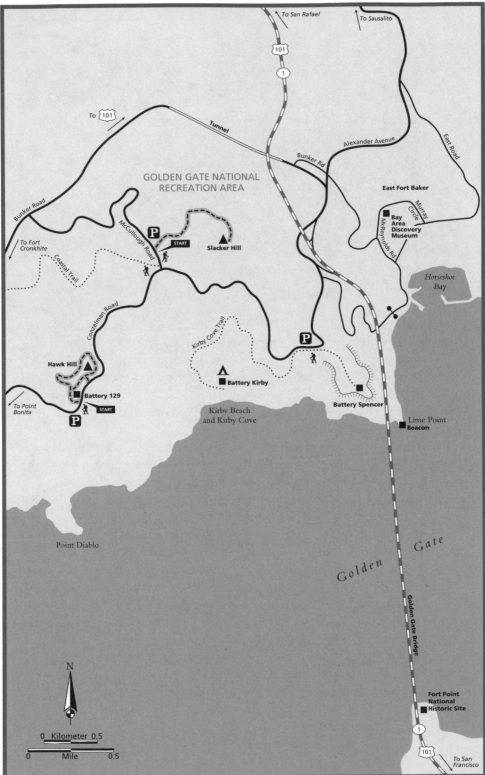

The summit of Slacker Hill offers some of the best bird's eye views of San Francisco and the Golden Gate.

skyline, the wooded hills of the East and North Bays, graceful Mount Tamalpais, and the rolling headlands dropping into the expansive Pacific.

Though steep, the trail is mercifully short. Pass the gate at the trailhead and start climbing the broad track—a dirt road, actually, that is part of the Coastal Trail. Thick scrub grows on either side of the trail, and a balanced rock hovers on the hillside to the right (south); other gray-green outcrops jut from the hillsides as well.

Climb to a trail intersection at 0.3 mile, and stay right (southeast); the Coastal Trail heads off to the left (northeast), and eventually hooks up with the SCA Trail, which offers access to the trails in the Gerbode Valley. The route to the top of Slacker Hill stays right and climbs toward a bunker on the hillside then, at a slightly lesser pitch, bends to the south.

More climbing leads to the crest of the hill and the intersection with an unnamed road that breaks off to the left (north); a chain designates it off limits. Stay right (south) on the Slacker Hill trail, naming the landmarks as they come into view: Angel Island and Alcatraz Island, Tiburon and Belvedere, Treasure Island and the Bay Bridge, the East Bay hills, US 101 and the rainbow tunnels through Waldo Grade far below, then the Golden Gate Bridge and San Francisco. The trail ends on the broad, flat summit of Slacker Hill, from which, by walking in a long circle around the hilltop, you can see all you've already seen, plus Point Lobos and the Pacific Ocean to the west, Rodeo and Tennessee Valleys, and Mount Tamalpais rising to the north.

When (or if) you get your fill of the views, return as you came.

Hawk Hill at Battery 129

See map on page 201

HIGHLIGHTS: Marvels of humankind (the tunnels and platforms built for the defense of San Francisco Bay), and marvels of nature (raptors, shorebirds, songbirds) mingle on the short path around Hawk Hill and Battery 129.

TYPE OF JOURNEY: Loop.

TOTAL DISTANCE: About 0.5 mile.

DIFFICULTY: Moderate.

PERMITTED USES: Hiking.

MAPS: USGS Point Bonita; Golden Gate National Recreation Area Map; Marin Headlands Map and Guide to Sites, Trails and Wildlife; TOPO! San Francisco Bay Area, Wine Country, and Big Sur.

SPECIAL CONSIDERATIONS: The summit of Hawk Hill is a Hawkwatch observation post. Please respect the observers that gather on the hilltop to count migrating and resident birds.

PARKING AND FACILITIES: Another popular and easily accessible site, parking at Battery 129 can be difficult on weekends and other busy days. Parking is along the south side of the road, facing the Golden Gate. Please be cautious and courteous while parking or waiting to park.

FINDING THE TRAILHEAD: From U.S. Highway 101 southbound, take the Sausalito/Golden Gate National Recreation Area exit (the last exit before you drive onto the Golden Gate Bridge). At the stop sign, turn left, then quickly right onto Conzelman Road. Climb 1.8 miles on Conzelman Road to Battery 129. From US 101 northbound, take the Alexander Avenue exit. Go less than 0.1 mile on the exit ramp, then turn left (the first left turn you can make). Go 0.2 mile, passing under the freeway via a tunnel, to Conzelman Road. Turn right onto Conzelman, and follow the directions above to the trailhead.

NOTE: Conzelman Road becomes a narrow, steep one-way drive beyond the turnaround at the battery. While very scenic, its exposure might be intimidating for those with a fear of heights. For an alternative route to Rodeo Cove and the Point Bonita Lighthouse, turn around at Battery 129, drive back down Conzelman to the intersection with McCullough Road, turn right onto McCullough, and descend to Bunker Road. A right turn onto Bunker Road will lead to other destinations in the park.

KEY POINTS:

0.0 Trailhead.

0.4 Reach the top of Hawk Hill.

The trails encircling Battery 129 link an unlikely pair—the military legacy of the Marin Headlands and wildlife observation. Designed during World War II as the future home of huge guns with a range of 25 miles, the earthworks that crown the unfinished fortifications of Battery 129 now serve as the site of annual bird counts. The hilltop is on the Pacific Flyway, a route followed by raptors and other species as they migrate in fall and spring, their passage (and the passage of resident birds) noted by dedicated volunteers of the Golden Gate Raptor Observatory.

There are a couple of routes to the summit of Hawk Hill from Conzelman Road. The most direct (and shortest) begins to the left (west) of the western-most Battery 129 tunnel at the turnaround. Pass a gate and make a short, stiff arcing climb onto the summit of the hill, which you will find hosts a cluster of bunkers and gun platforms. A concrete and asphalt path leads along the summit ridge, offering great views south and east of the Golden Gate and the bridge, and north to the Rodeo Valley, Rodeo Lagoon, and Wolf Ridge.

As you near the east end of the hilltop, you'll cross a platform upon which the average wingspans of common birds that travel the flyway, from gulls to condors, have been drawn—an interesting illustration. Hawkwatch volunteers commonly set up their tripods, mounted with huge binoculars, on an expanse of concrete at the eastern tip of the ridge, where their views are unobstructed by trees. A sign here admonishes visitors to stay on the trail, as the surrounding scrub is habitat for the endangered mission blue butterfly. From this spot, you return to the parking area as you came, for a round trip of about 0.3 mile.

A longer, more circuitous, and arguably more scenic route to the summit begins at the same tunnel. Pass through the broad concrete passage to the cavernous gun platform. Outside the platform, an overlook shaded by cypress offers views down and west to Rodeo Cove and the Pacific. Turn right (northeast) and follow the flat dirt path along the hillside to a second cavelike gun emplacement. Beyond this fortification, the trail turns sharply south and mounts a staircase that leads to the summit of Hawk Hill at 0.4 mile. Turn left (east) to reach the bird-watching aprons.

You can return to the parking area via the steep access road, as described above, or retreat down the staircase to the second (easternmost) gun emplacement. Pass through the first of two concrete tunnels; a brief wooded saddle separates the first, shorter tunnel from the second, longer passage. The second tunnel ends on the shoulder of Conzelman Road overlooking the Golden Gate. Turn right (west) to return to the first tunnel at 0.6 mile.

South Rodeo Beach Trail

HIGHLIGHTS: Bird Island and its winged residents dominate the views from South Rodeo Beach.

TYPE OF JOURNEY: Out-and-back.

TOTAL DISTANCE: 0.6 mile.

DIFFICULTY: Easy.

PERMITTED USES: Hiking.

MAPS: USGS Point Bonita; Golden Gate National Recreation Area Map; Marin Headlands Map and Guide to Sites, Trails and Wildlife; TOPO! San Francisco Bay Area, Wine Country, and Big Sur.

SPECIAL CONSIDERATIONS: No dogs are allowed.

PARKING AND FACILITIES: The Battery Alexander Trailhead boasts ample parking, but no other facilities.

FINDING THE TRAILHEAD: From the Marin Headlands Visitor Center, head southwest on Field Road for 0.9 mile to the Battery Alexander parking area, which is on the right (north).

KEY POINTS:

0.0 Trailhead.

0.3 Arrive on South Rodeo Beach.

Often shrouded in fog and littered with debris carried in by the surf, South Rodeo Beach is a place for parkas, binoculars, and contemplation, not for beach blankets, umbrellas, and coolers. Those you will find farther north on Rodeo Beach proper. Sure, there are rocks you can sit on, or you can clear a spot in the sand for a picnic, but you'll most likely find yourself walking, gazing westward past the fishing boats in the cove to the flat horizon, or south and up at the gulls, pelicans, and cormorants that cluster on craggy Bird Island.

The trail to South Rodeo Beach begins on the west side of the large Battery Alexander parking area, and is marked with a small sign. Head west down the path, through the fragrant coastal scrub and ice plant.

About 75 yards down the path, the trail forks. Go right (west) on the South Rodeo Beach Trail; the left path leads southwest toward the YMCA Conference Center complex. Bird Island, stained white with droppings, rises directly to the west, and the chatter of the birds mingles with the beat of the surf pounding Rodeo Beach.

The path drops into a sandy gully; collapsed wooden braces litter the head of the ravine. You will see other remnants of construction as you wind down

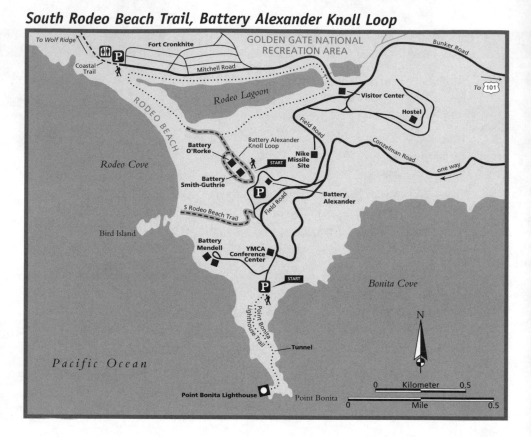

the ravine—unidentifiable concrete forms and scrap wood and metal stakes. A steep and deep-stepped staircase plunges down from the ravine to the beach at 0.3 mile.

The access path cleaves the beach almost exactly in the middle. If the tide is out, you can head right (north) onto Rodeo Beach, weaving through rock outcrops battered by the surf when it comes up. Or you can head left (south) across the streamlet that issues from the ravine to clamber on the rocks below Bird Island.

When you've finished exploring, return as you came.

Battery Alexander Knoll Loop

See map on page 206

HIGHLIGHTS: This short trail is battery-packed, visiting three separate sets of early twentieth-century fortifications.

TYPE OF JOURNEY: Loop.

TOTAL DISTANCE: 0.8 mile.

DIFFICULTY: Easy.

PERMITTED USES: Hiking.

MAPS: USGS Point Bonita; Golden Gate National Recreation Area Map; Marin Headlands Map and Guide to Sites, Trails and Wildlife; TOPO! San Francisco Bay Area, Wine Country, and Big Sur.

SPECIAL CONSIDERATIONS: Pets are permitted on the 0.3-mile section of trail on the west side of the knoll, but not allowed on the eastern portion of the trail.

PARKING AND FACILITIES: The Battery Alexander Trailhead boasts ample parking, but no other facilities.

FINDING THE TRAILHEAD: From the Marin Headlands Visitor Center, head southwest on Field Road for 0.9 mile to the Battery Alexander parking area, which is on the right (north).

KEY POINTS:

0.0 Trailhead.

0.2 Reach Battery Alexander.

0.4 Reach the first bunkers at Battery Smith-Guthrie.

0.6 Pass the trail leading down to Rodeo Beach.

0.8 Return to the parking lot.

This loop is perfect for those who want to combine a short hike with the exploration of several historic military batteries. The architecture is impressive, as are the views from the gun platforms atop the fortifications at Batteries Smith-Guthrie and O'Rorke.

To make the loop, leave the parking lot to the north and climb around the gate on the broad trail/access road. The trail forks almost immediately; signs divvy up the trail for those with dogs and those without. If you are pet-free, stay right (northeast) and climb the mildly steep track, bordered on either side by coastal scrub.

After about 100 yards the trail forks again; the road to the right (south) leads down to Battery Alexander at 0.2 mile. You'd never know it was there unless you followed this trail, because the side the battery presents to the parking area is camouflaged with grasses and eucalyptuses. Once open for camping, the battery is now like others in the headlands—lonely and formidable.

Climb back to the loop trail and go right (north), circling the top of the knoll to yet another trail fork at the ruins of Battery Smith-Guthrie at 0.4 mile. Like Battery Alexander, and its other neighbor, Battery O'Rorke, Smith-Guthrie dates back to the turn of the twentieth century, when coastal fortifications underwent extensive upgrades. Stay left (northwest) and climb the stairs onto the turret overlooking Rodeo Cove.

The gun emplacements are lined up with military precision to the north, marked with colorful graffiti and linked by narrow paths that cross the small grassy slopes that separate them. Head north along these narrow trails; the laughing calls of gulls, the ringing of a buoy, and the thumping of the surf washes up to you from the cove. Battery O'Rorke is poised at the northern end of the knoll overlooking Rodeo Lagoon and Beach. You can also follow the broad track that fronts the bunkers to the east, climbing steps onto the gun platforms for the views.

The trail continues around the knoll, circling west to intersect several paths that lead down toward the beach at 0.6 mile. The remainder of the trail offers views west of Bird Island and the Pacific; you'll reach the parking lot at 0.8 mile.

OPTION: You can add a relatively difficult 0.6 mile and about 160 feet of elevation change to this hike by taking a footpath from the Battery Alexander Knoll down to Rodeo Beach. Once on the beach, you can either return the way you came (a steep climb), or head south to the South Rodeo Beach Trail (if it's low tide), ascending that route back to the Battery Alexander parking lot.

Rodeo Lagoon Trail

HIGHLIGHTS: This easy jaunt circumnavigates Rodeo Lagoon, offering great views of the local bird life.

TYPE OF JOURNEY: Loop.

TOTAL DISTANCE: 2 miles.

DIFFICULTY: Easy.

PERMITTED USES: Hiking.

MAPS: USGS Point Bonita; Golden Gate National Recreation Area Map; Marin Headlands Map and Guide to Sites, Trails and Wildlife; TOPO! San Francisco Bay Area, Wine Country, and Big Sur.

SPECIAL CONSIDERATIONS: Dogs are permitted on this trail loop. Be considerate of wildlife and courteous to other trail users by keeping your pet on a leash.

Rodeo Lagoon Trail

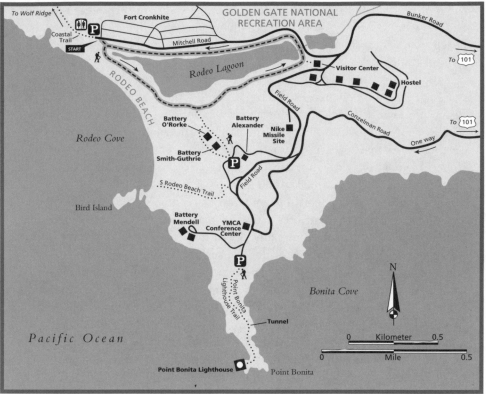

PARKING AND FACILITIES: Ample parking is available in the large lot at the end of Mitchell Road, and along the left (south) side of the road fronting the lagoon. Rest rooms and showers are provided.

FINDING THE TRAILHEAD: From the Marin Headlands Visitor Center, follow Bunker Road west for 0.6 mile, across the bridge spanning the eastern inlet of the lagoon, to its intersection with Mitchell Road. Continue west on Mitchell Road for 0.2 mile to the large parking lot at road's end.

KEY POINTS:

0.0 Trailhead.

0.5 Pass a large flat area.

1.0 Reach the east end of the lagoon.

1.5 Pass the intersection of Mitchell and Bunker Roads.

Think of the trail around Rodeo Lagoon as the perfect compliment to (or antidote for) a lazy day at Rodeo Beach. You've soaked up all the sun you can, the dog lies deflated in the sand after chasing a thousand Frisbees, and you need to work off a few calories before diving back into the cooler. Leave the beach gear where it lies, slap on the sandals, and spend an hour walking around Rodeo Lagoon.

The loop is described here in a counterclockwise direction, beginning by crossing the bridge that spans the lagoon outlet and deposits you on Rodeo Beach. Follow the beach south for about 0.25 mile to the base of the bluffs. The Rodeo Lagoon Trail climbs up and east onto the bluff, as does a social trail (farther west) that leads up onto the Battery Alexander knoll. Stay on the Rodeo Lagoon Trail; a sign warns that no bikes or horses are allowed on the route, and that dogs must be kept on leashes.

The bottle green lagoon drops away as you climb from the beach on the sandy path, passing through non-native ice plant that crowds the indigenous plants of the coastal scrub community. Social trails branch off to the right and left, petering out in the undergrowth. The surface of the path solidifies as you reach the top of the incline—you've just completed the hardest part of the hike.

The trail begins a gentle decline; the Nike Missile Site is to the southeast. Drop to a large open area at about 0.5 mile, where a barren platform the size of a football field spreads eastward toward the missile site before ending above a gully. Unmarked social paths lead into the undergrowth. Stay left (east and down) on the main path, which drops quickly to the edge of the lagoon and proceeds through a tangle of riparian growth.

At about 1 mile you reach a trail intersection at the southeast corner of the lagoon and its marsh. The path to the right (south) climbs to Field Road and, on the other side of the road, the Marin Headlands Visitor Center. Go left (north) and down the stairs, which end in a creek gully, dry in summer, but dense with fern, willow, and other riparian plants year-round.

Head north, alongside Bunker Road, crossing between the lagoon and Rodeo Pond on the right (east). The trail bears left (west) on the other side of the bridge; a parking lot and the Miwok Trailhead are on the opposite side of the roadway.

The remainder of the trail is squeezed between Bunker Road (and Mitchell Road), and the tall brush, reeds, and cattails guarding the lagoon. Climb past a Monterey pine; the trail is wedged between a guardrail and a drop-off (neither steep nor intimidating) to the lagoon. Climb to the intersection of Bunker and Mitchell Roads at 1.5 miles, then drop to the long, narrow parking area that parallels the roadway; the trail is now wedged between willows and the logs that form the lot's edge. Pass another Monterey pine and a scattering of picnic tables as you approach the Rodeo Beach bridge and parking lot at the west edge of the lagoon at 2 miles.

Coastal–Miwok Loop

HIGHLIGHTS: This route serves up an intriguing mix of grand views, challenging terrain, and abandoned military installations.

TYPE OF JOURNEY: Loop.

TOTAL DISTANCE: About 5.5 miles (the distance varies depending on how many side trips you include).

DIFFICULTY: Hard.

PERMITTED USES: Hiking. The Coastal Trail segment and the Miwok Trail segment are multiuse trails, but the Wolf Ridge Trail link is not.

MAPS: USGS Point Bonita, Golden Gate National Recreation Area Map, Marin Headlands Map and Guide to Sites, Trails and Wildlife.

SPECIAL CONSIDERATIONS: Dogs are permitted on all segments of this trail. Be considerate of wildlife and courteous to other trail users by keeping your pet on a leash. Observe proper etiquette when encountering other trail users.

PARKING AND FACILITIES: Ample parking is available in the large Rodeo Beach lot at the end of Mitchell Road, and along the left (south) side of the road fronting Rodeo Lagoon. Rest rooms and showers are available.

FINDING THE TRAILHEAD: From the Marin Headlands Visitor Center, follow Bunker Road west for 0.6 mile to its intersection with Mitchell Road. Continue west on Mitchell Road for 0.2 mile to the large lot at the road's end.

KEY POINTS:

0.0 Trailhead.

1.4 Pass the fortifications at Battery Townsley.

2.4 Reach the top of Hill 88.

2.5 Backtrack to the Wolf Ridge Trail junction.

3.2 Arrive at the Miwok Trail intersection.

5.0 Reach the intersection with the Rodeo Lagoon Trail.

I spend a lot of time alone on the trail, which gives me ample opportunity to muse. Most of the time I think about the beauty of the scenery around me, or about family and friends, or I just daydream. But I happened to hike this trail just after the terrorist attacks of September 11. And instead of using trail intersections or viewpoints as landmarks, I gauged my progress, mile by mile, with the derelict remnants of America's wars.

Coastal–Miwok Loop

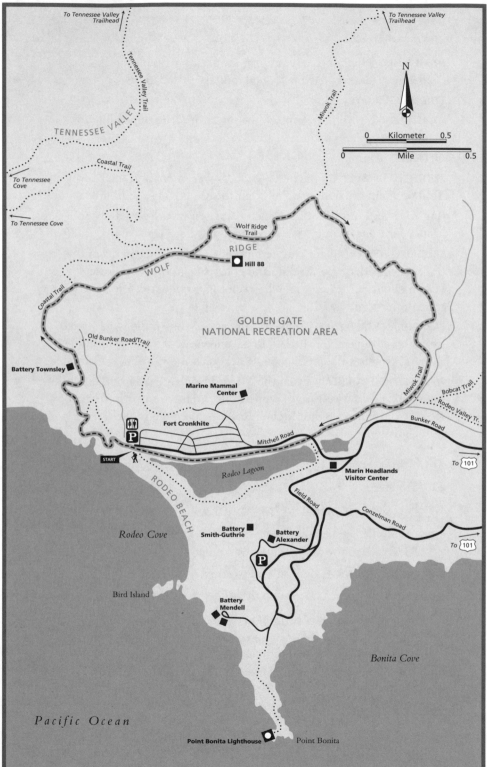

And when I stood amid the weather-beaten military installations atop Hill 88, their hospital-green paint peeling away and stained with rust, I had a hard time focusing on the spectacular views, or the raptors surfing the wind currents rising from the surrounding valleys. Instead, I was struck by how much humans have invested in the tools of warfare, and how quickly those investments—from hand axes to cannon to nuclear bombs and chemical and biological weapons—become obsolete. The ruins of war efforts dating back centuries are scattered throughout the GGNRA, stacked atop each other, rusty, clunky reminders of the white elephant humankind has nurtured for thousands of years.

I know that this is a guidebook, not a soapbox, but I challenge everyone exploring the trails of the headlands, regardless of their political or philosophical bent, to honestly consider the military legacy built so sturdily into these hills.

On to the trail: Follow the paved road that heads up and west through the gate at the western edge of the parking area. Maps designate this the Coastal Trail, but the sign calls it the Pacific Coast Trail. At the trail intersection about 100 yards above the gate, go left (west) on the dirt path, climbing to an over-look of Rodeo Cove and points south and west. Battlements hunker in the hill-side above and to the northwest.

The trail rounds a switchback and climbs to a slide area, where you can look down into a tiny cove. Climb a bit higher, away from the cliffside, onto a knoll where you can again look out over the Pacific and south past Rodeo Cove, with the Point Bonita Lighthouse white and bright on its rocky perch. Social paths branch this way and that; stay north and seaside on the wide, well-trodden route, which cuts through the fragrant coastal scrub.

The casemated gun platforms of Battery Townsley are carved into the hill-side above and on the right (northeast) of the trail; small sea stacks are pum-meled by the surf along the coast below and to the left (west). The overlook trail ends at about the 0.5-mile mark; the area beyond is blocked off by a rusty chain-link fence, though social paths lead through and around this barrier.

Return to the paved road via the same route (you'll reach it at about the 1-mile mark), or take an unmarked use trail up from the main dirt path to its intersection with the paved Coastal Trail. This is a bit shorter, but covers more challenging terrain. Once on the pavement, go left (north and up), passing through the sparse shade of a couple of cypress trees, to the gate at Battery Townsley at about 1.4 miles. The concrete gun emplacements here were part of the defensive fortifications built during World War II. Again, social trails invite exploration of the fortifications, which boast impressive views.

To continue, climb up and north on the paved trail, meeting the Old Bunker Trail about 100 yards from the battery entrance. If you want or need to abbrevi-ate your hike, you can follow the Old Bunker Trail back to the trailhead. Other-wise, go left (northwest), still ascending, then take a quick right onto the Coastal Trail at the sign behind a spreading evergreen tree.

The Coastal Trail climbs to the top of Hill 88, offering great views down to Rodeo Cove and the opportunity to explore Cold War–era fortifications.

The trail is now a dirt singletrack that rounds a switchback and offers views of the Golden Gate Bridge. A stone-and-wood staircase aids the ascent; a sign here admonishes you to walk your bike (as if you have a choice). At the top of the staircase you'll again meet the paved road—this series of staircases and single-track paths skirts a segment of the asphalt that has been washed out. Turn right (up and north), then quickly left, climbing a second staircase. Signs point the way.

At the top of the second set of stairs, the trail veers north to yet more steps. At the summit of the third flight, a use trail branches left to an overlook. Stay right (north) on the Coastal Trail (aka the Pacific Coast Trail). A World War II–era anti-aircraft battery is nestled in the hillside to the left (west). The singletrack ends at a T-intersection at the base of a road cut; go right (down and southeast) to continue on the Coastal Trail, then left (east) on the pavement (a white fence blocks the washed-out portion of the road to the right/west).

The paved Coastal Trail traverses the south-facing wall of the Rodeo Valley, climbing east toward Hill 88. It's worth taking a short aside, however, by turning left (north) at the T-intersection. Skirt yet more concrete installations, and climb a brief steep pitch on crumbling green stone to a cluster of fortifications on the ridgeline. From the summit, great views stretch both south to the Golden Gate and north into Tennessee Valley and to Mount Tamalpais.

You can either return to the paved Coastal Trail from here, or roller coaster along the ridgeline on a social trail that parallels the main route. The social trail meets the Coastal Trail just below the top of Hill 88.

The Wolf Ridge Trail junction is at 2.3 miles; it breaks off to the northeast, while the Coastal Trail switches back on itself to head northwest into Tennessee Valley. If you wish to visit the summit of Hill 88, ignore both these options and continue straight (east) on the paved path. The trail climbs through a colonnade of rusty fence topped with barbed wire for 0.1 mile, ending on the flat hilltop amid a cluster of Cold War–era radar installations used to guide Nike missiles that could be launched from Site 88 in the Rodeo Valley. Views from all points on the flat-topped hill are spectacular, sweeping from Mount Tamalpais to the Golden Gate and across the bay.

Return to the Wolf Ridge Trail intersection at 2.5 miles, and go right (northeast). The singletrack trail, restricted to hiking, descends swiftly at first, then climbs briskly, then follows the contours of the lush north-facing folds of the Tennessee Valley as it heads east. Pass through dense thickets of broom, poison oak, fern, blackberry brambles, grasses, and wildflowers, rolling up and down for 0.7 mile to the Miwok Trail at 3.2 miles.

Turn right (southeast) onto the broad service road that doubles as the Miwok Trail; you'll share the trail with cyclists and equestrians. Altitude is quickly lost as the track drops into the Gerbode Valley. The route is straightforward and shadeless, passing through sun-soaked coyote brush and sage.

As you near the base of the Gerbode Valley, where it spills into the Rodeo Valley, the sounds of the creek hidden in the sinuous line of willows below become louder, especially in winter and spring. Drop into the grassy bottomlands, strewn with wildflowers in spring. The trail flattens alongside the stream.

The Bobcat Trail meets the Miwok Trail at 4.6 miles in a dense stand of tall willow adjacent to the stream. Stay straight (west) on the Miwok Trail, which hugs the wind-flattened reeds and sedges of the marsh.

At the next trail junction, with a short spur to a trailhead on Bunker Road, pass an interpretive sign describing the Gerbode Valley. Again, stay straight (west) on the Miwok Trail, which meets Bunker Road at a warehouselike building labeled T1111 at 5 miles. Cross the road, and follow the Rodeo Lagoon Trail, which is wedged between the lagoon and Bunker and Mitchell Roads, back to the trailhead at 5.5 miles.

Marin Headlands Recreation

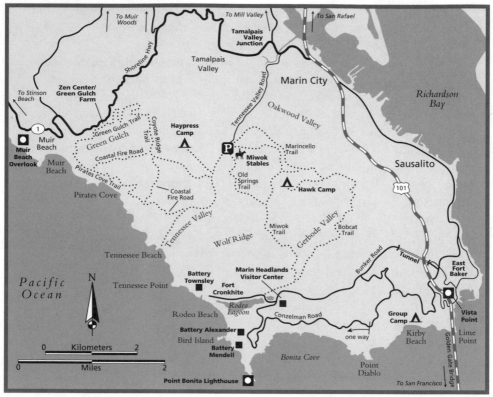

Marin Headlands Recreation

The trails of the Marin Headlands open doors to wonderful recreational activities. Beyond the great day hikes and fat-tire rides, the trails lead to wonderful walk-in camps, from the aerie of Hawk Camp to the beachside sites in Kirby Cove. The dirt tracks are also great fodder for equestrians, who saddle up at the Miwok Livery and head to the hills.

And beyond the trails there is the water, a venue for surfers and sea kayakers. Add in a very popular and well-used route for road bikers that tours the highlands and lowlands of the headlands, and you've got a mélange of recreational opportunities that will satisfy just about every desire.

Backpacking and Camping

The four camping areas within the Marin Headlands are perfect for a weekend getaway, or an introduction to the adventure of backpacking. Even Hawk Camp, the most remote of the four, is hardly difficult to reach, within 2.5 miles and an easy climb from the nearest trailhead. And the easiest, Bicentennial Camp, is a scarce 100 yards from the trailhead—perfect for those who want all the pleasure and absolutely none of the work.

General rules applying to all camps in the Marin Headlands include the following:

- Camping is permitted only in designated sites.
- Fireworks and weapons are prohibited.
- No pets are permitted, with the exception of service dogs for the disabled. Sites are not accessible to the disabled.
- No amplified music is allowed in camps.
- Please observe quiet hours between 10:00 P.M. and 6:00 A.M.
- The maximum stay at any camp is three nights per season.

Note: Some older maps of the headlands show a camp at Battery Alexander. No camping is currently permitted at the battery because hazardous conditions exist within the structures.

For more information on Bicentennial Camp, Haypress Camp, and Hawk Camp, or to make reservations for overnight stays at these camps, call (415) 331–1540. For Kirby Cove Camp, call (800) 365–2267. Information is also available at the GGNRA camping Web site at www.nps.gov/goga/camping.

Haypress Camp

Scarcely a mile from the Tennessee Valley Trailhead, Haypress Camp is tucked in a fold at the base of Coyote Ridge, hugged by steep scrub-covered slopes and shaded by a row of fragrant eucalyptuses. The five sites that make up the camp, laid out in a separate row parallel to the trees, line the edge of a no-name creek. The bustle of the Tennessee Valley Trail, one of the most popular in the Marin Headlands, is only a short walk distant but seems far removed from this sheltered enclave.

A grassy meadow spreads through the sites from the edge of the creek to the stacked split-rail fence that delineates the borders of the camp. The sites, which accommodate four people each, include a picnic table, tent site, and food storage box, and wonderful views of the rock-studded valley walls, which are dotted with wildflowers in spring. There is a single portable toilet at the camp, and a trash receptacle, but there is no water, and no fires are permitted.

The camp is open year-round, and there are no fees. Three sites can be reserved between April 1 and October 31; all sites may be reserved from November 1 to March 31. Groups must have a responsible leader who is more than twenty-one years old, and may camp between November 1 and March 31.

Haypress Camp is reached via the Tennessee Valley Trail, which begins in the southwest corner of the Tennessee Valley parking lot. Pass the gate and head downhill on the paved path. The signed trail to Haypress Camp leaves the Tennessee Valley Trail at 0.25 mile, breaking off to the right (northwest). The dirt road serving the camp climbs almost imperceptibly into a little valley. Pass a small grove of eucalyptus at the 0.5-mile mark; the trail curves lazily to the east, then back to the west, crossing a tributary stream before reaching the camp at 0.8 mile. The road/trail parallels the fence along the camp for about 0.1 mile before it heads into the hills and disappears in thick coyote brush.

Hawk Camp

Carved into the scrub overlooking the upper reaches of the Gerbode Valley, shaded by a cluster of Monterey pines, this aerie offers unsurpassed bird's-eye views that sweep down to the Golden Gate, Point Lobos, and beyond . . . and little else. The three small, spartan campsites are outfitted with picnic tables, food storage boxes, and tent platforms; a single portable toilet sits about 50 yards down a steep hill. No water is available, nor are fires permitted. In a touch of eccentricity, a palm tree grows amid the pines above the easternmost site. If you stay at Hawk Camp, be prepared to pack in everything you'll need, and to relish the seclusion.

Hawk Camp is open year-round, and no fee is charged. Four people may stay at each site. Only one site can be reserved between April 1 and October 31; all three can be reserved between November 1 and March 31.

To reach Hawk Camp by foot, horseback, or mountain bike, climb the Marincello Trail north, then east and south, for 1.5 miles to its intersection with the Bobcat Trail. Continue south on the Bobcat Trail for another 0.4 mile to its junction with the trail to Hawk Camp at 1.9 miles. This portion of the route is described in detail in the Marin Headlands Trails chapter; see the Marincello/Bobcat/Miwok Loop description.

Turn right (west) onto the Hawk Trail. The trail begins by dipping through a scoop in the scrub, climbs briefly, then descends and traverses to a more earnest climb. The steep, rocky path arcs northeast for the final pitch, which ends amid the trees at the lower campsite at 2.5 miles. A scrub-covered hillside—very steep—rises to the north of the campground, serving as habitat for the raptors, mountain lions, coyotes, and other wildlife that abides in the hills.

Kirby Cove Group Camp

A beach, a battery, and a group campground all find shelter within the narrow confines of Kirby Cove. The campsites—three total, each of which can accommodate up to ten campers—are scattered among the eucalyptus and cypress that grow at the interface of the headlands and the beach. This camp, like its Headlands brethren, has impeccable vistas: From the beach you can look out on the skyline of San Francisco, framed between the red towers of the Golden Gate Bridge.

Kirby Cove has a relatively limited season, open only between April 1 and October 31. It's also the only camp in the headlands that charges a fee: Check with the park for the going rate. Rest rooms, food storage lockers, barbecue braziers, picnic tables, and fire rings are provided. Though you cannot collect wood from the surrounding area for campfires, you may pack in your own. You can drive down to Kirby Cove, with three parking spaces per site available in the small parking area above the campground.

To reach the Kirby Cove Group Camp from U.S. Highway 101 southbound, take the Sausalito/Golden Gate National Recreation Area exit (the last exit before you drive onto the Golden Gate Bridge). At the stop sign, turn left, then quickly right onto Conzelman Road, which climbs steeply for 0.3 mile to the parking pullout on the south side of Conzelman Road at Battery Spencer. From US 101 northbound, take the Alexander Avenue/Sausalito exit. Turn left (west) at the first intersection, passing under the freeway to Conzelman Road and climbing to Battery Spencer. Finding a parking place here can be difficult; more parking is available farther up (west on) Conzelman Road.

Bicentennial Camp at Battery Wallace

Bicentennial Camp is cupped in a little dell below Battery Wallace and the sometimes-busy Conzelman Road. You'll be treated to marvelous views of the Golden

Gate Bridge and the San Francisco skyline on 100-yard walk down into the camp, but once tucked behind the cypress, you'd never know either was close by.

There are three sites in the camp, each of which can be used by two people. The sites are outfitted with tent sites and food storage lockers. There were two picnic tables at the site when I visited. Rest rooms and trash receptacles are provided. There is no water. The picnic area just up the trail from the camp, in the lee of Battery Wallace, has barbecue grills that campers are invited to use.

There is no fee to use the Bicentennial Camp, which is open year-round. Only one site can be reserved. No fires are permitted.

To reach the Bicentennial Camp from the Marin Headlands Visitor Center, follow Field Road southwest from the center for 0.5 mile to the short cutoff road that links Field to Conzelman Road above the Nike Missile Site. Turn left (south) onto the cutoff road, then quickly right (west) onto Conzelman, which is a one-way road. Follow Conzelman Road west for 0.1 mile to the signed access trail for the Bicentennial Camp. Parking is available on the north side of Conzelman Road.

Horseback Riding

That equestrians have a haven in Tennessee Valley is evident from the trailhead parking lot, which borders the outdoor arena of the **Miwok Livery and Stables.** Visit the park on any weekday morning, and riders will be in the arena, practicing their skills under the guidance of an experienced instructor from the livery. The great brown barn of the stables is just south of the parking lot, guarding the mouth of a steep scrubby side canyon. From the barn, riders have easy access to two of the most popular riding trails in the Marin Headlands: the Marincello Trail and the Old Springs Trail. But riders at the stables will tell you that any trail in the headlands that is open to equestrians is awesome.

The Marincello Trail is one of the easier favorites, featuring spectacular views of Mount Tamalpais and the North Bay. More advanced riders can head down into the Gerbode Valley via the Bobcat or Miwok Trails, or onto Coyote Ridge, which bounds Tennessee Valley on the north. The Marincello, Bobcat, Miwok, Old Springs, Coyote Ridge, and other popular trails are described in the Headlands Trails chapter.

The stables and livery are two separate entities, with the stables offering boarding services (there is currently a long waiting list), and the livery offering lessons and guided rides for children and adults, and popular summer camps for young riders. Operating out of the barns of a former dairy, the livery has been around since 1981 and has more than twenty horses available for lessons or guided trail rides.

Because the Marin Headlands see so much traffic, parking horse trailers in the lots at Tennessee Valley or at Rodeo Beach can be tight but is by no means

A rider and horse enjoy the morning sunshine as they train in the outdoor arena at the Miwok Livery and Stables.

impossible. That traffic also includes mountain bikers and hikers; be courteous to fellow trail users.

To reach the Miwok Livery and Stables from U.S. Highway 101, whether traveling northbound or southbound, take the California Highway 1/Stinson Beach exit in Marin City, at the border of Sausalito and Mill Valley. If approaching from the northbound lanes, follow the frontage road west for 0.7 mile to the arterial on the west side of the freeway. From the southbound exit, stay right, circling north to the intersection in 0.3 mile. Continue west for 0.3 mile on CA 1 to the Tennessee Valley Road turnoff. Turn left (southwest) onto Tennessee Valley Road, following it for 1.7 miles to its end at the Tennessee Valley Trailhead, and the Miwok Livery and Stables.

For more information on the Miwok Livery, call (415) 383–8048. The livery's address is 701 Tennessee Valley Road, Mill Valley, CA 94941, and the Web site is www.miwokstables.com. To reach the Miwok Stables, call (415) 383–6953.

The Marin Headlands is also home to the **Presidio Riding Club,** a private facility located on Bunker Road about 0.5 mile east of the Marin Headlands Visitor Center. The huge balloon hangar on the riding club's property now houses an indoor arena.

Road Biking

The main roads that wind through the Marin Headlands—Bunker Road and Conzelman Road—can be linked in a view-filled and challenging 8.4-mile loop. The route includes two steep climbs and one long downhill run, and can easily be coupled with a ride across the Golden Gate Bridge or to other destinations in the headlands.

Begin at the parking area at the base of Conzelman Road, which also serves the Golden Gate Bridge; this is located just off U.S. Highway 101 on the north side of the bridge. Follow winding Conzelman Road, which can be crowded on sunny weekend days, for 0.3 mile past Battery Spencer, then past the intersection with McCullough Road at 1.2 miles. The views are wonderful, south to the Golden Gate and San Francisco, and west to the Pacific. Pullouts along the roadway are nice places to stop and enjoy the vistas, or to catch your breath.

At 1.8 miles the two-way portion of Conzelman Road ends at Battery 129, as does the climb. The long snaking descent drops you past Battery Rathbone-McIndoe at 3 miles. At the first intersection, with a cutoff road that leads right (north) to Field Road, stay straight (west) on Conzelman, passing through the picnic area at Battery Wallace at 3.8 miles. Conzelman Road ends at its second intersection with Field Road at 4.1 miles. The YMCA Conference Center is dead ahead, and the trail to the Point Bonita Lighthouse is to the left (west) and 0.1 mile distant.

A cyclist enjoys a late-winter's ride along Bunker Road in Rodeo Valley.

Turn right (northeast) onto Field Road, passing the parking area for Battery Alexander at 4.2 miles and the Nike Missile Site entrance at 4.8 miles. The road drops a bit more steeply, with views down into the Rodeo Valley, to the Marin Headlands Visitor Center at 5.1 miles. The junction of Field Road and Bunker Road is 0.1 beyond the visitor center.

Turn right (east) onto Bunker Road and begin a deceptively flat climb. The Presidio Riding Club is on the right (south) at 5.6 miles, with the old balloon hangar looming over the paddocks.

At the intersection of Bunker Road and McCullough Road, at 6.3 miles, turn right (south) on McCullough and begin a more earnest, and winding, climb through the dry, open scrub. McCullough Road ends at Conzelman Road at 7.2 miles, where you will again have great city and bridge views. Drop left (east) down Conzelman for 1.2 miles to return to the parking area at 8.5 miles.

OPTIONS: If you like tunnels, you can remain on Bunker Road instead of climbing up McCullough Road. On the other side of the 0.7-mile-long, lighted tunnel, follow Bunker Road to Alexander Avenue, and turn right (south). Alexander Avenue climbs up to the freeway, passes under it, and meets up with Conzelman Road at 7.9 miles. Climb about 25 feet up Conzelman to the parking area. You can also easily add a jaunt across the mighty Golden Gate Bridge from the parking area at the beginning of the loop.

Sea Kayaking

From the grassy slopes of Yellow Bluff overlooking San Francisco Bay, you can watch sea kayakers play in the currents that swirl around the outcroppings at Fort Baker. From Kirby Beach or the overlooks on Conzelman Road, you can look down on kayakers who've ventured outside the Golden Gate, hugging the jagged shoreline of the headlands as they make their way westward toward Point Bonita. Whether you're an experienced kayaker, or a novice on a guided tour, exploring the waters surrounding the Marin Headlands is an exhilarating experience.

Sea kayaking off East Fort Baker, at the mouth of San Francisco Bay, is not for the beginner, though those with some kayaking experience may opt to play in the bay waters under the experienced eye of a guide. Sea Trek Ocean Kayak Center in Sausalito offers guided trips that launch from Horseshoe Cove in Fort Baker and cruise under the gate—a nice, safe option and a great opportunity to get some experience on open waters. For more information on kayaking options at Fort Baker or elsewhere in the bay (or even farther afield), or to hook up with a guided tour, contact Sea Trek. The phone number is (415) 488–1000; the Web site is at www.seatrekkayak.com.

A keyhole pierces the cliff wall high above the sands of Tennessee Beach.

Marin Headlands Beaches

Given its convoluted topography, beaches in the Marin Headlands are relatively abbreviated. They are uniformly tucked into rugged coves, generally no more than 0.5-mile in length and open to the volatile Pacific or, in the case of Kirby Cove, the equally volatile currents of the Golden Gate. Such ruggedness lends these strands an unsettling but irresistible beauty, an edginess that is a hallmark of these lovely escapes. The beaches are shown on the map on page 216.

Muir Beach

The crescent moon of Muir Beach is mounded with pale, inviting sand. A stretch of dark rocks streams out from the grassy bluff on its south boundary, and a wooded bluff flecked with homes, below which you'll find tide pools, forms the northern boundary. A thriving marsh fed by Redwood Creek backs the beach, the perfect place to look for frogs, toads, snakes, and songbirds.

A family friendly strand, Muir Beach is crowded with kids, beach blankets, and umbrellas when the weather permits. Amenities include fire rings (bring your own wood and contact the park about acquiring a permit), picnic facilities with barbecue pits, rest rooms, and a telephone. A couple of cautions: The beach fronts on the open ocean, so the surf is potentially dangerous. There is no lifeguard, so use caution if you choose to enter the surf. Dogs are permitted on the beach, but must be on a leash.

To reach the beach, follow California Highway 1 (the Shoreline Highway) west from U.S. Highway 101 for 8 miles to the signed Muir Beach turnoff. The scenic Shoreline Highway begins in Mill Valley, climbs up and over an arm of Mount Tamalpais, then drops through coastal scrub to the tiny coastal community of Muir Beach. The access road heads west from the Shoreline Highway for 0.2 mile to the beach parking lot, which is ample but can fill quickly when the sun is out.

Two access trails lead onto the beach. The northernmost passes through the marsh via a causeway, which may be closed seasonally. The southernmost traverses the marsh and creek on boardwalks and a bridge. In addition to offering access to the beach, which is to the right (west), you can also reach the Coastal Trail here, which heads south to the Tennessee Valley (2.9 miles distant), and reaches Rodeo Cove in 5.8 miles.

Tennessee Beach

The sun sets perfectly on Tennessee Beach. It washes the small cove in a bath of gold and red, and illuminates every divot and crease in the steep cliffs that enclose it. The northern cliff is notched with a small keyhole, a patch of blue (or gray) in the dark swirling oranges and browns of the rock; an old bunker hunkers in the scrub above. The cliffs to the south boast no unique formations or fortifications, forming a simpler boundary for the strand. Simple and serene whether splashed with sunshine or muted by fog, it's a powerful place.

The beach gets its name from the misfortune of a passenger ship named the *Tennessee*, which ran aground here in 1853. Bound for the Golden Gate, the hapless vessel was caught in the fog and strong currents that had been the bane of many ships before it, and would ensnare many ships to follow. When the tide is very low, beachgoers may glimpse the remains of the vessel offshore.

The Tennessee Valley Trail leads directly from the Tennessee Valley Trailhead to the beach. Two miles long, the trail is relatively flat and easy, perfect for a short family hike or mountain bike ride. The trail is detailed in the Marin Headlands Trails chapter.

To reach the beach from U.S. Highway 101 northbound or southbound, take the California Highway 1/Stinson Beach exit in Marin City, at the border of Sausalito and Mill Valley. Follow the frontage road to the intersection on CA 1 on the west side of the freeway. Continue west on CA 1, also known as the Shoreline Highway, to the Tennessee Valley Road turnoff. Go left (southwest) on Tennessee Valley Road for 1.7 miles to its end in the trailhead parking area.

Rodeo Beach

Surfers congregate like a colony of seals in the rolling surf of Rodeo Beach when the waves are good, uniformly sleek and black, patiently awaiting the perfect wave. Those who watch from the beach, on the other hand, are a colorful lot, decked out in bright bathing suits, lounging on vivid blankets. Laughter, the bellow of ship horns, and the bells of buoys mingle with the cries of birds and the drumbeat of the surf.

Rodeo Beach is wedged between Rodeo Lagoon and Rodeo Cove; it is whittled away and rebuilt annually by the action of the waves, usually at its broadest at midsummer, and breached by the surf in February. It is reached via an narrow bridge that spans the outlet of the lagoon. South Rodeo Beach, a relatively secluded appendage of the main beach, is best reached via a trail that drops from the parking area at Battery Alexander, but you can reach South Rodeo Beach at low tide from Rodeo Beach proper. If you linger until the tide comes in, however, your retreat will be awash in whitewater, resulting in a rather long walk along the Field Road and Mitchell Road back to the parking lot at Rodeo Beach.

Bird Island is the biggest of the sea stacks rising south of Rodeo Beach.

To reach Rodeo Beach from the Marin Headlands Visitor Center, continue west on Bunker Road for 0.6 mile to the stop sign at Mitchell Road. Go straight (west) on Mitchell Road for 0.2 mile to the parking area. A large lot is tucked between Fort Cronkhite and the coastal bluffs at the end of Mitchell Road, and is equipped with rest rooms and shower facilities. More parking is available along the left (south) side of Mitchell Road.

Kirby Beach

Kirby Beach, like other beaches in the headlands, is relatively small (maybe 0.25 mile long) and enclosed by imposing cliffs. But the setting is far from typical. The Golden Gate Bridge hovers above and to the east, framing a silvery San Francisco skyline that stretches all the way south and east to the Bay Bridge. Vessels of all sizes and shapes ply the waters beneath the bridge: lumbering freighters, sight-seeing ferries, graceful sailing ships—even tiny kayaks. It's a front-row seat at an endless regatta, with the grandest start/finish line on the planet.

Battery Kirby, compact but built to last, huddles behind the grass-topped dune that separates the beach from the Kirby Cove Group Campground. The campground, described in detail in the Marin Headlands Recreation chapter, is set above the beach in a grove of eucalyptus and Monterey cypress. Rest room facilities are in the campground. The beach also has a day-use picnic facility and a bike rack for those who chose to get to the beach on wheels.

Kirby Beach is reached via a 0.9-mile trail that drops from Conzelman Road. The trail is described in detail in the Marin Headlands Trails chapter, where you will also find directions to the trailhead.

Marin Headlands Beaches and Points of Interest

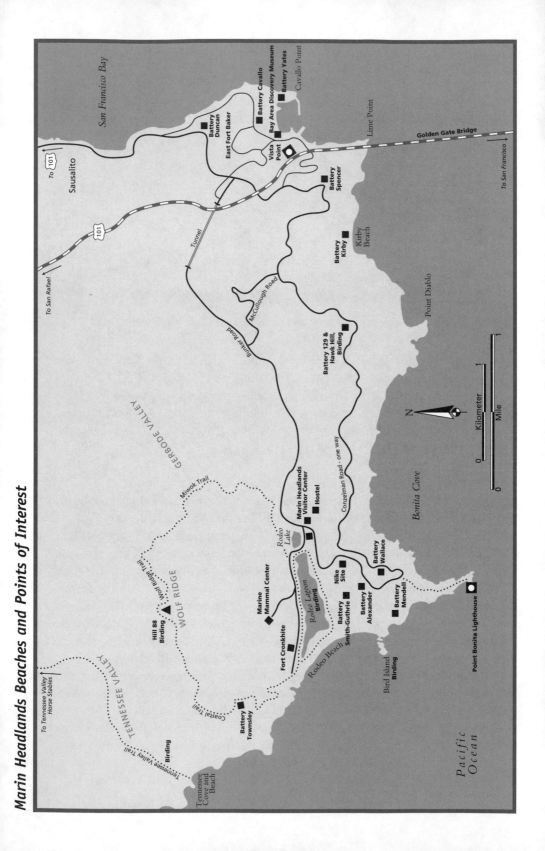

Sites with historical significance abound in the Marin Headlands. The stories of the military installations alone, some of which date back to the Civil War, is enough to engage both armchair historians and serious students of the history of coastal defenses around the San Francisco Bay.

But the headlands also host a wealth of sites with historical and cultural significance outside the military sphere, including the Point Bonita Lighthouse, the Bay Area Discovery Museum, and a youth hostel. The Marine Mammal Center is the centerpiece of the natural history sites in the headlands, but bird-watching sites vie for top billing in that category.

Historic and Cultural Sites

Point Bonita Lighthouse

White and red and a vast glittering blue. At the edge of the continent, where the headlands drop into the Pacific, the white walls and red roofs of the Point Bonita Lighthouse stand sentinel above the rolling waves of the Pacific—mute witness to the treacherous currents and unpredictable tides that have sent an armada to deep green graves.

The lighthouse, built in the middle of the nineteenth century, is an outpost of peacetime on a landscape otherwise built up with houses of war. The trail that leads down to the lighthouse begins on a bluff dotted with bunkers that, in World War II, were used by soldiers watching for foreign invaders. The hard architecture of Battery Mendell hulks in the hillside just to the north, and radio towers used by the marines rise from the lighthouse's original site. But at land's end, the lighthouse, relocated to the very edge of the continent in 1876, reflects only humankind's endless battle to assuage the dangers wrought by nature.

Originally built to help guide the flood of ships that poured through the Golden Gate during the gold rush, the lighthouse still operates, swinging seaward a powerful beacon created by 125 leaded prisms when the fog rolls in. The tankers, cargo ships, tugboats, tour boats, and pleasure craft that now share the complex waters at the mouth of San Francisco Bay glide over the wrecks of hundreds of wooden ships that went down before—and after—the light's installation in 1855.

A steep paved interpretive trail leads a 0.5 mile down to the lighthouse, which is open to the public on a limited basis (Saturday, Sunday, and Monday afternoons at the time of this writing). The trail begins on a hill of bunkers but descends swiftly into a more natural world, with the steep scrubby hillsides dropping swiftly below the trail into the cove below, and crumbling cliffs rising above.

The trail swings south at a sharp curve at about 0.1 mile, crosses a small nameless fault line, and passes beneath the radar towers. Monterey pines sink into the gulch that drops below the trail. The path descends to a bridge that spans a break in the rock wall that has sheltered the trail on its west side. To the right (west) you can look out onto the rocky coastline; on the left (east) you look down on the remnants of

The Point Bonita Lighthouse illuminates the dangerous coastline on the north side of the Golden Gate.

the Point Bonita Lifesaving Station; an interpretive sign extrapolates on the work of the"surfmen" who worked out of the station.

Orange lichen stains the rocks around the portal of a 125-foot-long tunnel carved by Chinese immigrants in 1877. Before the tunnel was built, a narrow walkway led around the east side of the sheer rock face. Beyond the tunnel, the trail crosses another gap, where the lighthouse comes into view. Pass an out-building and cross a smaller bridge before you arrive at the broad viewpoint from which you launch onto the whitewashed suspension bridge that will bring you across a final gap to the lighthouse itself.

Before you cross the bridge (or after, depending on your agenda), check out the views of the distant Golden Gate Bridge to the east, and the arch carved into of the pillow basalt to the left (south) of the suspension bridge. Views north up the rugged coast are also spectacular, and if the weather is clear, you'll have wonderful views west of the Farallon Islands.

Park rangers limit the number of people on the suspension bridge to five. The bridge is no place for those afraid of heights, slung as it is over jagged rocks and a thrashing surf, but is a great thrill for those with no fear, shimmying in the wind and under the weight of those treading its narrow walkway.

The trail and the continent end at the squat lighthouse. More light than house, the cylindrical building holds a gift shop and interpretive displays, including a description of the Fresnel lens that's been in use since 1855. Views are much the same as those at the viewpoint on the east end of the suspension bridge.

Once you've enjoyed the lighthouse, return as you came.

Interpretive signs line the path, and on weekends docents lead interpretive hikes to the lighthouse. There is limited parking at the trailhead, with more available at Battery Mendell, 0.1 mile west on Field Road. A portable toilet is located about 50 yards up the trail.

To reach the lighthouse from the Marin Headlands Visitor Center, follow Field Road for 0.6 mile to the signed trailhead on the left (southwest).

East Fort Baker

Occupying most of the bayfront property at the headlands on the east side of the Golden Gate, East Fort Baker is, most notably, home to the Bay Area Discovery Museum. But the fort, yet another facet of the comprehensive militarization of the Golden Gate that began before the Civil War, also encompasses Batteries Cavallo and Yates, the Presidio Yacht Club on Horseshoe Bay, barracks and a broad parade ground, a Coast Guard station, and a fishing pier. The Bay Trail—actually, more a series of linked roads and paths—wanders through some of these sites, offering glimpses into both Fort Baker's past and present.

The army acquired more than 300 acres at the strategic site in the mid-1800s, and planned to build a fort here, the last link in a triplex of defensive structures that included Fort Point and on the fort on Alcatraz Island. The fort was never completed: Instead, earthwork batteries were constructed at the site, of which the fenced-off Battery Cavallo is among the best preserved in the Bay Area. Battery Yates, which overlooks Horseshoe Bay, is one of a generation of fortifications built around the turn of the twentieth century. The fine white houses that frame the parade ground—permanent housing for soldiers stationed at the fort—date back to the same era.

Hardly a surprise, then, that East Fort Baker was added to the National Register of Historic Places in 1973. It is also a work in progress for the GGNRA: As this guide went to press, plans were afoot to expand the cultural and natural resources at the fort, including establishment of a conference and retreat center that would incorporate the historic buildings surrounding the parade ground.

To reach East Fort Baker and the Bay Area Discovery Museum from San Francisco and points south, cross the Golden Gate Bridge into Marin County and take the Alexander Avenue exit. Follow Alexander Avenue north for 0.2 mile, and turn left (west) onto Bunker Road. A quick switchback puts you on Bunker Road traveling east; follow the road for 0.6 mile to McReynolds Road. Turn right onto McReynolds Road, and follow it for 0.1 mile to Murray Circle. Turn left onto Murray Circle, and go 0.2 mile to the parking area for the Discovery Museum.

From the north, follow U.S. Highway 101 south to the Sausalito exit (the last exit before you get on the Golden Gate Bridge). Go right (northeast) on the frontage road, which leads 0.2 mile, passing under the freeway, to Alexander Avenue. Turn left (north) onto Alexander Avenue for 0.1 mile, then quickly left again, heading west on Bunker Road. Round the switchback to take Bunker Road east, and follow the directions above to Fort Baker and the museum.

Bay Area Discovery Museum

For anyone whose age has yet to reach the double digits, the Bay Area Discovery Museum is the shining star of the Golden Gate National Recreation Area.

Located in East Fort Baker, the museum is a favorite with the wee ones and with parents looking for a wholesome and memorable pastime for their children. It's a place where kids can watch water move through a see-through toilet tank, winch foam blocks from ground floor to second story in a mock construction zone, crawl through an "underwater" tunnel, and explore so much more.

The Bay Area Discovery Museum is structured for the entertainment and education of children ten and younger—and their families, of course. It is open Tuesday through Friday from 9:00 A.M. to 4:00 P.M., and from 10:00 A.M. to 5:00 P.M. on Saturday and Sunday. The museum is closed on Monday, as well as on Easter, Labor Day, the Fourth of July, Thanksgiving, Christmas, and New Year's Day. A $7.00 fee is levied for adults and children, with children under age one admitted free. The second Saturday of every month is free to all comers between 1:00 and 4:00 P.M.

The Discovery Museum's address is Fort Baker, 557 McReynolds Road, Sausalito, CA 94965. Recorded information is available by calling (415) 487–4398; you can call (415) 289–7266 to request an informational brochure. The Web site is www.badm.org.

Fort and Battery Tour

The forts and batteries erected during more than 200 years of military occupation at the Marin Headlands are inescapable. Some are well kept and obviously vital, housing international travelers, artists, and administrative offices. The rest are abandoned, in varying state of disrepair, melancholy artifacts of the fears and ingenuity of previous generations. They run the gamut from heavy bunkers burrowed into hillsides to sprawling structures whose gun emplacements offer the best views in the area to marks on a map, with no visible sign left that they ever existed.

The tour described below, which can be taken by car or by bicycle, with short, optional walks to and around the batteries and fort complexes themselves, covers the western portion of the headlands. East Fort Baker, on the inside of the Golden Gate, is described separately above.

Begin the tour at the foot of Conzelman Road near the northern entrance to the Golden Gate. To reach this point from U.S. Highway 101 southbound, take the Sausalito/Golden Gate National Recreation Area exit (the last exit before you drive onto the Golden Gate Bridge). At the stop sign, turn left, then quickly right onto Conzelman Road. From US 101 northbound, take the Alexander Avenue exit. Go less than 0.1 mile on the exit ramp, and turn left (the first left turn you can make). Go 0.2 mile, passing under the freeway via a tunnel, to Conzelman Road. Mileages, listed in parentheses after the battery name, begin at this point.

Fort Baker, established in the 1850s, encompasses rolling, scrub-covered acreage both inside and outside the Golden Gate at the north end of the Golden Gate Bridge. It's eastern reaches, described previously, include the historic structures and parade ground off Horseshoe Cove, with its adjacent batteries, Yates (completed in 1905), Cavallo (a Civil War earthworks), and Duncan (also early 1900s). Batteries on the west side of the Golden Gate are described below.

Battery Spencer (0.3): Battery Spencer, a relic of the military buildup that took place under two secretaries of war, William Endicott and William Taft, around the turn of the twentieth century, is perched on a bluff overlooking the north tower of the Golden Gate Bridge. Completed in 1897, the two-tiered structure was outfitted with three guns. To reach the battery, you pass through the Civil War–era earthwork-and-brickwork Ridge Battery, the remnants of which barricade the short trail.

Batteries dating back to the Civil War, the Endicott-Taft era, and World War II lie below Conzelman Road, along the trail to Kirby Cove and on Kirby Beach itself. A trail approximately 1 mile long leads down to these fortifications.

Fort Barry abuts Fort Baker to the west, and includes the bulk of the batteries and installations in the headlands. The nerve center of the park, the Marin Headlands Visitor Center, is housed in the Fort Barry's former chapel, while the Headlands Center for the Arts, the Marin Headlands Youth Hostel, and administrative offices are housed in old barracks nestled into the hills on the south side of Rodeo Valley.

Battery 129 (1.8 miles): The never-completed gun emplacements at Battery 129 were part of a system of seacoast fortifications built during World War II and designed to withstand bombardment from the air. The guns were protected within heavy concrete casemates, then topped with up to 20 feet of earth, according to park documents. Two tunnels lead from Conzelman Road to the casemates, which offer stunning vistas of the Rodeo Valley and the Pacific beyond. The top of the battery is known as Hawk Hill; volunteers gather here each fall to observe the thousands of raptors that migrate through the headlands. Though never completed, Battery 129 holds the dubious distinction of being the most expensive coastal fortification ever built in the United States.

Battery Rathbone-McIndoe (3.0): Another product of the Endicott-Taft era, Battery Rathbone-McIndoe looks down on the strait leading through the Golden Gate. Built in 1905 and decommissioned in 1948, four guns were mounted on platforms separated by concrete shelters and storage areas. During World War II, its guns were intended to protect the minefields that were laid outside the Golden Gate. Use trails link the gun emplacements, and the park service has, thoughtfully, placed a bench at the eastern end of the battery, where views of the Golden Gate Bridge are best.

Battery Wallace (3.8): This battery dates back to World War II, with two tunnels leading through the tree-covered earthworks to the casemated gun mounts. Only one of those tunnels is open now, shaded by stands of Monterey pine and bordered on the east by a picnic area with lovely views of the Golden Gate Bridge. Guns mounted at Battery Wallace when it first was completed, in 1919, could target ships 17 miles out to sea. The original gun sites were casemated in 1942; by 1948 it was considered obsolete and the guns were removed.

Conzelman Road ends at Field Road at 4.1 miles. The following batteries lie along Field Road, and are listed from west to east.

Battery Mendell (0.0): Views from the gun emplacements at Battery Mendell, constructed in 1905, are uninterrupted: On a clear day, you (or a soldier) can see miles out into the Pacific. This battery was outfitted with disappearing guns (an example of which remains at Battery Chamberlin off Baker Beach in the Presidio). Its amphitheaterlike gun platforms allowed for the recoil of the disappearing gun, which could then be reloaded by artillerymen protected from enemy fire by concrete barricades buttressed by earthworks. Though defaced with graffiti, its setting, views, and architecture, with covered walkways linking the gun platforms, set Battery Mendell apart.

Batteries Alexander, Smith-Guthrie, and O'Rorke (0.3): These three batteries all were constructed during the Endicott-Taft period, and all were ready for service in 1905. From the parking lot, you'd never know Battery Alexander existed; it lies behind a hillock overgrown with grass, brush, and eucalyptus. Armed with eight mortars (muzzleloading cannon), Battery Alexander, along

Fort Cronkhite and Rodeo Cove lie below and northeast of Battery Mendell.

with its neighbor, Battery Smith-Guthrie, remained in service until 1948. Battery O'Rorke, the farthest north in this triplex of fortifications and outfitted with four guns, was the first to be abandoned, in 1943. Battery Smith-Guthrie also boasted four guns.

A short loop trail leads around the knoll upon which these batteries perch. It is described in detail in the Marin Headlands Trails chapter.

Battery Bravo (0.9): Also known as SF-88, this Nike missile site is open to the public on a limited basis and is described in detail below.

Field Road descends from Battery Bravo, past the Marin Headlands Visitor Center, to its intersection with Bunker Road at 1.3 miles. To reach Fort Cronkhite and its batteries, turn left (west) on Bunker Road, and drive 0.9 mile, past the intersection of Mitchell and Old Bunker Road, to the parking area for Fort Cronkhite and Rodeo Beach.

Overlooking Rodeo Beach and Rodeo Lagoon, **Fort Cronkhite,** established in 1937 on the site of the former Tennessee Point Military Reservation, was a "mobilization barracks" in the 1940s, according to park documents. The orderly barracks are very well preserved, and house a number of park offices as well as the Headlands Institute, an organization that works in concert with the National Park Service to provide environmental education programs at the headlands.

Another relic of the Cold War, **Nike missile launch site SF-87** has been outfitted with tanks and pens for marine mammals being rehabilitated through the Marine Mammal Center. The center is located uphill from the barracks on Old Bunker Road.

Both **Battery Townsley** and the radar installations for Nike missile site SF-88 are perched on Wolf Ridge, high above the Fort Cronkhite barracks. Townsley, with its casemated gun emplacements trained on the Pacific, dates back to World War II; the lonely radar site was erected during the Cold War. A visit to these sites involves a rather long, steep hike on the Coastal Trail, which begins at the west end of the parking lot at Rodeo Beach. The trail is detailed in the Marin Headlands Trails chapter.

Also of note is the **balloon hangar,** built in 1919 to house hot-air balloons used by the military to survey the coast. Now serving as the indoor arena for the Presidio Riding Club, this vast structure is located about a 0.5 mile east of the Marin Headlands Visitor Center on the south side of Bunker Road.

Nike Missile Site

In their last incarnation, the fortifications at the Marin Headlands were outfitted for the Cold War. At the Nike Missile Site, one of eleven such sites in the Bay Area, artifacts of the nuclear age are preserved and, more spectacularly, on display. What once was secret is now in the open, the simplicities and intricacies of a devastating technology set forth with respect and care.

These displays—of the missiles themselves (now inert), the underground storage magazine where they were kept at the ready, the radar vans—are fascinating and thrilling, even for someone who is uneasy in the presence of a gun made of Lego, like myself. In the building once used for assembly and testing, a Nike missile's architecture is laid open, from the vacuum tubes in its computerized guidance system to the linkages in its belly. A short elevator ride at the underground magazine, one hand on a rail that is fixed to the armor of a missile, drops you into a vault where five more missiles are stored, ready to be moved by hand into position for a deployment that, thankfully, never came.

Docents, many of whom were involved in the missile program when it was active, have restored the area, and now conduct tours of the site—indeed, you can only visit the fenced-off underground magazine when accompanied by a docent or ranger. These experts are a wealth of information on Nike technology, including the missile's formidable range, how it achieved its supersonic speed, and the destructive capabilities of its warheads, both nuclear and conventional, among other things.

The Nike Missile Site is open Wednesday through Friday from 12:30 P.M. to 3:30 P.M., and on the first Sunday of each month from 12:30 P.M. to 3:30 P.M. The site is located on Field Road, about 0.3 mile west of the Marin Headlands Visitor Center. For more information, call (415) 331–1453, or visit the Web site at www.nikemissile.org.

Natural History Sites

Marine Mammal Center

Situated on an old Nike missile site overlooking the Rodeo Lagoon, the Marine Mammal Center, a nonprofit hospital for injured, orphaned, or ill marine mammals, provides sanctuary for hundreds of animals in need every year. The patients may change—the goal, of course, is to heal the wounds or cure the sickness, then return the animal to its ocean home—but the needs remain urgent.

The most evident and pressing facet of the Marine Mammal Center's work is rehabilitation. Outdoor pens at the headlands facility allow visitors to observe some of the seals, sea lions, and otters currently undergoing treatment, as well as for the patients to observe the visitors. Sometimes noisy and engaging, sometimes quietly resting, the plight of the soft-eyed animals recuperating in the pens can't help but touch those looking in on them, and inspire more than 800 volunteers to help out at the center.

Other marine mammals, including dolphins and whales, also receive aid here, and some are treated where they are found—the center has rescued creatures from a lengthy stretch of California coast, from Mendocino in the north to San Luis Obispo in the south. The numbers are astonishing: More than 9,000 animals have been rescued since the center was established in 1975, with between 600 and 800 animals receiving aid each year.

But the mission doesn't end with caring for animals in need. The center also studies the sick and injured, hoping to further an understanding of the diseases and environmental issues that affect their well-being. Educational programs provide the opportunity for visitors to learn about the natural and human-made dangers faced by these fascinating creatures, and include informational and interpretive displays at the headlands site and guided educational programs for visitors and schoolchildren.

To reach the Marine Mammal Center from the Marin Headlands Visitor Center, follow Bunker Road west for 0.4 mile to its intersection with Mitchell Road. Turn right (northwest) onto Old Bunker Road for 0.2 mile to the Marine Mammal Center driveway. Park alongside the 0.1-mile-long access drive. The center, which also includes a visitor center and gift shop, is open every day from 10:00 A.M. to 4:00 P.M., except for Thanksgiving Day, Christmas Day, and New Year's Day. The telephone number is (415) 289–SEAL (7325); this is also the rescue hot line, if you need to report a stranded marine mammal. The Web site is www.marinemammalcenter.org.

Birding Sites

A huge number of birds flock to the Marin Headlands during the year, some to rest, some to nest, some to take up permanent residence, and some simply to fly over. Seabirds, shorebirds, songbirds: They are all here at one time or another. Egrets wading in the shallows of Rodeo Lagoon in the heat of July. Gulls waddling along Rodeo Beach looking for castoffs from picnics. Cormorants crowding the guano-capped crown of Bird Island. Pelicans swooping over Kirby Beach under a glowering fog bank. Warblers and wrentits and sparrows and towhees filling the scrub with birdsong.

But it is the birds of prey—the falcons, harriers, ospreys, kites, and turkey vultures—that bring out the big crowds. And the hawks, of course—red-tailed hawks and red-shouldered hawks, Cooper's hawks and sharp-shinned hawks, all using the Pacific Flyway to migrate from winter to summer feeding and breeding grounds, and back again.

Some of those observing raptor migration, especially in September and October, are members of Golden Gate Raptor Observatory (GGRO), an organization that uses a volunteer force of 250 to observe the fall raptor migration. On weekends during the height of the migration, GGRO offer educational programs on Hawk Hill, which is the hub of raptor migration observations in the headlands. For more information on the GGRO, call (415) 331–0730 or visit the Web site at ggro.org.

Of course, Hawk Hill is not the only birding hot spot. Rodeo Lagoon and Tennessee Valley also offer plenty of opportunities to view a variety of species, including brown pelicans and a variety of wintering ducks. Bird Island, at the southern boundary of South Rodeo Beach, is another avian haven. Directions to all these locations are provided in the Marin Headlands Trails chapter.

Muir Woods National Monument

Muir Woods National Monument bears well the legacy of its namesake, famed naturalist and wilderness advocate John Muir. The park protects a stunningly beautiful pocket of old-growth redwood trees nestled in a steep canyon at the foot of Mount Tamalpais. These ancient trees, blessedly, escaped the logging frenzy that decimated redwood forests in the North Bay in the 1800s, spared by virtue of their inaccessibility—a seclusion that now is more valuable than the lumber that might have been harvested here ever would have been.

To reach the trailhead for the three trails described in this chapter from U.S. Highway 101 traveling either northbound or southbound, take the Stinson Beach/California Highway 1 exit. Follow the frontage road west to the stoplight at CA 1 (also known as the Shoreline Highway). Go west on the highway, which winds through the southernmost reaches of Mill Valley to another stoplight at Tamalpais Junction, the intersection of CA 1 and Almonte; this intersection is about 0.5 mile from the arterial at the freeway. Turn left (west), staying on the Shoreline Highway. The road winds through residential areas for 2.7 miles to its intersection with the Panoramic Highway. CA 1/Shoreline Highway continues straight (west) to Stinson Beach and Muir Beach; make a sharp right (north) turn onto the Panoramic Highway. Climb the Panoramic Highway for 0.8 mile to its intersection with Muir Woods Road at Four Corners (large signs indicate destinations here). Turn left (west) onto Muir Woods Road, dropping steeply to the parking area at 1.5 miles.

The monument boasts two huge paved parking lots, but on busy weekends and summer days you should be prepared to hunt for a spot. Rest room facilities, a visitor center, a cafe, and a gift shop are located near the trailhead and entry kiosk. A small fee is levied.

The three routes described here offer access to an extensive network of trails on Mount Tamalpais and in the watershed of the Marin Municipal Water District that begs for further exploration.

For information about Muir Woods National Monument, call (415) 388–2595, or visit the Web site at www.nps.gov/muwo.

Natural History

Redwoods thrive on moisture. In winter that's not a problem, as rainstorms regularly soak the redwood forests, like the one in Muir Woods, that line the northern California coast—the inland valleys too, for that matter. But in summer the marine influence of the Pacific becomes all-important to the health of these grand trees, for they are nurtured by dense fog that sweeps in off the ocean almost every day. The fog shrouds them in a cooling mist that condenses on the leaves and boughs, then falls like rain onto the forest floor.

Nourished by the fog and hardy by nature, the trees in Muir Woods reach heights of more than 240 feet, and measure as much as 12 feet in diameter. Though their cousins, the giant sequoias, can lay claim to the title of the largest living things on earth, the coast redwoods grow taller, with the tallest measured at nearly 370 feet.

While redwoods are clearly the main attraction in Muir Woods, the forest supports a variety of other flora and fauna. The undergrowth of the redwood forest includes several varieties of fern, including the impressive sword fern, as well as huckleberries, azaleas, miner's lettuce, and cow parsnip. Alders, a staple of riparian habitats, grow along the shores of Redwood Creek, and other trees, including the fragrant bay laurel, the flowering buckeye, the big-leaf maple, and the hazelnut, also contribute to the abiding shade on the canyon floor. Wildflowers bloom fitfully in that shade, including the yellow-flowered redwood violet and the broad-leafed trillium.

Wildlife within the monument includes deer, chipmunks, squirrels, raccoons, foxes, bobcats, skunks, and wood rats. Bird life ranges from the ubiquitous and raucous Steller's jay, a wild variety of songbirds including

Hikers pass through a patch of sunlight on the Ben Johnson Trail in Muir Woods.

towhees, juncos, sparrows, and warblers, and the rare and embattled northern spotted owl. Ladybugs gather in masses within the forest in summer. And in recent winters, coho salmon have returned to spawn in Redwood Creek, a welcome return of a threatened species.

Cultural History

Muir Woods was the gift of Congressman William Kent, a wealthy Marin County resident who aspired to the ideals of conservationist John Muir. The legacy of this remarkable man includes not only Muir Woods but also neighboring Mount Tamalpais State Park and portions of the mountain's watershed. Kent also authored the bill that established the National Park Service in 1916.

Kent and his wife purchased the land that would become the national monument in 1906, planning to develop it as a resort. Those plans were threatened by a water company that wanted to dam the creek and bury the old-growth redwoods under a reservoir. To protect the redwoods, Kent donated the 295 acres he'd purchased for $45,000 to the federal government, and in 1908 President Theodore Roosevelt declared the donation a national monument.

Later, another Roosevelt would be recognized beneath the canopy of Muir Woods. Franklin Delano Roosevelt died before the first conference of the newly chartered United Nations in 1945, but on May 19 of that year, delegates from the UN gathered in Muir Woods to dedicate a plaque honoring his memory.

Muir Woods Trails

People really do hug trees. I've seen them. On my last stroll along the nature trail in Muir Woods, I watched a middle-age man, dark skinned and dark haired, wearing a red button-down shirt and khaki slacks, spread his arms wide around a mighty redwood, grab a ripple of bark in each hand, and gaze upward in awe. He was hugging a tree of such girth that he would have had to be a giant himself to encircle it. Hugging a tree, and as oblivious to the manifold implications of his act as passersby, also enchanted by the green spell of the forest, were to him. Some of them too, at some point along the interpretive trail that crisscrosses the forest floor, might lose their inhibitions, and, instead of simply touching the rough bark with fingertips or pressing their backs against a trunk for a picture, hug a tree. Hiking any of the three trails desscribed below offers you a chance to get up close and personal with the redwood and its environs. Hugging a tree, of course, is optional.

Interpretive Nature Loop

HIGHLIGHTS: From the gargantuan (old-growth coast redwoods stretching to the heavens) to the minuscule (tiny ladybugs that gather in the forest in October in preparation for mating), this path through the forest of Muir Woods provides sanctuary.

TYPE OF JOURNEY: Lollipop loop.

TOTAL DISTANCE: 2 miles.

DIFFICULTY: Very easy.

PERMITTED USES: Hiking.

MAPS: USGS San Rafael; Muir Woods National Monument Map (National Park Service); Muir Woods Map and Guide to Trails, Plants and Wildlife (Golden Gate National Parks Association); A Rambler's Guide to the Trails of Mt. Tamalpais and the Marin Headlands (The Olmsted Bros. Map Co.); TOPO! San Francisco Bay Area, Wine Country, and Big Sur.

SPECIAL CONSIDERATIONS: No pets are permitted. This is a National Park Service fee area. The paved path is wheelchair and stroller acces-

Interpretive Nature Loop, Interpretive and Hillside Trail Loop

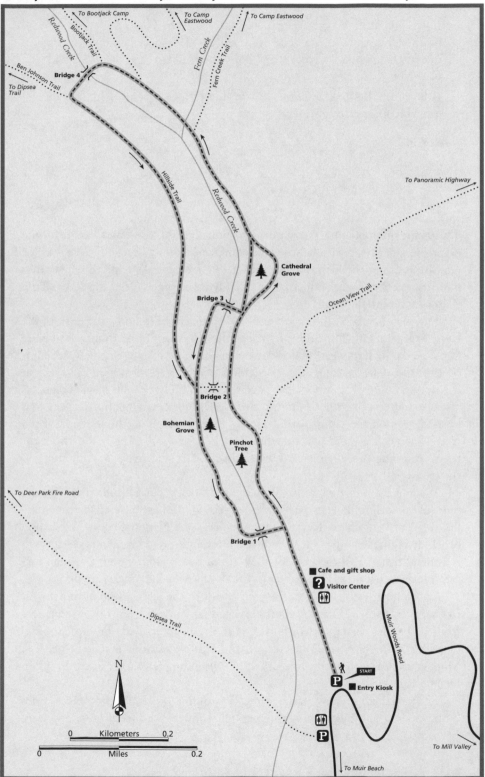

sible. The Muir Woods Map and Guide to Trails, Plants and Wildlife, produced by the Golden Gate National Parks Association, includes an interpretive guide keyed to stops along the trail between Bridge 2 and Cathedral Grove.

FINDING THE TRAILHEAD: Directions to the trailhead are presented in the introduction to this chapter.

KEY POINTS:

0.0 Trailhead.

0.5 Reach Cathedral Grove.

1.0 Arrive at Bridge 4.

This is the quintessential route through Muir Woods, winding through all the big groves, outfitted with benches for contemplation and interpretive signs for education. It's invariably crowded, especially on weekends and during summer months, but the magic of the trees invariably renders the forest hushed and the visitors reverential.

The path begins at the visitor center, leading past, in quick succession, the Kent Tree, the gift shop and cafe (off to the right), and rest rooms. Redwood Creek is on the left (west) side of the trail. The trail forks at Bridge 1, which is on the left (west), forming a loop. Stay on the right (east) side of the creek at the outset; you will return via the paved path on the west side of the creek.

The route is lined with interpretive signs, benches, and short fences that keep visitors on the paved path. Pass the Pinchot Tree on the left side of the trail at about 0.2 mile; beyond, the Ocean View Trail takes off to the right (east), climbing the steep face of the Redwood Creek canyon. Stay straight on the paved path.

At about 0.3 mile pass Bridge 2 on the left (west). The Hillside Trail (see the next hike description) terminates here. Stay straight on the paved path; the interpretive signs begin here. Keyed to the Golden Gate National Parks Association brochure available for a fee at the visitor center, interpretation covers old-growth redwoods, fish in Redwood Creek, the roles of water and fog on the ancient forest, human impacts, and the nature of the flora and fauna of the canyon.

At Bridge 3, again, stay on the paved trail to the right, heading northwest to Cathedral Grove. The trail splits here, so that you can enjoy the grand giants from both sides. Interpretive signs discuss the history of the monument, and plaques commemorate the meeting of the United Nations that took place at Muir Woods, as well as the memory of UN founding father President Franklin Delano Roosevelt.

The pavement gives way to boardwalk, still lined with benches. Here, trees both standing and fallen show the scars of wildfire; the interpretive brochure describes how fire is beneficial to the redwood forest.

The boardwalk ends near the intersection of the interpretive trail with the Fern Creek Trail at 0.8 mile. Fern Creek breaks off to the right (north) as the nature trail curves westward. Again, stay on the paved route, which remains creekside. The crowds thin beyond the Cathedral Grove, rendering the forest even more still than it was previously.

The trail to Camp Alice Eastwood branches off to the right (north) at about 0.9 mile, and at the 1-mile mark, you reach the end of the paved route at Bridge 4. If you cross the bridge, you gain access to the Ben Johnson Trail and the Hillside Trail (see subsequent hike descriptions); if you stay straight, you'll enter Mount Tamalpais State Park on the Bootjack Trail. To complete the interpretive route, however, this is the turnaround point.

Retrace your steps to Bridge 3, and go right (west), crossing the bridge to the west side of Redwood Creek. Stay right (west) until you reach Bridge 1 at the visitor center, passing through, most notably, the Bohemian Grove just south of Bridge 2. Here, a tree hollowed by fire and open to brief splashes of sunshine is the perfect frame for a pictures. You'll also pass the Bicentennial Tree, which began life at about the time of the American Revolution.

Bridge 1, and the end of the line, is at the 2-mile mark. Cross the bridge and turn right (south) to reach the visitor center and the parking area.

Interpretive and Hillside Trail Loop

See map on page 243

HIGHLIGHTS: Break away from the route more traveled by—and get a topside view of Redwood Creek and the groves that cluster along its banks—by adding the Hillside Trail to your Muir Woods tour.

TYPE OF JOURNEY: Loop.

TOTAL DISTANCE: 2 miles.

DIFFICULTY: Easy.

PERMITTED USES: Hiking.

MAPS: USGS San Rafael; Muir Woods National Monument Map (National Park Service); Muir Woods Map and Guide to Trails, Plants and Wildlife (Golden Gate National Parks Association); A Rambler's Guide to the Trails of Mt. Tamalpais and the Marin Headlands (The Olmsted Bros. Map Co.); TOPO! San Francisco Bay Area, Wine Country, and Big Sur.

SPECIAL CONSIDERATIONS: No pets are permitted. This is a National Park Service fee area. The paved section of the route is wheelchair and stroller accessible. The Muir Woods Map and Guide to Trails, Plants and Wildlife, produced by the Golden Gate National Parks Association, includes an interpretive guide keyed to stops along the nature trail between Bridge 2 and Cathedral Grove.

FINDING THE TRAILHEAD: Directions to the trailhead are presented in the introduction to this chapter.

KEY POINTS:

0.0 Trailhead.

0.5 Reach Cathedral Grove.

1.1 Cross Bridge 4 and climb stairs to the Hillside Trail.

1.7 Return to Bridge 2 and the end of the Hillside Trail.

If you'd like to sample a more rustic route through Muir Woods without climbing one of the steep paths that switchback up the canyon walls, venture onto the Hillside Trail. Etched into the fern and sorrel on the east-facing slope of the canyon, this unpaved singletrack sees less traffic than the interpretive path and allows you to gaze through the forest as opposed to up at it. Some words of caution: Though the trail is easy, it's also rough, and not for the sandal-footed. It's also not a "gawk and walk" trail; please stop walking if you want to look up into the canopy.

Begin on the Interpretive Nature Trail, described in detail previously. In short, this paved path begins at the visitor center, quickly passing the Kent Tree, the gift shop and cafe, and rest rooms. The trail forks at Bridge 1, which is on the left (west), forming a loop. Stay on the right (east) side of the creek; you will return via the paved path on the west side of the creek.

The trail, which traces the bed of Redwood Creek and is outfitted with benches, interpretive signs, and short fences that keep hikers on track, leads past the Pinchot Tree at about 0.2 mile. The Ocean View Trail breaks right (east), and beyond, at about 0.3 mile, Bridge 2 crosses Redwood Creek on the left (west). The Hillside Trail ends or begins here, depending on whether you chose to follow the loop portion of the route in a clockwise or counterclockwise direction. It's described here counterclockwise, but either works.

Remain on the paved nature trail; signs keyed to the Golden Gate National Parks Association interpretive brochure begins at this point. Continue to Cathedral Grove, where the trail splits and rejoins. A boardwalk, which begins at Cathedral Grove, ends near the Fern Creek Trail intersection at 0.8 mile. Again, stay on the paved route, passing the trail to Camp Alice Eastwood on the right (north) at about 0.9 mile.

At the 1-mile mark, you reach the end of the nature trail at Bridge 4. Cross the bridge to reach the Ben Johnson Trail and the Hillside Trail. If you stay straight, you can follow the Bootjack Trail into Mount Tamalpais State Park.

A short flight of stairs leads to the Hillside Trail, which branches left (south). The Ben Johnson Trail, described next, begins its climb on the right (northwest). A portal of trees welcomes you to the trail.

The narrow singletrack traverses the hillside, then switchbacks into a gully, crossing a bridge and passing a bench. The tributary stream is dry by late summer, but runs clear and vigorous in winter and spring. Out of the gully, you can look down (left) onto the nature trail below, as voices waft up through the redwoods that cluster along the Hillside Trail's edge.

At about 1.3 miles the trail reaches a second footbridge. A rustic staircase leads up and over the roots of a fallen tree. Beyond, the trail begins a gentle descent. Traverse a boardwalk, from which you can see Bridge 3 below.

Broad dirt and timber terraces lead down to the final staircase, which drops you to Bridge 2 at 1.7 miles. Follow either fork of the paved route back to the trailhead, though I recommend that you stay on the west side of Redwood Creek so you can enjoy the Bohemian Grove and Bicentennial Tree on the return.

Ben Johnson Trail to the Dipsea Trail

HIGHLIGHTS: Linking the deep forest of Muir Woods with ocean views and rolling meadows, the Ben Johnson Trail is a spectacular challenge for the energetic hiker.

TYPE OF JOURNEY: Loop.

TOTAL DISTANCE: 4 miles.

DIFFICULTY: Difficult.

PERMITTED USES: Hiking. Horses and mountain bikes are permitted on the Deer Park Fire Road, but do not have access to this loop within the boundaries of the national monument.

MAPS: USGS San Rafael; Muir Woods National Monument Map (National Park Service); Muir Woods Map and Guide to Trails, Plants and Wildlife (Golden Gate National Parks Association); A Rambler's Guide to the Trails of Mt. Tamalpais and the Marin Headlands (The Olmsted Bros. Map Co.); TOPO! San Francisco Bay Area, Wine Country, and Big Sur.

SPECIAL CONSIDERATIONS: No pets are permitted. The Muir Woods Map and Guide to Trails, Plants and Wildlife, produced by the Golden Gate National Parks Association, includes an interpretive guide keyed to stops along the paved nature trail between Bridge 2 and Cathedral Grove.

FINDING THE TRAILHEAD: Directions to the trailhead are presented in the introduction to this chapter.

KEY POINTS:

0.0 Trailhead.

0.5 Reach Cathedral Grove.

1.0 Arrive at Bridge 4.

2.1 Reach the Dipsea Trail intersection.

2.5 Climb to the Deer Park Fire Road.

3.5 Begin the descent back into Muir Woods.

4.0 Arrive at the bridge over Redwood Creek.

The undeniable, and well-deserved, focus of Muir Woods is the coast redwood forest. But these woods are intrinsically tied to a completely different and infinitely complex ecosystem—one that stretches from the California shoreline west to China—that of the Pacific Ocean, with its cooling winds and nurturing fog.

The steep, steep Ben Johnson Trail leads up through the fog-tied woodlands to a windswept ridge overlooking the Pacific Ocean; a ridge that traces the border of the redwood forest and the grassland and shrubland that sweeps down to the coastline. From the ridge, on a clear day, you can look south over the Marin Headlands to San Francisco, and west out across the ocean to the Farallon Islands and beyond.

The route begins on the Interpretive Nature Trail, described in detail in the first hike of this section. The paved path begins at the visitor center, quickly passing the Kent Tree, the gift shop and cafe, and rest rooms. The trail forks at Bridge 1, which is on the left (west). Take either fork; the trail loop will reconnect at Bridge 3.

The trail, lined with benches, interpretive signs, and short fences that keep hikers on track, follows Redwood Creek north. If you've taken the right-hand (east) section of trail, you will pass the Pinchot Tree at about 0.2 mile, the Ocean View Trail intersection, and, at about 0.3 mile, Bridge 2. If you are on the left side, you'll pass the Bicentennial Tree and Bohemian Grove before reaching Bridge 2. The Hillside Trail, described previously, terminates here.

Continue on the paved nature trail, which is linked to an interpretive brochure produced by the Golden Gate National Parks Association between Bridge 2 and Cathedral Grove. The trail splits and rejoins in Cathedral Grove, then passes over a boardwalk that ends near the Fern Creek Trail intersection at 0.8 mile. Remain on the paved route, passing the trail to Camp Alice Eastwood on the right (north) at about 0.9 mile.

Ben Johnson Trail to the Dipsea Trail

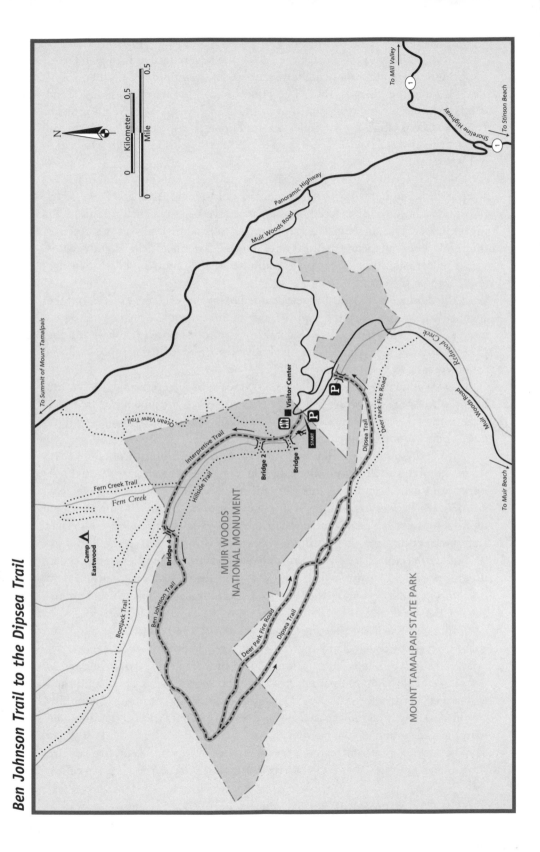

At the 1-mile mark, you reach the end of the nature trail at Bridge 4. Cross the bridge and climb a short flight of stairs to the beginning of the Ben Johnson Trail and the Hillside Trail. The Hillside Trail branches left (south), and the Ben Johnson Trail leads up to the right (northwest). A trail sign informs you that you'll climb for 1.1 miles to the Dipsea Trail, famed for its steeps, stairs, and a brutal annual race from Mill Valley to Stinson Beach, which is 4 miles distant.

Climb to a split-log bridge that spans a gully, and continue climbing. The steep path is augmented with short staircases of log and rock, and is edged by redwoods whose roots, exposed on the path, have been polished to a shine by hikers' boots. The singletrack is carved into a hillside that falls away steeply to the right. The trail incline mellows after about 0.25 mile, tracing a gully that is wet in winter and usually dry by midsummer. Cross another split-log bridge and continue the climb.

A third bridge spans another seasonal tributary; beyond, fallen trees and the scent of bay laurels spice the trail. Weave in and out of the ravines, passing a bench and working both up and westward. The forest grows brushier and the green more vibrant as you leave the redwood forest and the canopy allows more sunlight to reach the forest floor.

Cross a couple of footbridges, passing beneath a fallen redwood. Just as you begin to wonder if the climb will never end, you reach the junction with a spur trail to the Dipsea Trail at 2.1 miles. The Stapleveldt Trail continues straight (west) into Mount Tamalpais State Park.

Turn left (south) onto the spur trail, and climb a thigh-throbbing set of stairs and nine switchbacks to the ridgetop and the intersection with the Deer Park Fire Road. Turn left (southeast) onto the Deer Park Fire Road, which is also part of the Bay Area Ridge Trail. The Dipsea Trail parallels the fire road on its southwest side, and can be reached by crossing the fire road at the spur trail intersection, or at its plentiful intersections with the fire road.

Finally flat, the route passes through oaks, redwoods, and firs, with ocean breezes washing over the ridge. The fire road leads through a burn, where openings in the trees hint at the vast openness to the west, but you can't actually see the sea (yet).

Roller coaster along the ridge, then drop past the boundary of the state park, marked by a sign, and into an open area with dramatic ocean views sweeping south to Lands End and west down the steep ridges to the ocean. As you descend through alternating clearings and forest, views open south and east as well, across the bay to Angel Island, the Bay Bridge, and the distant hills of the East Bay. Fragrant coastal scrub now dominates, wildflowers mingled with the grasses and coyote brush in spring.

The Dipsea Trail runs parallel on the right (west) side of the fire road to start, then loops back and forth across the broader track. You can skip off on these short sections of the trail to vary the descent, tunneling through bowers of brush and negotiating uneven singletrack, or remain on the fire road. At about 3.5 miles both routes reenter the woods. At a trail sign the Dipsea breaks off to the left (east) and descends back into Muir Woods. Leave the fire road at this point (if you've been following it instead of the Dipsea), or you will continue southeast to the Muir Woods Road.

The Dipsea drops as earnestly as the Ben Johnson climbed, with stairs and roots demanding concentration. The undergrowth is complex, clogged with fern and poison oak, oaks and bay laurels arcing overhead. The descent is relatively short, however, dropping 0.5 mile to the Redwood Creek crossing, with the overflow parking area for the national monument just beyond. A plank footbridge spans the creek easily in summer, when the water is low, but when the creek is swollen with winter rain, the crossing is at best challenging, and at worst (though relatively infrequently) impossible. Check with the rangers to make sure passage is safe if you are traveling this route in the rainy season.

A short flight of stairs leads up to the overflow parking lot. If you've parked near the trailhead, turn left (north) on the paved path to return to the visitor center.

Presidio of San Francisco

A unique conglomerate of open spaces and historic structures, the Presidio of San Francisco occupies nearly 1,500 acres of valuable real estate on the northern tip of the San Francisco peninsula. The complex includes 870 buildings, many of which are architecturally intriguing, and approximately 800 acres of open space, including beaches, restored natural areas, and the stately Presidio Forest.

The Presidio's uniqueness extends beyond the diversity of its landscapes, however. It is managed in a one-of-a-kind partnership between the National Park Service and the Presidio Trust. The trust, a federal agency created by Congress when the Presidio was transferred by the army to the Golden Gate National Recreation Area in 1994, has a two-pronged mission: It must make the park financially self-sufficient by 2013, as well as bolster the natural and cultural resources that make it a valuable and prized asset of the national park system. To learn more about the Presidio Trust, write to P.O. Box 29052, San Francisco, CA 94129, or call (415) 561–5300. The Web site is at www.presidiotrust.gov.

Military History

The military history of the Presidio is rich and fascinating—and so well documented that it could be a book unto itself. Other writers have undertaken that task in volumes that can be picked up in visitor center bookstores; information is also available on the National Park Service's Web site. I'll whet your appetite with the summary that follows.

The Spanish established the Presidio in 1776, initiating a military presence on the site that would continue for more than 200 years. The northernmost outpost of the Spanish empire in California, the site was selected by Juan Bautista de Anza during his overland exploration of California in 1775; his lieutenant, José Joaquin Moraga, returned to build the adobe Presidio the following year.

The Mexicans took over from the Spanish in 1822, but abandoned the fort when General Mariano Vallejo moved the Mexican garrison north to Sonoma. By the time Mexico ceded California to the United States in 1848, Americans had already occupied the vacant Presidio buildings.

After gold was discovered, the Presidio's strategic location became even more important, and a period of expansion and improvement of fortifications that would last until World War II was under way. Fort Point and a sister fort on Alcatraz Island were completed by the time the Civil War began; construc-

Presidio of San Francisco

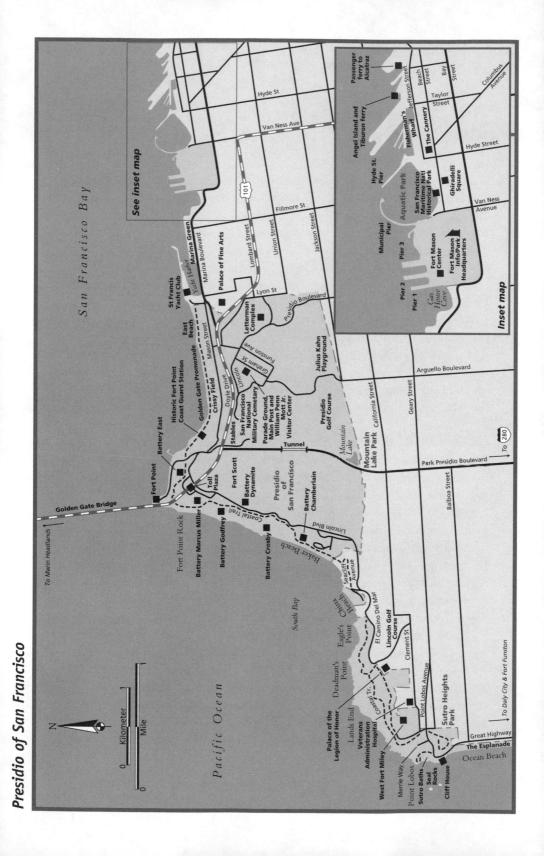

N

Kilometer
0   1
Mile
0   1

Pacific Ocean

San Francisco Bay

See inset map

Inset map

Golden Gate Bridge

To Marin Headlands

Fort Point
Battery East
Historic Fort Point Coast Guard Station
Golden Gate Promenade
Crissy Field
Stables
Battery Marcus Miller
Battery Godfrey
Fort Point Rock
Toll Plaza
Fort Scott
Battery Dynamite
Presidio of San Francisco
Battery Crosby
Battery Chamberlain
Coastal Trail
Baker Beach
Lincoln Blvd
Tunnel
Mountain Lake
Mountain Lake Park

St Francis Yacht Club
Yacht Harbor
East Beach
Palace of Fine Arts
Marina Green
Marina Boulevard
Mason Street
Doyle Drive
Lincoln
Graham St
Funston Ave
Lombard Street
Union Street
Lyon St
Letterman Complex
Presidio Boulevard
San Francisco National Military Cemetery
Parade Ground, Main Post and William Penn Mott Jr. Visitor Center
Julius Kahn Playground
Presidio Golf Course
Jackson Street

Hyde St
Van Ness Ave
Fillmore St
101

Arguello Boulevard
California Street
Geary Street
Balboa Street
Park Presidio Boulevard
To 280

South Bay

Seacliff Avenue
China Beach
Eagle's Point
Deadman's Point
El Camino Del Mar
Lincoln Golf Course
Point Lobos Avenue
Clement St
Sutro Heights Park
Lands End
Coastal Tr.
Palace of the Legion of Honor
Veterans Administration Hospital
West Fort Miley
Merrie Way
Point Lobos
Sutro Baths
Seal Rocks
Cliff House
The Esplanade
Ocean Beach
Great Highway
To Daly City & Fort Funston

Passenger ferry to Alcatraz
Angel Island and Tiburon ferry
Hyde St. Pier
Fisherman's Wharf
Jefferson Street
Beach Street
Bay Street
Taylor Street
The Cannery
Ghirardelli Square
Hyde Street
Van Ness Avenue
Columbus Avenue
Aquatic Park
San Francisco Maritime Natl Historical Park
Municipal Pier
Pier 3
Pier 2
Pier 1
Gas House Cove
Fort Mason Center
Fort Mason Info/Park Headquarters

tion of Victorian-style military housing at the Presidio began then as well, the first in a series of distinctive architectural styles that would be characteristic of each defensive era that followed.

Expansion of facilities at the Presidio was closely tied to the progression of wars fought by the United States. Following the Civil War, the Presidio troops were sent to fight in the Indian Wars of the 1870s and 1880s. In the Spanish-American War, which began in 1898, the Presidio served as a staging area for troops sent overseas. After a treaty ended the war with Spain, the United States remained in the Philippines, and troops sent to the islands to defend U.S. colonial aspirations were processed at the Presidio until 1902. The Letterman Hospital complex and the redbrick barracks that line Montgomery Street on the Main Post both date back to these years.

In the late 1800s and early 1900s, construction of coastal defense batteries intensified under the supervision of secretaries of war William Endicott and William Taft. Fort Winfield Scott was established 1912 to oversee these batteries. Meanwhile, from the Presidio, troops were sent to Mexico in search of the rebel Pancho Villa, and to the battlefields of World War I. In 1920 Crissy Field was added to the Presidio, supplementing already impressive coastal defenses. During World War II, the Presidio served as headquarters for the Western Defense Command. And during the Cold War the Presidio oversaw the Nike missile system that was put into place on military lands from the Marin Headlands south to Milagra Ridge. When more sophisticated weapons rendered Nike missiles obsolete, they also heralded the end of the era of coastal defense—and the Presidio's long history as a military post.

The Presidio was included in the boundaries of the Golden Gate National Recreation Area when the park was established in 1972, but the transfer of the property from the army to the park service wasn't completed until the fall of 1994. The core of the Presidio, excluding farther-flung outposts at Fort Mason, Fort Funston, and on Lands End, was placed under the joint jurisdiction of the National Park Service and the newly created Presidio Trust, which is charged with making the park self-sufficient by 2013. That process, the subject of much research, debate, and controversy, is still evolving, and involves proposals to lease buildings to private entities while demolishing others that are deemed to have little or no historic value.

Natural History

Prior to the mid-1880s, the landscape of the Presidio was one of marsh and coastal bluff. That changed dramatically during the late 1800s, when more than 100,000 trees—eucalyptus, Monterey cypress, Monterey pine—were planted on the post. This massive "beautification" project resulted in a majestic and orderly forest, albeit one that is not native to the area.

Indeed, the native habitats that once provided all the sustenance needed by local animals as well as the native Ohlone people exist today only in tiny pockets on the Presidio. Otherwise paradise has been paved, planted, or turned into a golf course.

The dearth of wild areas should not be unexpected in an urban park. And in those areas where the native habitats are being restored, such as the tidal marsh at Crissy Field and along Lobos Creek, visitors can see the floral species that were once common in the scrublands and dunes bordering the San Francisco Bay, like coyote brush, blackberry brambles, coffeeberry, and bush lupine. The hope is that rarer species, like the dune gilia, Presidio clarkia, and Raven's manzanita, can also flourish in rehabilitated areas within the park.

Visitor Centers and Amenities

William Penn Mott Jr. Visitor Center

The William Penn Mott Jr. Visitor Center is housed in one of five orderly red-brick barracks that front the former parade ground in the Main Post. The barracks, built in the mid-1890s, were originally designed as quarters for up to 200 men, but the simple, open architecture serves just as well as a visitor center. Inside, you'll find a gift shop and bookstore, as well as interpretive exhibits that concisely document the history of the Presidio. Park rangers and volunteers are on hand to impart information and recommend trails, sites, tours, and events that you may want to check out during your visit.

The William Penn Mott Jr. Visitor Center is in Building 102 on Montgomery Street, the fourth building from the right (second from the left) as you look west at the barracks row. It is open from 9:00 A.M. to 5:00 P.M. daily, with the exception of Thanksgiving, Christmas, and New Year's Days, when it is closed. For more information, call (415) 561–4323.

Note: As this book went to press, the visitor center was temporarily housed in the Presidio Officers Club, Building 50, on Moraga Avenue in the Main Post, while its permanent home was undergoing an earthquake retrofit. Repairs to the barracks were scheduled for completion in the spring of 2003.

Crissy Field Center

Located in a large, handsome building that once served as an army commissary and a photo lab, the Crissy Field Center is dedicated to environmental education and community outreach. Toward those ends, the center hosts a variety of programs aimed at the environmentally curious of all ages, ranging from "garbology" (the study of garbage at Crissy Field through archaeology) to an exploration of the impacts of bridges and airports on the bay ecosystem. In addition, the center holds a cafe that overlooks the restored Crissy Field marsh, a bookstore, rest rooms, an exhibit gallery, and interactive computers that provide information about Crissy Field and other features of the park.

The center is open Wednesday through Sunday from 9:00 A.M. to 5 P.M. Educational offerings are outlined on the center's expansive Web site at www.crissyfield.org, or you can call the center at (415) 561-7752.

The Warming Hut, located on the Golden Gate Promenade about 1 mile west of the Crissy Field Center, also offers visitors information, gifts, and a small cafe. It is open seven days a week from 9:00 A.M. to 5 P.M.

Gulf of the Farallones
National Marine Sanctuary Visitor Center

The Gulf of the Farallones National Marine Sanctuary includes more than 1,200 square miles of coastline and open ocean west of San Francisco Bay and the Point Reyes National Seashore. The sanctuary's visitor center, housed in the historic Coast Guard Station at Crissy Field, is microscopic by comparison—but it is packed with fascinating exhibits and information, including interpretive displays, printed information about the inhabitants of the sanctuary, and books and gifts for sale.

The Farallones Marine Sanctuary Association manages the visitor center, located at West Crissy Field in the Presidio. Limited parking is available along the western reaches of Mason Street, but however close you get by vehicle, you'll still have to travel a short section of the Golden Gate Promenade to reach the center. The visitor center is open Wednesday through Sunday from 10:00 A.M. to 4:00 P.M. Rest rooms are available. For more information, call the sanctuary association at (415) 561-6625 or visit the Web site at www.farallones.org.

Getting around the Park

Several major highways and roads run through the Presidio, as well as a web of lesser roads that offer access to various sites and trailheads. The main thoroughfare along the San Francisco Bay coastline is U.S. Highway 101, offering relatively easy access to the Golden Gate Promenade, Fort Point, and the Main Post. California Highway 1, also known as Park Presidio, bisects the park but offers no direct access. And Lincoln Boulevard skirts the coastal bluffs overlooking the Pacific Ocean, offering access to Baker and China Beach, Lobos Creek, and the Coastal Trail.

Directions to trailheads are provided with trail descriptions in the Presidio Trails chapter. Still, I advise anyone traveling in the Presidio, or any other park in the Golden Gate National Recreation Area on the San Francisco peninsula, to pick up a good street map (like a Thomas Bros. map). The Presidio has also produced an excellent map of the park, showing both trails, points of interest, and, most important, parking and access roads. These are available at any visitor center within the park. And don't forget PresidiGo, the free shuttle service offered by the Presidio Trust, which stops regularly at many of the Presidio's premier destinations.

Camping

The Presidio has one group campground, located in a grove of eucalyptus south of Fort Winfield Scott. Rob Hill Group Camp is open from April 1 to October 1, and offers two sites that can hold as many as thirty people for a fee of $50 per site per night. The camp has rest rooms, picnic tables, barbecue braziers, and a campfire ring. Water is available. For more information, call (415) 561–5444.

Impressive brick barracks line Montgomery Street in the Presidio's Main Post.

Approximately 15 miles of developed trails meander through the Presidio, with every mile varying wildly from the next, from the highly developed and extremely popular Golden Gate Promenade to the relatively remote and natural Lobos Creek Trail. The park's master plan calls for more trails to be developed over time; given the nature of the landscape upon which these new trails will ride, the variety will only increase.

Bicycles are allowed only on paved routes within the Presidio, with the exception of the Golden Gate Promenade and portions of the Bay Area Ridge Trail. A couple of the trails are not marked with trail signs; pick up a map at any of the park's visitor centers to help you stay on route.

Golden Gate Promenade

HIGHLIGHTS: The restored marsh at Crissy Field is at one end of the promenade, and the arcing supports of the Golden Gate Bridge are at the other. Views of San Francisco Bay fill the space between beautifully.

TYPE OF JOURNEY: Out-and-back.

TOTAL DISTANCE: 3.4 miles.

DIFFICULTY: Easy.

PERMITTED USES: Hiking, cycling.

MAPS: USGS San Francisco North; Golden Gate National Recreation Area Presidio of San Francisco Map; Golden Gate National Recreation Area Map; TOPO! San Francisco Bay Area, Wine Country, and Big Sur.

SPECIAL CONSIDERATIONS: This trail can be very congested, especially when the sun shines. Please be considerate of your fellow users. Pets are permitted on leash, but many dog owners allow their animals to run off-leash.

PARKING AND FACILITIES: The large East Parking Area, adjacent to the St. Francis Yacht Club, serves as the easternmost end point for the Golden Gate Promenade. The lot fills quickly on sunny weekends, in which case you may have to range farther afield for parking. There are rest rooms at the trailhead.

Golden Gate Promenade

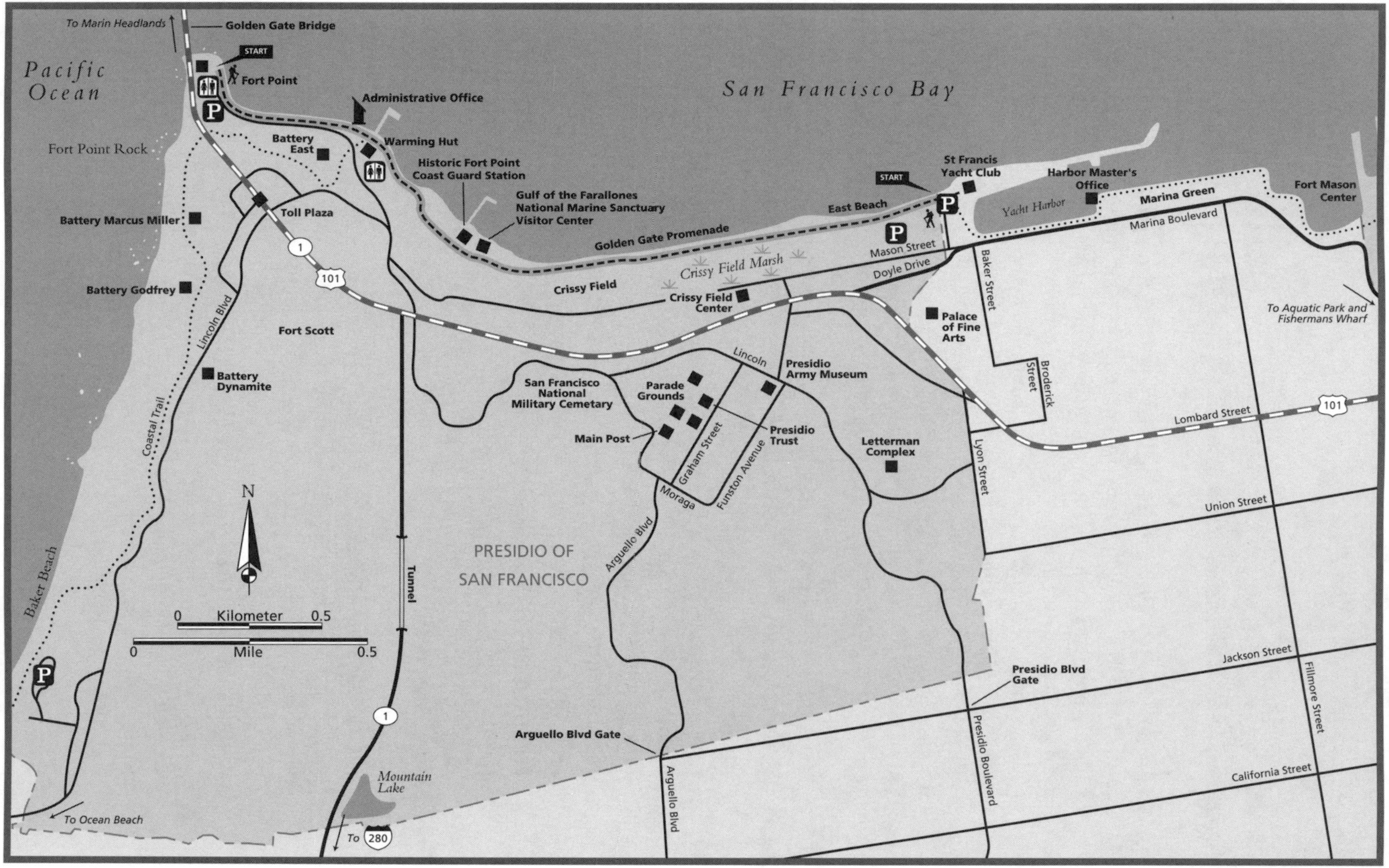

FINDING THE TRAILHEAD: The East Parking Area is off Mason Street less than 0.1 mile east of the intersection of Mason and Marina Boulevard.

KEY POINTS:

0.0 Trailhead.

0.1 Pass the trail to the Crissy Field Center at the border of the marsh.

0.6 The trail parallels the former airfield.

1.0 Pass the Gulf of the Farallones visitor center.

1.3 Arrive at the Warming Hut and Fort Point Pier.

1.7 Reach Fort Point and the end of the line.

Watching the sea mist retreat westward from San Francisco Bay is a privilege. The veil lifts slowly, revealing first the ghostly forms of sailboats hugging the shoreline, then the dark shapes of Alcatraz Island and Angel Island, and finally the graceful architecture of the Golden Gate Bridge. It doesn't matter whether you're a San Francisco native or a visitor watching the curtain rise for the first time, the scene is unforgettable.

To obtain a front-row seat for the unveiling, take a walk or bike ride along the Golden Gate Promenade. This wide, flat multiuse trail traces the bayshore from the Marina to Fort Point, and the views from its benches, beaches, and picnic grounds are unsurpassed.

The trail begins adjacent to the St. Francis Yacht Club; a small stone plaque engraved with a poem by Carl Sandburg marks the beginning of the path. The broad unpaved track heads west along the water, crowded with walkers, runners, people pushing strollers, cyclists, people in wheelchairs, people with dogs. A side trail leads left (south) to the Crissy Field Center at 0.1 mile; you can use this cutoff trail to link up with the paved path on the south side of the marsh, designated for faster travelers on bikes or in-line skates. The restored marsh area begins to the trail's left (south), marked by the first of several interpretive signs.

Cross a bridge over the marsh's outlet stream at 0.2 mile, continuing west toward the Golden Gate. Interpretive signs describe the dynamics of the marsh, and little side trails branch off to the right (north), giving access to the bayfront beach. Concrete benches have been placed along the promenade, as well as at the waterside. A cluster of Monterey cypresses shelters bayside benches at 0.4 mile.

The boardwalk leading to the Golden Gate Overlook breaks off the promenade to the right (north) at 0.6 mile, and a narrow dirt track heads left (south) onto a huge grass-covered platform—a re-creation of the historic Crissy airfield. The broad main path stays to the right (north), wedged between the field and the waterfront. East Beach, the strand that extends the length of the promenade, slowly gives way to a rockier shoreline as the trail continues westward.

The Gulf of the Farallones National Marine Sanctuary Visitor Center is on the right (northeast) side of the trail at the 1-mile mark. At 1.1 miles several paths converge with the promenade; these spurs lead into and out of the West Bluff Picnic Area, which sports tables, interpretive signs, an amphitheater of concrete risers nestled into the grass, and little hillocks that are not only interesting features of the landscape architecture but also serve as windbreaks. Stay right (bayside) on the promenade.

The Warming Hut is at 1.3 miles, along with the Fort Point Pier (aka Torpedo Wharf), which breaks off to the right (north), jutting into the bay. The wharf is often crowded with anglers—fathers and sons, husbands and wives, seated on camp stools or overturned milk crates, with one bucket full of bait and another awaiting the catch.

The Warming Hut, which is rather more than a simple "hut," is on the left (south) side of the trail, and houses a cafe and bookstore, as well as rest rooms. Informational and interpretive billboards are stationed around the building. The Coastal Trail breaks off to the left (south) on the west side of the hut, climbing stairs onto the bluff that holds Battery East.

The Warming Hut is the end of the Golden Gate Promenade as a separate entity, but you can continue west on the access road to Fort Point, which rides atop the rock-faced seawall. If you choose to proceed, watch for cars.

The gates of Fort Point are at 1.6 miles. Pass a little grassy knoll on the left (south) side of the road; both road and trail end in the parking lot below the towering brick walls of the fort at 1.7 miles. Return as you came.

Anglers try their luck on the Fort Point Pier (aka Torpedo Wharf).

HIGHLIGHTS: Visit the San Francisco National Cemetery and Mountain Lake on this route through the western reaches of the Presidio.

TYPE OF JOURNEY: Loop.

TOTAL DISTANCE: 3.4 miles.

DIFFICULTY: Moderate.

PERMITTED USES: Hiking. Portions of the trail are also open to cyclists.

MAPS: USGS San Francisco North; Golden Gate National Recreation Area Presidio of San Francisco Map; Golden Gate National Recreation Area Map; TOPO! San Francisco Bay Area, Wine Country, and Big Sur.

SPECIAL CONSIDERATIONS: This route encompasses dirt tracks, sidewalks, and roadways. Watch for cars and bicyclists. Dogs must be leashed.

PARKING AND FACILITIES: Parking is available in the parking lot for the Officers Club at the intersection of Finley Road and Arguello Boulevard. Parking is also available at Inspiration Point, which is just north of the Officers Club. There are no facilities.

FINDING THE TRAILHEAD: To reach the trailhead from the William Penn Mott Jr. Visitor Center on the Main Post, follow Montgomery Street south to Moraga Avenue. Go left (east) on Moraga for one block to Arguello Boulevard. Turn right (south) onto Arguello Boulevard, and go about 0.9 mile to Finley Road, which is on the right (west). The trailhead is in the northwest corner of the intersection.

KEY POINTS:

0.0 Trailhead.

0.3 Reach Washington Boulevard.

0.5 Arrive at the San Francisco National Cemetery.

1.0 The Presidio Golf Course is on the left (south) side of the trail.

1.2 Reach the Compton Road intersection.

1.4 Arrive at the junction with Battery Caulfield Road.

1.8 Pass the Public Health Service Hospital.

2.6 Visit Mountain Lake Park.

3.2 Pass the Presidio Golf Course Clubhouse.

The good, the so-so, and the ugly. The Presidio is a work in progress, and this loop showcases its metamorphosis from base to park without any sugar coating, passing through some areas that are scenically satisfying, and others that

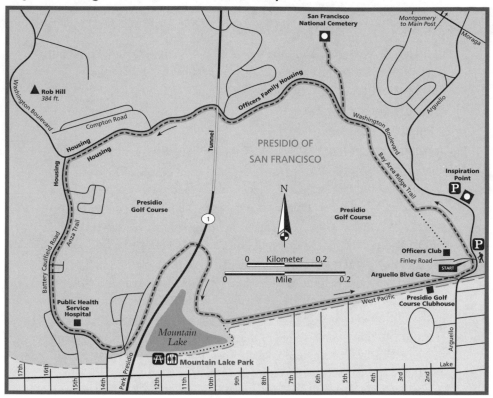

could be bolstered a bit—or a lot. A rehabilitated area like Mountain Lake contrasts starkly with the derelict Public Health Service Hospital, though they lie within 0.25 mile of each other. Refurbishing parklands like those around Mountain Lake is relatively straightforward—the park service has much experience in this area—but revamping historic structures that have fallen into disrepair is another thing entirely. The provocative contrasts, which may generate revolutionary ideas, make this a must-do route for all who care about the park.

Portions of the route follow two regional trails. It begins on the Bay Area Ridge Trail, which, when completed, will link ridgetops around San Francisco Bay. When the loop hooks south, down Battery Caulfield Road, it follows a portion of the Juan Bautista de Anza National Historic Trail, which traces the route followed by this Spanish explorer on his expedition to northern California in 1775 and 1776. Anza and his entourage reached the shores of San Francisco Bay in early 1776, and chose sites for the future Mission Dolores and Presidio before returning to Mexico.

The Bay Area Ridge Trailhead is marked with distinctive blue-and-white signs, one of which is at the trailhead. Go north on the obvious path, climbing along a ridge through stands of stately Monterey pine. Stay right (northwest) when another broad track merges with the ridge trail at 0.1 mile, then go right (north) again when the trail diverges from the road it has been following at 0.2 mile. A gate and Bay Area Ridge Trail sign mark the route.

Drop through the woods to Washington Boulevard at 0.3 mile, crossing the street to the Bay Area Ridge Trail sign. Go left (west) along Washington Boulevard to its intersection with Nauman Road. The trail sign directs you onto the sidewalk on the other side of Washington, but ignore that temporarily, breaking right (north) from the ridge trail on Nauman. Pass behind the residences to a little signed path that leads north through the eucalyptus to the top of the San Francisco National Cemetery at 0.5 mile.

You could spend hours wandering through the cemetery, reading the plain white headstones, most marked only with the name of the man buried beneath it, his rank, the date of his death, and the state in which he was born. The names of soldiers' wives are engraved on the backs of the stones. The rows of white markers spill down a gentle slope like a waterfall, with the Golden Gate Bridge rising above the trees at the cemetery's northern border.

When you can pull yourself away, head back to Washington Boulevard and continue west on the sidewalk, passing between columns of neat white residences. At about the 1-mile mark, the Presidio Golf Course borders the route on the left (southwest); a trail departs to the left as well, dropping into the golf course. Stay straight (west) on the signed Bay Area Ridge Trail, now a dirt path that runs alongside the road. You will know you've passed over California Highway 1 by the growing, then receding, roar of the cars; the tunnel through which the highway passes is underfoot.

At about 1.3 miles the Bay Area Ridge Trail crosses to the north side of Washington Boulevard onto Compton Road, and continues north to the Golden Gate Bridge and beyond. Stay straight (west) on Washington, passing through a cluster of unremarkable housing to the junction with Battery Caulfield Road at 1.4 miles.

Turn left (south) onto Battery Caulfield, now on the Anza Trail. The route certainly looks nothing like what the explorer would have seen, passing through another residential development and skirting the industrial-looking facilities of Battery Caulfield, a former Nike missile site. The road plunges down to the hulking husk of the Public Health Service Hospital at 1.8 miles. Though an impressive building, it is a vagabond—run-down, windows broken, barricaded.

The route circles east around the south side of the hospital and crosses North Fifteenth Avenue. Stay straight on Wedemeyer Street, passing the Jewish Community Center, to a service road overlooking CA 1 at 2 miles. A dog litter pickup station marks the trail, which arcs northward on the frontage road.

At the gate at 2.2 miles, stay left (down and northeast), crossing under the highway. The other paved path leads up into the golf course and back to Washington Boulevard.

Beyond the highway underpass, the trail curls south toward Mountain Lake. Lush riparian plants and trees—berries and willows and reeds—buffer the trail. To reach the tiny Mountain Lake Park, which is on the south shore of the lake and features a little beach, picnic tables, rest rooms, and swarms of ducks and pigeons, turn right (west) at the trail intersection at 2.6 miles. In the 0.1 mile between the intersection and the lake, the trail goes from dirt to pavement. Pause here to refresh, watch the birds, and read the interpretive signs, one of which describes de Anza's journey.

Return to the main trail at 2.8 miles, continuing straight (east) on the paved route. The trail climbs between a eucalyptus-lined drainage on the left (north) and a rustic stone wall on the right (south), with houses behind. This section of the route is popular with dog walkers, not all of whom keep their pets on leashes.

At 3.1 miles the trail empties onto West Pacific Avenue. Continue climbing, with the golf course and driving range on the left (north), and parked cars on the right (south). Pass the Presidio Golf Course Clubhouse at 3.2 miles. The Arguello Boulevard Gate is just beyond; turn left (north) onto Arguello Boulevard, and return to the trailhead at about 3.4 miles.

Ecology Trail–Lovers' Lane Loop

HIGHLIGHTS: This scenic passage takes you through the woods to a superb viewpoint and down a historic lane bordered by picturesque military housing.

TYPE OF JOURNEY: Loop.

TOTAL DISTANCE: 2.3 miles.

DIFFICULTY: Moderate.

PERMITTED USES: Hiking.

MAPS: USGS San Francisco North; Golden Gate National Recreation Area Presidio of San Francisco Map (available at visitor centers throughout the park).

SPECIAL CONSIDERATIONS: Pets must be on leashes.

PARKING AND FACILITIES: Parking is available behind Pershing Hall, which is at the intersection of Moraga Avenue and Funston Avenue, or in the large parking lot in the parade grounds at the Main Post. There are no other facilities.

FINDING THE TRAILHEAD: To reach the trailhead from the William Penn Mott Jr. Visitor Center on the Main Post, drive south on Montgomery Street to its intersection with Moraga Avenue. Turn left (east) onto Moraga, and drive to its end at its junction with Funston Avenue. The parking area is behind Pershing Hall.

KEY POINTS:

0.0 Trailhead.

0.4 Reach the restored serpentine grasslands.

0.5 Climb to Inspiration Point.

1.2 Drop into El Polin Spring picnic area.

1.6 Reach Lovers' Lane.

2.1 Cross the footbridge and climb to Presidio Boulevard.

Winding through the southeastern corner of the Presidio, the Ecology Trail and Lovers' Lane loop captures scenic diversity of the park. From the dark woodlands to the vista point, from a pocket of rare habitat to a historical lane that linked the Presidio to Mission Dolores during the Spanish occupation, the route presents the park's treasures in a compact and mildly challenging package.

I give you fair warning: No trail signs had been erected along this route in early 2002, and social trails collide in confusing tangles, especially in the stands of eucalyptus above El Polin Spring and around the intersection of Lovers' Lane and the Ecology Trail. Consult a map to keep on track, unless you like to stray. That, after all, is what exploring is all about.

Begin by passing a gate and climbing the paved trail. The path turns to dirt within 50 yards, and then intersects other trails amid a stand of eucalyptus. Stay left (southwest) on the main track, which ascends through a remarkably dense and diverse mixed evergreen forest. The climb is rigorous for the first 0.2 mile or so, then the pitch eases amid a redwood grove. A use trail drops off to the left (north); stay right (southeast) on the Ecology Trail.

The trail breaks out into an open area at about 0.4 mile. The park is in the process of restoring the serpentine grasslands that once covered this area; the flora being reintroduced here includes eleven rare and endangered plants, including the Presidio clarkia and the Marin dwarf flax. The trail forks at the base of the open hillside. Stay right (south) and climb through the restoration zone to another trail intersection. Again, go right (northwest), leaving the Ecology Trail to climb a brief but steep staircase to the overlook at Inspiration Point.

The overlook, a broad platform paved with flagstone, outfitted with benches, and prefaced with a bank of interpretive signs, offers views across the treetops to San Francisco Bay, Alcatraz Island, and Angel Island. One of the signs describes the trees that fringe the view: More than 100,000 trees, mostly non-natives, were

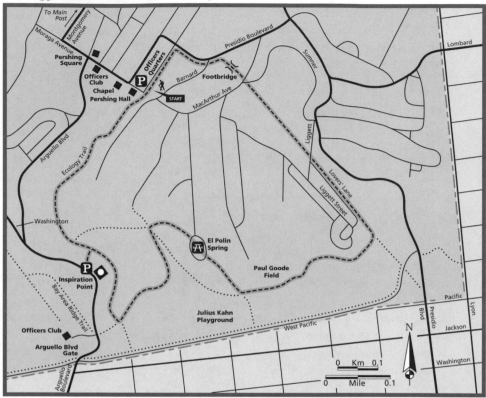

planted on the Presidio as part of a beautification project in the 1800s. The forest is lovely, but the juxtaposition of the trees with the tiny patch of reclaimed serpentine grassland spilling from the vista point is a bit poignant.

Retreat down the stairs to the Ecology Trail and turn right (south), gently climbing toward the south boundary of the park. At the trail intersection at about 0.9 mile, turn sharply left, switchbacking to the north on a wide unsigned path that drops steeply to the base of the serpentine grassland area. Stay straight (down and north) at the next trail intersection, dropping to a trail that breaks off to the right (east) and down into the El Polin Spring picnic area at 1.2 miles. (If you take the first right, you will pass above the spring and picnic area, traveling on sandy paths for about 0.2 mile before reconnecting with the route to Lovers' Lane.) The spring is located near the head of a narrow drainage, and was a water source for the Spanish and Mexican forces at the Presidio.

The trail climbs out of the spring area to the east, leaving the riparian zone for a clearing below the Julius Kahn Playground, which is out of sight behind a screen of trees, but not out of earshot. Stay left (east) at the trail intersection, circling the Paul Goode Field on the dirt track on its south side.

The unsigned trail then begins a moderate climb into a mixed forest of eucalyptus and Monterey pine, passing a use trail that breaks off to the right (south), offering access to the streets on the south side of the park. Stay left, heading eastward and upward, to the next cluster of social trails. Stay left (east) at these junctions too, intersecting Lovers' Lane, marked by a line of light poles, at 1.6 miles.

Turn left (north) onto Lovers' Lane, which is bordered on the east by stands of eucalyptus, and on the west by a row of homes once used by officers and enlisted men. The trail surface changes from dirt to broken asphalt before it crosses Liggett Street at 1.8 miles. Again dirt, and then, finally, paved, the lane crosses MacArthur Avenue at 2 miles. A quaint brick footbridge spans El Polin Creek at 2.1 miles, just before the lane ends on Presidio Boulevard.

To return to the trailhead, go left (northwest) on Presidio, then left (southwest) on Funston Avenue, passing the quaint houses of Officers Row, some of the oldest structures on the Presidio, before returning to the trailhead at 2.3 miles.

Coastal Trail at the Golden Gate

HIGHLIGHTS: Consider this a battery tour—the trail links fortifications from Battery Chamberlin at Baker Beach to Battery East inside the Golden Gate.

TYPE OF JOURNEY: Out-and-back.

TOTAL DISTANCE: About 3.6 miles.

DIFFICULTY: Moderate.

PERMITTED USES: Hiking, cycling on a portion of the trail.

MAPS: USGS San Francisco North; Golden Gate National Recreation Area map; GGNRA Presidio of San Francisco Map; TOPO! San Francisco Bay Area, Wine Country, and Big Sur.

SPECIAL CONSIDERATIONS: Pets must be kept on leashes.

PARKING AND FACILITIES: Ample parking is available at Baker Beach, the western end of this portion of the Coastal Trail, along with rest rooms, water, and picnic facilities. The eastern end point of the trail, at the Warming Hut near Crissy Field, also has rest rooms and picnic facilities, as well as a cafe and gift shop. Parking is more limited here, and is located alongside Crissy Field.

FINDING THE TRAILHEAD: To reach Baker Beach from U.S. Highway 101 at the Golden Gate Bridge, follow Lincoln Boulevard west for 0.9 mile to Bowley Street, which is signed for Baker Beach. Turn right (north) onto Bowley Street and drive down to Gibson Road. Turn right

Coastal Trail at the Golden Gate

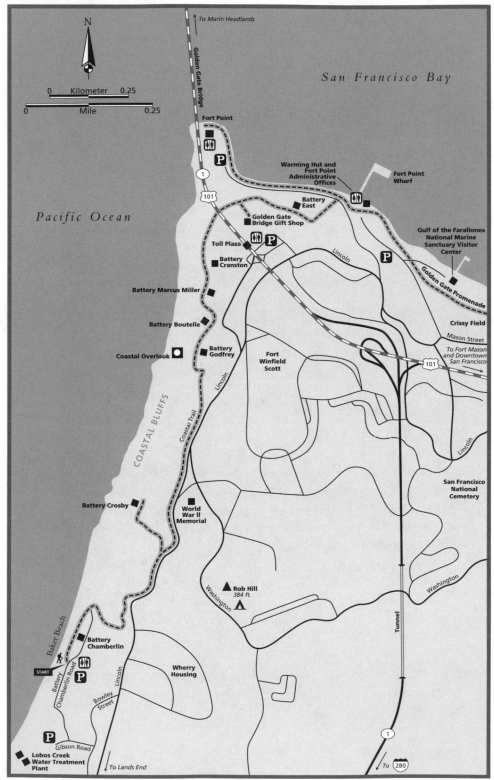

(north) onto Gibson, which drops into the parking area adjacent to the big brick Lobos Creek Water Treatment Plant. More parking is available by turning right (east) from Gibson Road onto Battery Chamberlin Road, which empties into another large lot.

KEY POINTS:

0.0 Trailhead.

0.2 Climb away from Baker Beach.

0.5 Reach Battery Crosby.

1.2 Arrive at Batteries Godfrey and Boutelle.

1.5 Pass under the Golden Gate Bridge.

1.7 Pass Battery East.

1.8 Arrive at the Warming Hut on the Golden Gate Promenade.

The batteries along this stretch of the Coastal Trail generally predate the great wars of the twentieth century. The brick-work and earthworks of Batteries East and West were erected just after the Civil War in response to advances in technology that rendered earlier fortifications, like those at Fort Point, obsolete. These batteries, in turn, were outdated by the end of the nineteenth century, and more "modern" fortifications, including Batteries Crosby, Boutelle, and Cranston, were erected along the coastal bluffs.

The route described here is a portion of the Coastal Trail, which stretches from the Golden Gate south for more than 9 miles to Fort Funston. It can be hiked in either direction, but is described here heading east from Baker Beach to the Warming Hut.

Begin the hike by visiting Battery Chamberlin. Chain-link fencing surrounds much of the battery, but the gates are open, allowing free exploration of the site. A restored "disappearing" gun is mounted in the first emplacement; this weapon was designed to drop out of sight after discharging so that artillerymen could safely reload it.

After checking out the battery, drop onto Baker Beach and walk south on the sand for about 0.2 mile to the end of the chain-link fencing at Battery Chamberlin. A trail sign points you to the Coastal Trail, which climbs a roadway up and south to the edge of Lincoln Boulevard, then links up with a dirt path that runs alongside the westbound lane of the roadway.

Climb east on the roadside path, passing a beach access trail. The trail to Battery Crosby breaks left (north) off the Coastal Trail at 0.5 mile. Head down the dirt path to the battery, which is set amid fragrant scrub filled with birdsong. This battery, which was in service between 1900 and 1943, was also outfitted with disappearing rifles. Stairs lead up to the gun emplacements, which

With unobstructed views of the Golden Gate, Battery Crosby, located just off the Coastal Trail, clearly occupies an ideal location for a defensive fortification.

are now filled with weeds and flowers. Wonderful views of the Golden Gate open from the top of the battery.

Return to the Coastal Trail, and turn left (northeast), continuing up along-side Lincoln Boulevard. A number of signs warn you to stay on the path and off the sensitive plants of the dune habitat, which is studded with wildflowers, including the vibrant California poppy, as early as February. Use trails break off the main path to cliffside overlooks; fight the temptation and protect both your safety and the habitat.

The trail flattens at about the 1-mile mark, and curves left (north) into the trees. Numerous use trails branch into the underbrush; stay on the path most traveled, which passes the brick entryways of Battery West, overgrown with brambles on the left (north) side of the route.

At 1.2 miles the trail empties into a parking lot at Battery Godfrey. The wide concrete apron atop the battery faces the Golden Gate and makes a mar-velous bench from which to enjoy the views and contemplate an interpretive sign that describes the landscape of San Francisco Bay in the last ice age. Pick your way through Battery Godfrey, climbing up and down the stairs onto and off the apron. The trail arcs northward and becomes one with the Bay Area Ridge Trail as Battery Godfrey melds into Battery Boutelle. The trail splits again beyond Battery Boutelle; stay left (north) on the main trail, which drops down a flight of steps and passes the shrub-covered aprons of Battery Marcus Miller and Battery Cranston. (If you take the right trail, you can check out the elegantly curved covered walkway at Marcus Miller, then retrace your steps to the main route.)

Beyond the batteries, the Golden Gate Bridge becomes the primary focus. At 1.5 miles the Coastal Trail merges with the paved path that leads right (east) onto the pedestrian walkway/bikeway of the bridge, and left (northeast) under the huge iron girders that support it. A trail sign here indicates that the route is also part of the Juan Bautista de Anza National Historic Trail, as well as the Bay Area Ridge Trail.

Follow the pavement to the left (north, then east), dropping down under the roadbed of the bridge. The sound of the cars passing overhead is hollow, muffled, and echoing; the architecture is massive, solid, and insulating. Watch for speeding cyclists.

As you emerge from the shadow on the bridge on the east side of the Golden Gate, Fort Point comes into view below and to the left (north). The trail forks at an interpretive sign; go left (northeast) and sharply downhill through a picnic area. Walk through the brick tunnel at the southeast end of the picnic area, which opens into the mounded earthworks of Battery East. This battery, like Battery West, dates back to the post–Civil War era, and was abandoned when new weapons of war could easily breach their defenses. A viewing platform rises at the far end of the fortifications, offering grand views of the bay and Golden Gate.

The trail arcs northward, through an area that has been stripped of non-native eucalyptuses. Stay left (northeast) at the trail intersection, dropping down a flight of stairs to the Warming Hut and the Golden Gate Promenade at 1.8 miles. Check out the sights, then return as you came.

Presidio Beaches

Four vastly different beaches fall under the umbrella of the Presidio or are close enough to its borders to warrant inclusion in this chapter. Ocean Beach fronts directly on the Pacific, and thus is the wildest in terms of weather, as well as host to the best sunsets. Both Baker Beach and China Beach are tucked into coves on the steep headlands west of the Golden Gate, offering great views of the Golden Gate Bridge and the Marin Headlands. East Beach at Crissy Field is on San Francisco Bay, the perfect place upon which to sit and watch sailboats, sailboarders, and other activities on the water.

China Beach

Once the domain of the Chinese, who anchored their fishing boats offshore and camped here in the late 1800s, China Beach attracts a more diverse crowd these days. The cultural mix that makes San Francisco so dynamic is captured in a snapshot in the tiny cove, unified by common beach occupations like sun-bathing, playing in the sand, exploring, and, of course, fishing.

This spare, sharp-featured beach, marked with a monument that acknowl-edges the contributions of the Chinese to San Francisco, is tucked below the homes of Sea Cliff. There isn't a lot of parking—enough for perhaps fifty cars—and the lot fills quickly when the sun is out. But the lack of abundant parking, coupled with the beach's relative seclusion, means it is seldom overcrowded.

The beach sits about 100 feet below the parking area, and is reached either via a steep staircase or paved switchbacking road. A large yellow bathhouse occupies a concrete landing above the beach; you'll find rest rooms and picnic facilities here. Down on the beach, families lay out beach towels, dig sand cas-tles, and dodge the surf (swimming, however, is dangerous and discouraged). The beach is no more than 0.25 mile long, and pocked with dark rocks, espe-cially on the west side. When the tide is low, you can walk west among these rocks, exploring nooks and little coves carved into the cliffs below Sea Cliff.

Finding the beach can be a little tricky. From the Golden Gate Bridge, fol-low Lincoln Boulevard (which becomes El Camino Del Mar) west into Sea Cliff. The beach is about 1.8 miles from the bridge toll plaza. Pass the stop sign at the intersection of El Camino Del Mar and Twenty-seventh Avenue, and go two blocks farther, where El Camino Del Mar swings sharply left (south). Turn right (north) onto Sea Cliff Avenue, then quickly left (west) onto an extension of Sea Cliff Avenue that drops to the parking area within 0.1 mile.

Baker Beach

Sunshine is a precious commodity in San Francisco, and Baker Beach is the ideal place to enjoy it. Its orientation, facing north with great views of the Marin Headlands and the Golden Gate, with bluffs rising both to the west and east, protect the beach from a direct onslaught of ocean breezes. The sand is soft and generous, stretching for more than 0.5 mile from rocky bluff to rocky bluff, with the grand homes of Sea Cliff rising above the western reaches of the strand. And while some come to walk—both with and without their dogs—and others to play, and yet others to fish, a good many simply sprawl in the sand, clothed or unclothed, and soak up the rays.

Yes, I said *unclothed*. There is no formal boundary between the G-rated portion of the beach and the R-rated, but in general the east side of the beach, beyond the fencing around Battery Chamberlin, is "clothing optional."

Battery Chamberlin was built in 1904 as part of the bay's defensive fortifications. A restored "disappearing" gun is mounted in one of the emplacements; park rangers demonstrate the gun once a month. Baker Beach is also part of the extensive Coastal Trail, which climbs east toward the Golden Gate Bridge, and west to Lands End.

The surf at Baker Beach is dangerous; beachgoers are advised not to swim. Facilities include picnic tables, rest rooms, barbecue grills, and drinking water.

To reach Baker Beach from U.S. Highway 101 at the Golden Gate Bridge, follow Lincoln Boulevard west for 0.9 mile to Bowley Street, which is signed for Baker Beach. Turn right (north) onto Bowley Street and drive down to Gibson Road. Turn right (north) onto Gibson, which drops into the parking area adjacent to the big brick Presidio Water Treatment Plant. More parking is available by turning right (east) from Gibson Road onto Battery Chamberlin Road, which empties into another large lot.

East Beach at Crissy Field

East Beach may not be the biggest strand in the Golden Gate National Recreation Area, or boast the biggest surf, but it certainly is the best place from which to watch sailboats and board sailors skim the surface of San Francisco Bay. On foggy days sailboats hug the shoreline, their lofted canvas ghostly white on white. Once the fog lifts and the winds pick up, the whole bay is theirs; they spread west to the Golden Gate and beyond, sails full, on parade. Sailboarders also patiently await the winds: When it begins to blow, they throw it into overdrive, dashing across the bay at unbelievable speeds, as zippy and flashy as hummingbirds flitting from a flower at one end of the yard to another at the opposite end.

East Beach is gentle, both in its slope and the lack of ferocity in its surf. This kindliness, coupled with the fact that the Golden Gate Promenade is at its back, brings a lot of traffic to the narrow strand—dogs chasing balls into the water, families with picnics spread on blankets, cuddling couples, and more. It offers access to the promenade itself, and to the tidal marsh, the Crissy Field Center, the restored historic airfield, and various other amenities.

Sailboarding on the bay is exhilarating, and East Beach is a favorite launch. But those in the know advise that sailing here is best left to the experienced. Hardcore board sailors ply the waters year-round, weather permitting, but the season generally runs from early spring to early autumn. If the sun is out, chances are good that the winds will kick in, but once (or if) the fog rolls in, the winds die off. Tides also affect the quality of the sailing; sailors are advised to check with local shops on conditions. Information, including info on shops, rentals, and lessons, is available through the San Francisco Boardsailing Association; visit the Web site at www.sfba.org or write SFBA, 1592 Union Street Box 301, San Francisco, CA 94123.

Sea kayakers may also take to the bay from the East Beach, but they, like board sailors, should consider winds and tides before heading out. For more information on sea kayaking opportunities on the bay, contact Sea Trek at (415) 488–1000; the Web site is www.seatrekkayak.com.

The waves that roll around the rocky promontory at Fort Point entice experienced surfers. The surf at the mouth of the bay is dangerous, subject to dangerous currents and tides (like so many beaches on the north coast)—not to mention that there is no sandy beach upon which to rest here, but rather a seawall composed of unforgiving rock.

Still, experienced locals say surfing at Fort Point can be great, given the right conditions. And this is also a wonderful place to watch wave riders. The shallow water in which waves break is close in at Fort Point, so the surfers are close in as well—as close as 50 yards to the rocky shoreline. Sometimes the conditions dictate that surfers paddle out under the yawning Golden Gate Bridge to catch the best rides.

East Beach at Crissy Field is located just inside the Marina Gate, off Mason Street near its intersection with Marina Boulevard, adjacent to the St. Francis Yacht Club. A large parking lot is available here, but on sunny days this fills quickly. Parking is available at other lots within the Presidio, but you may find yourself walking a bit to reach the beach.

Picnic facilities and rest rooms are located at both the east and west ends of the beach. For more information, contact the Crissy Field Center at (415) 561–7690, or visit the Web site at www.crissyfield.org.

Ocean Beach

Weather sweeps off the Pacific unhindered onto Ocean Beach. There is no protective cove, no cliff to huddle against, no brace of dune. On a foggy day the sky lowers and surrounds beachgoers in a Siberian moisture; when a storm kicks up, the surf becomes intimidating, eating away at the strand and heightening the hazards at the tideline; and when the sun shines, the city spills forth on to the warming sands, walking, surfing, spreading blankets to sunbathe . . .

In many ways Ocean Beach mirrors the complexity of the city it borders: It is dynamic, beautiful, and a little dangerous. It boasts all the best of beaches in northern California: great sunsets, heavenly vistas, stimulating surf. But it's not a beach upon which you'd want to walk barefoot—broken glass and dog poop could be the least of your worries. Signs warn you of the dangers posed by sneaker waves and riptides, but such hazards don't deter the wet suit-clad surf-sport aficionados who flock to the beachfront when the surf is up.

Ocean Beach is profoundly urban. A seawall of concrete forms an abrupt barrier between the beach and the Great Highway, which parallels the strand

A kite boarder rides the surf at Ocean Beach.

for several miles. The Esplanade, a walkway and parking area, lies atop the seawall, offering easy and pleasurable seaside strolling or cycling. The Sunset District of San Francisco abuts the Great Highway on the east, with the bay windows of its orderly pastel houses looking out over the beach to the sea. The Cliff House and Seal Rocks form the beach's northern boundary.

From the Cliff House, Ocean Beach stretches south for 4 miles to Fort Funston, passing Golden Gate Park and the San Francisco Zoo along the way. Fort Funston boasts its own set of activities, which are described in the Points of Interest in San Francisco and Points South chapter.

Dangerous surf precludes swimming and body surfing, but the beach's proximity to the city and the quality of its waves make it very attractive to local expert surfers, who negotiate frigid waters and notoriously tricky currents to partake of waves that can be twice as big as those at nearby beaches. In addition to your run-of-the-mill surfers, you will also find sailboarders and kite boarders, who use a parasail to catch the wind. Given the hazardous surf, only experienced wave riders should venture into the water. For information about conditions at the beach, check out the Web sites at www.surfline.com or www.stormsurf.com. You can also call for recorded surf reports, updated daily, at Wise Surfboards (415–273–1618), or SF Surf Shop (415–437–6683), among others.

Perhaps the most direct way to get to Ocean Beach from within the city is via Geary Boulevard, a straight shot west from Van Ness Avenue (U.S. Highway 101) to the Great Highway. In addition, you can head west from Nineteenth Avenue (California Highway 1) on Geary, Lincoln Way, or Sloat Boulevard to reach the Great Highway. A good road map will show you a multitude of alternative routes to the beach both from within the city and from without.

The beach is open daily year-round. Dogs are allowed if they're leashed. Fires, which can be built only after obtaining a permit, are allowed between the surf line and the high tide line on the stretch of beach between Fulton and Sloat Boulevard. Fires must be less than 3 feet by 3 feet, and must be extinguished with water. Use only clean wood; wood that's been varnished, painted, or contains nails or screws is not permitted. Call the GGNRA's Office of Special Park Uses at (415) 561–4300 for more information.

Presidio Points of Interest

The Presidio's points of interest fall easily into two categories: military installations and natural areas. The military sites range from a Civil War–era fort to batteries that were constructed in World War II. Natural attractions include areas that have been restored or are in the process of being restored. The overview map of the Presidio on page 252 will help you get oriented.

Historic and Cultural Sites

Fort Point National Historic Site

From the outside, Fort Point doesn't look like much. Blocky and plain, it resembles a big, brick warehouse, albeit one with a lighthouse and some narrow, odd-looking windows. The intricate latticework supporting the Golden Gate Bridge, which was built over the fort in the 1930s, holds more visual intrigue than the building below it.

But on the inside, the fort is an architectural marvel. Thick, graceful arches are mounted in three tiers, one atop the other, surrounding an open courtyard that echoes with the sounds of cars crossing the bridge. Towers rise in three corners of the court, housing spiral staircases of thick granite that ascend to the top of the fort, which is open to the Golden Gate and views of San Francisco Bay and the San Francisco skyline.

The empty shadowy corridors on the west, north, and east sides of the fort, bordering ocean and bay, are lined with alcoves, known as casemates, that once housed Civil War–era cannon. The casemates are now devoid of armature, their openings either bricked over or blocked with clouded glass through which filters a smoky light that barely relieves the gloom. Living quarters—rooms with arched ceilings linked by a long corridor of open doors—line the southern side of the fort on the second tier. Long emptied of the trappings of the officers who once resided there, the rooms now house interpretive displays describing the fort's past.

The history of a defensive post at Fort Point dates back to the Spanish, who erected Castillo de San Joaquin on the site in the early 1790s. That fort was razed to make way for the present edifice, built between 1853 and 1861 by the U.S. Army Corps of Engineers. The fort was designed to house 126 cannon, with casemates for thirty guns on each tier, and was intended to defend San Francisco Bay in the event of an invasion that never materialized.

The fort became obsolete quickly. By 1900 its cannon had been removed, and the building was used for training, for storage, and as an base during construction of the Golden Gate Bridge. It was staffed briefly during World War II, then again fell into disuse. Its current revival as a National Historic Site began in 1970, and today it is one of the biggest attractions within the Golden Gate National Recreation Area.

Interpretative displays explaining the history and operation of the fort begin when you walk through the sally port. From illustrated signs to displays of Civil War-era uniforms to historical photographs, the fort's identity is revealed as you walk its dark corridors and climb from tier to tier. Attractions range from the garrison gin, a spindly tripod that towers above the southeast corner of the courtyard on the ground level, to the stubby Fort Point Light, which stands on the westernmost border of the top, or barbette, tier.

Fort Point is open Friday, Saturday, and Sunday from 10:00 A.M. to 5:00 P.M.; it is closed Monday through Thursday, and on Thanksgiving, Christmas, and New Year's Day. The bookstore is open from 10:00 A.M. to 4:30 P.M. on the same days that the fort is open. An audio tour of the fort is available at the bookstore for a small fee. A printed interpretive guide of the fort is also available at the bookstore, as well as through the fort's Web site at www.nps.gov/fopo. For more information, call (415) 561–4395.

Crissy Field

Looking down the flat expanse of the Crissy airfield, re-created as it appeared in the 1920s as part of the restoration of the Presidio's bayfront, it's easy to see why it became a hub of military aviation during the 1920s and 1930s.

Fronting the Presidio, the airfield was a strategically located addition to the coastal defense network around San Francisco Bay. Aviators could expeditiously get aloft to scout the coastal regions for enemy ships that might not be seen from coastal fortifications located on land. From the cushiony grass runways, aviators flew reconnaissance, took aerial photographs, went on search-and-rescue missions, patrolled for forest fires, and even took part in dedication ceremonies for Lassen Volcanic National Park. The field was also used during record-breaking flights, including the first "Dawn to Dusk" transcontinental flight in 1924, and the first flight from the mainland to Hawaii, according to park service historian Stephen A. Haller.

By the mid-1930s, however, enthusiasm for Crissy Field as a "first-line air base" was waning. Fog and wind had always plagued the fliers (and are still responsible for delays at San Francisco International Airport); the construction of the Golden Gate Bridge, which compromised flight lines, sealed its demise. Airplanes and fliers moved north to Hamilton Field in Marin County, and Crissy Field was used as barracks, its hangars as classrooms, and its paved runways for medical flights. It was closed to air travel in 1974, and became part of the Golden Gate National Recreation Area when the Presidio was turned over to the park service in 1994.

Crissy Field stretches for about 3 miles along the waterfront, with the Golden Gate Promenade (described in the Presidio Trails chapter) running along its northern boundary. Though kites are now the only "aircraft" launched from the grass, it's easy to stand at either end of the elevated platform and imagine the thrill aviators must have felt as they took off or landed from the airstrip.

To reach Crissy Field from the Golden Gate Bridge, follow U.S. Highway 101 east, staying left (east) on Doyle Drive when the highway swings south to Lombard Street. Turn sharply right (west) onto Mason Street at the stoplight at Marina Boulevard, and follow Mason west to either the East Parking Area, at about 0.1 mile, or the Crissy Field Center, at about 0.3 mile.

For more information on Crissy Field, contact the Crissy Field Center by calling (415) 561–7690, or visiting the Web site at www.crissyfield.org. Information on Crissy Field is also available on the national park's Presidio Web site at www.nps.gov/prsf/history/crissy.

Main Post

The Main Post has, since the Spanish colonial era, been the nerve center of the Presidio. It overlays the original adobe presidio built by the Spanish in 1776, which overlooked the recently "discovered" San Francisco Bay. The views that were so crucial to its success as a fort are now blocked by the span of U.S. Highway 101 as it approaches the Golden Gate Bridge, but the post's historical significance is more than borne out in its buildings, and the interpretive signs that explain their importance.

The location of the original Spanish fort is near Pershing Square, but the adobe structure is long gone; a boulder on the sidewalk near the flagpole marks the approximate location of the building's northwest corner. The Spanish occupation is commemorated in the square by two brass cannon, which according to the park service were forged in the 1600s, and were part of the defensive batteries at Castillo de San Jóaquin, now the site of Fort Point.

The post contains some of the oldest structures still standing in the Presidio, including the row of officers' housing that fronts Funston Avenue. These charming little homes were built in the 1860s, during the Civil War. More elaborate Queen Anne and stick Victorian homes are located across the street near the intersection of Funston Avenue and Presidio Boulevard.

The parade ground of the post now serves as its parking lot. Infantry Row, with its distinctive redbrick barracks, was constructed in the 1890s; the well-maintained buildings line the west side of the then-new parade ground. The William Penn Mott Jr. Visitor Center is located in one of the former barracks.

The Main Post is bounded on the north by Lincoln Boulevard, on the west by Montgomery Street, on the south by Moraga Avenue, and on the east by Funston Avenue, through these delineations are by no means hard and fast. A walking tour of the post is outlined in a brochure available at the visitor center.

Fort Winfield Scott

Harking back to the Presidio's Spanish roots, the parade ground at Fort Winfield Scott is ringed with three-storied barracks built in the Spanish or Mission Revival style that was popular when the fort was established in 1912. With its U-shaped parade ground open to San Francisco Bay, Fort Scott was established as a headquarters for the plethora of coastal batteries being constructed during the Endicott-Taft period. During its heyday, when it was considered separate from the Presidio to the east, Fort Scott oversaw Batteries Marcus Miller, Boutelle, Godfrey, and Dynamite, among others. Battery Dynamite, the ruins of which are located just west of the parade ground, served as the Bay Area's harbor defense command center during World War II.

With the advent of the Cold War, the batteries overseen by Fort Scott lost their importance, and so did the fort. In the mid-1950s it was incorporated into the Presidio, and later used as an education center. Today one of the barracks serves as the park police headquarters. Interpretive signs at the parade ground, which can be circumnavigated in an easy 0.5-mile walk, explain the fort's significance and elaborate on its history.

San Francisco National Cemetery

Situated between the Main Post and Fort Winfield Scott, the San Francisco National Cemetery commands spectacular views of the Golden Gate. The first

Flowers decorate the graves of veterans buried in the San Francisco National Cemetery.

national cemetery on the West Coast, it was formally established in 1884, though the oldest graves on the site predate its founding by nearly forty years. By the time the cemetery closed in 1992, more than 30,000 veterans and their family members were buried on the site. Their uniform headstones, marked on the front with the names, ranks, and dates of the veterans buried there, and on the back with the names of spouses, march in orderly rows down the well-tended lawn, their neatness only enhanced by the bouquets of calla lilies, roses, and daisies sprinkled among them. More elaborate memorials are also present on the site, dating to the days of the Civil War.

The cemetery is a poignant and profound place, worthy of hours of exploration. It is located just west of the Main Post, reached via Sheridan and Lincoln Boulevard.

Batteries at the Golden Gate

Since the arrival of European explorers on its shores—and probably even before that, when the Ohlone and Coast Miwok thrived in the area—San Francisco has been coveted. And things of value, once claimed, must be defended.

Defensive fortifications at the Golden Gate date back to the Spanish occupation, when the Castillo de San Joaquin was established on the site where Fort Point now stands. Fort Point, with its sister fort on Alcatraz Island, was armed in 1861, and was intended to protect the entrance to the bay from enemies intent on stealing the wealth of the city after the discovery of gold in 1848, and from the Rebels during the Civil War.

Improvements in weaponry developed during the Civil War rendered these huge brick forts obsolete, and new fortifications, able to withstand new technologies, were built into the headlands at Batteries West and East in the 1870s. Earthworks, now covered in grasses and flowers, protected the guns in these batteries—and the men who manned them—from enemy ordnance. For a while, at least.

By the late 1800s the earthwork batteries had also become dangerously passé. Under the direction of two secretaries of war, William Endicott and William Taft, the Presidio broke out in new batteries like it had the chicken pox. From Baker Beach east to the Marina, over a period of about twenty years, the Presidio (actually, technically, Fort Winfield Scott, which was later incorporated into the Presidio), gained Batteries Chamberlin, Crosby, Stotsenburg-McKinnon, Stafford, Dynamite, Godfrey, Boutelle, Marcus Miller, Cranston, Howe-Wagner, Lancaster, Baldwin, Sherwood, Slaughter, and Blaney. A hike along the Coastal Trail from Baker Beach to the Golden Gate Promenade, detailed in the Presidio Trails chapter, offers access to some of these pre–World War I fortifications.

Battery Chamberlin, located on the southeastern boundary of Baker Beach, is home to the famous disappearing gun. On the first Sunday of each month, the gun, which was originally placed in 1904 and remounted by the National Park Service in 1977, is fired. The display demonstrates how the recoil of the shot pushed the gun back and below the defensive barrier, when artillerymen could safely reload it. The middle two mounts at the battery were fitted with barbette tiers, which look for all the world like wedding cakes, especially the one that's been painted white. A small military museum is open on the first weekend of the month as well, from 10:00 A.M. to 2:00 P.M. For more information, call (415) 561–4323.

For all that was invested over the years in military fortifications around the Golden Gate, there was never a need to use them. A shot was never fired on an enemy from any of the batteries at the Presidio, nor from any others on the Golden Gate headlands. There are those who might assert that the apparent strength of these fortifications deterred potential attackers, but I think San Francisco has just been lucky.

Natural History Sites

Gulf of the Farallones National Marine Sanctuary

Anyone who has lived in the Bay Area gauges the clarity of the air—or the proximity of San Francisco's seemingly omnipresent fog bank—by whether the Farallon Islands can be seen on the western horizon. Cross the Golden Gate Bridge, look for the islands. Visit Lands End, look for the islands. Stand on the beach at Rodeo Cove, look for the islands. Gaze southwest from the tip of Point Reyes or Limantour Beach, look for the islands. It's just the thing to do.

But the Farallones are the crux of a far more important endeavor than amateur weather forecasting: They are at the heart of the Gulf of the Farallones National Marine Sanctuary, a huge preserve that stretches along the coast from the mouth of Bodega Bay south to Half Moon Bay, encompassing Bodega Head, Tomales Bay and Point, Point Reyes and Drakes Bay, Bolinas Point, Lagoon, and Bay, and Stinson Beach. It extends 12 nautical miles west from the coastline to envelop its three namesake islands and Noonday Rock, which rises just north of the Farallones proper. And it includes the busy shipping lanes leading in and out of San Francisco Bay through the Golden Gate.

The sanctuary, and the archipelago, which has been designated a national wildlife refuge, supports huge populations of sea- and shorebirds, large colonies of pinnipeds (seals and sea lions), and vast fisheries. The species list is staggering in its variety, ranging from plankton to humpback whales. Its most infamous resident is the great white shark, which preys on the seals and sea lions that rest and breed on the islands.

Established in 1981, and falling under the purview of the National Oceanic and Atmospheric Administration, the Gulf of the Farallones National Marine

Sanctuary abuts the Cordell Bank National Marine Sanctuary to the north and the Monterey Bay National Marine Sanctuary to the south. Together the three sanctuaries cover more than 5,300 square nautical miles of the Pacific Ocean off the coast of northern California—an area twice the size of Yellowstone National Park, according to sanctuary literature.

In addition to habitat and environmental protection, the sanctuary also engages in research, studying such subjects as population fluctuations among the various species that inhabit the coastal waters, and habitat assessment and monitoring. The Farallones Marine Sanctuary Association, in partnership with the national sanctuary, offers educational and outreach programs to both youths and adults. It also manages the sanctuary's visitor center on West Crissy Field in the Presidio (described in the Presidio's introduction).

For information on how to contact the Gulf of the Farallones National Marine Sanctuary, or the Farallones Marine Sanctuary Association, see appendix A.

Crissy Field Marsh

Before it was filled in to make way for the explosive growth of San Francisco, a large marsh, covering an estimated 130 acres, stretched along the beachfront from Fort Point to the Marina District. The Ohlone people harvested food and supplies from the wetlands, which brimmed with bird life and the huge family of plants that typically thrives in a tidal marsh.

The marsh had disappeared long before its former site was paved over for the Crissy Army Airfield in the 1920s. But once the airfield became part of the Golden Gate National Recreation Area, park officials began work to re-create at least a portion of the former salt marsh.

After years of planning, work began on a twenty-one-acre site between East Beach and the Crissy Field Center. The area was cleaned, sculpted, opened to the bay, and blessed by a member of a Native tribe that once thrived here. It was replanted with arrow grass, rushes, pickleweed, saltgrass, sea-pink, and other salt-water marsh plant community members, as well as with plants from the coastal dune scrub community, which includes bush lupine, coyote brush, and monkey flower. The plants were propagated in the Presidio's native plant nursery.

The opening of the restored wetlands took place in May 2001, and today visitors can look out over the protected marshlands and observe both the bird life and the plant life that thrives in and around the marsh.

The restored marsh is located between the Crissy Field Center and East Beach. Parking is available in the East Parking Area, which is located off Mason Street less than 0.1 mile east of its intersection with Marina Boulevard. More parking is available at the Crissy Field Center, which is located about 0.2 mile farther west on Mason Street.

Lobos Creek Boardwalk

The last free-flowing creek in San Francisco is kept safe behind a chain-link fence, as you might expect a pristine area to be in a big city. But just above the northern bank of Lobos Creek, wedged between the fence line and the parking lot of a maintenance facility, the Presidio has performed a small miracle.

In the Lobos Creek Valley, the coastal dune scrub community has been restored, and plants that are rare or endangered are being given a chance to reestablish themselves. A wheelchair-accessible boardwalk winds through the restored habitat, and small signs identify the species that once covered about 14 square miles of the San Francisco waterfront.

The more common plants in this community are familiar shrubs, like coyote brush, bush lupine, and mock heather. Drought-resistant perennials like yarrow and Indian paintbrush spice a color scheme otherwise dominated by pale shades of green. Thrown into the mix are rare and endangered plants that have been fostered in the Presidio's native plant nursery, including Delores campion, dune gilia, San Francisco spineflower, and San Francisco wallflower.

An easy 0.6-mile loop that incorporates the boardwalk and a nearby single-track path offers access to the revitalized area. The trail begins in the southwest corner of the parking lot at an interpretive sign describing the dune restoration project. The boardwalk first heads east through the dunes, then arcs northward. A short spur boardwalk leads left (west) to a platform surrounded by

Visitors stroll through restored coastal dune scrub on the Lobos Creek Boardwalk.

plants with identification signs. When you've completed your botany lesson, return to the main boardwalk and continue northward to the end of the walkway at a staircase and trail intersection at about 0.3 mile.

Turn left (west) onto the sandy singletrack, which traces the interface of the dune scrubland and the evergreen woodland that covers the hillside to the north. The path heads into the trees behind a maintenance facility, and splits just before it reaches Lincoln Boulevard. Take the little trail to the left (southwest), climbing a wooded hillock into the trailhead parking area.

To reach the Lobos Creek Trailhead from U.S. Highway 101 at the Golden Gate Bridge, follow Lincoln Boulevard west for 1.3 miles to an unsigned right (southeast) turn into the parking lot of a maintenance facility. The turn is opposite the second Bowley Street intersection at Baker Beach. The trailhead is just inside the entrance to the parking lot, on the south side.

The coastal dune scrub community also thrives on the coastal bluffs that reach from Baker Beach north to the Golden Gate. The landscape is not as carefully restored as that along Lobos Creek, but in some ways it feels even wilder, perched as it is on the edge of the continent. Not to mention that you'll see more bird life here, shorebirds and seabirds, along with the occasional hawk, scouting the cliffs and surveying the waters below for an easy meal. The Coastal Trail, also described in the Presidio Trails chapter, edges between the scrub and Lincoln Boulevard, offering another option for those seeking to familiarize themselves with this ecosystem.

Serpentine Grasslands at Inspiration Point

When I visited Inspiration Point in early 2002, it was tough to visualize what was going to happen on the barren slopes dropping northeast from the viewpoint. The slope was studded with tiny flags, mostly white and yellow, with other colors scattered here and there. It looked barren and sterile, but interpretive signs and pale green rock outcroppings hinted at its ultimate fate. One day, like the Crissy Field marsh and the Lobos Creek Valley, this will be a restored native habitat. It will once again be a serpentine grassland.

The chemistry of serpentine, a rock specific to the Franciscan formation that underlies this part of the Presidio, is toxic to many plants. Those that do grow in serpentine soils have developed special adaptations to survive there, making up a very specific, and relatively rare, plant community. Several species found within the Presidio's remnant serpentine grasslands, including Presidio clarkia and Raven's manzanita, are rare and endangered.

To reach Inspiration Point from the Main Post, follow Montgomery Street south to Moraga Avenue. Turn left (southeast) onto Moraga to its intersection with Arguello Boulevard. Turn right (south) onto Arguello and climb for 0.5 mile to Inspiration Point, which is on the left (east) side of the road.

Points of Interest in San Francisco and Points South

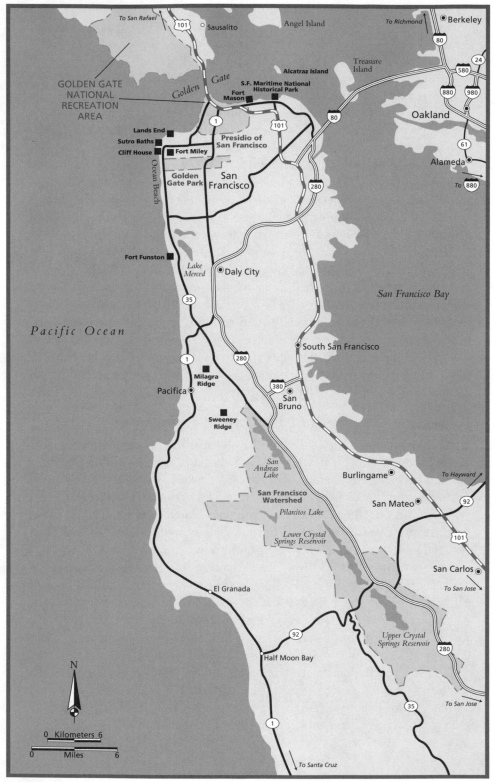

Points of Interest in San Francisco and Points South

The Golden Gate National Recreation Area (GGNRA) on the San Francisco peninsula extends east from the Presidio to Fort Mason and the San Francisco Maritime National Historical Park, west to Lands End, site of the Cliff House and Fort Miley, north to Alcatraz Island, and south to Fort Funston, Sweeney Ridge, and other points on the peninsula. Consider this chapter a catchall for those portions of the park that don't fit neatly into other categories, a potpourri of parks, forts, and trails that both defies easy categorization and, as always, invites exploration.

Alcatraz Island

Alcatraz Island, anchored in the middle of San Francisco Bay like a giant buoy, is a uniquely attractive and provocative landmark. The setting is exquisite, yet the site was chosen for a federal penitentiary that would house some of the most dangerous and notorious criminals of the twentieth century. The villains may have been behind bars, but they had really, really great views.

Like just about everything else in California, Alcatraz's history is closely linked to the discovery of gold. With the gold rush came another rush—one to defend the bay from anyone who might want to raid America's new promised land. An extensive defensive fortress, eventually outfitted with more than one hundred cannon, a citadel (or barracks), and a lighthouse, was built on Alcatraz Island in the 1850s. These military fortifications were manned by more than 400 soldiers during the Civil War, but some of the island's inhabitants, even this early in its illustrious history, were prisoners—a harbinger of things to come.

The island was still part of the bay's defensive complex when it made the formal transition from fort to prison in 1907. The citadel atop the island was replaced by a cellhouse and Alcatraz was dubbed a disciplinary barracks. But by the 1930s, the army deemed Alcatraz too expensive to maintain. The prison was transferred to the federal Bureau of Prisons in 1934 and transformed into a maximum-security facility. As "The Rock," Alcatraz housed some of the most notorious criminals of the time: Al Capone, "Machine Gun" Kelly, and the "Birdman of Alcatraz," Robert Stroud, to name a few.

By 1963 increasing costs forced the closure of the penitentiary on Alcatraz. The complex languished as federal officials discussed its future—proposals included making the island a monument, a casino, a space museum. Before any of these plans could be implemented, the island caught the attention of Native American activists, and more than one hundred occupied it in November 1969.

The Indians of All Tribes sought to purchase the island from the government, to establish a cultural center there, and to bring attention to the concerns of Native peoples. Initially they got that attention, but time eroded their hold on the government and media, internal conflicts arose, and tragedy struck when a child was killed in a fall. Still, the occupation lasted until June 1971, when federal agents removed the remaining few Indians from the island. After the Indian occupation, Alcatraz passed into the hands of the National Park Service and was incorporated into the Golden Gate National Recreation Area in 1972.

The modern Alcatraz experience begins with a ten-minute ferry ride from Pier 41 to the floating dock on the east side of the island. Upon disembarking, a ranger directs you to the theater on the lowest, oldest floors of the barracks building for a brief orientation to the amenities and restrictions on the island. You can also watch a short video that covers the evolution of the island, from its geologic formation to its modern incarnation as a national park site. After that, you are free to roam.

To reach the cellhouse, you must climb the equivalent of thirteen stories over a third of a mile on a switchbacking road. The road leads through the Civil War–era sally port and guardhouse, past the military chapel, the barracks building, and the military morgue. The cellhouse entrance is at the top of the roadway. A wheelchair-accessible tram is available for those unable to make the climb.

Inside the cellhouse you can tour each of the four cell blocks, including D block, which contains the solitary-confinement cells. I highly recommend the self-guided audio tour, available in six languages; it does an excellent job of bringing rooms in the cellhouse alive, and compels you to spend more time in the building and on the grounds, immersing yourself long enough in Alcatraz's atmosphere to make an indelible impression.

Outside the cellhouse you can explore short paths that wander through wild gardens and past buildings long fallen into disuse. On the south side of the island, the parade grounds offer stunning views of the cityscape, the Golden Gate, and back up at the cellhouse and lighthouse. The ubiquitous western gull, which nests here, patrols the area, keeping close tabs on an invading army of tourists.

Though subject to closure in spring and summer, the Agave Trail, which skirts the tide line on the south side of the island, offers great views and an intimate interface with a narrow strip of tide pools that cuddle up against the island. From this vantage point, it's difficult to imagine anyone trying to escape by swimming off The Rock. The trail, no more than 0.25 mile long, begins at the boat dock and circles up onto the parade ground.

Ferry service to and from Alcatraz is offered from the San Francisco waterfront at Fisherman's Wharf. Departures are scheduled throughout the day. The round-trip fares are $9.25 for adults ($13.25 with the cellhouse audio tour), $7.50 for seniors ($11.50 with the audio tour), and $6.00 for children ($8.00 with the audio tour). Space on the ferries sells out quickly, so it's recommended you secure tickets in advance. Visit the park's Web site (www.nps.gov/alcatraz) for access to the link to ferry details.

No food is allowed on the island. No pets, other than service animals, are allowed either, and scooters and bicycles are prohibited as well. The island has several bookstores, where you can also purchase memorabilia.

Alcatraz is closed on Christmas and New Year's Day. Fierce weather may also force closure of the island. In addition to the various brochures available for purchase in the bookstores, the Alcatraz Web site contains extensive historical and modern information about the island. Call (415) 705-1045 if you need to speak to an Alcatraz ranger.

San Francisco Maritime National Historical Park

San Francisco Maritime National Historical Park, which includes a fabulous maritime museum, Aquatic Park, and the Hyde Street Pier, is the easternmost outpost of the Golden Gate National Recreation Area, and abuts one of San Francisco's biggest tourist attractions, Fisherman's Wharf.

Dedicated to preserving and sharing the story of maritime endeavors along the Pacific coast, the park has two hubs—the Hyde Street Pier, along which are docked six vessels dating from different shipping eras, and the Maritime Museum, which houses models and artifacts that document maritime history in and outside San Francisco Bay.

At the Hyde Street Pier, you can check out a Cape Horn sailing ship from the late 1880s; a paddle tug from 1914; and the "last San Francisco Bay scow schooner still afloat," according to park documents, among others. The San Francisco Maritime National Park Association, which works with the park, maintains other ships along the waterfront as well. For more information on the association, visit the Web site at www.maritime.org, or call (415) 561-6662.

The Maritime Museum, fronting Aquatic Park, houses wonderful and unusual displays. Inside, you will find figureheads, detailed model ships, and historic pictures. It's a fabulous voyage through maritime history. Located on Beach Street at the end of Polk Street, the museum is open daily from 10:00 A.M. to 5:00 P.M. and closed on Thanksgiving, Christmas, and New Year's Day. Call (415) 561-7100 for more information.

The maritime park also includes the J. Porter Shaw Library, home to thousands of volumes covering maritime history, and Aquatic Park, the premier site for those interested in rowing and swimming on the bay. Buoys have been set up in the frigid bay waters for the enjoyment of the very thick-skinned, some of whom are in training for the annual Escape to Alcatraz Triathlon or a swim under the Golden Gate Bridge from San Francisco to Marin County. Those not interested in getting their feet—or any part of their bodies—wet can enjoy Aquatic Park from the narrow beachfront or by walking out on the municipal pier. The pier, which arcs for 0.25 mile across the mouth of the cove, boasts great vistas of Alcatraz Island, Angel Island, the North Bay, and the Golden Gate Bridge.

The maritime museum and Aquatic Park, like most attractions in the touristy sections of San Francisco, are plagued by parking problems on weekends, holidays, and during the summertime. There is limited parking available in the lot just west of the museum on Beach Street, and on along Van Ness Avenue as it plunges toward the pier. But if the spaces are occupied, you will have to park farther afield and walk to the museum, or take public transportation.

Fort Mason and the Fort Mason Center

Fort Mason was a military post for more than 200 years. In that time, its buildings and piers witnessed the passage of thousands of soldiers, weapons, and other trappings of war, a point of departure and return for men, women, and equipment bound for distant locales. But, as has been the case throughout the Golden Gate National Recreation Area, these batteries and buildings now have an altogether different focus—in this case, the arts.

The Spanish first fortified Black Point, upon which the present fort stands, but it is the Americans who have made a lasting mark on the once pristine landscape, starting with the construction of batteries during the Civil War. In the aftermath of the great earthquake of 1906, Fort Mason was the site of a tent city for residents forced from their homes either by the quake itself, or by the inferno that followed. During World War II large numbers of troops and tons of cargo were loaded onto ships at the Fort Mason piers and shipped off to the dangerous battlegrounds of the Pacific.

Since it's become part of the GGNRA, the historic buildings of the upper fort, including Civil War-era barracks and a former post hospital, are used for park administration; the barracks now house a youth hostel. Lower Fort Mason, with three huge piers jutting out into the bay and five warehouselike buildings on land, houses the Fort Mason Center, a hub for arts, entertainment, and environmental programs in the city. These theaters, art galleries, museums, bookstores, and restaurants—more than thirty of them—are a microcosm of the cultural richness that distinguishes San Francisco. The center is run by the Fort Mason Foundation in cooperation with the National Park Service; check out the foundation's Web site at www.fortmason.org for a calendar of events and other information about facilities and programs at the center.

The Fort Mason Center is open every day from 8:00 A.M. to midnight, with the exceptions of the Fourth of July, Thanksgiving Day, and Christmas. The

During World War II, the piers at Fort Mason bustled with soldiers and cargo headed to the battlegrounds of the Pacific.

mailing address is Fort Mason Foundation, Landmark Building A, Fort Mason Center, San Francisco, CA 94123; the phone number is (415) 441–3400. Park headquarters can be contacted by writing to the GGNRA, Fort Mason, Building 201, San Francisco, CA 94123; the telephone number is (415) 561–4700, and the Web site is www.nps.gov/goga.

The main entrance to the Fort Mason Center is at the intersection of Laguna and Bay Streets, at the east end of the Marina Green. The entrance to the administrative facilities, including park headquarters and the youth hostel, is at the intersection of Bay and Franklin Streets. The parking lots at the center and within the administrative complex are generally packed on weekends or when there is a special theater or art event. You can either park farther afield and walk to the center, or take public transportation.

Fort Mason also features the Great Meadow, a sprawling lawn that extends down and west from upper Fort Mason to Laguna Street. Studded with palm trees, shade trees, and benches, the Great Meadow is a splash of greenery amid the bustle of the Marina district. A short, easy-to-follow trail circumnavigates the meadow, and features wonderful views, interpretive signs, and a statue of Congressman Phillip Burton, who championed establishment of the GGNRA in the 1970s. Rest rooms are located along the south side of the meadow.

Cliff House and Seal Rocks

My family's Cliff House picture hangs in my brother's house now. It's a classic shot of the building's second incarnation—the Gothic-style Cliff House built by San Francisco millionaire Adolph Sutro and opened in 1896. The image of the castlelike structure hung in the home of my grandfather, who was almost old enough to have visited the structure. It's a picture of romance and mystery that remains potent in my imagination to this day.

That Cliff House was destroyed by fire in 1907, but a new Cliff House stands in its place. The present building, designed in a neoclassic style and remodeled over the years, overlooks Seal Rocks, where California sea lions and harbor seals regularly gather to sun, swim, and entertain San Franciscans and tourists from out of town. Those seals, which had been attracting sight-seers since the middle of the nineteenth century, initially inspired a New York investor to build a resort at the site in 1863.

The first Cliff House, built in the same year, was a relatively low-key structure, but still drew to its dining rooms some of the finest families in San Francisco, as well as three presidents. It was purchased by Sutro in 1881, part of his acquisition of much of the land at Point Lobos. The first structure was heavily damaged when a schooner carrying dynamite ran aground on the rocks below the building and exploded.

Sutro rebuilt the Cliff House, and his spectacular turreted structure stood on the site for a little more than ten years before it too was destroyed by fire. The third Cliff House was opened in 1909 by his daughter Emma and renovated several times before being acquired by the GGNRA in 1977. The park plans an extensive remodel of the Cliff House, slated to be completed in 2003, that will reveal the original 1909 facade, include a new gift shop and dining room, and add viewing terraces.

Always the site of spectacular dining experiences, the Cliff House holds a fine restaurant. Outside, a little paved path leads around the west side of the building, below the banks of windows that frame its dining room, to overlooks of Seal Rocks. The path leads around the building that houses a giant camera obscura—a relic of the Playland amusement park that once sat on the northern edge of Ocean Beach—which was added to the National Register of Historic Places in 2001. A flight of stairs leads up to the street and the front of the Cliff House; follow the sidewalk north for more views of Seal Rocks and down into the ruins of the Sutro Baths, with the Golden Gate and the Marin Headlands beyond.

Information on the Cliff House is available on the Golden Gate National Recreation Area Web site at www.nps.gov/goga. The Cliff House restaurant and banquet facilities also have a Web site at www.cliffhouse.com. The phone number for the restaurant is (415) 386–3330. The address is 1090 Point Lobos, San Francisco, CA 94121.

To reach the Cliff House from U.S. Highway 101 at the Golden Gate Bridge, follow Lincoln Boulevard west for about 1.5 miles to where it becomes El Camino Del Mar in the upscale neighborhood of Sea Cliff. Continue west on El Camino Del Mar for about 0.9 mile to its intersection with Legion of Honor Drive. Turn left (south), passing the Palace of the Legion of Honor, to Clement Street. Go right (west) on Clement Street for 0.9 mile to its intersection with Forty-eighth Avenue and El Camino Del Mar. Turn left (south) onto El Camino Del Mar for less than 0.1 mile to Point Lobos Avenue. Turn right (west) onto Point Lobos Avenue, which drops in front of the Cliff House before turning south and becoming the Great Highway. Parking is available alongside Point Lobos Avenue, in the Merrie Way parking lot above the Cliff House, or along the Esplanade below the Cliff House near Ocean Beach.

Sutro Baths and Sutro Heights

The extravagance of Adolph Sutro's vision for Lands End is evident even in its ruins. The spectacular structures he built here drew thousands of people to Point Lobos at the turn of the twentieth century; at the turn of the twenty-first century, his legacy is one of nostalgia and open spaces.

Sutro began buying property on Point Lobos by 1879, eventually purchasing more than 2,000 acres. Once he owned the land that had captured his heart, he set about transforming some of it into a fabulous resort. He rebuilt the Cliff House in Gothic style after it was destroyed in 1894, then turned his attention

Reclining stone lions guard the Forty-Eighth Avenue entrance to Sutro Heights.

to Sutro Baths, where he built six pools that could be filled with ocean water at high tide (a seventh pool was filled with fresh water). The pools were heated to different temperatures and enclosed in a greenhouse made of stained glass. On Sutro Heights, the bluff overlooking both the Cliff House and the baths, he built a fabulous house, a conservatory, and elaborate gardens dotted with statues of Roman gods and goddesses. He also built a railroad line, Cliff House & Ferries Railway, to bring visitors out to the Cliff House, baths, and heights.

After Sutro's death in 1898, all of his works fell into decline. The structures on Sutro Heights were derelict by the 1940s. Sutro Baths enjoyed a short-lived renaissance as an ice rink in the 1950s; they were destroyed by fire in the 1960s. Inclusion in the Golden Gate National Recreation Area in the 1970s has ensured that Sutro's vision will never be obliterated.

To explore the baths and heights, park in the large lot at Merrie Way, which also serves as the trailhead for the Coastal Trail at Lands End (described later in this chapter). A steep staircase departs from the northwest corner of the lot, dropping to an asphalt roadway overlooking the ruins of Sutro Baths. The pools are now open to the sun and frequented by the birds; a perch on their foundations offers wonderful ocean views.

Sutro Heights is on the south side of Point Lobos Avenue; a small parking area, usually full, is available here, and offers easy access to the park. A broad footpath circles the well-manicured park, accented with benches and interpretive signs that describe Sutro's vision for the heights. You can also climb onto the foundation of the "parapet," a viewing platform Sutro built on the site in 1910. Views westward, of course, are of the ocean, but lovely vistas spread south as well, of the green swath that is Golden Gate Park, the old windmills that stand sentinel on either side of the swath, and Ocean Beach.

To reach Sutro Heights and Sutro Baths from U.S. Highway 101 at the Golden Gate Bridge, follow Lincoln Boulevard west for about 1.5 miles to where it becomes El Camino Del Mar in the upscale neighborhood of Sea Cliff. Continue west on El Camino Del Mar for about 0.9 mile to its intersection with Legion of Honor Drive. Turn left (south), passing the Palace of the Legion of Honor, to Clement Street. Go right (west) on Clement Street for 0.9 mile to its intersection with Forty-eighth Avenue and El Camino Del Mar. Turn left (south) onto El Camino Del Mar for less then 0.1 mile to Point Lobos Avenue. Turn right (west) onto Point Lobos Avenue, and then right (north) again almost immediately into the Merrie Way parking lot.

Fort Miley

The soldiers stationed at Fort Miley may have been on the front lines of any potential assault on the Golden Gate, but they probably didn't complain too much. In the first place, that assault never came. And in the second place, Fort Miley, located on Lands End overlooking the Golden Gate, with Seal Rocks,

Sutro Baths, Ocean Beach, and the Cliff House within walking distance, has a setting that would be hard to grouse about.

Several batteries are located within the bounds of the fort, which was established in 1901, in the midst of the battery-building frenzy that characterized the Endicott-Taft period. These days Fort Miley is a peaceful place, site of a memorial to the USS *San Francisco*, which sustained heavy casualties in the Battle of Guadalcanal, as well as the old batteries. Parking for, and access to, the Coastal Trail at Lands End is available from the fort.

To reach Fort Miley from U.S. Highway 101 at the Golden Gate Bridge, follow Lincoln Boulevard west for about 1.5 miles to where it becomes El Camino Del Mar in the upscale neighborhood of Sea Cliff. Continue west on El Camino Del Mar for about 0.9 mile to its intersection with Legion of Honor Drive. Turn left (south), passing the Palace of the Legion of Honor, to Clement Street. Go right (west) on Clement Street for 0.9 mile to its intersection with Forty-eighth Avenue and El Camino Del Mar. Go right (north) to the parking area for the USS *San Francisco* monument.

Fort Funston and Battery Davis

Fort Funston crouches in the dunes on the cliffs above Ocean Beach. The southernmost outpost of the Golden Gate National Recreation Area within the boundaries of San Francisco, the fort's attractions are varied: Walking is popular with both humans and dogs, military installations await exploration, and, when the conditions are right, the skies above the fort fill with hang gliders.

Fort Funston was yet another part of the extensive system of military defenses built to protect San Francisco Bay, and was named for Major General Frederick Funston, who died just before the United States entered World War I in 1917. Battery Davis is typical of the defensive works erected during World War II, its casemated gun emplacements camouflaged within the slopes of the dunes. During the Cold War the fort was outfitted as a Nike missile installation; the park's parking lot is on the former launch site.

When the winds come up, all eyes look skyward. Fort Funston is the premier site in San Francisco for hang gliders, and the observation deck at the fort is the premier place to watch these fliers. They swoop up and down the southern reaches of Ocean Beach, butterflies caught mid-transformation, with their colorful wings spread but their bodies still wrapped in cocoons. They buzz the observation deck, thrilling observers, whose camera shutters work overtime trying to capture the action.

The easy, 1-mile long Sunset Trail loop is a good way to enjoy the aerial gymnastics of the gliders, Battery Davis, and views across Ocean Beach and the Pacific. The trail departs from the northwest corner of the parking lot near the informational billboard and map. The paved path sweeps north into the dunes to a Y-intersection at an interpretive sign about Battery Davis. You can go

The great wings used by hang gliders at Fort Funston look skyward.

either way; if you stay right (northeast) on the paved portion of the trail, you will curve around the backside of the overgrown battery, a long mound topped with eucalyptus and flanked by picnic tables. Pass the first tunnel through the battery; at the next intersection, stay left (north) on the Sunset Trail. The second tunnel through the battery beckons to the left (west) just beyond the trail junction; pass through the casemated gun emplacement and out onto the sand near the cliff's edge. Turn left (south) on the sand path, which returns you to the pavement, and thence to the parking lot.

As you'll no doubt gather walking the Sunset Trail, Fort Funston is extremely popular with dogs and their owners. Though the signs request that dogs be kept on leashes, the rule is almost universally ignored, and canine revelry is always in full swing. Remarkably, the area hasn't been completely trashed: Dog walkers have formed a group that organizes cleanup days, and numerous trash cans and dog litter stations have been set up so owners can clean up after their pets. Still, GGNRA regulations require that all dogs be kept on leashes.

Other amenities at the fort include a visitor center and a native plant nursery, which has been operating on the site for twenty years, growing plants native to the Fort Funston area. The Environmental Education Center on the site is used by school groups and is not open to the public.

Fort Funston is on Skyline Boulevard at the southern end of the Great Beach, about 4.5 miles south of the Cliff House. The fort's entrance can only be reached from the southbound lanes of Skyline Boulevard, and is located about 1.7 miles south of Sloat Boulevard. To reach the fort from the northbound lanes of Skyline Boulevard, turn around at John Muir Drive (there is also a trailhead here), and head south to the park entrance. The park is open from 6:00 A.M. to 9:00 P.M. daily. For more information, call (415) 239–2366.

Trails in San Francisco and Points South

The three trails described in this section encompass great views, interesting landscapes, and significant cultural or natural history sites on the San Francisco peninsula. The Coastal Trail at Lands End traces the route of an historic rail line and offers great views of the Golden Gate. Milagra Ridge is home to threatened and endangered species. And at Sweeney Ridge, at the site of the "discovery" of San Francisco Bay, you'll encounter spectacular vistas of both the bay and the Pacific Ocean.

Coastal Trail at Lands End

HIGHLIGHTS: The trail at Lands End combines easy hiking with great views of the Golden Gate and the Marin Headlands.

TYPE OF JOURNEY: Out-and-back.

TOTAL DISTANCE: 4 miles.

DIFFICULTY: Easy.

PERMITTED USES: Hiking.

MAPS: USGS Point Bonita and San Francisco North; Golden Gate National Recreation Area Map; TOPO! San Francisco Bay Area, Wine Country, and Big Sur.

SPECIAL CONSIDERATIONS: Pets must be kept on leashes. Mountain bikers can ride portions of the gravel trail, but the steep sets of stairs preclude uninterrupted time in the saddle.

PARKING AND FACILITIES: There is a huge parking lot at Merrie Way, but this fills quickly on weekends; you may have to park along Point Lobos Avenue or at West Fort Miley. There are no facilities at Merrie Way; rest rooms are located at West Fort Miley.

FINDING THE TRAILHEAD: From U.S. Highway 101 at the Golden Gate Bridge, follow Lincoln Boulevard south, then west, for about 1.5 miles to where it becomes El Camino Del Mar in the upscale neighborhood of Sea Cliff. Continue west on El Camino Del Mar for about 0.9 mile to its intersection with Legion of Honor Drive. Turn left (south), passing the Palace of the Legion of Honor, to Clement Street. Go right (west) on Clement Street for 0.9 mile to its intersection with Forty-

Coastal Trail at Lands End

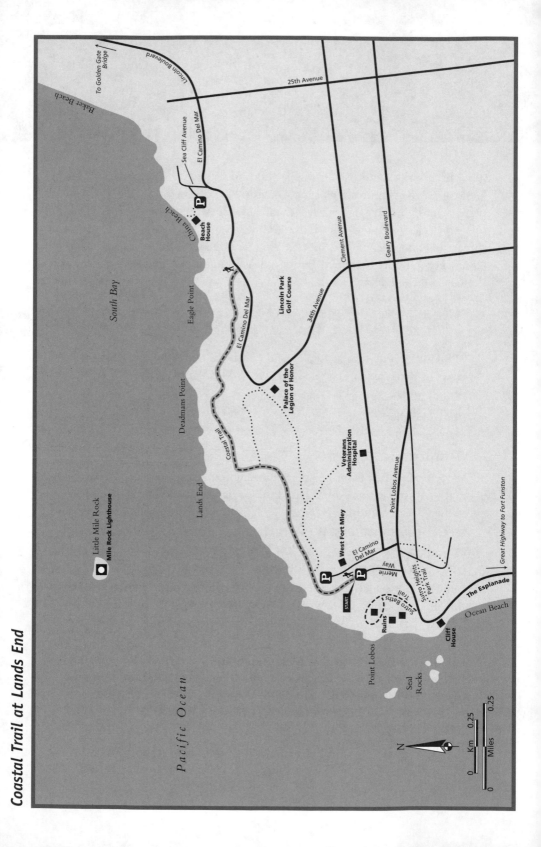

eighth Avenue and El Camino Del Mar. Turn right (north) to the parking area at West Fort Miley, or, to reach the Merrie Way trailhead, go left (south) on El Camino Del Mar for less than 0.1 mile to Point Lobos Avenue. Turn right (west) onto Point Lobos Avenue, and then turn right (north) again almost immediately into the parking lot.

KEY POINTS:

0.0 Trailhead.

0.5 Pass below the Veterans Administration Hospital.

0.8 Climb the staircase.

2.0 Reach the Eagle Point observation deck and the turnaround point.

Adolph Sutro, wealthy philanthropist and onetime mayor of San Francisco, left his mark on Lands End in powerful ways. His works are most evident in the ruins at Sutro Baths and Sutro Heights, but the Coastal Trail at Lands End is also part of his legacy. The path follows the bed of the Cliff House & Ferries Railway, a steam-powered railroad that Sutro built to bring residents from downtown San Francisco out to his spectacular enterprises at Lands End.

Landslides forced the railroad to shut down in the mid-1920s, after about 40 years of service, but both the GGNRA and the Rails-to-Trails Conservancy, an organization that facilitates the transformation of former railroad lines into trails, recognized its recreational value. The railbed is now a portion of the Coastal Trail, which stretches for 9.1 miles from the Golden Gate Bridge south to Fort Funston. With its stunning views of the Golden Gate Bridge and the cliffs of the Marin Headlands, and its relatively wild feel, the inspiration for Sutro's love affair with Lands End quickly becomes clear to anyone on the Lands End trail.

To walk the route, begin at the interpretive sign at the north end of the Merrie Way parking lot on the wide, obvious road heading right (north). The grade is shaded by stands of Monterey cypress. Use trails scatter from the main trail, which proceeds to a major trail intersection at 0.2 mile. Stay left (north) on the railroad grade.

The trail climbs past a staircase that leads up and south to the parking area at the West Fort Miley, site of the USS *San Francisco* Memorial and several defensive batteries that were built between the turn of the twentieth century and World War II. A quick side trip into the fort is more that worth the short climb.

Continuing east on the Coastal Trail, you will be treated to vistas of the wild coastline and the Golden Gate Bridge. Monterey pines and cypresses provide abundant shade, but enough light penetrates the canopy to nurture a colorful understory of wildflowers and brush.

The trail passes below the Veterans Administration Memorial Hospital at about 0.5 mile. Again, ignore the use trails that leave the railroad grade at this point, as well as a paved road that drops to the trail from the hospital grounds, remaining on the unpaved railroad grade.

The trail skirts Painted Rock Cliff, where signs warn you to stay on the main trail, which climbs a long flight of stairs made of, appropriately, railroad ties at about 0.8 mile. You can rest and enjoy the views from a bench located about halfway up the staircase. From the top of the stairs, the trail drops to a trail junction. Go left (northeast) toward the coastline, again enjoying vistas of the mouth of the bay, as well as of China Beach and the fine homes of Sea Cliff. The path narrows amid dense brush, then skirts the fairways of the Lincoln Park Golf Course near the Palace of the Legion of Honor. Trail's end is at about 2 miles, just beyond the wooden overlook at Eagle's Point.

Return as you came, enjoying views westward, out to sea, on the journey back to the Merrie Way parking lot.

Milagra Ridge

HIGHLIGHTS: A tiny scoop of the wilderness that dominated the San Francisco peninsula before development encroached has been preserved at Milagra Ridge.

TYPE OF JOURNEY: Loop.

TOTAL DISTANCE: About 1.2 miles.

DIFFICULTY: Easy.

PERMITTED USES: Hiking; bicycling on the paved trails.

MAPS: USGS San Francisco South; Golden Gate National Recreation Area Milagra Ridge brochure; TOPO! San Francisco Bay Area, Wine Country, and Big Sur.

SPECIAL CONSIDERATIONS: This is a fragile habitat. Please remain on trails. Paved trails are wheelchair accessible. To volunteer for habitat restoration programs, contact the GGNRA's Site Stewardship Program at (415) 561–3034, extension 3437.

PARKING AND FACILITIES: Limited parking is available alongside College Drive at the trailhead. A portable rest room is located about 0.25 mile north of the trailhead on the paved trail.

FINDING THE TRAILHEAD: Milagra Ridge can be reached either from Skyline Boulevard (California Highway 35), or California Highway 1 in Pacifica. Heading south out of San Francisco, follow either Skyline or CA 1 to its intersection with Sharp Park Road. If on Skyline Boulevard, turn right (west), and drive 0.9 mile to its intersection with Col-

Milagra Ridge

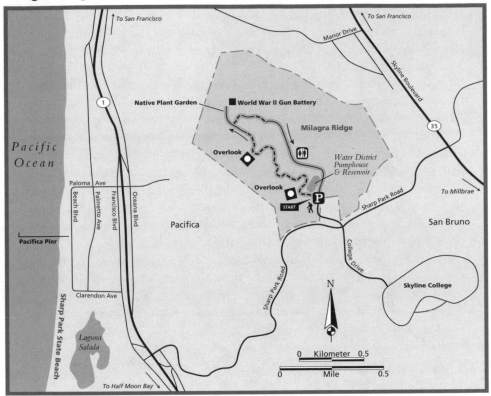

lege Drive. Turn right (north) onto College Drive and continue for 0.2 mile to the end of the road at the trailhead. If traveling on CA 1 from San Francisco, head south to the Sharp Park Road exit in Pacifica. Go east on Sharp Park Road for 1.5 miles to the intersection with College Drive. Turn left (north) onto College to reach the trailhead.

KEY POINTS:

0.0 Trailhead.

0.6 Arrive the native plant garden at the bunker.

0.8 Reach the overlook at the concrete pad.

1.0 Drop to the paved road at the rest rooms.

The GGNRA calls Milagra Ridge "an island ecosystem." Standing amid the grasses on the windy ridgetop, its relative isolation is clearly illustrated. A sea of development stretches in all directions, truncated only on the west side, where another sea—the Pacific—stretches to the horizon.

Only 240 acres in size, the ridge was added to the park in 1984. The park, along with a group of dedicated volunteers, has been working since then to rehabilitate and maintain a natural habitat on the site—a habitat that supports rare and endangered species including the mission blue butterfly, the San Bruno elfin butterfly, the California red-legged frog, and the San Francisco garter snake.

A network of singletrack trails and paved roads winds through the scrublands on the ridgetop. The loop described here links some of the paths, but none ranges so far afield that you have to worry about getting lost if you stray.

Begin by mounting the stairs on the left (west) side of the road and gate. Climb past the fenced-off covered reservoir on the right (north) to an overlook with great 360-degree views, with the Pacific Ocean spreading endlessly westward and the pastel mosaic of the suburbs in all other directions. The trail turns north, traverses the ridgetop, then drops down a flight of stairs to a saddle. Veering west again, the trail wanders through the blooming scrublands, rolling on to meet the paved road at about the 0.3-mile mark.

Turn left (west) onto the unpaved path, which drops westward to another overlook before looping inland. Pass a lone Monterey cypress—the only tree you'll see along the route—then cross a clearing to intersect the paved road again. Go left (west) on the paved route, dropping to an old battery and native plant garden overlooking the ocean at 0.6 mile.

Backtrack up the paved road to a staircase that climbs to a concrete pad at 0.8 mile—yet another spectacular overlook. Head east down the paved road to a footpath that breaks off to the left (northeast); follow the footpath down to its junction with the pavement.

Once on the asphalt, turn left (southeast) and follow the road to its intersection with the main paved road at about the 1-mile mark. You will find a portable rest room, a trash can, and informational billboard at this juncture.

Unless you plan to do laps, turn left (south) on the main paved road to return to the trailhead at about 1.2 miles.

Sweeney Ridge and Portola Discovery Site

HIGHLIGHTS: Enjoy panoramic views of San Francisco Bay and the Pacific coastline from the summit of Sweeney Ridge.

TYPE OF JOURNEY: Out-and-back.

TOTAL DISTANCE: 3.6 miles.

DIFFICULTY: Moderate.

PERMITTED USES: Hiking, horseback riding, mountain biking.

MAPS: USGS Montara Mountain; Golden Gate National Recreation Area Sweeney Ridge brochure; TOPO! San Francisco Bay Area, Wine Country, and Big Sur.

SPECIAL CONSIDERATIONS: Dogs must be kept on leashes.

PARKING AND FACILITIES: There is parking for about fifteen cars at the Sneath Lane trailhead. No other facilities are available.

FINDING THE TRAILHEAD: Approach the trailhead from the north or south via Skyline Boulevard (California Highway 34) in San Bruno. Sneath Lane heads west from Skyline Boulevard, climbing through a residential area for 1.1 miles to the trailhead parking area.

KEY POINTS:

0.0 Trailhead.

0.3 Start the long climb to the ridgetop.

1.7 Reach the summit of the ridge.

1.8 Take in the views from the Portola Discovery Site.

Spanish explorer Gaspar de Portola was on a mission. He was charged by his country to establish settlements in California that would cement its status as a Spanish colony. One of the settlements was to be at Monterey Bay, but his expedition, traveling by land, overshot that mark by about 100 miles. On November 4, 1769, the band of explorers climbed atop Sweeney Ridge and beheld a bay of colossal proportions. A bay that would become one of the most important harbors on the West Coast. A bay that would one day be the site of a famously cosmopolitan city surrounded by spectacular parklands.

Though not nearly as pristine as it appeared to the explorers who stood at what would later become the Portola Discovery Site, San Francisco Bay still sprawls magnificently below the vista point. To the west is the Pacific Ocean, and to the south rise the undeveloped hills and mountain of the San Francisco watershed. The cylinder of granite that tops one of the monuments at the site is inscribed with images of the surrounding landmarks, enabling visitors to identify and name them.

The climb to the top of Sweeney Ridge begins on Sneath Lane. Use the stile to pass around the gate; the northern reaches of San Andreas Lake are visible ahead. The trail heads south toward the lake, passing a gated side road at 0.25 mile, then arcs southwest, and begins an unbroken ascent to the ridgetop.

The climb begins moderately, winding up the pavement through coastal scrub and offering brush-framed views of the lake, with San Francisco International Airport and the waters of the bay in the distance. Pass the fog line at 0.8 mile; beyond this marker painted on the asphalt a single yellow line runs up the middle of the road.

The route swings slowly to the northwest, climbing at a fairly steep pitch, with San Bruno Mountain rising to the northeast. The steepness mellows as the road heads back southwest, then passes through the shade of a stand of

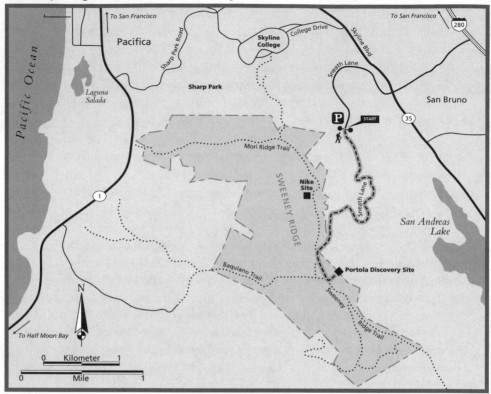

eucalyptus at 1.3 miles. A final push, this time heading directly west, lands you atop the ridge at 1.7 miles.

Sneath Lane ends on the Sweeney Ridge Trail, which runs from north to south along the ridgecrest. The pavement curves right (north) toward the water towers and the remains of a Nike missile site; the Portola Discovery Site is reached by heading left (south) on the dirt service road that doubles as the trail. A pair of benches is perched on the west edge of the trail amid the scrub, looking west out over the Pacific.

To reach the discovery site, follow the Sweeney Ridge Trail south for less than 0.1 mile to a smattering of use trails that mount a knob on the east side of the route (opposite the Baquiano Trail, which drops off the ridge to the west). The serpentine monument that commemorates the Portola Expedition is on the north side of the little clearing atop the knob; a second monument, to Carl McCarthy, who escorted more than 11,000 people to the site as part of his efforts to get it preserved, is on the south side of the clearing. McCarthy's monument is topped with engravings that identify landmarks on the horizon.

Appendix A

For More Information

Point Reyes National Seashore
Point Reyes Station, CA 94956
(415) 464–5100
www.nps.gov/pore

Point Reyes National Seashore
Association
Point Reyes Station, CA 94956
(415) 663–1200
www.ptreyes.org

Golden Gate National
Recreation Area
Fort Mason, Building 201
San Francisco, CA 94123
(415) 556–0560
www.nps.gov/goga

Golden Gate National Parks
Association
Building 201, Fort Mason
San Francisco, CA 94123
(415) 561–3000
www.ggnpa.org

Crissy Field Center
Building 603,
Corner of Mason and Halleck Streets
P.O. Box 29410
San Francisco, CA 94129
(415) 561–7690
www.crissyfield.org

Farallones Marine Sanctuary
Association
The Presidio, P.O. Box 29386
San Francisco, CA 94129
(415) 561–6625
www.farallones.org

Fort Mason Foundation
Landmark Building A,
Fort Mason Center
San Francisco, CA 94123
(415) 441–3400
www.fortmason.org

Gulf of the Farallones
National Marine Sanctuary
Fort Mason, Building 201
San Francisco, CA 94123
(415) 561–6622
www.gfnms.nos.noaa.gov

Presidio Trust
Presidio of San Francisco
34 Graham Street
P.O. Box 29052
San Francisco, CA 94129
(415) 561–5300
www.presidiotrust.gov

Appendix B

Sources and Further Reading

The list that follows is by no means inclusive. Some of the books, pamphlets, and maps listed below are available for purchase, but park visitor centers offer a number of free pamphlets and maps, many of which offer similar information.

Books and Pamphlets

2002 Tidelog: Northern California, Mark Alan Born. Pacific Publishers, 2001.

A Civil History of the Golden Gate National Recreation Area and the Point Reyes National Seashore, Vol. 2, Anna Coxe Toogood. National Park Service, 1980.

Alcatraz: Island of Change, James P. Delgado. Golden Gate National Parks Association, 1991.

A Good Life: Dairy Farming in the Olema Valley, D. S. (Dewey) Livingston. National Park Service, 1995.

An Annotated Checklist of Mammals, Point Reyes National Seashore, Gary M. Fellets and John Dell'Osso. Coastal Parks Association, 1986.

An Incomplete Dairy Ranching History and Outline of Land Use in the Marin Headlands, Darcie Luce. Golden Gate National Recreation Area, 1993.

Discovering Francis Drake's California Harbor, Raymond Aker and Edward Von der Porten. Drake Navigators Guild, 2000.

Farming on the Edge, John Hart. University of California Press, 1991.

Fort Mason: A Park Walk of One Mile, Marilyn Straka. On the Level San Francisco Excursions, 2000.

Fort Point: Sentry at the Golden Gate, John A. Martini. Golden Gate National Parks Association, 1991.

Geology of the Golden Gate Headlands, William P. Elder. National Park Service, 2001.

Golden Gate National Recreation Area Guide to the Parks, Ariel Rubissow Okamoto. Golden Gate National Parks Association, 1995.

Headlands: The Marin County Coast at the Golden Gate, Miles DeCoster, Mark

Klett, Mike Mandel, Paul Metcalf, Larry Sultan. University of New Mexico Press, 1989.

Marin Headlands: Portals of Time, Harold and Ann Lawrence Gilliam. Golden Gate National Parks Association, 1993.

Muir Woods: Redwood Refuge, John Hart. Golden Gate National Parks Association, 1991.

National Audubon Society Field Guide to California, Peter Alden, Fred Heath, Amy Leventer, Richard Keen, Wendy B. Zomlefer. Chanticleer Press, 1998.

Place Names of Marin, Louise Teather. Scottwall Associates, 1986.

Point Reyes National Seashore: A Hiking and Nature Guide, Don and Kay Martin. Martin Press, 1997.

Point Reyes: A Guide to the Trails, Roads, Beaches, Campgrounds, and Lakes of Point Reyes National Seashore, 3rd edition, Dorothy L.Whitnah. Wilderness Press, 1977.

Post and Park: A Brief Illustrated History of the Presidio of San Francisco, Stephen A. Haller. Golden Gate National Parks Association, 1997.

Point Reyes Secret Places & Magic Moments, Phil Arnot. Wide World Publishing/Tetra, 1992.

Ranching on the Point Reyes Peninsula: A History of the Dairy and Beef Ranches Within Point Reyes National Seashore, 1834–1992, D. S. (Dewey) Livingston. National Park Service, 1994.

San Francisco's Wilderness Next Door, John Hart. Presidio Press, 1979.

Saving the Marin-Sonoma Coast, L. Martin Griffin, M.D. Sweetwater Springs Press, 1998.

Shipwrecks at the Golden Gate, James Delgado and Stephen Haller. Lexikos, 1989.

The Coast Miwok Indians of the Point Reyes Area, Sylvia Barker Thalman. Point Reyes National Seashore Association, 2001.

The History and Architecture of the Point Reyes Lifeboat Station, Dewey Livingston and Steven Burke. National Park Service, 1991.

The Natural History of the Point Reyes Peninsula, Jules G. Evans, Point Reyes National Seashore Association, 1993.

The Ohlone Way: Indian Life in the San Francisco-Monterey Bay Area, Malcolm Margolin. Heyday Books, 1978.

Wildflowers of Point Reyes National Seashore, Katherine H. Holbrook and Elisabeth Ptak. Point Reyes National Seashore Association, 1996.

Maps

A Rambler's Guide to the Trails of Mt. Tamalpais and the Marin Headlands. The Olmsted Bros Map Co., 1986.

Map and Guide to the Seacoast Fortifications of the Golden Gate. Golden Gate National Parks Association.

Marin Headlands Map and Guide to Sites, Trails and Wildlife. Golden Gate National Parks Association.

Muir Woods Map and Guide to Trails, Plants and Wildlife, including Key to the Self-Guiding Nature Trail. Golden Gate National Parks Association.

Nike Missile Site. Golden Gate National Parks Association, 1999.

Official Map and Guide to Alcatraz: Its History as a Fort, a Prison, and a Park. Rufus Graphics in cooperation with the Golden Gate National Parks Association, 2000.

Pictorial Landform Map, Point Reyes National Seashore and the San Andreas Fault. Wilderness Press, 1999.

Point Reyes National Seashore Trail Map. Tom Harrison Maps, 2000.

About the Author

Tracy Salcedo-Chourré is virtually always on the trail, whether hiking, mountain biking, or skiing. When she's not outdoors, she can be found at her desk, writing, or volunteering at the local school or for the Marin Agricultural Land Trust. In addition to working as a newspaper reporter and editor, and authoring a number of magazine articles, she has written fifteen hiking guides covering areas in Colorado, where she lived for 12 years, and her native California, where she currently resides with her husband and three sons.